World of Science

THE ILLUSTRATED WORLD ENCYCLOPEDIA YEARBOOK

World of Science

Bobley Publishing Corp.

WOODBURY, NEW YORK

LC 77-93707
ISBN 0-405-13094-5

Book Design: Lynn Yost

Editor: Arleen Keylin
Assistant Editor: Douglas John Bowen
Editorial Assistant: Jonathan Cohen

Manufactured in the United States of America

Contents

Contributors

Lawrence K. Altman is a reporter for *The New York Times*.
Penicillin
1979 Nobel Prizes in Science—Physiology and Medicine

Edward M. Brecher is a longtime writer on science and medicine.
Opting for Suicide

Jane E. Brody is a reporter for *The New York Times*.
Inbred Mice
Plant-Animal Interaction

Michael H. Brown is a reporter for *The Niagara Falls Gazette*.
Love Canal, U.S.A.

Malcolm W. Browne is a reporter for *The New York Times*.
The Solar Eclipse
Man-Powered Flight
1979 Nobel Prizes in Science—Chemistry and Physics

William E. Burrows is an associate professor of journalism at New York University.
Cancer Safety

Laurence Cherry writes frequently about medicine and science.
Anesthesiologists
Medical Technology
New Hope for Burn Victims

Glenn Collins is an editor of *The New York Times Magazine*.
Life With Father

Patricia Curtis is a freelance journalist who writes frequently about animals, and has just completed a book about animal rights.
Animal Experiments
Pet Therapy

Timothy Ferris is a professor of English at Brooklyn College and author of *"The Red Limit: The Search for the Edge of the Universe"* and co-author of *"Murmurs of the Earth: The Story of the Voyager Interstellar Record."*
Mysteries of Deep Space
Crucibles of the Cosmos

Franklin Folsom, a freelance writer, is author of *"America's Ancient Treasures"* and *"Science and the Secret of Man's Past."*
"Space-Age" Archeology

Robin Marantz Henig is the features and news editor of *BioScience Magazine* in Washington, D.C.
The Myth of Senility
Mother's Milk

Richard D. Lyons is a correspondent for *The New York Times.*
Skylab

D. H. Melhem, author of *"Rest in Love,"* is a New York poet.
A Family Works a Miracle

Anthony J. Parisi is a business reporter for *The New York Times.*
The Energy-Efficient Society

Boyce Rensberger was a reporter for *The New York Times.*
The Ebla Ruins
Rival Anthropologists

Maggie Scarf has just completed a book to be published by Doubleday, on stress points in the lives of women.
Shocking the Depressed

Harold M. Schmeck Jr. is a reporter for *The New York Times.*
The Manic-Depressive Cycle
Aging

William Stockton is director of science news and editor of *Science Times* at *The New York Times.*
Smallpox is Not Dead

Walter Sullivan is the science editor of *The New York Times.*
Fusion
The Elephant Seal

Bayard Webster is a reporter for *The New York Times.*
The Biggest Dinosaur

Marietta Whittlesey is a freelance writer and author of "Killer Salt."
Antibiotics

Roger Neville Williams is a freelance writer living in Telluride, Colorado.
Tiny Town vs. Mining Giant

Introduction

by Walter Sullivan

The year 1979 was memorable for developments applicable to such diverse questions as the essential character of nature's laws, the well-being of mankind and the ultimate fate of the universe.

It was a year for looking back—at the revolutionary contributions of Albert Einstein, born a century earlier—and ahead toward the possible fulfillment of his dream, incorporating all natural phenomena into an integrated fabric of understanding.

1979 was a year when, because of a major nuclear accident and increasing concern at the affect on climate of heavy fuel burning, the prospects for an easy solution to the energy crisis became even more remote.

With more pedestrian forms of exploration obsolete, attention turned upward, as some of the most dramatic space discoveries to date revealed the amazing diversity of Jupiter's moons, and downward to the deep sea floor, where remarkable hot-water geysers were observed in action.

In medicine the day drew nearer when genetic manipulation could be used to deal with genetic disorders and fears for the hazards of such research diminished. Further evidence was found that the brain produces its own pain-killers.

The Basic Laws

The first step toward Einstein's dream of unification came a decade or two before he was born, when James Clerk Maxwell showed that two of the forces with which his contemporaries were familiar—the electric and magnetic forces—are manifestations of the same phenomenon, electromagnetism. Maxwell's reasoning was a special inspiration for Einstein and for the generations that followed. They had, however, to deal with two additional forces, unknown to Maxwell. One is the force that holds together particles (protons and neutrons) forming the atomic nucleus. It is the "glue," some of which is left over and converted into energy when atoms are split (as in an atomic bomb or nuclear power plant) or when they are fused (as in a hydrogen bomb or the core of the sun).

The other force also functions on the atomic level, and is very weak (although not as feeble

ix

as gravity). It accounts for certain forms of radioactivity and is known as the "weak" force. Both it and the nuclear or "strong," force act only at distances on the atomic scale whereas the range of gravitational and electromagnetic forces is limitless. In the years leading up to 1979 a succession of diverse experimental findings had lent increasing support to the idea that the weak force is really a form of electromagnetism. The two, together, would constitute the "electroweak" force. In that year three men largely responsible for that proposition received the laurel wreath of the world scientific community, the Nobel Prize in Physics. They were two Harvard University physicists (who had worked independently of one another), Drs. Sheldon L. Glashow and Steven Weinberg, and a Pakistani, Dr. Abdus Salam, Director of the International Centre for Theoretical Physics in Trieste, Italy. Earlier in the year, before the prize was awarded, all three had independently written the United States Department of Energy, urging that it provide funds for a bold experiment to test the plausibility of what had come to be known as "the grand unification" theories. While variously stated, they all proposed ways to incorporate the nuclear force with the electroweak force. Only gravity would still lie outside this formulation.

An implication of these theories is that even the particles forming all atomic nuclei are unstable, although disintegrating radioactively at an almost unimaginably slow rate. The proposed experiment was to monitor a cube of water 70 feet on each side to see if any of the nuclear particles within it decayed. Such a volume of water would contain so many billions upon billions of nuclei (three for each molecule of water) that a few of their constituent particles should decay each year if the theory is correct. The water would fill a chamber carved out of a salt mine extending under Lake Erie east of Cleveland and operated by the Morton Salt Company. Approval was given for the $2 million project. Less ambitious ones were already under way or planned, both in the United States and Europe, including one in a Utah silver mine. In all cases subterranean sites were chosen to minimize background radiation from cosmic rays. If a nuclear particle decays in one of the ways predicted it will generate telltale flashes of light or other signals. Their observation would be revolutionary, for it would mean that eventually all matter in the universe must disintegrate.

A landmark series of experiments during 1979, conducted with the PETRA colliding beam facility near Hamburg, West Germany, provided strong evidence for the existence of gluons—particles manifesting the force that glues quarks together to form the particles of the atomic nucleus (protons and neutrons). The gluon force is remarkable in that, whereas other forces become weaker at greater distances, it seems to become stronger, possibly reaching infinity within a short enough range to make it impossible to pry quarks apart. The experiments were done by an international team of more than 250 physicists, presumably the largest such effort in history.

The year ended with expressions of concern at the proliferation of particles assumed to be the basic building blocks of matter—quarks and leptons. Until a few years ago only one lepton was known—the electron—but by 1979 two heavier versions had been discovered— the muon and tau particle. Likewise, although it had been assumed that all nuclear particles are formed from variants of two quarks (the "up" quark and "down" quark), by the end of the year three more were known (the "strange," "charmed" and "bottom" quarks). The existence of a matching sixth, or "top," quark was widely assumed. All seemed to carry a property analogous to the electric charge that occurs in three forms or "colors." The added quarks are heavier than the original two. Like the heavy leptons they only occur from high energy collisions and survive hardly longer than an instant, although they were probably common when the universe was young, compact and highly energetic.

Why do they exist? Why, as Victor F. Weisskopf of the Massachusetts Institute of Technology has put it, does nature "need" them? Do they imply that the truly basic building blocks are even tinier? "Will we," he has asked, "find an unending series of worlds within worlds when we continue to penetrate deeper into matter to smaller distances and higher energies?" The answer can only come from further experiments.

Space Exploration

Four planets, apart from the earth, were subjected to close scrutiny during 1979. The most surprising discovery being the continuous, sulfurous volcanism of Jupiter's moon Io. Two spacecraft, Voyager 1 and Voyager 2, flew past that giant planet in March and July, passing among the large inner, or Galilean, moons. Each proved radically different from the others and, closer than any of the moons, a ring of debris was found to be orbiting the planet. The Great Red Spot evident for many years near the Jovian equator proved to be rotating like a ball-bearing between two bands of turbulent clouds moving relatively in opposite directions. Three of the four Viking craft that reached Mars in 1976—two landers and an orbiter—were still sending data. For the first time a spacecraft, Pioneer 11, passed close to Saturn, twice traversing the plane of its rings without damage. The planet was found to have a magnetic field roughly aligned with its spin axis and one or two additional small moons were observed.

As noted in the pages that follow, the fall of Skylab into the earth's atmosphere caused much excitement because of uncertainty as to where it might come down. Meanwhile two Soviet cosmonauts established a new record of 175 days in orbit aboard Salyut 6.

On September 22 one of the surviving Vela satellites, launched by the United States a number of years earlier to watch for clandestine nuclear weapons tests in the atmosphere, recorded the characteristic, two-peaked flash of such an explosion somewhere in the vicinity of South Africa. With no observation by another satellite it was impossible to determine the location within less than several thousand miles. It could have been over the ocean on either side of Africa or even as far south as Antarctica. Some scientists suspected that it was a superbolt of lightning. The Vela satellites had, in fact, documented the occurrence of such bolts in various parts of the world, notably off Japan. With an energy release comparable to that of a small atomic bomb, their existence had only been recognized in the past few years, but one had been reported off New York State's Long Island only a short time before the Vela observation. Detailed analysis of the flash

recorded over the African area, however, showed it strikingly similar to dozens of documented bomb tests (particularly French and Chinese). Some sort of clandestine nuclear explosion therefore seemed the probable explanation, although no other reliable evidence for it was reported (apart from what proved a spurious report from New Zealand of fresh radioactive fallout). South Africa denied any knowledge of the event.

Astronomy

On March 5 an extraordinary burst of gamma rays from somewhere far out in space was recorded by an international network of eight farflung space stations. The burst was fifty times more intense than any of this kind previously recorded. Because the observing sites were scattered around the solar system and arrival times of the burst at each of them was precisely known, it was possible—in contrast to the single Vela recording of a suspicious flash—to determine the precise direction from which the rays had come. This suggested an origin within the Large Magellanic Cloud, a small neighboring galaxy. The most likely source was thought to be a catastrophic event of some sort involving the remnant of a star that blew up there in a so-called supernova. The observations were made by gamma ray detectors aboard two Soviet Venus probes (Venera 11 and 12), an American Pioneer craft orbiting Venus, three Vela satellites and two international craft orbiting the sun (Helios and International Sun-Earth Explorer 3).

As befit the centennial of Einstein's birth, an effect predicted from his general theory of relativity was reportedly observed for the first time. This was the action of a gravitational lens in splitting the image of a distant source of light—a quasar presumably out near the limits of the observable universe. As first demonstrated in 1919 during attempts to confirm one of Einstein's predictions, strong gravity, like that close to the sun, bends light waves. The effect in 1919 was to make stars past the sun, visible when the latter was covered by the moon, appear out of place. It was assumed that similar light bending by an extremely massive object might act as a lens, splitting the light from a very distant, pin-point source. The finding was based on observations with British radio telescopes and two optical telescopes on Kitt Peak in Arizona.

The astronomical world was somewhat shaken in November when three astronomers presented preliminary findings suggesting that the yardstick used to measure large astronomical distances had led to distance estimates twice too large. The implication, when this was applied to estimates of the rate at which the universe is expanding, was that the universe is only about nine billion years old, rather than between fifteen and eighteen billion years, as widely supposed. The new yardstick depends, in part, on estimating the intrinsic brightness of many galaxies at infrared wavelengths and then using the observed brightness of each to judge its relative distance. The intrinsic brightness is estimated by recording the rotation rate of the galaxy (from the extent to which wavelengths of radio emissions from its hydrogen clouds are altered by such rotation) and using the rate to calculate the total mass of the galaxy. It is assumed that this mass determines how many stars it has and therefore its total brightness. The method was greeted as innovative and useful, but the deduced time scale was widely questioned. It would mean the universe is only twice the age of the earth and much younger than estimated ages for slowly decaying radioactive elements and the globular clusters of very old stars.

Two startling reports concerned the sun. One said it appears to be vibrating at a rate of once every 160 seconds. The other said the sun is shrinking and has been doing so for at least a century. This was deduced from published measurements of the sun's vertical and horizontal diameters made routinely by the Royal Greenwich Observatory in England from 1836 to 1953. The solar diameter of 865,000 miles was said to be shrinking by about 8.3 miles each year. As early as 1854 it had been proposed that the sun might derive its energy from the internal heat generated by gradual contraction. It was noted that, from modern calculations, the solar eclipse of 1567 should have been total, yet chronicles of the period describe it as annular—an eclipse where the face of the sun is not completely covered because the apparent size of the moon is not larger than the apparent size of the sun. This could be explained if the solar diameter in 1567 was considerably larger than today.

It has also been proposed that the sun may expand and contract in a long-term cycle. In recent decades it has been assumed that the sun derives virtually all its energy from a chain of fusion reactions in the sun's core that convert hydrogen into helium. These reactions should produce neutrinos—ghostlike particles that could pass out of the sun and reach the earth. Yet efforts to detect the predicted output of such neutrinos have been unsuccessful. It was proposed that current shrinkage of the sun might coincide with a respite in fusion reactions, providing the sun, instead, with energy derived from contraction.

Climate

After years of debate on whether a new ice age is imminent, whether supersonic transports, spray can propellants or carbon dioxide from increased fuel burning will alter the world climate, leading climate specialists from throughout the world met in Geneva during February to compare notes and chart a "World Climate Program." The latter, under the auspices of the World Meteorological Organization, based in Geneva, is designed to collect enough data on factors determining climate and climate change to make possible at least moderately reliable projections.

It was widely agreed that no clearcut trend can currently be projected. Weather records, chiefly from the Northern Hemisphere, have shown a slight warming from the late nineteenth century to about 1950, followed by a slow drop in mean annual temperatures. In at least parts of the Southern Hemisphere, however, opposing trends were recorded, so the global effect seems to have been minor. Masking such trends were regional extremes such as the paralysis of Chicago by snow shortly before the conference, a report from Russia that the month of December was colder than at any time in a century, and records from Britain and Western Europe showing the summer of 1976 to have been the hottest in 250 years. The meeting coincided with a five-week period of intensified worldwide weather studies forming part of the year-long Global Weather Experiment. Balloons were released from 40 ships strung out along the Equatorial Zone, including thirteen ships from the Soviet Union, six from the United States and two from China. Planes parachuted instruments down through the tropical atmosphere. In the Southern Hemisphere 220 buoys provided by six nations were set adrift. Data from the buoys and balloons were collected by a French data-processing system riding the Tiros-N satellite, placed in an orbit passing near both poles by the United States. Additional oceanic data were collected by 80 specially equipped, wide-bodied transports of ten airlines. It was such intensive collection of data from a large portion of the earth's atmospheric and water envelopes, combined with processing by new generations of computers, that, it was hoped, could serve the projected World Climate Program.

The conference took note of recent suggestions that pollutants from various human activities are depleting the stratospheric ozone layer that protects the earth and its inhabitants from harmful wavelengths of ultraviolent sunlight. Among the pollutants under suspicion are oxides of nitrogen from high-flying aircraft and from heavy use of nitrogen fertilizers as well as synthetic substances (known as chlorofluoromethanes or Freons) used as refrigerants and spray can propellants. The conferees also took note of the concern expressed in the previous year at the increasing use of fuel burning as an energy source, adding to the carbon dioxide content of the atmosphere. Carbon dioxide, as a gas, acts much in the manner of the glass in a greenhouse, allowing sunlight to reach the earth unimpeded but preventing the return of heat into space as infrared radiation. The result, it was assumed, would be to warm world climates. Plants, as they grow, remove carbon dioxide from the air and release oxygen. When plants or plant derivatives (such as petroleum products) are burned, the process is reversed (oxygen is consumed and carbon dioxide released).

In their final declaration the conferees stated that during the past century fuel burning and changes of land use, such as felling forests for new farmland, had increased the carbon dioxide content of the air by 15 per cent. Currently it was rising at 0.4 per cent yearly, the declaration said. Forests remove carbon dioxide from the air and place it in long-term storage. When they are felled, the wood is burned or decays, returning that gas to the air. It "appears plausible," said the declaration, that the projected increase of atmospheric carbon dioxide will lead to a gradual warming of the lower atmosphere, especially at high latitudes. In conclusion the declaration stated: "The long-term survival of mankind depends on achieving a harmony between society and nature. The climate is but one characteristic of our natural environment that needs to be wisely utilized. All elements of the environment interact, both locally and remotely. Degradation of the environment in any national or geographical area must be a major concern of society because it may influence climate elsewhere. "The nations of the world," it continued, "must work together to preserve the fertility of the soils, to avoid misuse of the world's water resources, forests and rangelands, to arrest desertification, and to lessen pollution of the atmosphere and the oceans."

The concern over climate change caused by fuel burning raised grave concerns regarding future American energy policy. The reactor accident at Three Mile Island in Pennsylvania, while threatening a serious release of radiation, was controlled and public health specialists concluded that there had been little or no effect on the surrounding population. Nevertheless, the accident and the highly critical report by the investigation commission that looked into it struck a severe blow at plans to increase dependence on nuclear energy. The most readily accessible alternative was the burning of coal and its liquid or gaseous derivatives, but widespread concern developed regarding serious climate changes that might affect global food production, starting some time in the next century.

With energy production by atom splitting in trouble, attention turned to atom fusing—the reaction that powers the sun and hydrogen bombs. Large fusion machines built, with variations, on the Soviet Tokamak principle, were under construction in Britain, Japan and the Soviet Union, as well as at Princeton, and it appeared that most, or all, would "break even" in releasing more fusion energy than is injected into the fusion fuel through magnetic compression. On the basis of these hopes an international consortium of those building these machines was formed to develop the world's first fusion reactor—a machine that would produce energy in usable form. It would be purely experimental and fusion was not expected to make a substantial contribution to energy needs until some time in the next century.

The Sea Floor

In a series of dives during the spring of 1979 the deep submersible *Alvin* hit the jackpot in its search for ore-forming eruptions on the sea floor. Evidence had been found that metal-rich layers are being laid down by eruptions of hot water along the East Pacific Rise and the central rift valley of the Red Sea. The island of Cyprus bears witness to the fact that some of the world's most valuable mineral deposits were formed in this way. Most of the early Mediterranean civilizations—Phoenecian, Egyptian, Greek and Roman—derived their copper from Cyprus and the Romans called the metal cyprum (later modified to cuprum from which "cu," the chemical symbol for copper is derived). The metal deposits on Cyprus, as in many other regions, are in the form of sulfur compounds (sulfides).

Along the Galapagos Rift Zone, west of Ecuador, sea floor explorers aboard the *Alvin*, operated by the Woods Hole Oceanographic Institution in Massachusetts, had already found evidence of hot spring activity and colonies of specialized deep-sea creatures dependent on the eruptions, such as giant clams and worms living inside ten-foot tubes of their own making. They had not, however, witnessed anything to compare with the tall stacks emitting jets of metal-blackened water that they saw on the East Pacific Rise south of the southern tip of Baja, California. The East Pacific Rise is a gently sloping ridge that bisects the South Pacific, paralleling the coast of South America. It is a "spreading center" on either side of which the sea floor pulls away, opening the oceanic crust and allowing molten rock to rise into the gap. Sea water percolating through this newly erupted rock becomes greatly heated and leaches various

minerals from it. The geysering water observed from *Alvin* was at about 700 degrees Fahrenheit, erupting from stacks six to fifteen feet high. As soon as the erupted water encountered the frigid oceanic bottom water, only a few degrees above freezing temperature, the sulfides of copper, iron and zinc in the geyser plume precipitated and fell to the sea floor, forming mounds 50 or 60 feet high. As one scientist aboard *Alvin* said later of the spectacle, "it was like Pittsburgh in 1925 with all those blast furnaces going full tilt."

South of the Galapagos Rift Zone the drill ship *Glomar Challenger*, under two miles of water, sank a hole 1,100 feet into sea floor that had presumably been formed along the rift (itself a spreading center) some five and a half million years earlier. The ship had drilled 800 holes at 501 sites throughout the world's oceans and, while primarily financed by the United States National Science Foundation, was now an international enterprise, with million-dollar-a-year contributions from Britain, France, Japan, West Germany and the Soviet Union. This hole, however, was special in that for the first time it was used for an extended period as a laboratory within which a variety of experiments could be conducted including efforts to sample water that had percolated through the deep rock, imaging of the hole's walls by a special sonic device and the lowering of a Soviet magnetometer the full length of the hole. By sampling the sediment layers laid down on various parts of the sea floor as well as the bedrock beneath them the *Glomar Challenger* has probably added more than any other vessel to what is known of the history of the oceans and their inhabitants.

Apes, Hominids and Endangered Species

Excavations and explorations in Africa and Asia continued to cast light on man's ancestry. Near Lake Turkana in northern Kenya, Mary D. Leakey reported that solidified footprints of two humanoids had been discovered alongside those of early hippopotamuses, indicating that human ancestors (or members of a dead-end side branch) walked upright at least 3.6 million years ago. This is 1.5 million years before man is known to have begun using tools. Finds reported from Burma were said to confirm earlier speculation that anthropoids may have originated there as early as forty million years ago.

Microscopic study of ancient teeth at the Johns Hopkins University was reported to have shown that the human ancestral line did not become omnivorous (eating both animal and plant material) until the appearance of modern man's most immediate ancestor (Homo erectus).

Light may have been cast on the manner whereby man and the apes evolved through the chance mating of two species of ape at an Atlanta zoo. The successful mating, reported during the summer, was between two separate but closely related species: a male gibbon and a female siamang. Both live in the forests of Southeast Asia. Hybrids of this sort are rare with such exceptions as the mating of a male ass with a mare, producing a (usually sterile) mule. The event was seen by researchers at the Human and Behavioral Genetics Research Laboratory of the Georgia Mental Health Research Institute as supporting the hypothesis that relatively abrupt evolutionary developments can occur through the juggling of genetic material. The classic view has been that evolution is a very slow process, occurring in tiny steps as small mutations alter individual genes, or pieces of genetic information.

Mindful that the present diversity of life on the earth, the product of millions of years of evolution, is threatened in many ways by human activity, wildlife specialists from 50 nations met in Costa Rica in March to draft regulations for the protection of more than 130 species of plants and animals, ranging from orchids to whales. Researchers at the University of California in Santa Cruz reported that one endangered species, the Northern Sea Elephant, was making a dramatic comeback, but that its genetic diversity had probably been irreparably damaged when its numbers were reduced to a handful of animals.

Health

Advances in surgery, psychotherapy, burn treatment, cancer prevention and medical technology are described in the pages that follow. The agonizing debate over surgery for breast cancer continued through 1979 with no clear statistical evidence resolving the issue of whether or not survival rates for those undergoing the more radical surgery exceed those for conservative surgery followed by radiation therapy. Many women were reported to be asking for the latter approach if the disease is not far advanced.

From a Mayo Clinic study it appeared that the incidence of stroke had declined considerably over the past half century. Progress was also reported in efforts to understand how pain signals are transmitted and processed by the brain as well as the role of the nervous system's own pain suppressors (such as endorphins and enkephalins). Researchers in China told of experiments suggesting that the release of such substances might account for the success of acupuncture as a form of anesthesia.

The opening of China to visitors brought to light several medical developments there. One is a new, massive effort to control schistosomiasis or "snail fever," testing new drugs for its treatment in human beings and engaging in large-scale efforts to destroy the moist or shallow-water environment in which the snails thrive. Part of the life cycle of the disease parasite must be spent within snails. The Chinese are also seeking to account for three localized "epidemics" of cancer. In the lowlands around Canton there are "hot spots" where cancers of the nasal passage and pharynx are disturbingly frequent. In the same general area and especially around the mouth of the Yangtze River north of Shanghai cancer of the liver is common. One researcher reported that it seemed to occur most often in communities where drinking water was taken from irrigation ditches and other stagnant sources fed by runoff from fields where pesticides had been used. The rate was close to normal where well water was used. Particularly dramatic is the occurrence of cancers of the esophagus, or food pipe, among residents of Linxian County southwest of Peking. The incidence is fifty times the world average and is the leading cause of death. It has been found to affect chickens who live on table scraps, suggesting that an element of the local diet is to blame. If the factors responsible for these "epidemics" can be identified, the information could be of help in combatting such cancers in areas where the incidence is less remarkable.

An area of biomedical research with special promise for the future is the use of genetic manipulation, or "engineering," to modify bacteria, such as those inhabiting the intestine (Escherichia coli), so they produce substances useful in treating disease. In 1979 biochemists at the University of California in San Francisco reported inserting genes into bacteria for the production of human growth hormone.

Similar steps were taken toward bacterial production of human insulin for the treatment of diabetics. In a joint project of Rockefeller

University and the National Institutes of Health Laboratory-cultured mouse cells with a genetic defect were "cured" by the insertion of an appropriate gene. The long-term hope is to treat genetic defects in human beings by such manipulation.

Was 1979 more productive, scientifically, than other years? One cannot judge from so short a perspective. But new tools of research, such as those in biomedical laboratories for transferring genes or the most powerful particle accelerators and orbiting spacecraft, are opening new frontiers so rapidly that the momentum is likely to sustain such advances into what may become a period of considerable budgetary austerity.

Voyager Encounters Jupiter

In March 1979 Voyager 1 swept past Jupiter, photographing both the giant planet and five of its moons. Four months later, a companion spacecraft, Voyager 2, made a similar encounter. Now, with Jupiter receding behind them, both spacecraft are headed toward the outer reaches of our solar system. In November 1980, Voyager 1 will fly past Saturn. Voyager 2, traveling at slower speeds, will reach the same way station in August 1981. Beyond there, the itinerary is less certain. In January 1986, eight years after its departure from Earth, Voyager 2 may sail within range of Uranus, taking closeup pictures of that distant planet for the first time. Long after they have exhausted their fuel supplies and their radios have fallen silent, both spacecraft will continue their traverse through space and beyond our solar system, on an endless journey.

The Voyager mission is focused on the exploration of the Jupiter and Saturn systems. The alignment of these large planets permits the use of a gravity-assist trajectory in which the gravity field of Jupiter and Jupiter's motion through space may be used to hurl the spacecraft on to Saturn. In 1977, a rare alignment (once every 176 years) of our four outer planets —Jupiter, Saturn, Uranus, and Neptune—may permit a gravity-assist trajectory to Uranus and even to Neptune for Voyager 2.

Voyagers 1 and 2 began their journeys in the late summer of 1977, catapulted into space by a Titan/Centaur launch vehicle from Cape Canaveral, Florida. With them went the hopes and dreams of thousands of people who had worked to create them and their mission.

The Voyager spacecraft are unique in many respects. Since their journeys are taking them far from the Sun, the Voyagers are nuclear powered rather than solar powered. The Voyagers are the fastest man-made objects ever to have left Earth. In fewer than ten hours, they had crossed the Moon's orbit. This compares to about three days for an Apollo flight and one day for the Mariner and Viking spacecraft. Their launches marked the end of an era in space travel—the end of the planned use of Titan/Centaur launch vehicles. With the advent of the Space Shuttle in the 1980's, future spacecraft will be launched from the Shuttle Orbiter.

Jupiter is the largest planet in our solar system, with a diameter 11 times that of Earth. Jupiter rotates very quickly, making one full rotation in just under ten hours. Composed primarily of hydrogen and helium, Jupiter's colorfully banded atmosphere displays complex patterns highlighted by the Great Red Spot, a large, circulating atmospheric disturbance. Three of Jupiter's 13 known satellites are also visible in this Voyager 1 photograph taken in February 1979. The innermost large satellite, Io, can be seen in front of Jupiter and is distinguished by its bright, orange surface. To the right of Jupiter is Europa, also very bring but with fainter surface markings. Callisto is barely visible beneath Jupiter.

Two photos of Jupiter taken by Voyager 2 in May 1979 contrast with the small inset photo by Voyager 1, taken almost four months earlier. They demonstrate that planet's atmosphere undergoes constant changes, and that, although individual clouds are long-lived, winds blow at greatly different speeds at different latitudes, causing clouds to move independently over each other.

The Great Red Spot on Jupiter is a tremendous atmospheric storm, twice the size of Earth, that has been observed for centuries. The "Great Red Spot rotates counterclockwise with one revolution every six days. Wind currents on the top flow east to west, and currents on the bottom flow west to east. This Voyager 1 picture shows the complex flow and turbulent patterns that result from the Great Red Spot's interactions with these flows. The large white oval is a similar, but smaller, storm center that has existed for about 40 years.

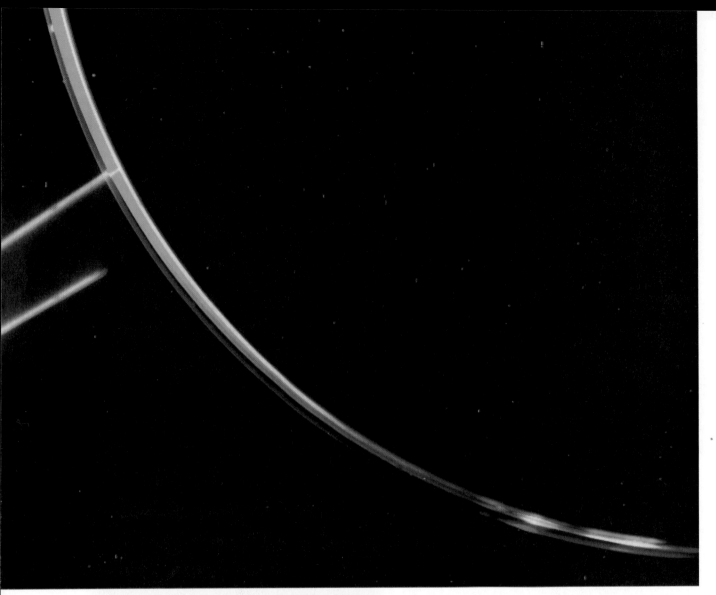

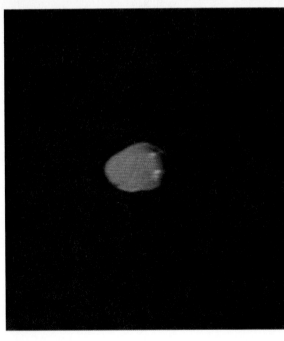

Because of Voyager 1's discovery of a ring around Jupiter, Voyager 2 was programmed to take additional pictures of the ring. Jupiter's faint ring system is shown in this color composite as two light orange lines protruding from the left toward Jupiter's limb. This picture was taken in Jupiter's shadow through orange and violet filters. The colorful images of Jupiter's bright limb are evidence of the spacecraft motion during these long exposures.

Amalthea, Jupiter's innermost satellite, was discovered in 1892. It is so small and close to Jupiter that it is extremely difficult to observe from Earth. Amalthea's surface is dark and red, quite unlike any of the Galilean satellites.

Io, Jupiter's innermost Galilean satellite, displays great diversity in color and brightness. This Voyager 1 picture shows Io's complex coloration of red-orange, black, and white regions, and the two major topographic features: volcanic regions, the most prominent of which is the "hoofprint" (volcanic deposition feature) in the center, and the intervolcanic plains that are relatively featureless. Io's vivid coloring is probably due to its composition of sulfur-rich materials that have been brought to the surface by volcanic activity.

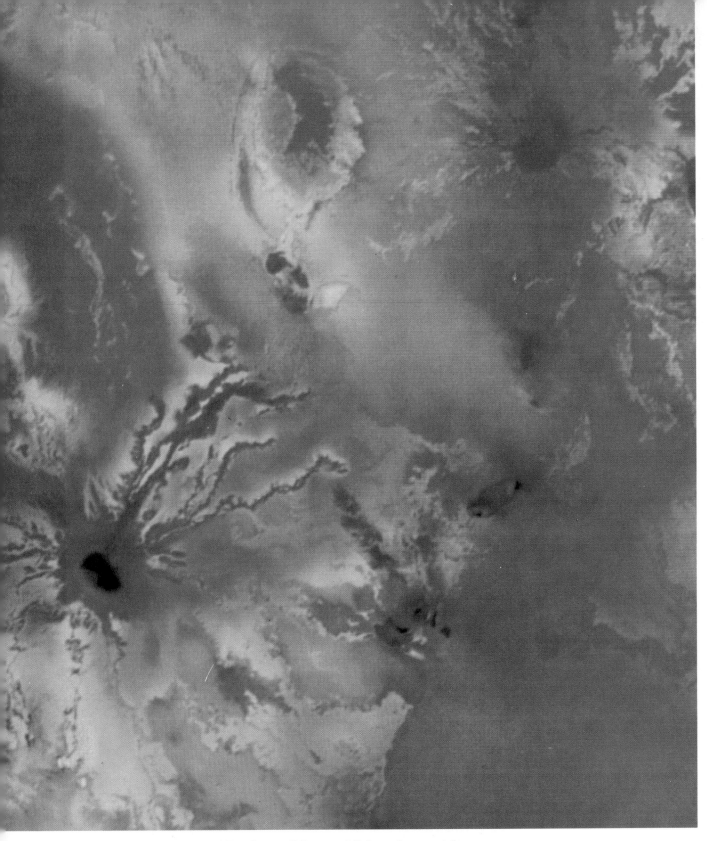

This color picture of Io, shows diffuse reddish and orangish colorations which are probably surface deposits of sulfur compounds, salts and possibly other volcanic matter. The dark spot with the irregular radiating pattern near the bottom of the picture may be a volcanic crater with radiating lava flows.

Special color reconstruction by means of ultraviolet, blue, green, and orange filters allowed scientists to study the amount of gas and dust and the size of the dust particles that erupted from the volcano on Io shown in this Voyager 1 image.

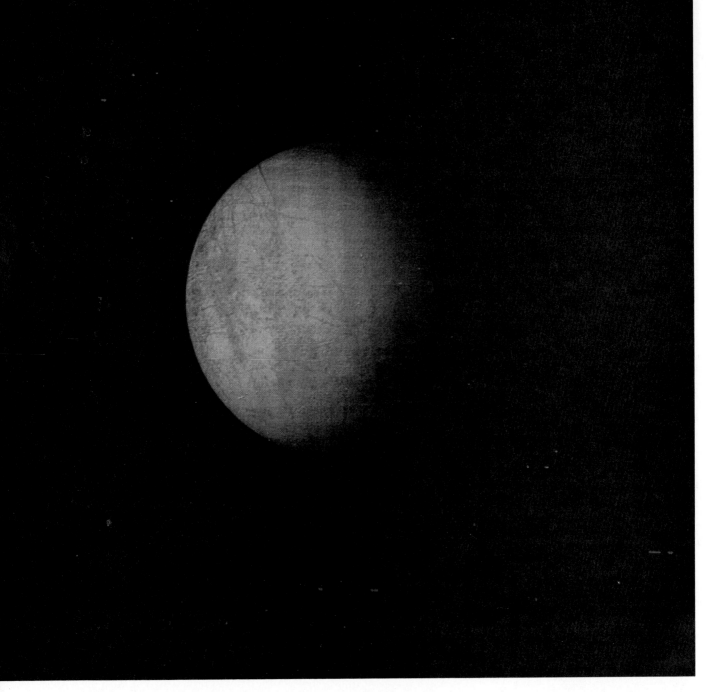

Europa, approximately the same size and density as our Moon, is the brightest Galilean satellite. The surface displays a complex array of streaks, indicating that the crust has been fractured. In contrast to its icy neighbors Ganymede and Callisto, Europa has very few impact craters. The relative absence of features and low topography indicate that the crust is young and probably warm a few kilometers below the surface. The regions that appear blue in this Voyager 2 image are actually white.

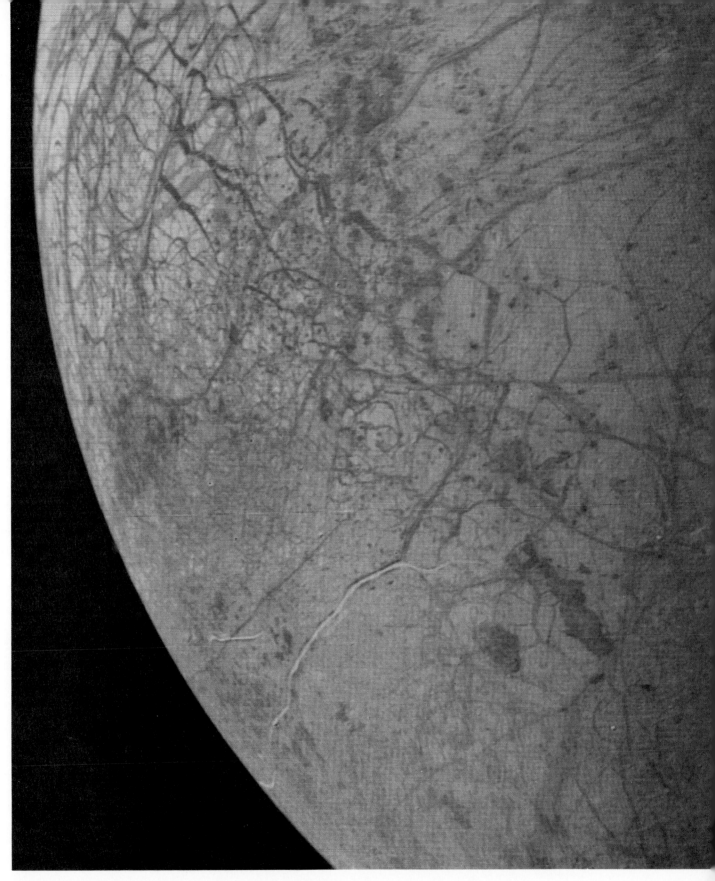

A close-up of Europa's surface which scientists believe is a thin ice crust overlying water or softer ice (slush).

Ganymede, Jupiter's largest satellite, is about one and one-half times the size of our Moon but only about half as dense. It is composed of about 50 percent water or ice and the rest is rock. The bright surface of Ganymede is a complex montage of ancient, relatively dark and cratered terrain, grooved terrain that resulted from a dramatic history of tectonic movement in the icy crust, and bright young ray craters that expose fresh ice. In this photograph, taken by Voyager 1, there are several dots of single color (blue, green, orange) which are the result of markings on the camera used for pointing determinations and are not physical markings.

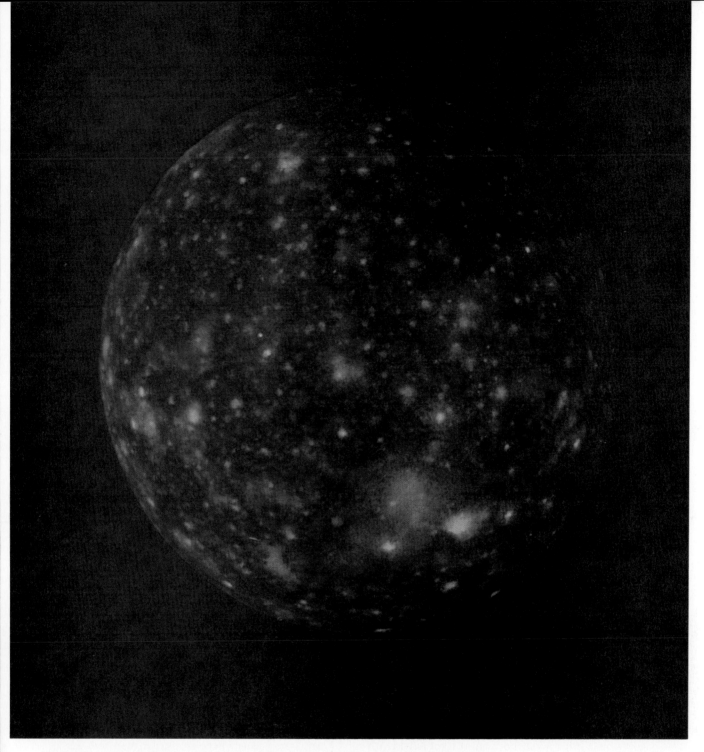

Callisto, only slightly smaller than Ganymede, has the lowest density of all the Galilean satellites, implying that it has large amounts of water in its bulk composition. Its surface is darker than the other Galilean satellites, although it is still twice as bright as our Moon. This Voyager 2 false-color-photograph shows Callisto to have the most heavily cratered and therefore, the oldest surface of the Galilean satellites, probably dating back to the period of heavy meteoritic bombardment ending about four billion years ago.

VOYAGER ENCOUNTERS JUPITER

Voyager 1 was launched 16 days after its sister ship, but because of a different trajectory, it arrived at Jupiter four months ahead of Voyager 2. Both spacecraft spent more than nine months crossing the asteroid belt, a vast ring of space debris circling the Sun between the orbits of Mars and Jupiter. During their 16- and 20-month journeys to Jupiter, the spacecraft tested and calibrated all of their instruments, exercised their scan platforms, and measured particles and fields in interplanetary space. As the spacecraft neared the planet, the cameras showed the dramatic visible changes that had taken place in the five years since Jupiter had been photographed by Pioneer 11. And for the first time, we got a close look at some of Jupiter's moons: Amalthea, Io, Europa, Ganymede, and Callisto.

Targeted for the closest look at Io, Voyager 1 flew the more hazardous course, passing between Jupiter and Io, where the radiation environment is the most intense. Voyager 2's flight path gave Jupiter and its intense radiation a much wider berth. Unlike Voyager 1, which encountered the five innermost satellites as it was leaving Jupiter, Voyager 2 encountered the satellites as it was approaching the planet, thus providing closeup photography of opposite sides of the satellites.

Arriving at Jupiter from slightly different angles, both spacecraft measured the large, doughnut-shaped ring of charged sulfur and oxygen ions, called a torus, encircling the planet at about the orbit of Io. Then, both spacecraft disappeared behind Jupiter, out of view of Earth and Sun, for about two hours. During this time, measurements were taken on the planet's dark side. Each spacecraft took over 15,000 photographs of Jupiter and its satellites.

From the moment of launch, the Voyager spacecraft have been monitored by a worldwide tracking system of nine giant antennas strategically located around the world in California, Spain, and Australia to ensure constant radio contact with the spacecraft as the Earth rotates. Radio contact with Voyagers 1 and 2 has not been instantaneous, however. When Voyager 1 flew past Jupiter, radio signals between Earth and the spacecraft took 37 minutes; when Voyager 2 arrived, the signals took 52 minutes because by then the planet was farther from Earth.

The pictures presented here were taken by a shuttered television-type camera. Each picture is composed of 640,000 dots, which were converted into binary numbers before being radioed to Earth. When the signals reached Earth, they were reconverted by computer into dots and reassembled into the original image. Most of the color pictures are composed of three images, each one taken through a different color filter: blue, orange, or green. The images were combined and the original color was reconstructed by computer. The computer eliminated many of the imperfections that crept into the images, and enhanced some of the images by emphasizing different colors.

Designed to provide a broad spectrum of scientific investigations at Jupiter, the science instruments investigated atmospheres, satellites, and magnetospheres.

□

After their closest approaches to Jupiter, both spacecraft fired their thrusters, retargeting for their next goal, the Saturn system. Scientists will still be studying the wealth of new information about Jupiter when Voyager 1 reaches Saturn in November 1980, and Voyager 2 follows in August 1981. After Voyager 1 encounters Saturn, Voyager 2 may be retargeted to fly past Uranus in 1986. Upon completion of their planetary missions, both spacecraft will search for the outer limit of the solar wind, that boundary some where in our part of the Milky Way where the influence of the Sun gives way to other stars of the galaxy. Voyagers 1 and 2 will continue to study interstellar space until the spacecraft signals can no longer be received.

Pioneer Saturn

We have entered into a new era of space exploration. Missions undertaken during the lunar exploration of the 1960's typically lasted a matter of days with commands issued and carried out in near real time. Now, a decade later, planetary voyages may last for many years as the spiraling trajectories of the spacecraft make periodic intersections with the orbits of the planets. Communicating with us across the vastness of space, these spacecraft report to us their experiences as they traverse the outer reaches of the solar system.

Among these deep space travelers, Pioneers 10 and 11 are appropriately named, for they truly are pioneering the exploration of the outer solar system. Launched in 1972 and 1973, respectively, they were the first spacecraft to fly by Jupiter (in 1973 and 1974). At Jupiter, Pioneer 11's trajectory was carefully targeted to swing it toward Saturn for an encounter in September 1979.

Pioneer Saturn (Pioneer 11) has given us our first close view of the spectacular ringed planet Saturn and its system of moons. The spacecraft began its journey to the giant planets Jupiter and Saturn on April 5, 1973. It reached Jupiter on December 2, 1974, passing within 42,760 km of the Jovian cloud tops and taking the only existing pictures of Jupiter's polar regions. Jupiter's massive gravitational field was used to swing Pioneer 11 back across the solar system toward Saturn. Additional maneuvers were executed in 1975 and 1976 to place the spacecraft on a suitable trajectory, with the final aimpoint selected in 1977.

From the many possible targeting options for the first Saturn flyby, two aimpoints were considered, both of which would result in a near-equatorial flyby that would give the best mapping of the high-energy particles and the magnetic field near the planet. The difference between these two aimpoints, which came to be known as the "inside" and "outside" options, was their relationship to Saturn's unique ring system first discovered by Galileo in 1610. The "outside" option was finally selected because it was considered to be of less risk to the spacecraft and more valuable in planning the subsequent encounter of Saturn by Voyager 2, which will reach Saturn in 1981. Final targeting was

13

Shown here is the best view yet available of Saturn and its rings, returned by Pioneer 11 during its encounter with the planet.

This image of Saturn's rings photographed by Pioneer 11 on August 31, 1979, shows the structure of Saturn's ring system in detail never before seen.

completed during early 1978, when a series of timed rocket thrusts locked Pioneer into the desired trajectory.

On September 1, 1979, the spacecraft, now designated Pioneer Saturn, reached Saturn after 6 years of flight. It passed through the ring plane outside the edge of Saturn's A-ring and then swung in under the rings from 2,000 to 10,000 km below them. At the point of closest approach, it attained a speed of 114,100km/h (71,900 mi/h) and came within 21,400 km of the planet's cloud tops. While it was approaching, encountering, and leaving Saturn, the spacecraft took the first closeup pictures of the planet, showing 20 to 30 times more detail than the best pictures taken from Earth, and made the first close measurements of its rings and several of its moons, including the largest moon, the planet-sized Titan. Titan, along with Mars, has been considered by many scientists to be the most likely place to find life in the solar system.

Pioneer Saturn unraveled many mysteries. It determined that Saturn has a magnetic field and trapped radiation belts, measured the mass of Saturn and some of its moons, and studied the character of Saturn's interior. It confirmed the presence and determined the magnitude of

15

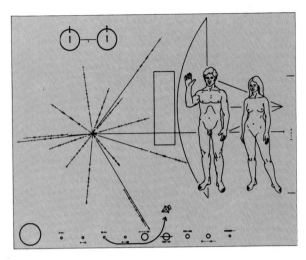

The Pioneer spacecraft carries a message, engraved on a plaque, from Earth to any inhabitants of another star system who might discover it.

an internal heat source for Saturn. Its instruments studied the temperature distribution, composition, and other properties of the clouds and atmospheres of Saturn and Titan, and took photometric and polarization measurements of Iapetus, Rhea, Dione, and Tethys. Pioneer may also have discovered a previously unknown moon of Saturn. The spacecraft measured the mass, structure, and other characteristics of Saturn's rings, and passed safely through the outer E-ring, which posed a potential hazard for Pioneer. It also discovered new rings. One of these rings, called the F-ring by the Pioneer team, lies just outside the A-ring. The gap between the F-ring and the A-ring has been tentatively designated the Pioneer Division. The other new ring has been called the G-ring, which lies well outside the F-ring.

Pioneer carries a scientific payload of 11 operating instruments; another instrument, the asteroid/meteoroid detector, was turned off in 1975. Two other experiments, celestial mechanics and S-band occultation of Saturn, use the spacecraft radio to obtain data. Pioneer Saturn is a spinning spacecraft, which gives its instruments a full-circle scan 7.8 times a minute. It uses a nuclear source for electric power because the sunlight at Jupiter and beyond is too weak for a solar-powered system.

Two booms project from the spacecraft to deploy the nuclear power source about 3 meters from the sensitive spacecraft instrumentation. A third boom positions the magnetometer sensor about 6 meters from the spacecraft. Six thrusters provide velocity, attitude, and spin-rate control. A dish antenna is located along the spin axis aand looks back at Earth throughout the mission, adjusting its view by changes in spacecraft attitude as the spacecraft and Earth move in their orbits around the sun.

Tracking facilities of NASA's Deep Space Network, located at Goldstone, California, and in Spain and Australia, supported Pioneer Saturn during interplanetary flight and encounter. Pioneer's radio signals, traveling at the speed of light, took 85 minutes to reach Earth from Saturn, a round-trip time of almost 3 hours, somewhat complicating ground control of the spacecraft. Almost 10,000 commands were sent to the spacecraft in the 2-week period before closest approach. Continued communications should be possible through at least the mid 1980's.

After the spacecraft passed Saturn, it headed out of the solar system, traveling in the direction the solar system moves with respect to the local stars in our galaxy and in approximately an opposite direction from its sister spacecraft, Pioneer 10. Both spacecraft have plaques attached to them which contain a message from Earth for any intelligent species that may intercept the spacecraft during their endless journeys through interstellar space.

Other spacecraft are following along the trail blazed by Pioneer Saturn. Voyager 1 passed by Jupiter in March 1979 and will reach Saturn in November 1980. Voyager 2 has also passed beyond Jupiter and will encounter Saturn in August 1981, with the further possibility of traveling on to Uranus (a 1986 encounter). Under development are the Galileo orbiter and atmospheric entry probe, destined to journey to Jupiter where the orbiter will return more detailed information, including high-resolution pictures of the Galilean satellites, and the probe will penetrate deep below the Jovian clouds.

In the coming years, each of these follow-on missions will enrich our understanding of the solar system, greatly supplementing the observations of Pioneers 10 and 11. But one thing will never change. The Pioneers were first.

Skylab

by Richard D. Lyons

On July 11, 1979, the Skylab space station, at 77 tons the largest object ever orbited, flashed through the atmosphere and disintegrated in a blaze of fireworks over the Indian Ocean, showering tons of debris across the Great Australian Desert, one of the world's most remote places. Officials of the National Aeronautics and Space Administration estimated that the area of re-entry into the earth's atmosphere began over the north Atlantic and that disintegration began over Ascension Island in the south Atlantic. Many accounts of sighting of debris filtered from the sparsely populated desert region, but no reports of either injury or property damage. Should either occur, the United States is bound by treaty to indemnify those hurt.

President Carter sent the Australians a message of apology and proffered assistance, saying:

"I was concerned to learn that fragments of Skylab may have landed in Australia. I am relieved to hear your Government's preliminary assessment that no injuries have resulted. Nevertheless, I have instructed the Department of State to be in touch with your Government

immediately and to offer any assistance that you may need."

The threat that the disintegrating space station could rain havoc over a wide area had captured attention around the world as space agency controllers tried to predict and control when and where it would fall. In making its 34,981st and final orbit of the earth, Skylab provided some anxious moments for space officials who had sought to steer it away from populous areas.

Skylab re-entered the atmosphere several thousand miles farther down its orbital track than had been expected, and sent flaming debris onto the barren desert of Western Australia and, presumably, into the sea off southwestern Australia. Earlier, it had been expected to land in the ocean. A decision to maneuver the craft as it moved closer to re-entry enabled it to fly safely over southern Canada and Maine, but may have been responsible for its Australia landing.

"We had a tougher bird than expected," said the Skylab project director, Richard G. Smith, several hours after re-entry had occurred at

17

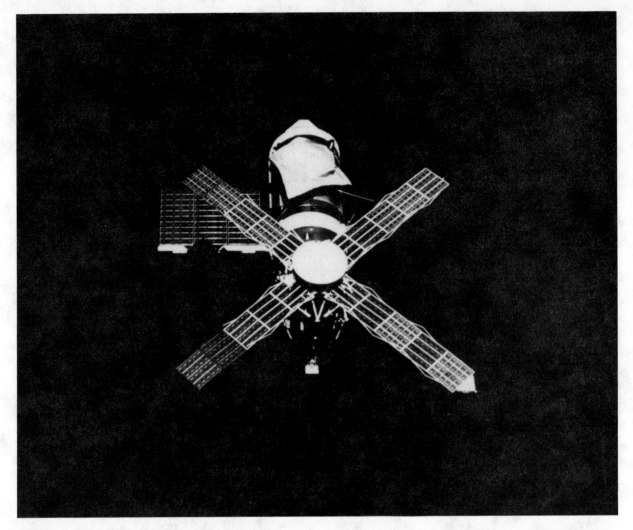

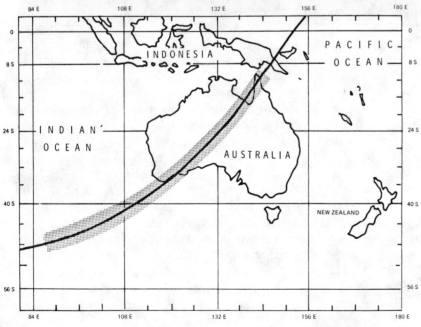

A view of the Skylab space station in orbit (above), as it appeared before its fiery re-entry into the atmosphere.

These pieces of Skylab debris (right) were recovered from the backyard of Stanley Thornton, Jr., of Esperance, Australia.

The grey area indicates the "footprint" of Skylab debris, as estimated by NASA (left). Despite fears of injury, no one was reported hurt.

12:37 P.M., Eastern daylight time. "We're glad it's down, but we would have liked to have seen it never sighted over Australia."

The decision on re-entry involved a command to the spacecraft six hours before re-entry that put it into a sort of wobble, which was designed to extend its re-entry track by about 5,000 miles and 30 minutes. The maneuver virtually assured that no debris would land on Canada and the northern United States, as had been feared late last night, but re-entry was prolonged so that chunks did shower down near Australia.

On the final pass shortly before noon, Skylab sped eastward over Portland, Ore., flew in an arc across the continent, descended over Maine and Nova Scotia, re-entered the atmosphere at

11:44 A.M., went farther down its track over the South Atlantic, and then started breaking up over Ascension Island at 12:11 A.M.

While Skylab was on this final pass, the Federal Aviation Administration closed a 150-mile-wide path of airspace east of Kennebunkport, Me., to minimize the possibility that debris might hit an aircraft. It later proved that the precautionary measure was unnecessary. "We're in the last hour of the descent of Skylab," said the flight director, Charles Harlan, at the Johnson Space Center in Houston, just before disintegration.

First evidence that friction was heating up the satellite's surface—temperatures eventually reached several thousand degrees—came from the South Atlantic when the Ascension tracking station reported that telemetry data from the spacecraft were "becoming garbled and intermittent."

"The solar panels folded like a little duck's wings," said Bob Kapustka, a Skylab engineer at NASA's Marshall Space Flight Center in Huntsville, Ala.

As the satellite headed beyond Ascension Island, around the Cape of Good Hope and into the Indian Ocean, a general uneasiness settled over the Skylab situation room at NASA headquarters across from the National Air and Space Museum along Independence Avenue in Washington. Though not articulated, the fear was that through some gross miscalculation the spacecraft would continue to fly past Australia, over the Pacific and then re-enter somewhere near Vancouver Island in the Pacific Northwest. To complicate the problem, while flying over the western regions of the Indian Ocean, Skylab was out of reach of civilian tracking stations, although as it neared Australia it was picked up by the radars of the secret spy satellite ground station at Pine Gap near the center of the country.

Then at 12:42 P.M., Eastern daylight time, officials of NASA announced that the easternmost edge of the debris footprint had landed at about 43 degrees south latitude and 106 east longitude, perhaps 750 miles southwest of Perth, on the southwest Australia coast.

Almost six hours later NASA officials set the final break-up point more than 1,000 miles farther east, about 31.8 degrees south latitude and 124.4 degrees east longitude. "Entering debris believed to have been the heavier pieces of Skylab was sighted over the area of Western Australia," said a NASA announcement late this afternoon, adding: "No reports of accident or injury have been received." If true, the larger pieces of the expected 26 tons of debris would then have fallen in the desert, an outback area largely inhabited by aborigines. According to previous calculations by the space agency, the pieces, of which at least 500 would have weighed at least a pound, would land along a "footprint" about 4,000 miles long and 100 miles wide.

But according to prior estimate, the largest pieces would land first on the easternmost end of the landing site because they had the greatest weight and thus the greatest momentum, at about 260 miles per hour. By contrast, the smaller pieces had been calculated to enter at a speed of perhaps 30 miles per hour. The later calculations would have a footprint extending hundreds, perhaps even thousands of miles over the Australian continent.

Injury or property damage, in the event that it did happen, also would open to question the early-morning decision to wobble the spacecraft deliberately. Mr. Smith said the decision was made about 3 A.M. after consultations with a group of experts, including Dr. Robert A. Frosch, the administrator of NASA. "We made the decision on the basis of all the information we had, the best analysis we had, and I'd make that same decision again based on absolutely the same information," Mr. Smith said.

Noting that, "apparently, there has been some debris overfly of Australia," Mr. Smith conceded that a margin of error had crept into

Richard G. Smith, Skylab project director.

the calculations because of too little information being fed into the forecast computers at the start of the final orbit. "We have been saying for weeks that we have an uncertainty around the point of predicted re-entry that is fairly large and this illustrates the point," Mr. Smith said. "The best information we had, the best information NORAD, everybody had predicted that it would come down before Australia." NORAD is the North American Air Defense Command, which supervises the tracking. But for the wobble or tumble maneuver being made, Mr. Smith told newsmen later, there was a possibility that some debris might have struck North America.

"It was a worst-case situation," he said. "We were trying to prevent the creation of a worse condition than we started with." For many weeks, NASA scientists had conducted a series of intricate calculations aimed at providing Skylab controllers with estimates of the numbers of people living beneath any given track of the vehicle. The final orbit was one of the best, since it was almost totally over ocean.

The final plunge thus ends the $2.6-billion Skylab project that began over a decade ago. The huge cylindrical space station was placed in orbit in 1973, and was visited by three parties of astronauts who carried out long scientific and medical experiments. The longest of the three-man groups stayed aloft for 84 days.

At present, NASA has no firm plans for the development of another space station like Skylab. Operations will center, starting this year, on the space shuttle, which blasts into orbit like a spacecraft and lands like an airplane.

Mysteries of Deep Space

by Timothy Ferris

The reconnaissance of Jupiter by Voyager 1 has yielded a treasure of scientific discovery and sheer spectacle. As it sailed past Jupiter the spacecraft took a close look at what is virtually a mini solar system—the lordly planet itself, which harbors 90 percent of the mass of all the planets, its moons, some of them almost as hefty as planets, and (as Voyager discovered) a ring of particles that calls to mind the rings of Saturn and Uranus, and the vast belt of asteroids that circle the sun.

Data from instruments designed to assess the composition of Jupiter and its surroundings will take time to be fully analyzed. The impact of the photographs is more immediate. Scientists cried out in delight as the Voyager cameras presented them with sights no eye had ever seen. The gaseous outer layers of Jupiter were resolved into a roiling stew of salmon pink, brick red and ice blue whose intricate filigree offered fresh evidence that the more closely one looks at nature, the more beautiful it becomes. The moons, previously known as little more than dots of light swimming in a telescope's field of view, turned out to be as individualistic

as flowers. Ganymede is an agate wreathed in veins of white, Europa a cracked ocher ball that bears a passing resemblance to Mars. Callisto, a lonely outpost, is the color of a corroded Roman coin, while Io, a garish orange and cream, looks as whimsically decorative as a hot-air balloon.

The success of the Jupiter encounter produced elation at the Jet Propulsion Laboratory, the organization that managed the mission and guided the twin spacecraft on their long journey for the National Aeronautics and Space Administration. J.P.L. people have a unique specialty: They take over responsibility for interplanetary spacecraft once they have been launched into space and guide them out into the realm of the planets, thus realizing a dream that goes back to the time of Kepler. They are very good at what they do. They have tracked the probes which were dropped into the maelstroms of Venus, dispatched others to take close-up photos of Mercury and to brave scorching near encounters with the sun, have assayed the solar system out almost to the orbit of Saturn and have helped soft-land the mechanical emissaries on Mars, 300 million miles away, to

22

An artist's conception of Voyager spacecraft in interplanetary cruise configuration.

within 6 miles of their target. "Life seems very rich, just now," said the forceful, youthful-looking director of J.P.L., Dr. Bruce Murray, 47, as praise for Voyager's success poured in from around the world.

Dr. Murray felt he could use a little richness. When he took over J.P.L. in 1976, the lab had fallen on hard times. So few interplanetary space missions were planned for the 1980's that the survival of the lab as a space-faring center stood in jeopardy. Now, however, he hopes that J.P.L.'s fortunes are improving.

The Voyager mission itself had begun in a climate of uncertainty. The launch of the first of its twin spacecraft was attended by a series of near disasters, the most disturbing of them a crisis that came to be known ruefully as the "software affair." "It was no idle matter," Dr. Murray recalled. "It was a $400 million mission and we were in deep trouble."

"Software" is computer jargon for the myriad instructions programmed into a computer. For a "smart" spacecraft like Voyager, software constitutes what might be called the computer's world view—its sense of where it is, what is happening, its alertness to problems and its acumen in solving them. Properly programmed, Voyager can carry out complex assignments—such as locating and photographing Jupiter's moons —and can manage its affairs with little human help. Improperly programmed, the spacecraft computer can become, in effect, psychotic. To a psychotic computer, perfectly normal events can take on a sinister cast, like that of a human psychotic who, say, interprets the dripping of a leaky faucet as the ticking of a bomb.

That is what happened on the occasion of the first Voyager launch. Because of a programming oversight, the spacecraft interpreted its own launch as a disaster, and duly reported to the ground that it had suffered a massive electrical breakdown. The mission seemed to be over almost as soon as it had begun.

The thunderous launch of Voyager atop a Titan Centaur rocket from Cape Canaveral, Fla., overwhelmed the delicate sensibilities of the spacecraft's internal guidance system, a package of gyroscopes designed to cope with the far less violent accelerations Voyager would experience once it had left Earth behind. This raised no concern on the part of humans involved in the mission, who knew that the gyroscopes would sort themselves out as soon as the launch phase ended and Voyager was cruising in space. But it raised grave concern on the part of the computer. The software people had neglected to tell the computer that there would be such a thing as a launch. Voyager didn't know that it was being swamped by the acceleration of its powerful booster rocket. All it knew was that it couldn't tell where it was.

In mounting alarm, the main Voyager computer tested each set of gyros in turn and found that all were behaving crazily. Since the simultaneous failure of all the gyros was extremely unlikely, the computer checked to see whether the fault might lie in the electronic circuits that reported on the condition of the gyros. The circuits seemed fine. If the problem wasn't the gyros and wasn't the circuits, the computer was obliged to reach the galling conclusion that it must itself be to blame. Voyager carries two identical master computers, one of which lies dormant and waits to take over should the other fail. With the mission only an hour and 13 minutes old, Voyager's A computer diagnosed itself as faulty and abdicated control of the spacecraft to the B computer. The B computer in turn performed the same sequence of tests, arrived at the same conclusion, and reported to the ground that all was calamity.

It took time for Voyager personnel to untangle this story and satisfy themselves that the spacecraft's problem had been emotional rather than physical. Meanwhile, more tangible problems appeared as the spacecraft sped out beyond the orbit of the moon. An on-board radio receiver failed. A sensor designed to signal the deployment of a boom carrying scientific instruments failed to report: Had the boom itself failed to deploy or, which turned out to be the case, had only the sensor failed?

Problems like these are diagnosed at J.P.L. by reference to a vast set of records that detail the history of each of the space vehicle's 61,000 parts. Ultimately, a technician who suspects an obscure spacecraft subassembly of misbehaving millions of miles out in space can look up the names of the people who built that particular part, call them, and ask them how the unit "seemed" back when they held it in their hands. So thorough a system works well, as witness the

William H. Bayley manages the Deep Space Network at JPL.

Dr. Bruce C. Murray is Director of the Jet Propulsion Laboratory, the organization that managed the Voyager 1 mission for NASA.

sterling performance of Voyager today after its shaky start—but it takes time and money to operate. As they untangled Voyager's problems, the project people got farther and farther behind schedule. NASA, footing the bill, expressed concern. With the help of a J.P.L. review board made up in part of veterans of the spectacularly successful Viking mission to Mars, the Voyager problems were ironed out and the mission was running smoothly by the time Voyager 1 approached Jupiter.

But the memory of the software affair lingers, a symbol of the problems faced by the interplanetary navigators in the days of the shrinking dollar. Voyager's cry of alarm came at a time when the fortunes of J.P.L. had ebbed. The laboratory had but a single iron in the fiscal fire, a proposal for a mission known as the Jupiter Orbiter Probe (now renamed Galileo) and that proposal had been voted down by the House Appropriations Committee. The Viking landing on Mars the summer of 1976 was a brilliant success, and the data being returned from Mars were adding volumes to human understanding of the solar system. But Viking had cost nearly a billion dollars, and the word from Washington was to bring off subsequent missions on the cheap. "Voyager was an understaffed, underplanned mission," said Dr. Peter Lyman, one of the Viking veterans drafted to help straighten out the Voyager mission. "They had been pressured to do it as cheaply as possible. As a result, in the long run, it cost more to set things right than it would have to have done them right in the first place."

Having achieved the opportunity to realize the ancient dream of understanding the solar system, the nation seemed uncertain whether it wanted to go through with it. The White House was at best lukewarm on the subject of unmanned space exploration. Congress was wary of appropriating money for space probes at a time when many Americans were finding it difficult to put beef on the table. And NASA, which funds J.P.L., had amassed a notoriously poor record of selling the public on unmanned space exploration, an effort it undertook by arguing the unlikely hypothesis that taxpayers should support the investigation of other worlds because the resulting technology might produce wrist radios and efficient coatings for

Scientists at JPL helped soft-land the devices on Mars which sent back photos such as this.

frying pans.

"It's remarkable when you think about it," said Gentry Lee of J.P.L. We sat talking in a sunlit central plaza at the laboratory, a cluster of steel and glass buildings nestled in the foot-hills in Pasadena that looks like a junior-college campus but for the nests of microwave dish antennas. Dr. Lee looked upward, rolling his eyes in a gesture of incomprehension. "Imagine that you were living in the Pleiades star cluster, writing a history of our world in the second half of the 20th century," he said, "and you found

that here an intelligent species developed the capacity to extend its senses out to touch all the planets of its solar system. And yet for some strange reason, that species decided not to employ that ability. Instead it turned its back on this adventure."

As we sat up one night in a building that hummed with the musings of computers alert to the status of spacecraft from the sun to Saturn, another top J.P.L. staff member admitted, "I'm not optimistic about the future of planetary exploration. I think the public appreciates its

The Titan-Centaur-7 that lifted off from Cape Canaveral at 10:29 a.m. (EDT) on August 20, 1977 sent the 1,800-pound Voyager II on its odyssey through the outer planets.

value—understands its grandeur and excitement —and perhaps Congress understands it. But NASA doesn't seem able to understand it, and President Carter seems to have all but written it off. I get discouraged sometimes. But then I come into the lab and a new photo of Jupiter is on the screen, and we're seeing things that no human being ever saw before, and I get such a boost."

Dr. Murray admits to similar bouts of pessimism. A tall, square-jawed man more comfortable giving orders than listening to advice, he brought to the lab an aggressive—some would say abrasive—style of leadership under which its fortunes have sharply improved. Dr. Murray calls the process "climbing out of the bathtub," referring to a chart of laboratory funding that descended to a low plateau by 1977 and now is slowly ascending. The ascent began when Congress, in a House floor vote, rare in such matters, finally approved Galileo, a mission to drop an instrumented probe into the seething atmosphere of Jupiter in 1985.

The probe will carry a mass spectrometer (an instrument that measures the masses of atoms and molecules accurately) which may provide the first direct information on the presence of the large molecules that could be building blocks of living matter. This instrument should be able to get down at least to the level of the water clouds on Jupiter, where the density of the atmosphere is high, collisions are more frequent, the temperature is comfortable, and conditions for the onset of chemical evolution are fairly favorable.

Galileo will bring us to the threshold of a serious search for life in the outer reaches of the solar system. A plan on the drawing boards calls for the subsequent exploration of Titan, largest moon of Saturn, which is important to that search because, unlike any other moon, it possesses its own atmosphere. Titan, like Jupiter, is also rich in methane and other gases helpful to the evolution of life. It may be even more favorable than Jupiter for the onset of evolution because it is likely to have a solid surface on which pools of liquid can accumulate for more rapid progress in nature's experiments.

There are two further missions in the wings for J.P.L. One is a comet-chasing probe powered by an ion engine driven by sunlight. The other,

Solar Polar, funded jointly by NASA and the European Space Agency, calls for looping a pair of spacecraft high above and below the plane in which the planets orbit to survey these previously unexplored regions of the solar system. With the bottom of the bathtub behind him, Dr. Murray might be expected to rejoice. Instead, he is worried about the future of unmanned space flight, frustrated by the limitations of bureaucracy, and impatient with the rate at which humans are piecing together an understanding of their cosmic surroundings.

Dr. Murray recalls his early years at J.P.L. with the air of someone remembering a bad dream. When he took over the lab in 1976, his previous administrative experience was limited to having run a geology project at the California Institute of Technology that employed six persons and spent $200,000 a year. J.P.L. employs 4,000 on a budget of roughly $250 million a year. The lab is a hybrid, technically part of Cal Tech but funded primarily by NASA, a situation that some at J.P.L. view as resembling the grip of contending talons. Yet Dr. Murray found that he lacked for advisers on either side. The president of Cal Tech, Harold Brown, had gone off to become President Carter's Secretary of Defense. The head of NASA, James Fletcher, a Nixon appointee, had resigned and was yet to be replaced, J.P.L.'s only source of substantial income aside from space exploration was a contract to help the Energy Resource Development Administration research cheap solar energy, but President Carter, soon after entering office, eliminated E.R.D.A. (It later became the Department of Energy.)

Feeling rather lonely in his lofty new post, Dr. Murray was subjected to a prompt education in the hazards of administration. Much of it came in the form of what he called "torpedoes in the night," bureaucratic warheads that reached his desk in the morning mail. The Internal Revenue Service audited Cal Tech and challenged the nonprofit status of J.P.L. The Federal affirmative-action program charged the laboratory with hiring too few members of minorities and threatened to cut off its Federal funds. (This is a perennial problem in the aerospace industry, where educational requirements are stratospheric and starting salaries usually unimpressive.) There followed the earthquake

This giant tracking antenna, located at Goldstone, California, is part of NASA's Deep Space Network of stations located around the world to maintain 24-hour radio contact with planetary and interplanetary space vehicles.

"torpedo." A group of consulting engineers warned that J.P.L. was vulnerable to earthquakes. The director of the Viking project, Jim Martin, a crew-cut perfectionist with the bearing of a career military officer, got wind of the report and ordered top mission personnel to keep their passports and vaccination certificates up to date so they could fly to deep-space tracking stations in Australia or Spain and carry on with the Mars mission should J.P.L. crumble into rubble. This struck Dr. Murray as amounting to something less than a vote of confidence. "After all, I'm a geologist—God, this is so agonizing to talk about—and I know about these things," he said recently as we talked in his home in Pasadena. "J.P.L. did not appear to me to be in any particular danger. At any rate,

we drilled holes all over the place. And we earthquake-proofed the buildings. Now it's better understood geologically than almost any place in the region."

Dr. Murray was discovering that space exploration had its unglamorous side. As the Viking spacecraft approached Mars, a bomb scare forced evacuation of the entire laboratory. Bubonic plague was found being carried by squirrels in the foothills near the lab. J.P.L. began losing personnel to sects, notably Scientology. "The problem isn't when they quit," Dr. Murray grumbled. "The problem is the ones that don't quit—if they stay on, but stop thinking."

In Washington, Dr. Murray lobbied from a final redoubt: Unless further unmanned space

Another antenna of the Deep Space Network is in Canberra, Australia. A third, similar tracking antenna is located near Madrid, Spain. The control center for these giant tracking antennas is located at JPL, which designed, built and manages the network for NASA.

missions were funded, he said, the laboratory would be unable to continue to employ the men and women who had learned how to navigate to the planets. Some would be laid off; others, assigned to nonspace projects. As Gentry Lee put it, "The engineering feats involved in interplanetary space flight can be compared to the building of the Roman aqueducts or the medieval cathedrals. If you dismantle the teams that landed Viking on Mars and steered Voyager to Jupiter, then try to pick up where they left off again in a few years, you'll find that it's no mean trick. You may well not be able to do it."

Is interplanetary space flight as practical as the Roman aqueducts, or as fanciful as the cathedrals? Both, Dr. Murray answers: "We do it for international prestige. What has reflected better on the United States than Viking and Voyager? This has a practical result—other nations here on Earth must believe that we have a good and positive side to us, and they have to believe in our technical prowess. We do it for the sake of our domestic self-esteem; unmanned space exploration is a popular thing with Americans, especially when you remember that the cost of doing it amounts to about a dollar or so per person per year. We do it because by setting such challenging tasks for ourselves we drive our technology to otherwise unattainable accomplishments, and this in turn strengthens

This view of Venus was taken by Mariner 10's television cameras and computer-enhanced at JPL's Image Processing Laboratory.

The Galileo orbiter and probe mission to Jupiter in 1985 will expand upon the Voyager investigations of the Jovian system.

our entire technological and economic system. And finally, exploration has scientific and philosophical significance. The expansion of man's consciousness through space exploration will have no less significant effects on mankind's view of itself and of the reality in which we exist than have the explorations from the 14th to the 19th centuries when we explored the Earth and opened our minds to our environment."

This theme runs through many lines of conversation at J.P.L., that space ought to be explored because it *is* ultimately our environment. "Are we doing space research in order to understand the earth?" asks Moustafa Chahine, head of the earth and space sciences division of J.P.L. "No. We're trying to better understand our solar system, seeking knowledge for its own sake, for its own merit. Are we benefiting here on earth from this research? Are we coming to understand our planet better? Yes."

But given the economic climate of the times, the people at J.P.L. are not bashful about arguing in terms of cost-effectiveness, even when discussing missions whose public-relations appeal might seem to be chiefly romantic. Ask J.P.L.'s resident comet expert, Ray Neuburg, why we should spend money to send probes chasing after comets and he will note that they are made of material left over from the time when the sun and planets formed, that they are in a sense scraps from the cosmic workbench, and that understanding them could help us solve one of the great riddles of modern astronomy, that of how the solar system came into existence. Having set forth the scientific arguments in favor of the mission, he then promptly adds a remark in a cost-conscious vein: Since comets are buffeted by the solar wind, like sailboats blown off course by a terrestrial gale, the orbits of comets could tell us about the solar wind if we understood in detail just how they are affected by it. Says Dr. Neuburg, "If we can observe just one comet up close and understand how the solar wind acts upon it, then each subsequent comet will become a free interplanetary probe."

Arguments like these helped Dr. Murray and his colleagues persuade Congress to sustain the nation's commitment to a continuing reconnaissance of our solar system. But Dr. Murray's one disappointment in Washington involved the least expensive of his pet projects. This was the Search for Extraterrestrial Intelligence, or SETI, a plan developed jointly by J.P.L. and the NASA Ames Research Center near Palo Alto to use radio telescopes part-time to search the heavens for messages possibly dispatched by inhabitants of other worlds. Given its relatively modest cost of $20 million (as compared with more than $400 million for Galileo) and its enormous potential (if successful in receiving an alien signal, SETI could be expected to alter the course of human thought), Dr. Murray hoped that SETI would get through Congress. Instead, it attracted the unwelcome unattention of Senator William Proxmire of Wisconsin, who awarded his "Golden Fleece" award as a "ridiculous example of wasteful spending." Senator Proxmire noted that "there is not now a scintilla of evidence that life beyond our solar system exists." His remarks infuriated many advocates of SETI, since searching for such a "scintilla of evidence" was the whole idea of SETI. "The detection of evidence of extraterrestrial intelligence is the most significant fact that could be discovered," says Dr. Murray. "We are not likely to find something unless we look for it. If astronomers at the beginning of the 20th century had listened to arguments like Senator Proxmire's, many of the most important discoveries of this century—the discovery of pulsars, of quasars, the development of radio astronomy—never would have happened."

Whatever becomes of SETI and of more ambitious plans being hatched at J.P.L.—plans that include snatching up pieces of comets and asteroids and returning them to Earth, Dr. Murray has managed for the present to keep J.P.L. in business as the world's only full-time center of interplanetary exploration. Symbolic of this commitment is the Deep Space Network, the division of J.P.L. that stays in touch with interplanetary spacecraft as they wander, year after year, through the void.

The network stands as a monument to audacious precision. Its radio receiving stations in Australia, Spain and the Mojave Desert can pick up signals as weak as the energy given off by a safety match struck on the surface of Mars. Its computers sustain an awareness of space and time so precise that they can report on the location of a probe hurtling through space 100 million miles away with an accuracy of a few yards. J.P.L. navigators have found the very stars insufficiently constant to steer by—stars slowly swarm as our galaxy turns—and they now navigate by sighting quasars, brilliant beacons at the outposts of the cosmos whose light in many cases has been traveling through space since before the earth was formed. With their sights set on quasars and their clocks ticking with a precision in comparison to which the spinning of the earth is a mere drunken wallow, the D.S.N. navigators deserve much of the credit for space spectaculars like the Voyager encounter with Jupiter. Curious about what sort of people had built this monument to precision, I paid a visit to the D.S.N. headquarters at J.P.L.

To visit William Bayley who manages the D.S.N., and Mahlon Easterling, its architect, one negotiates a building filled with the trappings of futurism—the low hum of computers, the march of data like colored confetti across television screens, the perambulations of preoccupied technicians. But what one finds in the middle of all this is an office devoid of electronic gear, its lights dimmed, occupied by two men who would not be out of place playing checkers by the stove in a country store. Dr. Easterling is red-faced, with flowing white hair and a voice that ripples with the sound of a mountain stream just above a good distillery. Dr. Bayley carries himself with the quiet calm of a man whose most serious technical problem is deciding whether to bother his sleeping hounds long enough to get up and fetch his fly rig. Both were wearing sweater vests and plaid shirts, a theme Dr. Easterling had extended to include a pair of clashing plaid pants.

Dr. Bayley began his explanation of how the Deep Space Network works by jotting a few figures on a blackboard and frowning at them. "Now these figures are wrong, you understand," he said, "but they help me keep it in my head where everything is. Take Pioneer 11, for example. Pioneer 11 has a round-trip travel time of five hours . . ."

"I think you mean Pioneer 10, Bill," said Dr. Easterling.

"Yes, right, Pioneer 10. Anyhow, it takes two and a half hours for radio signals traveling at the speed of light to get to Pioneer 10, and an-

other two and a half hours for it to reply, so if you want to have a conversation with Pioneer 10 it takes five hours to send a command and find out if the spaceship has heard you."

Dr. Bayley grinned and shook his head. "It's hard for me to think of something a billion and a half miles away," he said. "I find it even harder to think of all those data streaming back from the spacecraft, that long thin trickle of data stretching across all that space."

Dr. Easterling chuckled. "There aren't too many of those bits of data, but they're sure going like the devil," he said.

"Yes, and that old Pioneer 10 is just going on out now," Dr. Bayley replied. "You know, it's an old spacecraft, and it has only a 10-watt transmitter. That's about like a refrigerator bulb. If you want to see something operating at 10 watts, look at the light in your refrigerator. So we get the data back pretty slowly from Pioneer, only about one thousand bits per second. We're rather proud of the way we've been able to improve the rate that we get data back from our spacecraft. When Mariner 4 flew past Mars in 1964, its photographs and scientific data came back at the rate of only 8.3 bits per second. With Voyager, we're getting 117,000 bits per second, and that from way out at Jupiter. Pretty soon we hope to be able to go as high as eight million bits per second."

"We're always improving the accuracy of our clocks, too," said Dr. Easterling. The two spoke in the tone of old friends swapping stories they had exchanged many times before. "Right now we operate at an accuracy of one second in three million years. That sounds pretty accurate, but believe it or not we have people who complain bitterly that it's not good enough."

"Soon we will have improved that to better than one second in three billion years," Dr. Bayley said. He hesitated. "Or is it one second in 300 million years? I forget." He went to the telephone and dialed his secretary. "Barbara? Will the next generation of D.S.N. clocks get us to one second in three *billion* or one second in three *hundred million* years?" He returned with a scrap of paper. "It's three billion years," he said happily.

I asked Dr. Easterling how he had come to be involved in building the Deep Space Network.

"To understand that, you should know that I

A solar electric propulsion spacecraft would eject an instrumented probe toward Halley's comet in 1986 and continue on to rendezvous with another comet, Tempel 2.

have every issue of Analog science-fiction magazine since 1948," he said. "In 1952 I read about interplanetary navigation for the first time. It was an article in Analog by John Pierce titled 'Don't Write: Telegraph.' There had been some science-fiction stories about using rockets to deliver the mail, and these had got John angered because they were so inefficient. So he worked out the design of an interplanetary communication system, using microwaves. It employed exactly the techniques we use today.

"I went to Columbia University as an electronics engineer, and then I worked on military radar. When Sputnik was launched I said, 'Whoops, now's the time.' I wanted to work on deep space. It took me a year to find the right place, which was J.P.L. I've been here ever since." Dr. Easterling looked out the window at the San Gabriel Mountains. "So you see, when it came to designing an interplanetary communication system, it was no trouble, because I'd read how to do it."

□

I left Drs. Bayley and Easterling, each of whom has logged more than 20 years at J.P.L., joking comfortably with each other. Fresh streams of data were pouring in from Voyager 1 and marching across the screens. While we had been talking, Voyager had traveled another 25,000 miles. In a few months it will reach Saturn, then it will leave our solar system. In 40,000 years it will have passed abeam of another star, a white dwarf designated AC + 79 3888. Unless someone or something snares Voyager at some future time and place, it will still be journeying among the stars billions of years from now, when the sun expands and consumes the earth.

Crucibles of the Cosmos

by Timothy Ferris

Dr. Allan Sandage sat up late one night at the Kitt Peak National Observatory in Arizona exposing photographic plates on the giant four-meter telescope and talking about galaxies. It was a dark, moonless night. It always is when Sandage is to be found observing, for his interests lie with starlight that has been journeying in space for millions of years and arrives in so feeble a condition that it can be analyzed and recorded properly only by the dark of the moon. Sandage is one of the bluewater sailors among astronomers.

The sky over Kitt Peak was full of stars. Sandage could see none of them. He was sealed in an observer's cage suspended within the telescope tube high above the observatory floor, his vista of the cosmos limited to its close black walls and to a single blob of light in the eyepiece that he scrutinized to assure himself that the telescope was tracking correctly while the plate was exposed. The plate is what matters in viewing galaxies. The human eye is insufficiently sensitive to view galaxies in detail and deep-space astronomers rarely *look* at them through telescopes. Nor do they spend much

time admiring the resulting photographs, though galaxies are indisputably beautiful and I have seen an ordinarily sober astronomer jump up and down with excitement at a photograph of a particularly striking one. Instead, they analyze the plates, counting and measuring thousands of star images on them, seeking to discern the anatomy of these cities of stars. As to the stars in the Arizona sky, Sandage appreciates their spectacle as do the rest of us, but he finds them rather . . . local. Astronomers like Sandage enjoy gazing at them casually but find them of such peripheral concern that many never bother to learn the constellations. Some would have trouble locating the Big Dipper. These stars are our neighbors. They crowd the foreground like leaves in a celestial tree that makes up the Milky Way galaxy. The deep-space astronomers are interested in peering out beyond, to the other galaxies. "Trees aren't important when you're interested in the forest," Sandage said over the intercom from the observer's cage. By "forest," he meant the universe.

Now astronomers are finding that galaxies

A team of researchers recently found what they believe to be a huge black hole in the nucleus of the massive galaxy M-87.

are stranger than anyone had suspected. Nesting in them may be creatures as provocative as black holes feeding on stars, and quasars, pouring out power with a vigor that astonishes physicists. They are enormous physical laboratories; by better understanding what goes on inside them, astronomers expect to gain fresh insights into the age, size and dimensions of the universe.

A team of researchers including Wallace Sargent of the Hale Observatories in Pasadena and C. R. Lynds of Kitt Peak recently found what they believe to be a huge black hole in the nucleus of the massive galaxy M-87, making the galaxy resemble a sort of cosmic sink with an infinitely deep drain in its center. Astronomer

Donald Hall of Kitt Peak, studying how stars form in galaxies, discovered a star so young that it has been shining, in Hall's estimate, only since Homeric times, a mere instant in astronomical terms. A host of investigators in galactic dynamics, among them Beatrice Tinsley and Richard Larson of Yale University, James Gunn of Cal Tech, and the veteran observer Halton Arp of the Hale Observatories, are finding that galaxies undergo startling transformations. Big galaxies swallow little ones. Galaxies collide. Some, it appears, explode. Some dance grand passacaglias, swapping stars by the millions. These transformations are less violent than they sound—we who are riding aboard a galaxy need worry little more about them than

Dr. Allan Sandage.

Jonah worried about the perambulations of the whale—but they add up to a picture of a universe in evolution, in whose story our own evolution plays a part.

It is beginning to look as if we are deeply connected with our cosmic surroundings, like birds perched in a galactic tree, our lives involved with the fortunes of the starry forest. Some of these connections may dictate matters as mundane as the weather. Several British astronomers, among them Sir Fred Hoyle, R. A. Lyttleton and William McCrea, suggest that the Ice Ages may have been triggered by the solar system's having passed through a cloud of dust and gas associated with one of our galaxy's spiral arms. A Colorado physicist, Lars Wahlin, has proposed that lightning bolts, those symbols of the caprice of fate, may be produced by cosmic rays—particles accelerated through interstellar space by our galaxy's magnetic field. If Wahlin is right, then the old commonplace is true, and lightning bolts really are, in a sense, dispatched from heaven.

Still deeper connections between ourselves and the galaxies are being discerned. Astrophysicists studying the chemical composition of stars, and biologists investigating the chemical composition of our bodies, have found that we are made up of much the same allotment of elements as is our galaxy: The metals found in trace elements in our bodies appear to have been formed in the explosions of stars that died

M-81, a spiral galaxy consisting of 90 billion stars, is a half million light-years away.

before the sun was born, seeding space with the metal-rich dust and gas from which our solar system and, eventually, ourselves were formed.

The story of galaxies is beginning to reveal itself to a new generation of astronomers, as well as to their elders, through the eyes and ears of new astronomical tools. X-ray satellites have made it possible to study the tenuous intergalactic gas through which galaxies pass, permitting analysis of how entire clusters of galaxies behave. Ultraviolet sensors, working in realms of the spectrum beyond the range of the human eye, have yielded clues to the puzzling quasars, which may represent galaxies in their early stages of development, shimmering with light that started on its voyage to our telescopes bil-

Our own galaxy and that of Andromeda (above) form a pair which spiral in opposite directions.

lions of years ago. Researchers aided by computer simulation techniques are taking steps toward cracking the highly complicated problem of how galaxies herded their billions of stars together in the first place. Says Gunn: "We've only just started looking at galaxies in analytical ways, but I have every faith that some real understanding will be reached and that it won't take terribly long. Tremendous effort is being dedicated to it." And Sandage, as we talked, said, "We see the story of the evolution of galaxies coming to a head in a remarkable way. Problems that had seemed impossible to understand are yielding, and a general picture of sorts is emerging. The subject is going to be very lively in the next few years."

The astronomers who know galaxies best tend to be careful in choosing their words about them. They are mindful of the contrast between the grand reality of the galaxies and the elementary nature of our understanding of them. Sandage, who in the estimation of many colleagues possesses the most accomplished mental picture of galaxies of any man alive, can be circumspect in the extreme. Sometimes he begins a conversation by denying he knows anything at all, a characteristically scientific sort of defense, the social equivalent of calibrating all meters to zero. That is what happened when I appeared at Kitt Peak and announced myself through the intercom.

"I don't work on galaxies anymore," said

41

A "small" galaxy passes near a large galaxy (M-51), tugging stars by the millions into the void of intergalactic space between them.

Sandage from his perch up in the dark. "I gave it up."

The night assistant sitting beside me grinned and pointed to the coordinates glowing in ruby numbers on the control console. They indicated that Sandage was photographing M-81, a spiral galaxy six and a half million light-years away.

"That looks like M-81 you're on now, Allan," I said.

"Oh well, it's not a big galaxy. Only 90 billion stars."

"The residents of M-81 might not be pleased to hear that. It's a beautiful galaxy."

"Yes. You know, beauty in galaxies appreci-

42

ates according to their mass. The more stars a galaxy has, the prettier its spiral arms."

We talked through the night. Like a guide spotting fishing holes, Sandage can show you where in a galaxy to find nurseries churning out young stars, or retirement homes of old stars nearly spent, or slowly winking variable stars that will help you chart the galaxy's distance. He is familiar with giant elliptical galaxies larger than our Milky Way, with paltry irregular galaxies that look like little more than thimblefuls of sand, with spirals of elegant beauty and galaxies whose eventful past has left them tattered. He can show you two spiral galaxies cocked to each other like an open pocket watch, and note that in such pairs, the two spiral in opposite directions. (Our own galaxy and the great spiral in Andromeda form such a pair.) "Galaxies are what they are," Sandage said, quoting a Zenlike remark of his mentor Edwin Hubble, one of the discoverers of the expansion of the universe. "You try to learn from them."

Sandage searches for similarities in galaxies, seeking to improve our estimates of the dimensions of the universe and the rate at which it is expanding; these numbers in turn ought to yield a prediction of the fate of the universe—whether expansion will go on forever. The approach stands in contrast to that of some younger researchers whose curiosity leads them to be concerned more with individual galaxies—how they formed and why they look the way they do. Many are physicists rather than astronomers. "We who came into the field from physics are not so much grand builders," says Wallace Sargent, a physicist at Cal Tech. ("Grand builder" in astronomical circles is more or less a code name for Sandage.) "The big picture is far too uncertain as yet. We tend more toward being explorers, toward looking for an interesting particular problem and going after it. We look for galaxies whose stars are bluer than average, or redder, or fainter than average, and try to see what the hell is going on there." A colleague put it more baldly and less seriously: "We physicists are opportunists."

Recently several of the physicists have been looking into the question of why some galaxies seem to be producing no new stars. In a "healthy" galaxy like ours, new stars form with regularity, but some spirals appear to have

closed up their star-making shops long ago; they contain only old stars. Our sun is itself a relatively young star. Had our galaxy stopped forming stars six billion years or more ago, we wouldn't be here to ask why. Two young Kitt Peak astronomers, Karen and Stephen Strom, suggest that the "unhealthy" galaxies may have suffered collisions with other galaxies or with clouds of intergalactic gas, collisions that swept them clean of the dust and gas they needed to make more stars. The Stroms and others have found evidence that "unhealthy" galaxies tend to be found in the crowded inner regions of galaxy clusters, where collisions would be most likely.

The question would be interesting to residents of an "unhealthy" galaxy if they were interested in developing technology, because metals apparently are available only to inhabitants of planets of younger-generation stars. According to this theory, widely accepted in astrophysics, metals are forged in the explosions of dying stars, which seed the interstellar medium with heavy elements that in turn condense to form new stars and planets. In galaxies where star formation ceased before the metals seeded space, all the planets would be metal-poor. Astronomers there, studying the skies with telescopes formed of bamboo or lignum vitae or whatever other light materials had been left them by their cosmic fortunes, presumably would ask themselves the same sorts of questions the Stroms are asking here: Why do galaxies turn out differently from one another? Says Stephen Strom, "We're trying to unravel what might be called the genetics of galaxies, their evolutionary processes."

One obstacle has been that galaxies conduct their affairs over such long periods of time that on a human time scale they appear frozen. If you want to know whether hawks nest on a particular cliff you can sit in a blind for a month or two and see if any hawks show up. But if you want to see two galaxies interact as they pass each other, you'll have to wait a few hundred million years, and that is more than even the most patient astronomers can manage. Recently scientists at several institutions have employed computer simulations to look into the past and future of galaxies. The computers are programmed with data on the mass and size and relative locations of galaxies. Then the programs are run to re-create events that took eons to unfold.

A pioneer in this endeavor, Alar Toomre, showed me a computer-generated film one afternoon in a darkened office at M.I.T. The subjects were M-51, a lovely spiral galaxy, and a small nearby irregular designated NGC 5195. The symmetry of M-51 is broken by one distended arm that reaches out toward the smaller galaxy; astronomers had wondered just what was going on there. Toomre's film appears to have solved the riddle.

Toomre started the film at a point millions of years ago. As the millenniums sped by (a counter in the corner off the screen, calibrated in millions of years, flickered faster than the eye could follow), the two galaxies churned across space toward each other. At first they looked as unperturbed as strangers approaching on a city street. Then their gravity began to make itself felt as the space between them narrowed. Each galaxy contorted like the face of a man who has been punched in the stomach. Their arms, each home to billions of stars, waved like tentacles, reached out almost to touch—and the film froze. We were at the present.

The computer rotated the model in one dimension, and we were treated to the sight, unprecedented on earth, of how a couple of galaxies look from another perspective. If Toomre's film is correct, the two galaxies have experienced their nearest encounter and NGC 5195 is continuing off into space, followed by one beseeching arm of M-51. A few million stars have been left homeless by the episode. They now ride alone in intergalactic space. If astronomers evolve there one day, they might, by recourse to the sort of analysis Toomre has applied, learn how they came to find themselves dwelling under starless skies, drifting between two galaxies and claimed by neither.

Computer analysis by Toomre, Roger Lynds of Kitt Peak and others has enjoyed at least preliminary success in explaining the curious ring galaxies. Dozens of these puzzling objects have been found, each resembling a smoke ring. The computer studies suggest that ring galaxies are formed when a smaller galaxy passes through the center of a large one, punching a hole in it. And indeed, near every known ring galaxy is found a smaller galaxy, slinking away from the scene of the accident.

Galaxies are mostly space, and collisions between them may take place with few if any stars running into each other. The exceptions to this rule are the nuclei of galaxies, their centers, the Grand Central Terminals of stars. What goes on there is not yet well understood. Some galaxies emit considerable light and natural radio noise from their nuclei, and our own galaxy's core rumbles a bit in radio wave-lengths. (Intervening dust clouds prevent our seeing the center of the Milky Way galaxy in visual light, but radio telescopes can "see" it.) A number of astronomers and physicists are interested in galactic nuclei, not least because what goes on there may tell us something about two of the most provocative subjects of modern astronomy, black holes and quasars.

Black holes were predicted indirectly by that cornucopia of gravity physics, Einstein's theory of general relativity. The theory implies that if mass is concentrated to a high enough density—as in the case of a giant collapsed star—its gravitation will be so intense that nothing, not even its own light, can escape from it. In Einsteinian terms, the black hole occupies a well in space-time whose sides are so steep that radiation cannot "climb out." Most theorists today take seriously the possibility that black holes exist, but actually finding one poses difficulties, as black holes are invisible. A black hole swallowing up gas from an interstellar cloud, or tearing it off the surface of a nearby star, might betray its presence by a sort of scream released by the doomed gas. Calculations show that the scream ought to be detectable in the zone of the electromagnetic spectrum known as X-rays, and observations of X-ray satellites have revealed several such sources that may signal the presence of genuine black holes.

Quasars, discovered by Sandage in 1960, appear to be very remote objects glowing with furious brightness. They are so bright that astrophysicists have trouble imagining how they turn out so much energy. One popular speculation is that they represent the nuclei of young galaxies, where the collapse of gas clouds formed massive black holes; their intense energy would result from tormented dust and gas heated as it spins into the black hole. More than one hypothesis urges that stars, too, are consumed by black holes at the center of these galaxies. Some quasars flicker; this might signal that they are gorging themselves on stars. "It would be quite a sight," says one physicist, "stars spiraling down into the hole like bowling balls, first dismembered and then disappearing in sheets of light."

Virtually all quasars lie at distances of a billion light-years or more, meaning that it has taken their light a billion years or more to reach us, so we are seeing a feature of the universe as it was that long ago. No quasars are known to exist in the modern universe. But some relatively nearby galaxies exhibit signs of lingering violence at their centers, like the thunder in a subsiding storm. If these nuclei once were quasars, and if the black hole concept of quasars is correct, we should find black holes at the nuclei of many galaxies today. With this in mind, astronomers in the United States and England recently examined two large galaxies, whose great mass makes them likely candidates, and found evidence of giant black holes sitting in the nucleus of each. Observations by an orbiting space telescope, scheduled for launch in 1982, should help decide the matter.

An alternative to looking for relics of ancient cosmic violence is to search out galaxies still in their birth throes. The more conspicuous galaxies, ours among them, were born billions of years ago and seem to have settled into calm middle age, but young galaxies may yet be condensing out of raw dust and gas, their violent adolescence still in the future. Looking for them will take time—the number of available telescopes is small, galaxies are strewn across the sky like beach sand, and very young ones are likely to be dim—but astronomer R. B. Larson of Yale calls it "the most intriguing and perhaps most promising possibility" in the field.

□

At Kitt Peak, Sandage and I talked on past midnight. His voice grew weary.

"I don't know what I'm accomplishing here, letting starlight put marks on a silver nitrate photographic plate," he said with a sigh. "But it sure looks pretty. I don't know why people have to try to do what they couldn't do before. I don't know what it's all about. All I know is that I feel awful bad if I don't keep working."

At 1 A.M. Sandage had exposed all the plates in the observer's cage. He ordered the telescope tilted down to the floor so he could reload with fresh film to keep him supplied till dawn. In the dark interior of the dome I watched the telescope heel over and down until the observer's cage reached a white steel scaffold. A door in the cage opened, spilling red night-vision light. Sandage's booted feet emerged. He climbed out, a case of plates under his arm. We shook hands. "This will take about 10 minutes," he told the night assistant. He hurried toward the darkroom to reload the plates. He did not quite run.

The Solar Eclipse

by Malcolm W. Browne

On February 26, 1979, the moon's dark shadow swept across the northwestern states, treating thousands of spellbound viewers to the last total solar eclipse the continental United States will see until the year 2017. "We had a beautiful corona, very active," said Dr. Charles F. Keller in a telephone interview from the Los Alamos Scientific Laboratory in New Mexico. Dr. Keller and his colleagues flew from Kirtland Air Force Base in New Mexico to North Dakota and, racing the moon's shadow, were able to stay in the zone of totality for four minutes.

The eclipse plunged the snow-covered prairies in Central Montana into darkness for slightly more than two minutes. The intensity of storms on the sun resulted in a spectacular display of flaming prominences from several parts of the solar disk at totality. Outside the fringe of solar storms, the ghostly white corona sprang into view, displaying many irregular spikes. The stark, rolling snowfields reaching to the peaks of the Rocky Mountains on the horizon added to the drama of the show.

In the last few seconds before the dark outline of the moon completely covered the sun, a great bluish mass seemed to sweep across the snow, swiftly darkening the scene into night and leaving a brilliant orange sunset on the horizon. The planet Venus suddenly came into view not far from the eclipsed sun. More than 500 astronomers and other eclipse enthusiasts riding in 15 buses selected a remote vantage point at the last moment, parking by the side of a country road near an abandoned farmhouse. The group's organizers, including two meteorologists, a former astronaut and a network of ham radio stations, coordinated information to guide viewers away from approaching storms and overcast skies. At the last moment, the eclipse was nearly obscured to some of the ground viewers by a group of hot-air balloons flown by eclipse watchers. Anxious astronomers yelled to the balloonists a few hundred feet above the ground to change altitude, and the balloonists obliged.

Also in the air was Dr. Keller, whose chief goal was to photograph the corona in such a way that it could be seen precisely where, and under what conditions, the solar wind forms. This rush of particles from the sun exerts a va-

Leaders of the bus caravan, From left: Marcy Sigler, Dr. Theodore Pedas, Dr. Phillip Sigler, and former astronaut M. Scott Carpenter.

Dr. Charles Keller

riety of effects on the earth's ionosphere and magnetic field. To do this, Dr. Keller used polarizing filters, which screen out unwanted optical effects. Similar efforts in previous eclipses have examined the corona outward to a distance of 12 solar radii. This time Dr. Keller extended the photography to 20 solar radii. When the moon's shadow had outdistanced their Air Force NC-135, a converted Boeing 707, Dr. Keller and his co-workers flew, without having stopped, back to New Mexico.

At totality on the ground, the red prominences and white corona were so striking that an appreciative murmur swept over the crowd. Seasoned eclipse watchers, including astronomers in the group, agreed that the day's show was one of the best they had seen.

Temperature Falls Sharply

As usual, the temperature fell sharply during the eclipse, and the bitter cold numbed photographers' fingers. Watchers took to skis, cars, airplanes, balloons and mountain trails to look at the eclipse, which was total in an arc starting in the Pacific Ocean and running northeastward through Washington, Montana, Manitoba, Canada, and the Arctic. Elsewhere in the continental United States, the eclipse was only partial. In New York City, 61 percent of the sun's disk was covered by the moon.

The bus caravan, which carried the largest single group of watchers, was organized by Dr. Philip Sigler, a professor of sociology at the City University of New York, with his wife and brother-in-law, Dr. Theodore Pedas, planetarium director at Youngstown State University in Ohio. The Siglers have organized eclipse expeditions on ships and land since 1972, all of which have successfully evaded bad weather and other obstacles to convey large numbers of enthusiasts and professional astronomers to the best vantage points. This year, they had hoped to use some 200 miles of Montana railroad to chase the eclipse, but negotiations for a special Amtrak train failed at the last moment. A bus caravan operating from Big Sky was used instead.

Experts on the expedition included Dr. John A. Eddy, solar astronomer at the High Altitude Observatory in Boulder, Colo.; Dr. Mark R. Chartrand 3d, chairman of New York City's Hayden Planetarium, and Dr. Frank D. Drake, director of the National Astronomy and Ionosphere Center at Arecibo, P.R. Dr. Edward M. Brooks, professor of geophysics at Boston College, maneuvered the convoy of buses through the snow-covered mountain passes and range land of western Montana near Yellowstone National Park, plotting tactics against the weather like a general up against a wily and unpredictable enemy.

With much of the North American continent under overcast skies, the task of finding a hole in the clouds large enough to look at the sun for two minutes proved a formidable task. For days in advance, Dr. Brooks, the meteorology guide on previous eclipse expeditions the group has made, plotted weather data and made dummy eclipse-chasing runs.

He reported to participants that of three dummy passes he had made during the last three days, viewers would have been able to see the eclipse on only one, but that he had learned about some peculiarities of local weather in the process. "It looks as if we have a fighting chance of seeing the eclipse," he announced at a final weather briefing. "Unfortunately, our [astronomer] friends in Canada are not going to be so lucky. The overcast will probably cover them completely." Dr. Brooks led the 15-bus convoy, escorted by sheriff's cars, from a radio-equipped jeep in continuous touch with weather stations in various parts of the country and with several aircraft in flight, including one in which the former astronaut M. Scott Carpenter was sending direct weather reconnaissance.

The overcast in Canada, besides being deeply disappointing to thousands of people along the path of totality in Manitoba Province, was especially unlucky for a research team from Williams College in Williamstown, Mass.

Data on Plasma Sought

The Williams team was headed by Dr. Jay M. Pasachoff, whose observations of the sun's corona during this eclipse were planned to yield data on the density of plasma within the huge shell of ultrahot gas surrounding the sun.

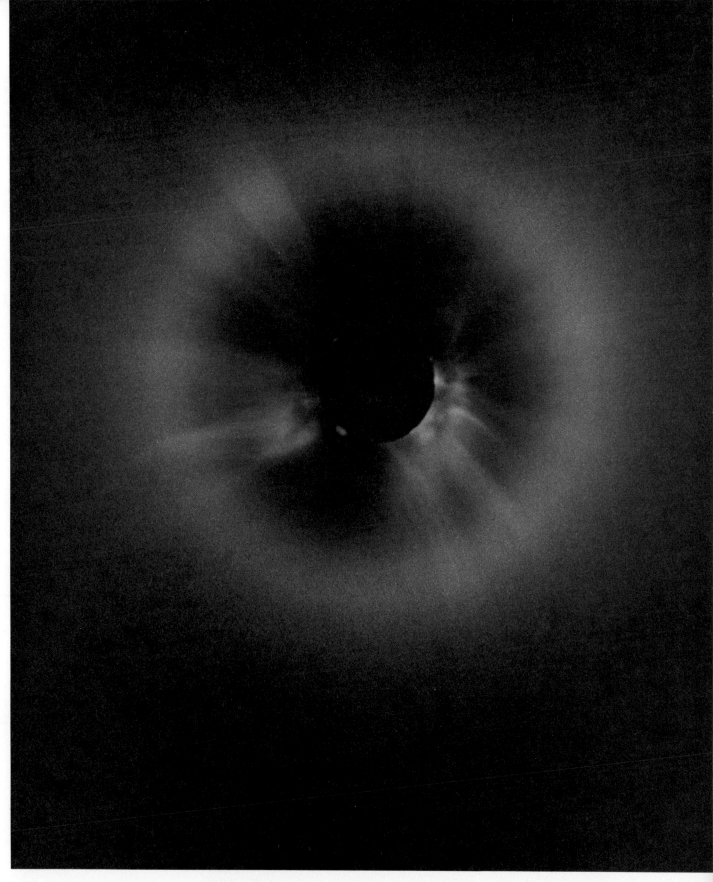

This photograph of the corona was taken from an aircraft by Dr. Keller's expedition, in an effort to determine where and how the solar wind forms.

The last sliver of sunlight creates a "diamond ring" effect just before the sun disappears behind the moon. The effect will reoccur as the total eclipse ends.

The solar corona, consisting of gas and plasma, can be seen by the naked eye only during eclipse.

Unusually large red prominences caused excitement among eclipse watchers. A filter was used for this photograph to eliminate the glare of the corona.

Plasma is gas in which normal atoms have been stripped of some or all of their electrons, thus becoming ions. This commonly occurs in extremely hot gases such as the solar corona, whose temperature is about 1 million degrees Fahrenheit. The plasma in the solar corona is strikingly similar to the plasma that would have to be heated, compressed and confined in a fusion reactor here on earth, and the irregular behavior of the sun's corona could hold clues to the proper design of a workable fusion reactor.

Dr. Pasachoff's observation point was among the more comfortable to be had by scientists observing this eclipse. He and his students sat on the balcony of the physics building of the University of Brandon in Manitoba. Although there was a thin cloud cover, Dr. Pasachoff said in a telephone interview, he was able to make usable measurements of the density of plasma at about 40 points throughout the corona before totality ended. His goal is to produce a map of coronal density variations. He said each eclipse added to such knowledge because the densities change in accordance with the 11-year

sunspot cycle. This time, he said, he saw a number of condensations, isolated regions of unusual brilliance in the corona where densities were unusually high.

Eclipses are not particularly rare. In the average century there are 237 solar eclipses, which includes 66 total solar eclipses, and 154 lunar eclipses, including 71 total lunar eclipses. But most of these are in out-of-the-way places, and many people pass their lives without seeing one. Allowing for the fact that in a total eclipse the path of totality is about 100 miles wide, a total eclipse of the sun is visible from the same spot on earth only once every 360 years.

During the last century or so, astronomers have been able to go to remote eclipses intentionally, rather than having to wait for each one. Shipborne astronomy added many more eclipses to those to which land-based observers had been limited, and the airplane and space vehicles have still further expanded access to eclipses. Consequently, there has been an explosion of knowledge about eclipses and the sun in recent years.

TECHNOLOGY

Fusion

by Walter Sullivan

Never before has the derivation of energy through the splitting of atoms been in greater disrepute. The accident at the Three Mile Island nuclear power plant in Pennsylvania has been followed by reports suggesting that even low-level radiation from such plants can be hazardous.

Might the answer be fusion—deriving nuclear energy by combining small atoms instead of splitting big ones? It should produce far less hazardous waste and, it is hoped, ultimately burn fuel that is virtually unlimited. Sufficient research progress has been made to embolden the Department of Energy to set a step-by-step timetable leading to construction of the first demonstration fusion reactor to generate power. However, that high point in the effort to harness the energy of the sun will have to be preceded by a succession of difficult decisions, progressively setting aside all but one of the potential paths toward fusion.

Fission is a contrived process. In a reactor, it generates a wide range of lethal byproducts whose safe handling is a problem. Fusion, on the other hand, is nature's way. It is what makes stars shine, providing the solar energy that has made life possible on earth. A fusion reactor would produce helium, which is not radioactive, although the process would generate radioactivity in the reactor's structural materials.

In fission, massive atoms such as those of uranium 235 are split. But in a fusion reactor, the nuclei of very small atoms, such as the two heavy forms of hydrogen (deuterium and tritium), would be fused into helium nuclei. In both cases, the resulting atoms weigh slightly less than those entering the reaction and the residual mass is converted into a great deal of energy.

Researchers in a half-dozen countries are trying to harness fusion reactions. Though some have been working on the problem for 30 years, they admit that fusion is for the next generation, not this one. Tempering their optimism is an awareness of the history of today's atomic reactors. What a generation ago seemed a golden path to cheap, almost unlimited energy has proved to be a costly, rocky road, still far from its goal and beset by difficulties. Neverthe-

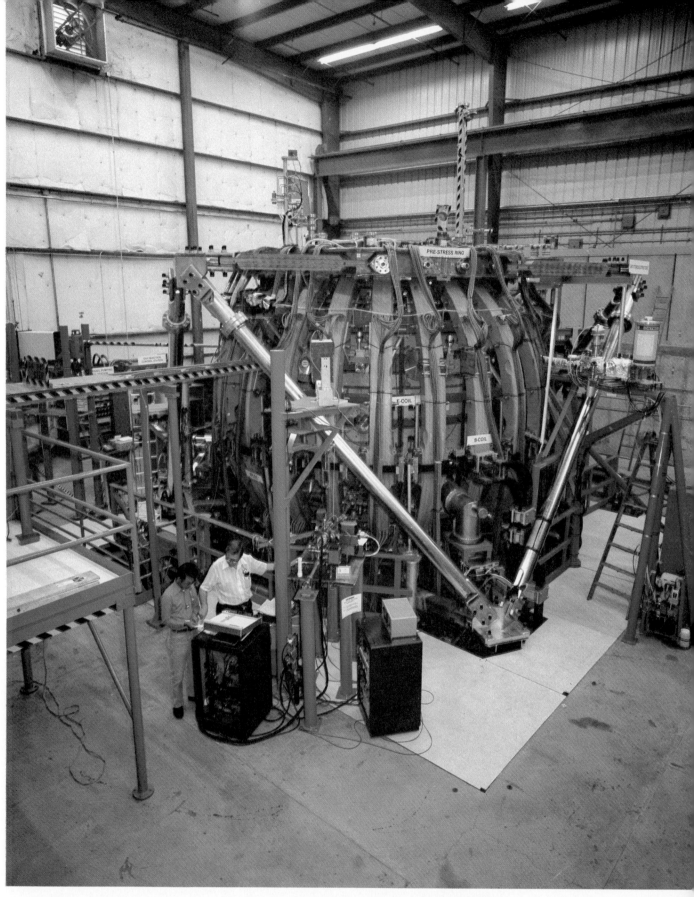

The Doublet III Fusion Machine at the General Atomic Company in San Diego.

FUSION

less, last April John W. Deutch, Assistant Secretary for Energy Technology in the Department of Energy, told a Senate subcommittee that "significant commercial development" of fusion should begin in about 2020.

Two Approaches to Problem

Two routes toward fusion are being pursued. One is magnetic confinement, which, in a "magnetic bottle," seeks to squeeze and heat fuel sufficiently for atomic nuclei to fuse and release energy. The other is "inertial confinement," in which converging high-energy beams crush a pellet of fuel to sufficient temperature and density.

Magnetic confinement, using the so-called Tokamak method, which originated in the Soviet Union, is the most advanced line of attack. Large-scale Tokamak devices are being built in Britain, Japan, the Soviet Union and at

Princeton University in the United States. The Princeton device, known as the *Tokamak Fusion Test Reactor*, has a projected cost of $240 million. It is to begin operation in 1981 and is expected to be the first fusion device to generate as much energy as is injected into the reaction chamber. It will not, however, "break even" by matching the power needed to run the entire operation. In a Tokamak, deuterium-tritium gas is heated until the atoms shed their electrons, forming a plasma of electrically charged particles that can be confined magnetically. In the Princeton reactor, the temperature and density of the plasma are increased by firing electrically neutral beams into the plasma. The neutral particles can traverse the magnetic fields confining the plasma.

In the summer of 1978, the predecessor of the giant machine being built at Princeton—the Princeton Large Torus—demonstrated that the high temperatures needed for a power-generating Tokamak could be achieved. In a parallel

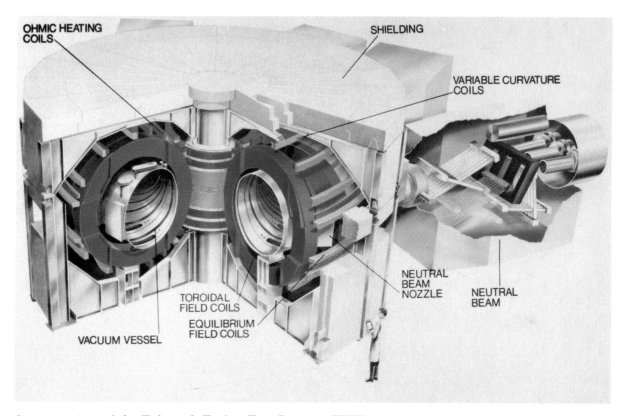

Cutaway view of the Tokamak Fusion Test Reactor (TFTR) in Princeton, N.J. It is scheduled to be operational in 1981.

54

The 2XII-B experiment, shown here, demonstrated the feasibility of fusion using mirror magnets.

The Mirror Fusion Test Facility, now under construction at the Lawrence Livermore Laboratory in California.

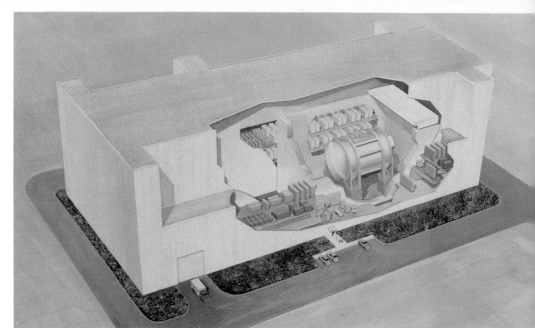

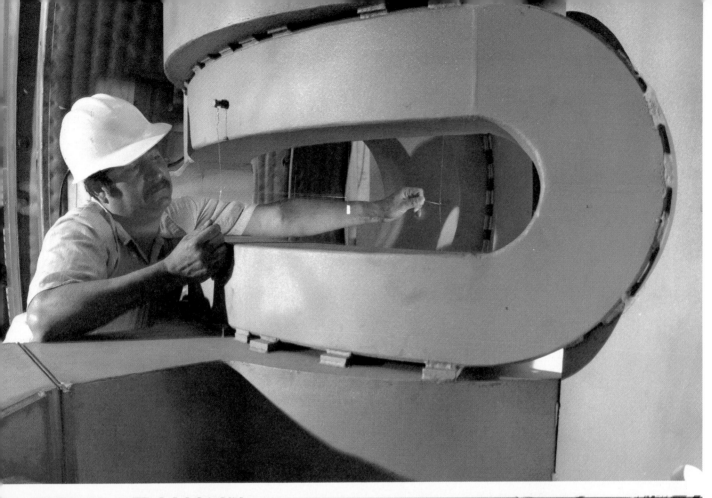

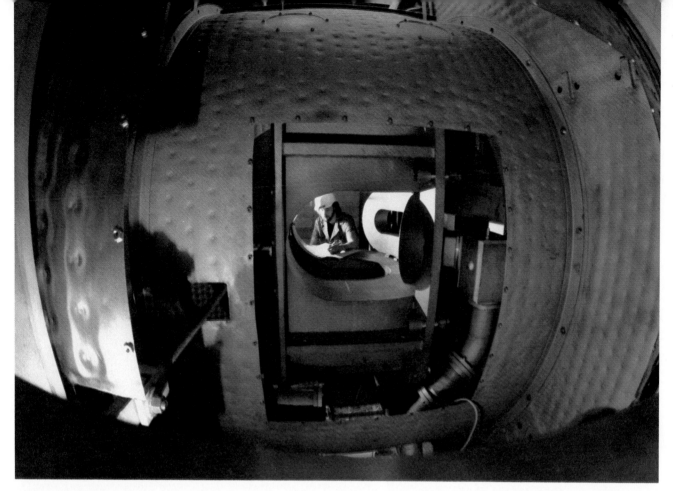

(Top, left) This magnetic mirror will generate magnetic forces that increase in every direction away from the center of the mirror region. A fusion plasma will be confined by the magnetic mirror, assuming the shape of a bow tie.

(Bottom, left) Technicians make final adjustments to one of two magnetic mirrors. These mirrors, placed on either end of the central tube, would contain plasmas, which would in turn aid in confining another plasma inside the tube itself. Most of the fusion would occur in the central tube.

(Above) This is a neutral beam's eye view of two magnetic mirrors. A beam would inject hot fusion fuel into the center of a mirror.

advance at the Massachusetts Institute of Technology, another Tokamak design substantially increased the combination of plasma density and confinement time.

Two other designs are being funded by the Department of Energy. These are the Doublet III machine being developed by the General Atomic Company in San Diego and the Elmo Bumpy Torus at Oak Ridge National Laboratory in Tennessee.

Scientists are also planning an international device that would go one step farther, exploring the problems of converting fusion energy into electricity. This facility, the International Tokamak Reactor, should achieve "ignition"—a situation in which helium, formed by the fusion of deuterium and tritium, becomes hot enough to sustain the reaction without further energy input.

Officials of the Department of Energy, concerned at the complexity and cost of the Tokamak approach and at the fact that it would generate power in pulses rather than continuously, have decided to support as well a rival approach using "mirror machines," in which heated plasma particles fly between intense magnetic fields that act as mirrors. A Mirror Fusion Test Facility is being built at the Law-

The Nova Laser Fusion Facility (top) at the Lawrence Livermore Laboratories in California. This project will incorporate the Shiva Laser Facility, already in existence.

Six of the 20 Shiva laser amplifier chains (bottom) are seen here, looking back from the target room.

An electron beam creates a spray of molten metal as it strikes a metal target plate on an accelerator at Sandria Laboratories outside Albuquerque, New Mexico.

rence Livermore Laboratory, which is operated by the University of California. The facility, to be completed in 1981 at a cost of $94.2 million, will explore the feasibility of two mirror configurations. If one proves practical, it could mean a device smaller, simpler and cheaper than a Tokamak that might be able to generate power continuously.

The first milestone in the Energy Department's timetable, set for 1983, is choosing between the Tokamak and mirror-machine approaches. The next major decision, slated for 1986, will be a choice between lasers and parti-

cle beams as the best way to smash fuel pellets.

At the Livermore Laboratory, another device, the Shiva-Nova laser machine, is expected to cost at least $197 million. The Shiva facility, which is already in operation, converges 20 laser beams on a fuel pellet, crushing its deuterium-tritium droplet to 10,000 times the original density. For a billionth of a second, it delivers more energy to the target than that in all the power lines of the United States.

Adding additional beams for the Nova phase of the project will more than double its power, and the device, when completed about 1983, should generate more fusion energy than is delivered to the pellet by the lasers. But because the lasers are inefficient, the power required to operate Nova will far exceed that produced.

Several laboratories—notably the Los Alamos Scientific Laboratory in New Mexico, the KMS Fusion Company in Ann Arbor, Mich., the University of Rochester in New York and the Naval Research Laboratory—are seeking to develop more efficient lasers. Efforts to do the job with converging beams of electrons are concentrated chiefly at Sandia Laboratories near Albuquerque, N.M., where the first phase of a giant Electron Beam Fusion Acclerator is to be completed soon. The Argonne National Laboratory in Illinois is exploring an approach using beams of heavier atoms.

In each case, when a choice between rival approaches has been made, an Engineering Test Facility will be built to develop the technology. The facility to test the winner in the Tokamak versus mirror-machine competition will cost

some $600 million. By 1995, these facilities should have advanced far enough for the Energy Department to make its choice between magnetic confinement and pellet crushing. Eight years will then be spent building an Engineering Power Reactor at a cost of $1 billion, to begin operation in 2004. A year later, a decision could be made on building a demonstration plant to begin generating power in 2015.

Fusion will not be without its problems, although they are expected to be far less difficult than those of fission energy. Tritium, required for the fuel of systems now under development, does not occur in nature in any abundance. It must be made in the reactor by transforming lithium, which itself is not abundant, although some believe enough can be found on land to last 1,000 years. Tritium, which is radioactive, is also hazardous if released. Ultimately, it is hoped fusion reactors will achieve sufficiently high temperatures to use pure deuterium fuel, available in all sea water.

Man-Powered Flight

by Malcolm W. Browne

For more than 40 centuries, men have tried to flap, pedal or crank their way into the air, unaided by beasts or engines. But without the technological advances of recent years, man-powered flight would have remained an unfulfilled dream.

The flight by Bryan Allen and his 70-pound aircraft across the English Channel represented a triumph for modern chemistry, physics and engineering, as well as for Mr. Allen's skill and powerful leg muscles. The whole of modern science and technology stood behind the builder of the Gossamer Albatross, Dr. Paul MacCready, and the others in his 35-member Pasadena, Calif., engineering team.

Man has not lacked for ingenious mechanical ideas for getting into the air. The Greek legend of Daedalus and Icarus, the father and son who supposedly flew with artificial bird wings attached to their bodies by wax, dates from about 3,500 B.C. Ancient Greeks, Babylonians, Indians and Chinese, among others, all apparently experimented with man-powered flying contraptions. They all failed, partly because of lack of understanding of aerodynamic principles and partly because of lack of the needed materials. Emperor Wen Hsiian Ti of China, who reigned from A.D. 550 to 551, had so little confidence in the bamboo-winged ornithopters (wing-flapping machines) of his day that condemned prisoners were assigned as their test pilots, launching themselves and their craft from a 90-foot tower. All suffered fatal crashes.

Leonardo da Vinci devised a number of clever mechanical devices for translating the power of a man's arms and legs into the flapping of artificial wings, and his designs for ornithopters seem entirely practical until one has a more sophisticated understanding of the problems. The main difficulty is that even the strongest man is extremely heavy and inefficient compared with the crudest internal combustion motor. The best athletes, all weighing more than 100 pounds, have been able by simultaneously pedaling and cranking to produce up to one-and-one-quarter horsepower for bursts of up to one minute. But after one minute their output rapidly falls to about one-half horsepower.

Experiments during the 18th and 19th centuries demonstrated that man-powered flight would probably require less energy if the craft had fixed wings like a glider, rather than flapping, birdlike wings. One of the great discoveries at the end of the 19th century was that a forward-moving wing would lift efficiently only if its upper surface was curved in such a way that the air was forced to travel over it faster than the air passing under the lower surface. This principle is exploited by sailboats, which are pulled by the wind in the direction of the outward curve of their sails. Its application to flying machines finally led to successful gliders and the airplane.

But even the most successful gliders were a long step short of man-powered flight. A glider constantly falls, and stays aloft by maneuvering itself into columns of warm air that rise faster than it is falling. A true man-powered craft must sustain itself without any help from nature. The problem was that any craft man could devise was heavier than that which could be kept aloft with only one horsepower or so of power. Frames made of spruce, bamboo or steel

The Gossamer Albatross lifts off (above), leaving the Dover cliffs behind.

An escort of project members and the press formed an honor guard for the aircraft (top, right).

Bryan Allen flew his plane over the French coast and into the record books (bottom, right).

62

and covering made of silk or doped fabric or metal worked if the power came from a light and efficient engine, but not from a man.

Breakthrough by the British

The first fully authenticated flight of an aircraft that took off and flew exclusively under human muscle power did not take place until 1961. The Sunpac plane, built by engineers at Southampton University in England, could not have been built without the ultralight aluminum alloys and plastic covering material that had been developed by then. Since then, one of the most important contributions to manned flight has been the development of ultrastrong polyester film. The Du Pont Mylar film used to cover the craft that flew the channel in 1979 is only five ten-thousandths of an inch thick, but is strong enough to reduce the requirement for supporting members. Structural parts were fabricated from a carbon-filament composite material, an extremely strong, light substance

developed in recent years to replace metal parts in high-performance combat planes.

While the Gossamer Albatross weighed 70 pounds including safety equipment, its basic weight was only 55 pounds, meaning that it required only about one-quarter horsepower to stay aloft. The best efforts to lighten an aircraft in the 1960's produced flying machines requiring one full horsepower—close to the limit a man can produce for a short burst. The margin of excess power provided by the ultralight Albatross and its 1977 predecessor, the Gossamer Condor, permitted maneuvering in man-powered flight for the first time. To turn a glider or airplane normally entails banking, dipping the wing in the direction of the turn. Banking not only reduces the lift of the wings but also slows the aircraft, reducing lift still further.

The Gossamer Condor overcame this problem in 1977, both through greater lift efficiency and eliminating the need to bank, becoming the first man-powered craft to complete a figure-eight course.

The seventy-pound craft (top, left) makes its way over the English Channel (side view).

Bryan Allen (top, right) pedaled the 70-pound Gossamer Albatross a distance of 22 miles, thus making the first human-powered flight across the English Channel.

Paul MacCready(right), the father of the Gossamer Albatross, also created the Gossamer Condor, in which the first human-powered flight was made.

Anesthesiologists

by Laurence Cherry

Seated on stools or standing at the head of operating tables, their features all but obscured by surgical masks, anesthesiologists until recently were only dimly perceived by patients, who thought of them simply as merciful dispensers of controlled unconsciousness.

Though they have always chosen their surgeons carefully, on the advice of family physicians and medical specialists, candidates for surgery traditionally have had little say about or interest in who would be administering anesthesia to them. Today, however, a new awareness and realization of the importance of the expanded role played by practitioners of this important, if still somewhat anonymous, adjunct of surgery has precipitated a trend toward greater patient participation in the selection of anesthesiologists.

Far from merely putting patients to sleep, anesthesiologists today are really the physicians in charge of patients during surgery, as well as the supervisors of special care and pain relief afterward. A patient's ease of recuperation and even survival often depends on the skill of the anesthesiologist in attendance. "That's precisely why we advise people to use as much caution in choosing their anesthesiologist as they do their surgeon," says Dr. Joseph Artusio Jr., anesthesiologist in chief at New York Hospital and chairman of anesthesiology at Cornell University Medical College.

Important developments in the field over the past few years have transformed anesthesiology from a rather primitive medical art solely concerned with keeping surgical patients unconscious during an operation into a complex and sophisticated specialty. New and safer chemical anesthetics have come into use; nerve-block techniques have been developed that relieve chronic postoperative pain; and in some places, hypnosis and acupuncture are being used on prescreened patients. There have also been improvements in technology, such as blood-gas machines that feed back vital information within 70 seconds about chemical changes taking place in the blood, and new jet ventilators that generate gentle jet streams of air at about the rate of two tiny puffs of air a second to facilitate breathing without creating harmful pressure in the lungs.

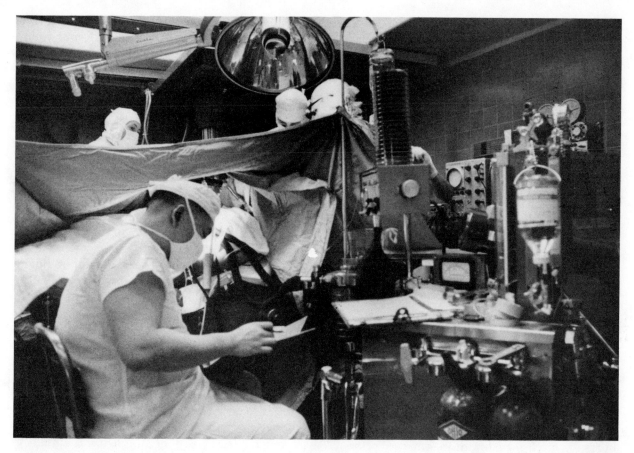

A patient's ease of recuperation and even survival often depends on the skill of the anesthesiologist.

These and other improvements have meant that now anyone can be a candidate for surgery, from newborn babies to people over 90. "We routinely operate today on patients who were considered too poor a risk for anesthesia and surgery a few years ago," says Dr. Artusio. In fact, information has accumulated so quickly that subspecialties, such as pediatric anesthesiology, neurosurgical anesthesiology, and obstetrical anesthesiology, have begun to form, each with its own particular kind of expertise. "This is a field where the explosion of knowledge is so rapid that an ever-greater degree of specialization is necessary," adds Dr. Artusio.

At Memorial Sloan-Kettering Cancer Center in New York, the intensive-care unit is under the joint supervision of an anesthesiologist and a surgeon. "This is a recent but logical extension of what we do in the operating room," explains Dr. Alexander Gotta, one of the center's

attending anesthesiologists. "The anesthesiologist has learned how to maintain the patient's vital functions, and what we do in these special units, in effect, is to take over these functions, sometimes for weeks at a time."

Unlike only a few years ago, anesthesiologists today have a wide choice of anesthetics. A pharmacological revolution has led to the development of a half-dozen new chemicals, safer and more effective than the ether used so commonly a generation ago. Most anesthesiologists have their preferences, but they obviously must also take a patient's health problems into account. The anesthetic methoxyflurane, for example, is not often used on those with kidney problems, because the fluoride ion it contains can damage kidneys. And halothane can be toxic to the liver, so it is never used during operations on those with hepatitis or a history of it.

Not uncommonly, patients feel pain following

their operations—pain that may not disappear for months or even years. In other cases, chronic pain seems to come for no fathomable reason and then refuses to disappear. Anesthesiologists have begun to deal with this problem by using drugs to block the most troublesome nerves, thereby abolishing the most persistent pain. "This is a kind of new frontier for anesthesiology," says Dr. Paul Goldiner, of Memorial's pain unit.

What anesthesiologists do when they use nerve blocks, in effect, is play medical detective. "We try to analyze the pain and determine which nerve out of several is responsible for the trouble," says Dr. Gotta. "This is where our experience in giving local anesthesia can help us— we know where to look." Not long ago, for example, he says, he treated a cancer patient with agonizing pains in her uterus by injecting a drug called lidocaine, which can control pain for only a few hours. Once he had established that blocking a particular nerve had temporarily freed the patient from pain, Dr. Gotta followed up a few days later with an injection of phenol, a substance whose effect is similar to alcohol which, in effect, destroyed the nerve. "It usually hurts like heck for a few days, but very often it does the job."

Most anesthesiologists have reacted cautiously to using acupuncture as a pain-control method. "Actually, nerve blocks and acupuncture are very closely related in their effect on nerves involved in the pain response," says Dr. Kinichi Shibutani, director of anesthesiology at Westchester County Medical Center and professor of anesthesiology at New York Medical College. "Unfortunately, acupuncture's been tainted by the media overexposure it received a few years ago, so many doctors still edge away from it. Certainly it's not reliable enough to use in place of chemical anesthetics during surgery, as some overenthusiastic people at first suggested. But it does seem to work well on chronic pain." Using electrically operated needles inserted at predetermined nerve sites, Dr. Shibutani has been able to eliminate pain in half of his patients complaining of chronic pain.

"Although acupuncture certainly *does* work," another anesthesiologist says, "you can never tell if it's going to work on a particular patient, so it just isn't reliable enough to be used during an operation, as even the Chinese are starting to admit. Also, it takes a good half-hour to induce acupuncture anesthesia so, at least for the moment, it's impractical for doctors to use during a busy surgical schedule."

And yet, despite all the advances of the past few years, the fact remains that the anesthetics used in surgery are far from being completely safe. "From the anesthesiologist's point of view, there is still no such thing as a completely safe operation," says Dr. Artusio. "Even a procedure as simple as a tonsillectomy carries a small but definite risk." Estimates about the number of deaths caused by anesthesia vary widely, partly because some experts define an anesthesia-related death as any that occurs within 48 hours after surgery—a definition many anesthesiologists consider unfair. "If someone comes in with a bullet wound in his heart and dies on the operating table, that's listed as anesthesia-related," says Dr. Gotta, "and yet of course it's nothing of the kind."

Out of the over 80,000 operations performed at Memorial Hospital during the last 10 years, there has been only one proven death caused by anesthesia; at New York Hospital, where twice as much surgery is done, the figure is similarly low. "But once you get outside the prestigious urban teaching hospitals, where standards are exceptionally high, the mortality rate begins to soar," says Dr. Gotta. Outside of big cities, patients are more likely to be given anesthesia by doctors who lack the anesthesiologists' specialized training, which includes three years spent learning how to use and evaluate anesthetics of all types. Technical errors are responsible for some of the deaths that do occur: pipes for conducting oxygen and the anesthetic nitrous oxide into operating rooms have been mixed up with disastrous results and sometimes monitors have failed to function properly.

Aware of all the possible mechanical complications involved in giving chemical anesthesia, some anesthesiologists feel that it should be avoided if possible—as, for example, during the delivery of a baby. A report issued in January by the National Institute of Neurological and Communicative Disorders and Stroke (a unit of the National Institutes of Health) found that the use of inhalant anesthetics during labor "had negative associations with certain aspects

Dr. Joseph Artusio, Jr., chief anesthesiologist at New York Hospital-Cornell Medical Center, advises people to use as much caution in choosing their anesthesiologist as they do when choosing their surgeon.

of development in the first year: enlarged liver and spleen, abnormal neural motor reflexes, some aspects of psychomotor development." Further findings indicate long-term effects: Many children were slow to sit, stand and walk, and by age 7 some lagged in language and learning skills. For these reasons, some experts have suggested that hypnosis, rather than drugs, be used to control pain during delivery.

Although many physicians still edge away from it as a kind of parlor entertainment or stage stunt, hypnosis has, in fact, been studied rather rigorously. About 70 percent of us, it turns out, can be hypnotized, although not all equally well. For those capable of entering deep trances, hypnosis is an obvious alternative to chemical anesthetics. "Eventually," one expert contends, "hypnosis is going to be used on suitable subjects for minor operations of all kinds." (At Walter Reed Army Medical Center in Washington, D.C., hypnosis is already being used to treat almost half of all patients referred to its pain clinic.)

Nevertheless, not everyone can be hypnotized, and still fewer can enter a pain-free deep trance. For the majority of patients, making chemical anesthesia safer seems to be the obvious priority, and improving the quality of those giving the anesthesia the obvious way to go about it. "Human error," says Dr. Artusio, "is still the greatest problem in anesthesiology. Good clinical judgment is so terribly important —noticing little things, like a slight change in blood pressure, that might signal a real crisis. By no means every anesthesiologist has it."

Precisely that question of complete medical competence has caused some to criticize the widespread use of nurses to administer anesthesia. "I'd much rather have a physician than a nurse give me anesthesia," says one anesthesiologist privately. "Although, of course, I'd prefer a good nurse, and there are several superb ones around, to a bad doctor. Nevertheless, if you compare them one against one, an anesthesiologist is far preferable to a nurse-anesthetist." Another doctor, who also prefers not to be identified, says, "Nurses are good technicians, but in a real crisis they just don't have the medical background to make some of the important decisions."

But most nurses angrily contest this unfavorable verdict. "I think it's all part of the old doctor-as-God mentality," says one nurse-anesthetist at Memorial Hospital. "Nearly all the nurses involved in anesthesia here are continually taking courses to improve their competence. I consider myself quite as well-trained as any anesthesiologist. Fortunately, we work as a team here, and very few doctors try to pull rank."

Until the late 1940's, usually only nurses administered anesthesia, under the direction of a surgeon. Today, about a third of the operations in this country are handled by anesthesiologists (who are always physicians); another third by nurse-anesthetists; and the others—usually in poor rural areas—by doctors who have little formal training in anesthesiology. At most of the better medical centers, anesthesia is usually administered by an anesthesiologist. At a few others, a combined approach is used: although nurses administer the anesthesia, they do so

69

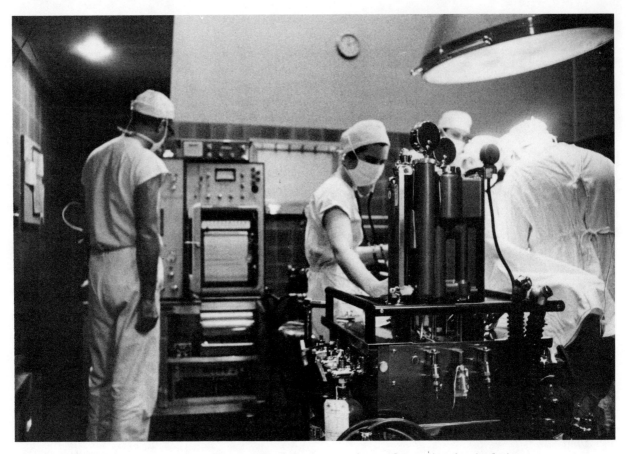

As the surgical team performs, the anesthesiologist monitors the patient's vital signs.

under the supervision of an anesthesiologist; one anesthesiologist is thus able to oversee two operating rooms at once.

As in most medical specialties, there are still few women anesthesiologists, although the number is rapidly growing. Anesthesiology has generally been more hospitable to women than some other areas in medicine, such as surgery. Many in the field feel this is because anesthesiology is less traditionally "masculine"—anesthesiologists, they contend, tend to be less flamboyant, extroverted and domineering than their surgical counterparts.

At many hospitals, patients are now being allowed to decide who will administer their anesthesia. Where this is not permitted, patients who feel uneasy about the anesthesiologist assigned to them are advised by Dr. Gotta to contact their surgeons at once and enlist their help in effecting a change. Hospitals generally try to

oblige, if they can. (In most hospitals, initial assignment is still done on a rotation basis. But in larger hospitals, where there is a tendency toward specialization, certain anesthesiologists are regularly assigned, for example, just to cardiac patients or pediatric patients.)

Obviously few laymen are knowledgeable enough to effectively judge the qualifications of an anesthesiologist. But there are a few useful things for those interested in taking a more active role in the selection of their anesthesiologist to consider, such as consulting a standard reference, The Directory of Medical Specialists, which lists medical backgrounds and also indicates whether or not an anesthesiologist is certified by the American Board of Anesthesiology (A.B.A.).

"For the most part, American, British and Canadian medical schools turn out anesthesiologists far superior to those from other coun-

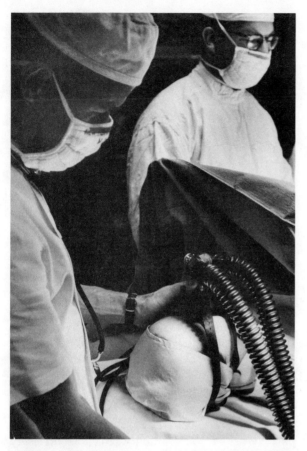

Far from merely putting patients to sleep, anesthesiologists today are really the physicians in charge of patients during surgery, as well as supervisors of special care and pain relief afterward.

tries," says one doctor, who prefers to remain anonymous since he works closely with graduates from foreign schools. His opinion reflects the views of many others in the field, who are equally reluctant to be identified. Although a very few certified anesthesiologists may choose, sometimes for reasons of personal privacy, not to be listed in specific reference books, virtually all are. Dr. Gotta advises patients to ask their anesthesiologist if he has been certified. "And if he isn't," says Dr. Gotta, "the patient should find out why. Certification is something most of us in the field want very badly, and if someone doesn't have it, it should be, at least provisionally, considered a bad sign."

Patients generally first meet their anesthesi-

ologist the day before surgery is scheduled. They should be concerned, says Dr. Gotta, if this preoperational visit is omitted, since that would indicate a disturbing lack of responsibility.

The Joint Commission on Accreditation of Hospitals—a prestigious, powerful and independent survey organization, headquartered in Chicago, which regularly conducts surveys of most American hospitals—now urges anesthesiologists to give patients an even greater voice, advising anesthesiologists to discuss the nature of the anesthetic to be used with patients and, if possible, to comply with their wishes. Some anesthesiologists, however, are frankly skeptical about whether most patients are yet ready to handle this kind of responsibility. "The continuing lack of sophistication about our specialty among the general public never fails to astonish me," says one. "Many people think that we just inject some sort of magic potion into them and disappear. They aren't yet qualified to make a truly sophisticated kind of decision. But, yes, today, if someone comes to me and tells me that he had an operation a few years ago with a spinal anesthetic and would prefer that approach be used again, I'd certainly try to do it."

Meanwhile, in response to criticism both within and outside the profession, many anesthesiologists are actively seeking to improve standards. Their goal is a requirement for all practitioners to pass tests every few years to demonstrate a continuing high level of skill in order to be recertified. "People entrust their lives to their anesthesiologist," says Dr. Gotta. "They have the right to expect that he knows what he's doing."

A PATIENT'S PROGRESS

Most patients have their first contact with an anesthesiologist on the day before their operation. It is at this time, after a brief examination and the taking of a short medical history, that a decision is made as to whether or not the operation will actually take place. "The surgeon has told us that the patient can get through surgery," says Dr. Paul Goldiner, an anesthesiologist at New York's Memorial Sloan-Kettering Cancer Center, "but we have to make up our own mind about whether or not the patient's in the best possible shape—if not, we may ask for a delay."

Another decision made then is whether or not to sedate the patient before he arrives in the operating room. "If the anesthesiologist handles the preanesthetic visit right, a patient won't need any tranquilizers beforehand," says Dr. Alexander Gotta, an anesthesiologist at New York's Memorial Hospital. "But if you pick up a sense of real agitation, you prescribe drugs to make sure that he comes to surgery very calm and relaxed."

In most cases, before a patient is taken to the presurgery holding area, an intravenous tube is inserted into his arm—partly to provide energy-giving fluids, and also as a way of easily introducing anesthetics during the operation. Soon afterward, unless the operation is very minor, a muscle relaxant is administered, which paralyzes all of the patient's muscles. To insure unhampered breathing, an endotracheal tube, connected to a mechanical ventilator, is then pushed through the mouth into the windpipe. At the same time, an airway—a plastic or rubber device to keep the patient from biting on the tube and later to prevent his tongue from obstructing his breathing—is put into his mouth. "From now on, until the operation's over," says Dr. Gotta, "we handle the patient's breathing for him."

Already, electrical monitors have begun to function, each demanding the anesthesiologist's full and continuing attention. An electrocardiogram above the operating table provides constant printed readouts of heart activity, filling the operating room with a steady beep, while other devices give digital readings of pulse and temperature. Blood pressure is taken, along with periodic blood samples. A tube may also be inserted through the esophagus behind the heart, to provide a core body temperature reading. If it seems to be dropping, the patient must be warmed, usually with blankets, since a cooler body responds differently to anesthetics.

Anesthesia is administered either intravenously or else is inhaled through a mask, depending on which drug is used. Spinal anesthesia, once widely used, is now only infrequently employed at most medical centers. Instead, the majority of patients are usually put to sleep, most often with a dose of sodium pentothal. "It's really an ideal drug," says Dr. Goldiner. "It puts the patient to sleep quickly and pleasantly. The only danger is that it can interfere with heart activity, so the anesthesiologist has to watch it very carefully."

The biggest danger during an operation, according to Dr. Gotta, "is a feeling of complacency. Things just seem to percolate along for a time, and there's a tendency to daydream. It's the easiest thing in the world to get in there, sit down on the stool next to the operating table, and mentally disappear. But, of course, you can lose a patient that way—which is why anesthesiology is not for everyone. You have to be constantly curious, always involved with what the surgeon's doing."

As the operation comes to an end, the anesthesiologist begins to give drugs chemically opposed to the anesthetics that first put the patient asleep. The amount given is precisely adjusted to time the awakening. Sometimes the patient has to be roused almost immediately; after a brain operation, for example, the surgeon may want to gauge the extent of neurological damage by measuring the patient's conscious reactions. But more often, still asleep, he's wheeled into the recovery room and placed in a bed with an oxygen respirator and monitor at his side. "Years ago, with the anesthetics then used, some patients would wake up in a tremendous amount of pain, and go absolutely berserk in the recovery room, but didn't remember it afterward," recalls Dr. Gotta. "With today's drugs, you don't see that sort of thing happening anymore." Less than 1 percent of today's surgery patients even become nauseous. In fact, within two hours most are returned to their rooms.

The Myth of Senility

by Robin Marantz Henig

The world seemed to be rushing past her. She couldn't concentrate and was failing miserably at the simplest task. What happened to the time when things moved at her pace? Her body ached. Why were her hands moving so slowly? Why did her mind creak so? Frustrated by her mistakes, angry that she couldn't remember details, she finally gave up, grumbling.

A crotchety old woman, long past her prime, obviously forgetful, rigid . . . senile? No, this was a young college student participating in a classroom psychology experiment conducted by Dr. Robert Kastenbaum at Wayne State University in Detroit. A group of 31 students between the ages of 18 and 24 was assigned the task of "rebuilding" a mock village supposedly shattered by war. Each student was given two sets of file cards—one set describing the jobs that needed to be done, and the other describing the available people to do it—and was told to match jobs with the individuals best suited to them. There were about 100 job cards and 150 manpower cards to manipulate.

To create a speeded-up environment he called "Pre-experiencing Age," Dr. Kastenbaum allowed students five minutes for each of the first three match-ups, then three minutes, then two. A hand bell signaled when it was time to move to the next pairing, but the students were not told that an acceleration was taking place.

"There was a marked paralysis of action by the end of the experiment," recalls Dr. Kastenbaum, now superintendent of the Cushing Hospital in Framingham, Mass. "The students began to engage in random actions—picking up a card, putting it down, picking it up again. Some narrowed their focus and kept working with the same few cards. Some became almost stultified; some jittery and agitated. Even though many of them were aware that we were speeding things along, they still took it out on themselves when they couldn't perform fast enough. They were angry at themselves, angry that what had started out as a manageable task had become so complicated."

In short, these young people began to act "old" and "senile" simply because they found themselves unable to keep pace with the world around them—a situation, Dr. Kastenbaum points out, that is "not too bad an analogy to

As a result of classroom experiments, Dr. Robert Kastenbaum has found that "so-called 'senility' is not age dependent, and is not inevitable with age."

Dr. Robert Butler believes that Americans expect their final years to be dismal, not even worth living.

the real-life situation of the aged." The experiment confirmed his belief that senile behavior is in large measure socially induced, and can be created in anyone stripped of roles, prestige, purpose, economic independence and physical well-being. "So-called 'senility,'" he says, "is not age dependent, and is not inevitable with age."

Yet Americans expect their final years to be dismal, not even worth living. "I believe more people fear senility, fear growing old and losing their minds and being put away, than fear cancer," says Dr. Robert Butler, director of the National Institute on Aging in Bethesda, Md. He recalls a recent survey that asked people how long they expected to live and how long they *hoped* to live; the majority of respondents wished for *shorter* lifetimes than they thought awaited them. It does no good to point to the continuing vitality of a Buckminster Fuller or a Georgia O'Keeffe. Such people are looked upon as the exceptions to the rule—the rule that equates age with rigidity, forgetfulness and confusion.

But Americans can no longer afford to equate harmless forgetfulness with irreversible senility. Society will soon have too many old people to be able to accommodate so much enforced enfeeblement. We are fast becoming a nation of old people. The 75-plus age group is the fastest-growing in America; it increased by 37 percent between 1960 and 1970, almost three times the rate of growth for the 65-to-75 age group. There will be 30 million elderly Americans by the year 2000—an estimated 15 percent of the population —and nearly half of them are expected to be over 75.

"We are not wrinkled babies," says 73-year-old Maggie Kuhn, leader of the militant Gray Panthers organization, in objecting to the pervasive discrimination Dr. Butler has labeled "ageism." As the Gray Panthers and other organizations have brought their "gray power" message to Congress, political, economic and medical institutions have gradually been nudged toward adjusting to the burgeoning number of the aged. The National Institute on Aging was created in 1974; the Age Discrimination Act was passed in 1975, and in April Congress raised the mandatory retirement age to 70.

Now a few gerontologists (experts in the scientific study of aging) have taken up arms against one of the most insidious forms of age-ism—the myth of senility. They are trying to disentangle myth from reality and to distinguish among the normal changes of aging, pathological changes that can accompany age, and the invidious effects our fears and expectations have on the behavior of the elderly.

Old brains, like old faces and old bodies, look different from young ones. Brain cells, or neurons, are among the few types of cells that do not replicate throughout life. By late childhood we have all the neurons we will ever have—billions of them—and, around the age of 30, we begin to lose them, scientists surmise, at the rate of 100,000 or so a day.

Losing neurons, though, need not mean losing our faculties. Most old people show no sign of mental deterioration no matter how long they live. A minority of the very old (30 percent of those over 80, according to Dr. Ernest Gruenberg, chairman of the department of mental hygiene at the Johns Hopkins School of Public Health in Baltimore) show evidence of forgetfulness and confusion, but usually this is a harmless side effect of the normal slowing down that comes with age. In some cases, the forgetfulness is due to a distinct neurological disease known as senile dementia, or to one of a handful of rare irreversible conditions that affect some aged brains. But in many cases, the loss of memory is due to a wide variety of factors having nothing to do with age per se: The stresses of retirement, bereavement, loss of income and social role, or diseases that can occur at any age but that, in the elderly, can produce symptoms of forgetfulness and confusion.

Often—tragically often—underlying physical diseases that may make an old person *seem* senile are unnoticed and untreated, and the old and sick are dumped into a wastebasket category of "senile" by families and doctors who have accepted the conventional wisdom that senility is inevitable with age. But as biomedical research, coupled with clinical experience, reveals that more and more old persons are perfectly alert and fully capable, the inevitability of senility is being questioned in ever-widening circles.

Research recently conducted in Great Britain, Scandinavia, Japan and New York has

Maggie Kuhn is the 73-year-old leader of the militant Gray Panthers.

shown that just 5 percent of the over-65 brains examined show evidence of severe senile dementia, and another 10 to 15 percent show signs to a lesser degree.

In June 1977, some 60 leading scientists and hundreds of clinicians from around the world attended a conference on senile dementia research, co-sponsored by the National Institutes of Neurological, Communicative Disorders and Stroke, of Aging, and of Mental Health, in Washington, D.C. A follow-up meeting on senile dementia, emphasizing service instead of research, was scheduled for December 1978. In July 1978, a conference on treatable brain diseases in the elderly was held at the National Institutes of Health.

Current medical consensus is that senile dementia is a distinct disease which constitutes a public-health menace that will become more serious as America ages. Dr. Robert Katzman, chairman of the department of neurology at the Albert Einstein College of Medicine in the Bronx, says an estimated 600,000 old persons suffer from the neurological disease known as senile dementia of the Alzheimer's type (SDAT). There is no cure for SDAT, and treatment, he says, is inadequate. In its most severe form, SDAT usually leads to mental deterioration—from loss of recent memory, inability to calculate, and disorientation, to profound memory loss, inability to care for oneself, and loss of control over bodily functions—and it may lead to death within five years. Dr. Katzman says that from 100,000 to 120,000 deaths a year are probably due to SDAT, making it the nation's fourth or fifth leading killer.

The characteristic manifestations of SDAT are distinctive brain lesions known as neurofibrillary tangles and senile plaques. Tangles and plaques are found to some extent in most very old brains (99 percent of persons over 80, according to one study, have some plaques and tangles). Most people, though, never develop *enough* of these lesions to lose memory or function. These plaques and tangles are the key to unlocking the mystery of SDAT. Researchers are now trying to formulate theories about how the lesions develop, how they interfere with mental functioning, and whether, once they occur, they can somehow be treated.

One of the most promising lines of thought is that the origin of SDAT may be related to a particularly puzzling infectious agent known as a slow virus. Slow viruses cannot be detected by ordinary laboratory procedures and do not manifest such signs as the antibody formation, pus or inflammation that characterize most infections. They can exist in harmless, latent states for many years, becoming pathological only when the internal environment changes. Some of the physiological changes that accompany aging, it is thought, might be enough to "turn on" these slow viruses and convert them into disease-producing substances, or pathogens. It is already known that some neurological diseases are caused by slow viruses. Brain disorders with exotic names such as kuru and Creutzfeldt-Jakob disease are caused by slow viruses and accompanied by brain plaques like those seen in SDAT. The slow-virus theory is particularly attractive because it suggests that someday a drug, perhaps even a vaccine, will be able to combat SDAT.

An effective drug therapy may also result from the recent finding that many patients with senile dementia suffer from an enzyme deficiency. Dr. Peter Davies, who works with Dr. Robert Terry, chairman of the department of pathology at Einstein, detected in SDAT patients a reduction by as much as 90 percent in the amount of the enzyme choline acetyltransferase. This enzyme manufactures acetylcholine, one of the most important neurotransmitters in the nervous system. This transmitter is responsible for conveying certain nervous impulses—such as those involved in memory, Dr. Davies believes—from one brain cell to another. Without it, the impulses are short-circuited.

To compensate for this enzyme deficiency, researchers have tried administering choline. Although initial results are said to be disappointing (subjects appear "brighter" but perform no better on tests), scientists at the University of Massachusetts and the Massachusetts Institute of Technology are pursuing some promising leads. Choline is present in large quantities in such foods as eggs, meats and some packaged desserts and cake mixes. Some scientists believe that a meal of a large omelet can, within hours, send choline directly to the brain. The possibility exists that, someday, dietary changes or enzyme replacement therapy will improve the memory and intellectual functioning of persons with senile dementia.

Thus far, more successful means have been found to treat another chronic form of senile dementia, known as multi-infarct dementia, or multiple strokes. This disease used to be popularly—and misleadingly—labeled "hardening of the arteries of the brain," and was mistakenly thought to account for most cases of senile dementia. Dr. Terry says multi-infarct dementia is only one-third as common as SDAT, affecting some 200,000 Americans, most of whom also display other symptoms of cardiovascular disease, such as hypertension. Anticoagulant medications have been used with some success in multi-infarct dementia. By thinning the blood, these drugs allow more of it to get to the brain, which is then able to get more oxygen and nourishment. Treatment of the co-existing hypertension may also be helpful.

For the moment, perhaps the most significant result of research into senile dementia has been the new role in which it casts victims of the dis-

We are becoming a nation of old people; the 75-plus age group is the fastest-growing in America.

ease. Patients with senile dementia can no longer be viewed as the ones to be blamed for their condition—a conclusion all too easy to reach when a disease makes its victims seem sloppy, lazy, out of touch, exasperating. Ironically, the fact that these people are sick and not simply old somehow dignifies their plight, and enables families and care-givers to treat symptoms of the disorder, to seek ways to stem its progress and minimize its attendant disabilities.

□

Nevertheless the message that senile dementia is a distinct disease and relatively uncommon is slow to spill over from the laboratories to the homes—and, more important, to the doctors' offices—of America. For every four elderly people correctly diagnosed as suffering from a chronic, irreversible form of senile dementia, there is one old man or woman who becomes an even more tragic statistic—someone misdiagnosed as irreversibly senile because of a "confusional state" that could be caused by any one (or several) of dozens of reversible conditions.

"A national catastrophe" is the way Dr. Richard Besdine, an assistant professor of medicine at Harvard Medical School, describes the frequent misdiagnoses of so-called "reversible dementias." Dr. Besdine, who is also chairman of a National Institute on Aging task force on reversible dementias, estimates that the misdiagnoses may account for 300,000 wasted lives and 100,000 needless institutionalizations.

"Whatever the percentage, even if it's just one patient in 100, that's one too many," says Dr. Thomas Kalchthaler, medical director of the St. Joseph's Nursing Home in Yonkers. "That's one patient too many who is stripped of his rights, incarcerated against his will, and left to live out life—often a shortened life—dependent and confused."

How are such tragic errors made? And why are they made so often? "Elderly brains are very vulnerable to insults elsewhere in the body," explains Dr. Besdine. "Diseases in the young and middle-aged may be straightforward; in the elderly, the brain might show the first signs of illness." When a 50-year-old has a heart attack, for example, chest pain is quick and direct. But 15 percent of elderly heart-attack victims, says Dr. Besdine, show no sign other than confusion.

Similarly, hypoglycemia—low blood sugar that can lead to diabetic coma—usually causes weakness, dizziness, cold clammy sweats and rapid heartbeat in the young and middle-aged. In the elderly, however, the only symptom may again be confusion. Infections can exist in the elderly without fever or an elevated white-blood-cell count. Hyperthyroidism may be present without the overactivity found in young hyperthyroid patients. Appendicitis may occur without pain. Malnutrition, anemia, renal failure, vitamin deficiency . . . in all, some 100 physical ailments can mimic senility in the elderly. And they must all be ruled out before a diagnosis of chronic, irreversible senile dementia can be confidently made.

Two of the medical problems most frequently misdiagnosed as senility are drug intoxication and depression. "Whenever a new patient comes in in a confused state, the first thing I do is check the medications," says Dr. Kalchthaler. "In my experience, iatrogenic—doctor-induced—confusional states do happen, and they happen quite frequently."

The elderly are particularly prone to drug intoxication for several reasons. Aging brings about changes in absorption, metabolism, excretion, tissue-binding and organ responsiveness—all factors to be considered when setting a therapeutic dosage for a particular medication. The proportion of fat cells, in which some drugs tend to accumulate, also increases with age. But pharmacology courses in medical schools, and drug manuals distributed to physicians, are usually geared to the middle-aged patient. A normal dose for a 40-year-old could be an overdose for an 80-year-old.

This problem is compounded by the fact that the aged are often multimedicated. One-quarter of all prescriptions are written for persons over 65, who are likely to take several different drugs at one time. "It's not at all unusual to find elderly people living in the community who take five or six different medications," Dr. Kalchthaler observes. "And as the number of medications increases, the incidence of adverse drug interaction increases exponentially." So does the likelihood of error in taking each pill or potion at the right time, in the right dosage—especially among old persons who live alone, have failing eyesight or tend to be forgetful.

Depression is so often mistaken for senility that many geriatricians say they "owe" their confused patients a trial of antidepressants before making a final diagnosis of senile dementia. Depression, the "common cold of mental illnesses," is even more prevalent in the aged than in the population as a whole. And no wonder: Old people are not only stripped of power, of a sense of productivity and purpose, they suffer frequent stresses—grief and bereavement, ill health and changed appearance, loneliness and isolation.

"These people have a pervasive sense of no-goodness," says Dr. Gruenberg, "and part of that sense of no-goodness comes out when they say, 'I can't remember. I don't know. I'm senile.'" Since depression is among the hardest of maladies to pinpoint, he adds, physicians must be willing to try vigorous antidepression treatments once other possible causes of symptoms of senility have been ruled out.

Vigorous medical treatment of the elderly is not taught in most medical schools today, nor is it particularly encouraged in the medical marketplace. The chronic, slow-to-mend nature of most geriatric ailments makes them unpopular in a health-care system that rewards, both emotionally and economically, quick cures.

At the New York University School of Medicine, a summer clerkship in geriatrics in 1977 attracted more than four applicants for each opening. But medical schools have been slow to respond to such evidence of student interest. Of the 20,000 faculty members at 116 medical schools, only 15 are primarily identified with geriatrics. And there is still only one endowed professorship in the field—the Irving S. Wright Professorship at Cornell Medical College in Manhattan—and just one residency training program—at the Jewish Institute for

Geriatric Care at Long Island Jewish-Hillside Medical Center in New Hyde Park.

The health-care system, however, will soon have to change. Already, one-third of the average physician's patients are over 65, and the proportion will rise steadily in the years to come.

The public at large must also learn more about the diseases of age—and, even more important, about normal aging—if such tragedies as the misdiagnosis of reversible senility are to be avoided.

One of the few generalizations that can be made about old age is that it is a time of slowing down—although this does not usually occur until well into the 70's or even 80's. Like the young college student in Dr. Kastenbaum's "Pre-experiencing Age" experiment, old people can become trapped in a time warp and may show signs of memory loss, confusion and disorientation when they are asked to perform too quickly. For years, the elderly person's inferior performance on tests of intellectual function has been used as evidence that intelligence diminishes with age. When they are allowed to set

their own pace, older test subjects have been shown to perform as well as their younger, more agile counterparts. On longitudinal tests designed to pick up age-related changes by testing the same individual over many years, older test subjects show little falloff in cognitive ability once speed has been adjusted to their level. Indeed, certain functions related to the accumulation of knowledge—vocabulary, for instance—actually improve with age.

For some people, slowing down is easily compensated for—a few changed habits, a better-organized life, greater reliance on notes and shopping lists. Some actually relish the chance finally to catch their breath and take time to reflect. But for old people without the physical, emotional or economic resources to make this adjustment, slowing down is cause for panic. They become terrified that this missed appointment, that forgotten phone number will send them on the long toboggan slide into senility.

If the elderly themselves don't worry, often their families will worry for them. The net effect is the same: Signs of normal aging are misinterpreted as signs of senility, and old people

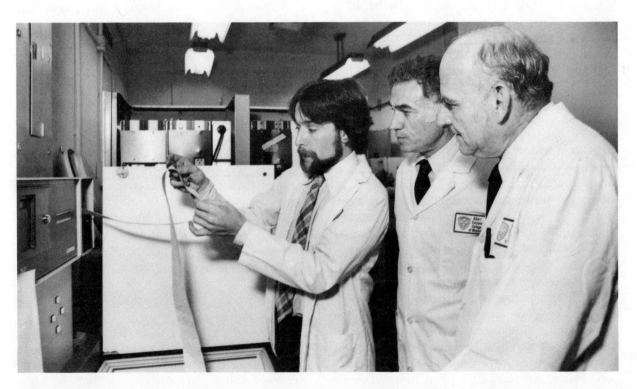

At Albert Einstein College of Medicine Drs. Peter Davies, Robert D. Terry, and Robert Katzman (left to right) are studying patients with the neurological disease known as senile dementia.

It is estimated that misdiagnoses of irreversible senility may account for 300,000 wasted lives and 100,000 needless institutionalizations.

become progressively more dependent. As people expect less of them, they expect less of themselves and they get out of the habit of thinking. They allow themselves to be cared for and are finally unable to care for themselves. With nothing to do, they spend their days catnapping and then, no longer tired, wake frequently at night, wandering in the dark, bumping into furniture, unsure of where they are. When they ask, "What day is today?" they receive only expressions of concern—never the date—and soon they lose all chance of fixing themselves in time and place.

"If you think you're going senile," says Dr. Besdine, "you probably aren't. Having the intellectual facilities to worry about it means you're probably O.K." According to Dr. Butler of the National Institute on Aging, "Even patients suffering from the progressive, chronic form of senile dementia can be helped if we reduce the excess disability. The belief that nothing can be done for them only hastens the progression of the disease."

If an aged parent asks what the date is, tell him, Dr. Gruenberg urges. "Don't just figure, 'Oh, well, there's no point telling him—he won't remember.' He *will* if he's told enough times. Constant reorientation is the single most important thing you can do to reduce the effect of a gradual decline in recent memory."

Home environments can be rearranged into safe places in which to be forgetful. "The blind do it, the deaf do it, the lame do it—and people with memory loss can do it," Dr. Gruenberg says. The most hazardous item in a forgetful person's home, he says, is a gas stove. Imagine an old woman who goes to sleep without turning off the stove. The kettle boils over and douses the flame, the apartment fills with gas, and an alerted neighbor calls the police. In no time at all, the woman is institutionalized because "she's become a hazard to herself and her neighbors."

Gerontologists agree that institutionalization, even in the best of nursing homes, is the surest way to speed the decline of memory and to hasten confusion and disorientation. Far better, says Dr. Gruenberg, to do everything possible to keep the elderly at home: "Why not buy an electric stove?"

As the myth of inevitable senility is dispelled, perhaps a clearer vision will allow us to perceive such simple solutions. The changes will not only improve the lot of our parents and grandparents, but will enrich our own lives as we ourselves move slowly toward old age.

Shocking the Depressed

by Maggie Scarf

In the three months before she entered the hospital, Margaret Garvey's* body weight had dropped an alarming 30 pounds. She was severely depressed, and appetite loss is a common symptom of depression. It can be tolerated well enough by a younger patient, but in an elderly person—and Mrs. Garvey was in her mid-60's— it can lead to an inability to use the life-giving energy that is in our food. If the depression, and the weight loss, continued unabated, the patient would, in effect, be committing a passive form of suicide.

Mrs. Garvey, moreover, had no idea what had *caused* her depression. Her husband had died six years earlier, but she hadn't become depressed at the time. "He was an alcoholic," she said, her voice so subdued that it was difficult to hear her. "We stayed together, but we were not happy." Her mother, whom she'd nursed through a long illness, had been dead for two years. "I grieved for her," she continued, "but I seemed to get over that, in time, pretty well. . . ."

Two years ago, she'd suffered a minor foot accident, and she had to have her leg put in a cast.

"I couldn't get around," she recalled, her voice expressionless. "There wasn't anyone to care for me. . . . My daughter lives in the apartment just above, but she works. And she has to look after her children. She's divorced. So. . . ." She shrugged helplessly. "I didn't want to be a burden to her, as my mother was to me. I felt so alone, as if I were going to die, or as if I *had* died."

Her foot and ankle injuries healed within six weeks, but by then her mood and her spirits had begun their relentless decline. In the 18 months before her hospitalization at Massachusetts General Hospital in Boston, she'd been through one form of treatment after another. Psychotherapy hadn't helped; the drugs, she felt, only made her sicker. They made her confused, faint and terribly dry in the mouth. She could no longer eat, sleep or concentrate. She lay in her hospital room, all alone, all day.

Mrs. Garvey was, in a word, immobilized.

The next morning she was scheduled to receive the first in a series of six to eight electroconvulsive treatments, the number depending on her response.

*The patient's name has been changed in order to protect her privacy.

81

How did she feel about it? "Very, very nervous," she said quietly. "But I can't go on like this anymore. I'm not well."

□

Electroconvulsive or "electric shock" therapy has not been relegated—like dunkings in cold water—to the trunkful of outmoded psychiatric modalities of a less scientifically sophisticated era. Though no one yet fully understands exactly how it works, ECT is still a form of treatment that is in relatively widespread use. Recent estimates made by a task force of the American Psychiatric Association, which has been studying the overall efficacy of the therapy, indicate that anywhere from 60,000 to 100,000 persons undergo a course of therapeutic brain stimulation each year.

ECT was first used in 1938, and the process was named "electroshock" by Italian psychiatrist Dr. Ugo Cerletti. In describing the therapy, Dr. Cerletti wrote: ". . . we observed the . . . instantaneous . . . spasm, and soon after, the onset of the classic epileptic convulsion." He noted the terrifying, momentary halt in the patient's breathing and the awful blueness of his face: "that moment . . . seemed to all of us painfully endless." When the patient started breathing again, wrote Dr. Cerletti, "the blood flowed better not only in the patient's vessels but also in our own. . . ."

Unfortunately, the initial success of the treatment—among the first effective somatic therapies available for the treatment of mental illness—led to instances of overuse and abuse, such as the use of ECT for alcoholism or very mild depression or to control antisocial behavior. Ultimately, the abuses of the therapy became mistaken for the therapy itself.

Perhaps more than any other form of medical treatment, electroshock therapy arouses fantasies and fears of the Frankenstein-style physician who is tinkering with matters that ought to be beyond human intervention. The misuses that have been described in novels and movies have made the treatment a synonym for "mind control" and "psychiatric punishment." In Soviet psychiatric institutions, the treatment is administered to dissenters. In the movie "One Flew Over the Cuckoo's Nest," the therapy is given in the same malevolent spirit.

The very notion of an electric current being passed through an organ so exquisitely sensitive as the human brain evokes the most profound anxieties. Critics of ECT contend that the brain ought to remain sacrosanct and that electrical therapy is a form of Mad Doctoring.

Such a critic is Dr. John Friedberg, a neurologist. In his book "Shock Treatment Is Not Good for Your Brain," he describes his own mounting aversion to it during the time of his medical residency. "The brain was a magic mushroom, two plus pounds of electrical jelly, the circuitry of consciousness. . . . I was teased by the notion that the brain is more quintessentially 'self' than any other part of the human anatomy. . . . And I came to conceive of the neurologist as a protector of the brain, not only from bacteria, viruses and trauma, but from overly ambitious fellow creatures—especially those who would harm the brain to help mankind, that is, the practitioners and proponents of electroconvulsive therapy."

Yet, according to a recent 200-page report of the American Psychiatric Association task force studying ECT, no one has actually demonstrated that ECT, properly administered, does cause any permanent damage to the nervous tissues. The report does stress that ECT be used only in cases of severe depression where the risk of suicide or death from malnutrition is exceptionally high. For the treatment makes a lot of very sick people a lot better, rather quickly.

Therapeutic brain stimulation is an excellent treatment with a terrible reputation, according to Dr. Michel R. Mandel, who is a member of the A.P.A.'s task force on ECT and the director of the somatic therapy unit at the Massachusetts General Hospital. ECT as now given, says Dr. Mandel, involves neither massive convulsions, breath-stopping electric shocks, nor memory losses so profound that they transform the reasoning and functioning human individual into an amnesiac vegetable. "The strange notions that so many people seem to have about the treatment correspond far more to the ECT of 40 years ago. But the ECT of today is so completely different. It's like comparing Kitty Hawk to Apollo 14."

Dr. Mandel cites one of the newer ECT innovations, a "low-energy apparatus" now being

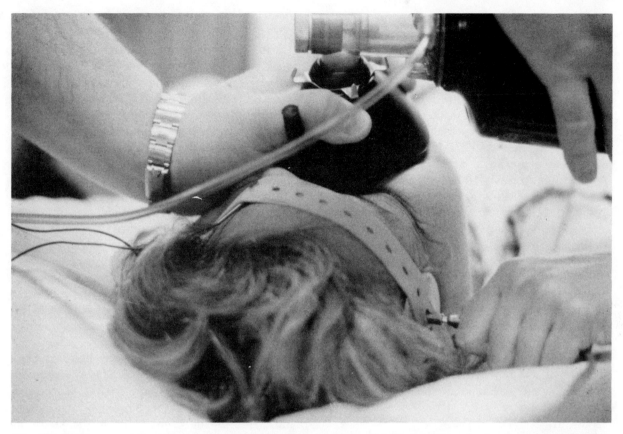

An electrical current is about to be delivered, through the electrodes, into the brain of a patient at Massachusetts General Hospital. The air supply is maintained throughout the procedure.

pioneered at Mass. General. The machine makes it possible to evoke the necessary seizure with what is, comparatively, a mini-current. The new apparatus provides a readout of total electrical energy in watts-second, and total seconds of seizure activity. With this machine, a seizure involving the two brain hemispheres can be elicited with an electrical stimulus as low as 4 or 5 watts-seconds—as compared to the minimum of 50 to 60 watts-seconds commonly in use —and reduces the temporary confusion and amnesia that can accompany the treatment. (In the past, electrical outputs were sometimes as high as many hundreds of watts-seconds.)

ECT is administered on the 11th floor of the Baker wing of the sprawling Massachusetts General complex. Baker-11 is actually an ordinary surgical day-care unit—a place in which routine procedures such as minor knee operations and tonsillectomies are carried out. The decision to give the electrical treatments here, Dr. Mandel says, was "made with a certain degree of self-consciousness. There are so many wild fantasies about the therapy, even medical personnel share them. That's why we like to give the treatments in this very public and undramatic setting."

Every Monday, Wednesday and Friday morning, at 8 A.M., the patients who are to be treated are wheeled into a line of beds that forms in the corridor just outside a large, combination operating-and-recovery room. On the morning that Margaret Garvey was to receive her first brain stimulation, a bright sunshine filled the room. She was the second of four patients in the waiting row outside.

The first patient was a frail-looking man in his mid-70's who was also suffering from a severe depression, and who, like Mrs. Garvey, had also had a recent, very dangerous, weight loss.

Although he had a mild heart condition, there were actually no medical counter-indications against this patient's receiving electroconvulsive therapy.

In terms of mortalities associated with the treatment, the rate of loss is about 1 in every 60,000 treatments; there is, on the other hand, 1 death for every 18,000 persons undergoing tonsillectomy. The low ECT-fatality figures are even more remarkable when one considers the populations from which each type of patient is drawn. Tonsillectomy patients are usually young and healthy, while ECT patients include elderly people who are both malnourished and exhausted from lack of sleep.

When it was time for Mrs. Garvey's bed to be rolled into the treatment area, Dr. Mandel leaned over the side of her bed. "How are you feeling this morning?" he asked gently. She looked pale and frightened. "Nervous," she answered, "terribly nervous." She gave him an almost childlike, imploring look. He patted her hand, spoke to her reassuringly. Jane Cahill, a psychiatric nurse clinician, raised Mrs. Garvey's right arm and wrapped a blood-pressure cuff around it.

Dr. Mandel, working at the head of the table with his associate, Dr. Charles Welch, had slipped a rubber strap—rather like an Indian's headband—around the patient's upper forehead. This strap would hold the recording electrodes, used to measure and record brain-wave activity, firmly in place. The recording electrodes, held by a conductive jelly paste, are merely a monitoring device: They record the rapid electrical firing of the grand-mal seizure (which involves both brain hemispheres), or a failure, if a proper seizure of both cerebral hemispheres has not been elicited.

The treatment electrodes, through which the current is actually delivered, would be held in place, when the time came, by Dr. Mandel's and Nurse Cahill's hands. At this moment the anesthetist, Dr. Bucknam McPeek, was assuring Mrs. Garvey that she would be unaware of most of the treatment: "The only thing you will actually *feel* will be the little pinprick when this needle goes in." The i.v. was in place.

Before Mrs. Garvey slipped completely into unconsciousness, the muscle relaxant succinylcholine—a drug like curare—was injected.

The electroconvulsive current had to be delivered to her brain during the brief period when (1) her musculature was completely relaxed, so that there would be no bodily convulsion, and (2) she was still completely asleep.

Succinylcholine essentially disconnects the muscles from their nervous innervations, rendering them flaccid to the point of total paralysis. It remains effective for about five minutes. Thus, when the seizure is elicited, the muscle spasms, or convulsion, that ordinarily follow a brain seizure will simply be prevented from happening. With one exception.

The patient will experience the convulsion in the right arm. "What we do," explained Jane Cahill, "is to inflate the blood pressure cuff up to a pressure that is greater than the person's systemic pressure. This prevents the muscle relaxant, which is going everywhere *else* in her body via the bloodstream, from getting through to the muscles in this one place."

Mrs. Garvey's right arm was therefore being used as a monitoring device. She was receiving unilateral brain stimulation—that is, the current was being delivered to only the nondominant side of the brain: This would spare the dominant hemisphere, where verbal abilities and skills reside, thus reducing memory loss and confusion. Because she was right-handed, and because brain functions cross over to the opposite side, Mrs. Garvey's dominant cerebral hemisphere was the left side of the brain. A convulsion of the *right* arm, then, would mean that the seizure elicited in the right, nondominant side of the brain had crossed over and spread to the dominant cerebral hemisphere—to produce the convulsive aftermath.

Mrs. Garvey was now soundly asleep. Dr. McPeek had moved to the top of the bed, behind Mrs. Garvey's head, and was holding an oxygen mask over her face, while rhythmically pumping a mixture of air and oxygen into and out of her lungs.

Several of the dials on the front of the square, compact low-energy console had lit up. "This new machine," Dr. Mandel explained, "has a self-test phase, which tests the intactness of the circuitry. If it's correct, and everything is O.K. and ready, then that red button lights up—and we push this button here, to treat."

Dr. Mandel placed one electrode toward the

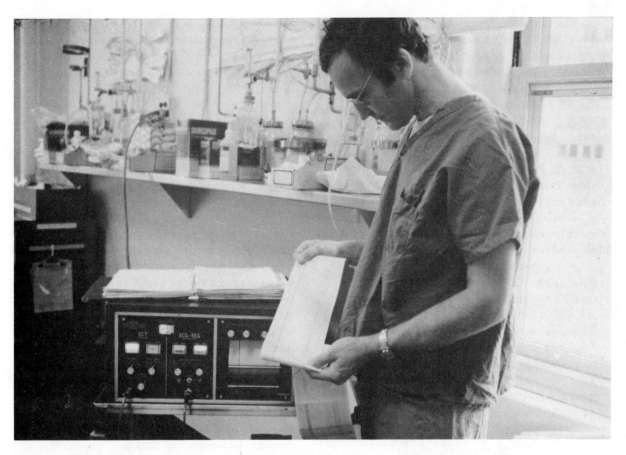

The duration of the patient's electrically induced brain seizure is checked carefully.

top of the patient's head, and on the right side; Nurse Cahill took the other electrode and held it on the right side of the face, midway between Mrs. Garvey's eye and her ear. Dr. Mandel pressed the button to deliver the current. Almost instantaneously, the patient's right arm shot up, the fingers clenched in upon themselves in an odd, clawlike fashion. "She's having a full convulsion," said Jane Cahill, who had reached out to hold and to support that rigid arm.

This was the tonic, or muscle clenching, phase of the convulsion, and it endured for the long breath of an instant. It was succeeded by the clonic phase, during which the muscles unclenched, in short bursts of movement. Slowly, guided gently downward by the nurse, Mrs. Garvey's arm underwent a series of spastic-seeming, fluttery motions. Within a few seconds it lay quietly at her side. Both the brain seizure and the convulsion were over.

The low-energy console, like a ticker tape, had been sending out a continuous record of brain-wave activity. Dr. Mandel, tearing off the paper, pointed out the seizure-activity and the length of its duration. It had lasted 40 seconds and had required 7 watts-seconds of electrical energy. This was fairly typical, he said.

"Mrs. Garvey? Mrs. Garvey?" Dr. Welch, who would attend the patient during recovery, was already calling her back into wakefulness. Her eyelids opened, and she looked surprised. "Is it all over?" she asked uncertainly. "Am I all right?" "Yes it is, and you are," said Dr. Welch, smiling.

A few minutes later, she was sitting up in bed. I glanced up at the clock on the wall, and saw that it was 8:26 A.M. She was already awake, alert and aware of who *I* was. The ECT treatment had begun at 8:15.

According to Dr. Mandel, ECT is one of the

most effective antidepressant treatments available—"especially in the treatment of the severe depressions of middle and later life." These depressions tend to have a different clinical "feel" from the depressions that are seen in younger patients, observes Dr. Mandel, who is also an assistant professor of psychiatry at Harvard Medical School. "The younger person doesn't, in general, show the same degree of severity. Nor does he or she tend to become so completely immobilized. It's as if the motor of living has . . . just stopped."

A series of short-acting electrical stimulations of that brain area which seems to mediate basic biological functions important to survival (such as sleep, appetite, energy levels, sexuality) can restore normal function. "This includes, of course," says Dr. Mandel, "the living organism's basic wish to survive."

There seems to be a very common belief, he notes, that there are drug cures now available that can effectively relieve most serious depressions. "In practice," says Dr. Mandel, "the drugs prove effective in about 65 to 70 percent of the more severe depressive illnesses. But that leaves a large 30 percent of these patients who are just not having any response. With ECT, as a number of studies have indicated, there's a much higher success rate—on the order of 90 to 95 percent. So we're talking about a group of people for whom nothing *but* brain stimulation is going to help." This may be the reason for ECT's survival, adds Dr. Mandel, in a climate of continuing public misunderstanding, distrust and antipathy.

Another explanation for the therapy's continued use has to do with the side effects of the antidepressant compounds. These drugs are powerful and not always easy to metabolize, especially for elderly people. Among the most troublesome symptoms produced by antidepressant drugs are delirious states. The person feels drunk, confused, unable to remember things. In addition, antidepressants can cause the blood to collect and to "pool" in the veins, which in turn can cause fainting spells. A serious problem is that of cardiac toxicity. Among those patients who are not only depressed but who have a pre-existing heart condition, the commonly used tricyclic antidepressants can bring about life-threatening arrhythmia, or irregular beating of the heart.

Severe depression can be a particularly difficult problem, Dr. Mandel says, since the body's immunological mechanisms are affected and altered by the depressive process—a process that is now known to affect virtually every organ system in the body, including sleep, appetite and sexual functioning, salt balance, brain biochemistry and endocrine function. Relieving a depression, notes Dr. Mandel, and restoring the body's physiology to its normal functioning, renders the individual far less susceptible to any of the more serious physical diseases.

And when the possibility of death from suicide is an issue, ECT, because it brings relief so much more rapidly than do the drugs—in days, as compared to weeks—can be a life-saving procedure. (ECT is also used in the treatment of catatonic schizophrenia and some chronic pain conditions associated with depression—such as severe backache—and mania.)

If electrical therapy has been modified and streamlined, it is largely because of an increasing understanding of just which aspects of the treatment are therapeutic and which aspects are "side effects." It used to be believed, for example, that memory loss and confusion were what made the patient better; in other words, the clearing of the depression was related to the blurring of painful thoughts and recollections. This has now been shown to be completely false. A series of researches, carried out in the late 1960's by J. O. Ottoson, a Scandinavian psychiatrist, have made it clear that it is *the series of brief brain seizures, and that alone, which bring about clinical improvement.*

As to the post-treatment "side effects," such as loss of memories and the capacity for retaining newly learned information, such difficulties are, for the most part, transitory. Many people, however, find them terribly disturbing, even though "memory loss" is another symptom of the depression itself, since the depressed person's entire ability to think is slowed down and impaired. In any case, memory loss does seem to correlate with the amount of electrical energy used to elicit the brain seizure. And the recent trend has been toward seeking methods of bringing about the grand-mal seizure, without the excess of electrical energy that may result in disturbances of memory and of thinking.

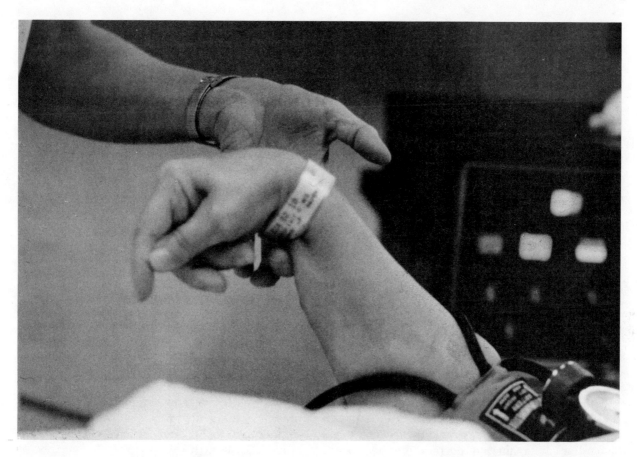

A blood pressure cuff is attached to the patient's arm and that arm is used as a monitoring device.

Unilateral placement of the stimulating electrodes is an excellent technique, says Dr. Mandel, even though, he acknowledges, the psychiatric community has been slow to accept this method. There is some controversy in medical literature as to whether this method is as effective as bilateral stimulation—i.e., delivering the current to both brain hemispheres simultaneously. But there is no dispute at all about the fact that the unilateral method does reduce amnesia and post-ECT confusion.

The task force of the American Psychiatric Association studying ECT has found that 75 percent of the American psychiatrists who administer ECT still use the bilateral method. This study group is recommending the wider use of the unilateral technique.

The new low-energy apparatus, in combination with unilateral electrode placement, has now been used on a series of 50 patients admitted to Massachusetts General Hospital who were suffering from depressive illnesses that had been resistant to drug and psychological forms of therapy. "The results thus far have been excellent," says Dr. Mandel. "We've not had one patient with a spontaneous memory complaint—and such complaints were fairly commonplace, prior to our use of this new 'combination' technique."

Why—and how—does ECT actually work? No one really knows for sure, says Dr. Fred H. Frankel, director of the adult psychiatry unit at the Harvard-affiliated Beth Israel Hospital in Boston, and chairman of the A.P.A. task force studying ECT. "Neither," he continues, "do we know why *aspirin* does what it does. We only know that there's a beneficial effect. And this is the case in much of medical therapeutics. We aren't sure why something helps; we just know that it does."

Dr. Frankel and his colleagues have now combed through all of the major research on the treatment. "The best that we can say," he says, "is that stimulation of the 'old' brain might be affecting its chemical or electrical activity, or both. And that a series of brief electrical stimulations then brings about that very marked clinical improvement."

Perhaps it is true, as some experts have suggested, that the brain cells in this critical hypothalamic region have become "sluggish"—unable, somehow, to produce their proper neurochemical secretions. What *is* known is that the brain seizures evoke a sudden large outpouring of catecholamines, including the important norepinephrine, into the bloodstream. These neurotransmitter substances are believed to be crucially involved in mood regulation. It may be, that by inducing a series of seizures in this particular area of the brain, the cells themselves are being helped to release their neurochemicals more effectively. An analogy might be to a biological pendulum which, stimulated by a series of short taps, began swinging regularly once again and now could do so by virtue of its own force.

"A current going into the brain can regulate heartbeat," observes Dr. Frankel, "as it does in a cardiac pacemaker. A current on the chest wall can defibrillate a heart in the midst of a life-threatening attack. So there are parts of the body where electricity *is* used therapeutically."

ECT *has* helped thousands of acutely suffering, debilitated, exhausted, often suicidally depressed people. One such person, a woman whom I interviewed at the University of Pittsburgh's Western Psychiatric Institute and Clinic, told me that she'd been desperately ill with depression two times in her life—once, after her son went away to college and once, after her husband's death—and that nothing but ECT had been able to help her. On both occasions it had, she said, "restored me to myself."

There is something eerie about seeing such a patient suddenly begin to improve. Or about seeing someone like Margaret Garvey, who had been dragging herself around for months, steadily reawakening into life. The transformation of the patient's entire way of being, taking place over such a brief period of time, is almost magical—more like wizardry than it is like the practice of psychiatry.

"I'm feeling so different, now," Mrs. Garvey told me, on the evening after her sixth treatment (she was treated three times weekly, over a period of two weeks). "When I came in here, I simply couldn't talk to anyone—I hadn't the strength. But now I feel I want to be with people, and I get into conversations all the time. I want to find out about everyone around here," she added, cocking her head to one side and smiling.

She was eating and gaining weight. The depressive emergency was over—she had begun coming out of it, she believed, around the fourth or the fifth treatment.

Mrs. Garvey's course of electroconvulsive therapy had effectively relieved her depression; what it hadn't done, clearly, was to solve all of her human dilemmas. She was a person who had spent most of her life in service to other people, and now she had to cope with the problem of "not being vitally needed by someone else." But she was beginning, in collaboration with the psychiatric staff, to plan the shape of the life she would lead on leaving the hospital.

The Abuse of Antibiotics

by Marietta Whittlesey

Over the past 30 years, antibiotics have permitted a control of infectious disease that would have been considered miraculous by earlier generations. And until recent years, the medical world made the comfortable assumption that antibiotics were a sure-fire weapon against bacterial infections. Now, however, doctors are beginning to have problems treating some of the diseases they thought they had defeated with antibiotics. There are, for instance, two new strains of gonorrhea that are resistant to even megadoses of penicillin.

What has been happening is that the indiscriminate prescribing and taking of antibiotics for anything from minor colds to venereal diseases have led to an alarming increase in drug-resistant bacteria. Highly controversial at the moment is the question of antibiotics as feed additives for livestock; antibiotics are fed to these animals in part to promote rapid growth. Critics of this practice contend that these additives only generate more resistant organisms.

The most dramatic demonstration that resistance to antibiotics could be life-threatening to large populations was a typhoid epidemic in 1972–73 in Mexico. Of the 100,000 who were afflicted in what became the largest typhoid outbreak in recorded history, says Dr. Ephraim S. Anderson, 20,000 died because the typhoid bacteria had already picked up resistance to chloramphenicol, the drug normally used to combat it. Dr. Anderson, now retired, who was at the time of the outbreak director of the Enteric Reference Laboratory in London—which identifies and records bacterial samples from all over the world—ran tests to determine which drugs were still effective against this resistant strain, and found that ampicillin was.

Epidemics in Guatemala and Brazil soon followed. In all three countries, the use of antibiotics is poorly understood and inadequately controlled. Though recently there has been an attempt to regulate all drugs in South America, outside the large cities it is still possible to obtain virtually any antibiotic over the counter; many pharmacists often dispense antibiotics for a variety of ailments, such as headaches and colds, for which the drugs are totally ineffectual.

Self-medication is not just a matter of eco-

Dr. William M. O'Leary in a microbiology laboratory at Cornell University Medical College where bacteria are freeze dried to keep them viable for research for long periods.

nomics (taking a pill is cheaper than seeing a doctor); it is a product of ignorance. And the ignorance isn't confined to developing countries. Doctors often dismiss the problem of resistance because, they insist, new drugs discovered daily can be relied upon to overcome resistance to antibiotics.

Resistance is not a new problem. Sir Alexander Fleming encountered it with strains of *Staphylococcus aureus* as far back as 1942. He issued a surprised warning at the time that some strains of that species of bacteria seemed "almost insensitive" to penicillin.

Originally it was thought that bacteria acquired resistance only through mutation. In most populations of bacteria there are only a few naturally resistant variants; in the presence of an antibiotic they flourish because the antibiotic kills or inhibits the drug-sensitive bacteria. Furthermore, in species of bacteria where resistance has not been known, researchers found something quite unexpected.

In 1959 it was discovered by a medical research team in Japan that a strain of *Shigella dysenteriae* that was resistant to four antibiotics could transfer its resistance to other bacteria. This type of resistance was not the result of a new mutation but the result of an actual transfer of genetic material from one bacterium to another (even of a different family) through physical contact. Resistance genes are transferred on a structure called a plasmid. Thus, a benign but resistant organism could transfer its drug resistance to virulent pathogens such as salmonellae, or to resident bacteria such as *E. coli.*

As antibiotic usage continued to rise, it became apparent that the plasmids could carry more than one resistance gene. While in the early 1960's plasmids carrying more than a couple were uncommon, it is now commonplace to see bacteria carrying genes for resistance to as many as 10 different drugs. Moreover, one research team has isolated an *E. coli* plasmid that carries genes for drug resistance *and* the production of enterotoxin (the substance that causes traveler's diarrhea).

This form of "natural" genetic recombination is far more real a threat to the general population today than the research in recombinant DNA. According to Dr. Anderson, "we have accomplished in half a century evolutionary changes that couldn't have happened in a million years under natural circumstances. Recombinant DNA research is tiddlywinks compared with what has been done ecologically to bacteria with the emergence of antibacterials."

The mechanics of drug resistance vary with the bacteria and the drug involved. One way bacteria become resistant is through changes in the cell membrane so that the antibiotic cannot enter the cell and take effect. Researchers in the microbiology department at Cornell University Medical College are working on a method of overcoming this type of resistance by using surfactants—surface-active agents similar to detergents—to break down the cell membrane. Dr. William M. O'Leary, professor of microbiology at Cornell, feels that this method is applicable to a large number of resistant bacteria.

Another way bacteria become drug resistant is through the production of enzymes that destroy the drug molecule. One such enzyme is beta-lactamase, which destroys penicillin by breaking up one bond of the penicillin molecule while it is in the body. An example of beta-lactamase-producing bacteria is the so-called "incurable" form of gonorrhea. Until recently, two new strains of gonorrhea that are resistant to penicillin and several other drugs could be controlled by spectinomycin, which is 10 times as expensive as penicillin. However, in 1973, spectinomycin-resistant strains were reported from Denmark.

While thousands of cases of penicillin-resistant *N. gonorrhoeae* have been reported in 18 countries around the world since 1976, when the bacteria acquired the penicillinase plasmid, there have been only 368 cases in the United States and Guam. For the most part, the American carriers were servicemen who had been stationed in the Philippines. It was discovered that Filipino prostitutes had been routinely taking low levels of penicillin as a prophylactic against the very disease they were incubating in their bodies.

What is responsible for the rise in resistant bacteria? There are those who believe that antibiotic feed additives play a major part. Antibiotics are fed to livestock for two reasons: (1) to promote rapid growth; (2) as prophylaxis against diseases, such as shipping fever, which can ravage herds in no time. When antibiotics are used in this way, they are said to cut down on the amount of space and feed needed per animal.

The "growth promotion effect" was discovered in 1949 by Dr. Thomas H. Jukes, now professor in residence at the medical physics division of the University of California at Berkeley. He found that the drug residue from the fermentation of antibiotics increased

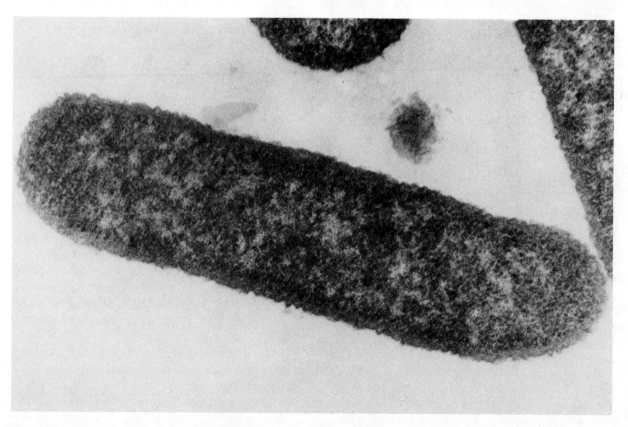

Certain antibiotic research is being focused on the E. coli *bacteria.*

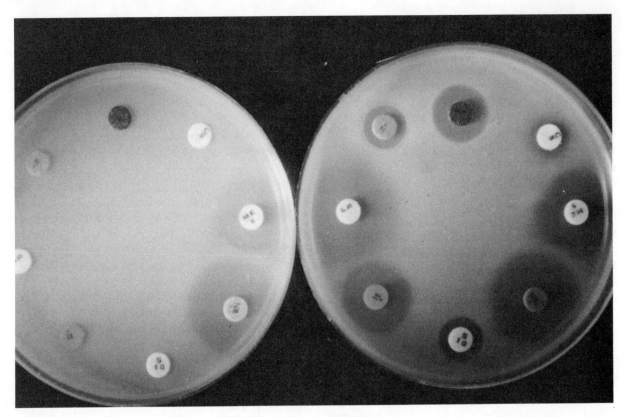

Dr. Novick's research involves antibiotic sensitivity tests. In this test six antibiotics are being tested on two strains of staphylococci. The petri dish on the right shows that bacteria is sensitive to all of these antibiotics. (There is a greyish film of bacterial growth surrounding the pills.) The one on the left shows that the bacteria is resistant to six of the drugs due to the presence of plasmids.

weights and size by about 10 to 20 percent. To this day it is not known how this effect works. The antibiotics may be suppressing the detrimental effects of certain resident bacteria, or they may be stimulating beneficial resident intestinal microflora, such as coliform bacteria and yeast cells, which synthesize nutrients. It is known that levels of these resident flora increase when an animal is fed by this method. These animals also show a thinner gut wall, which may be more capable of absorbing nutrients than that of untreated animals.

The growth effect does not yet appear to be jeopardized, as the bacteria involved in it have been slower to acquire resistance. Yet public-health experts warn that the plasmids have turned out to be very adaptable. "They were able to get into all sorts of bugs which never had them before," says Dr. Richard P. Novick,

chief of the department of plasmid biology of the Public Health Research Institute of the City of New York Inc. "It's taken a very long time," he continues. "What we've seen is a very rare event that is statistically improbable, but if you put the pressure on high enough you get very rare events, and once you have the first one, the rest can take off from there. So when people say that it's been 25 years without any trouble and we can be confident of safety, I would argue that no one has the right to make that assumption. In fact, it's just now that the trouble's starting."

Part of the trouble is the number of resistant organisms in these animals' bodies that could be transferred to humans. In a study of farm families who raised chickens that had been fed tetracycline-supplemented feed, Dr. Stuart Levy of Tufts University Medical School in Boston

Dr. Richard P. Novick of the Public Health Research Institute is among those who have been trying to discover what is responsible for the rise of resistant bacteria.

demonstrated that resistance plasmids and *E. coli* in the chickens were picked up by some farm handlers. In addition, the tetracycline-supplemented feed caused an increase in plasmids that imparted resistance not only to tetracycline but to several other antibiotics as well.

Many supporters of a ban by the Food and Drug Administration on antibiotic additives base their arguments on what happened in Britain in 1964–68 when an outbreak of salmonellosis swept through the cattle herds. Thousands of animals as well as seven humans died as a result of this epidemic.

Dr. Ephraim S. Anderson, who brought the situation to the Government's attention, traced the epidemic to one dealer, who denied having any infection among his livestock, but who was later found to have sent more than 800 carcasses to the knacker's yard—where old or sick

animals are sent to be slaughtered and sterilized for nonhuman consumption. His business was, in effect, the salmonellosis distribution center, as his stock was shipped all over England. The strain of *S. typhimurium* acquired resistance to each drug the veterinarians used to treat the disease. By the time the epidemic died out (mainly as a result of the dealer's death in an automobile accident in 1967), the strain was resistant to eight different drugs.

The Swann Committee was convened in London to discuss the additives problem, and out of it came a law that banned antibiotics as feed additives if they were of primary importance in treating humans. Other antibiotics require a veterinarian's prescription and are used as medicines only.

Influenced by the Swann Committee, the F.D.A. in 1977 and 1978 proposed rules that would make antibiotic additives available only on a veterinarian's prescription and made only from drugs with no use in human therapy. The F.D.A. also proposed that feeds with additives could be purchased only from F.D.A.-licensed feed mills, and that the diagnosis be stated on the prescription form. Right now, a veterinary medicine can be sold over the counter if the directions for use can be explained adequately to a layman in writing.

The proposed rules are not without their problems. In the vast meat-producing areas of the country, there are not always veterinarians within a few miles. Most smaller feedlot operators cannot afford their own veterinarians, and complying with F.D.A. rules, they say, would mean a lot of added costs, which might put them out of business, and which would certainly mean a rise in meat prices.

No action has yet been taken on the proposed rules, which are generally opposed by the drug industry. Dr. John Farnham, manager of quality assurance at American Cyanamid's agricultural division, points out that meat from animals not given antibiotics could be contaminated with pathogens, such as salmonella, which he feels would rise dramatically were prophylactic use of antibiotics to be curtailed. Members of the drug industry are also quick to point out that the British model has not worked well. There is a thriving black market in additives, and many farmers are able to evade the rules that the drugs not be given for growth-promotion purposes by giving the drugs as prophylactics.

The F.D.A., supported by large numbers of medical researchers, feels that the more resistant organisms are let into the environment, the more resistance will spread.

□

Once viewed as wonder drugs and miracles, antibiotics are now called overworked miracles. Perhaps more than any other group, the drug industry has been responsible for the overuse of these valuable drugs. All too often, pushy sales representatives offer free samples and glossy brochures promoting unneeded items to their customers. Not surprisingly, antibiotic use increases year by year. Americans use up enough penicillin to provide a weekly dose for every man, woman and child.

Patients are also responsible for antibiotic abuse. Many patients are resentful if their visit to a doctor does not result in a prescription for medication. And many doctors, to avoid losing these patients, have learned not to argue; they will dispense drugs for their placebo effect. However, in the case of antibiotics, this is not a harmless practice. To prescribe antibiotics for flu and viral infections, against which the drugs are useless, is to create a public-health hazard by raising the number of resistant resident bacteria.

Another dangerous practice is self-medication by patients. Often, drugs left over from previous illnesses are put to use two years later. And even though there should be no antibiotics left over from a prescription, too many patients have the habit of taking an antibiotic for a few days until they feel better and then halting medication. This is the perfect way to cause a relapse. The antibiotic is present just long enough to slow down or kill most of the sensitive ones, leaving intact the minority of resistant organisms. If the antibiotic is withdrawn at this point, the bacteria will rebound, more resistant for having to adapt to the antibiotic.

Self-medication is also unwise because not all antibiotics are effective against all bacteria. Some are known as "broad-spectrum antibiotics," and they are active against a wide range of bacteria. Broad-spectrum drugs kill off everything in their path, including normal intestinal flora. When this happens, one is open to invasion by other bacteria.

Furthermore, self-medication can be hazardous because of drug-food interactions. Until recently, little was known about this subject, and what information there was often wasn't passed on to patients. For instance, the combination of tetracyclines with milk or antacids can reduce drug absorption up to 100 percent; streptomycin and diuretics can cause temporary or permanent deafness.

Many physicians themselves often show a fundamental lack of understanding of recent findings in bacteriology and internal medicine. This was clearly shown by Dr. Harold C. Neu of the division of infectious diseases at Columbia Presbyterian Medical Center. Dr. Neu devised a self-assessment test on the diagnosis and treatment of infectious diseases, and he found that out of 4,513 physicians the median score was only 68 percent; residents and those in practice for fewer than five years scored best.

According to Dr. Georges Causse of the World Health Organization in Geneva, part of the reason for the spread of the beta-lactamase-producing strain of gonorrhea is that physicians have not kept up with medical research, and they continue to prescribe doses of penicillin that don't reach a high enough concentration in the body to eliminate even the sensitive bacteria. These patients become sources of highly resistant organisms and are threats to those around them.

In 1976, Dr. William Schaffner and his colleagues at the Vanderbilt University Medical School in Nashville did a study of office prescriptions of chloramphenicol by the state's doctors. Even though this antibiotic has been found to be so highly toxic to human tissues that it is indicated only rarely in office practice, 6 percent of the doctors prescribed it frequently, and most commonly for colds. For rural doctors the figure was 21 percent. Not only were the drugs dispensed unwisely, but in cases where they were indicated, they were often given in too low a dosage to treat an infection adequately.

One of the more serious manifestations of the resistance problem is that of nosocomial, or hospital-acquired, infections. Bacteria are present

Dr. Harold C. Neu (above) of Columbia-Presbyterian Medical Center has found that physicians often show a fundamental lack of understanding of recent findings in bacteriology and internal medicine.

Dr. Richard B. Dixon (right) of the Center for Disease Control in Atlanta estimates that there are two million cases of hospital-acquired infections a year.

everywhere, and hospitals are no exception. While sanitation can do much toward keeping these bacterial populations under control, bacteria can never be totally eliminated, and optimal sanitation is far from universal. During the 50's and 60's, the most common hospital bacterium was a strain of *Staphylococcus aureus.* Then, without anyone's knowing why, *Serratia marcescens, Klebsiella, Proteus* and *Pseudomonas* bacteria began to prevail. *Serratia,* which used to be considered so harmless it was given to medical students to learn from, is now epidemic in hospitals. It is often resistant to all drugs.

Dr. Richard B. Dixon, chief of the hospital infections branch at the Center for Disease Control in Atlanta, estimates there are two million nosocomial infections a year. In some instances, patients infected with these bugs cannot be treated, and in their weakened condition their bodies cannot fight off the bacterial invasion and they die. According to Dr. Schaffner, these infections prolong the average hospital stay by a week. At a minimum of $150 a day, another $1,000 is added to the patient's hospital bill. Nationally, the figure comes to $1.5 billion.

Dr. Edward Lowbury at the University of Aston in Birmingham, England, is emphatic in stating that in order to cope systematically with hospital infections, a strict antibiotic control program must be set up by each hospital.

He recommends that the hospital's antibiotic policy be run by an infection-control team that surveys the rate and type of infection present in the hospital, as well as the shifting patterns of resistance. Antibiotics are to be classified in categories of availability:

(1) *Relatively unrestricted drugs* which have shown little resistance, and drugs which are inexpensive or which have a low toxicity.

(2) *Relatively restricted drugs* which are available on general prescription but which have shown increasing resistance, or drugs which are toxic.

(3) *Reserved drugs* which are used only for severe infections where other antibiotics are inadequate, and are available only on a consultant's signature. Drugs are placed in this category to preserve their high value or to restore their activity when there has been widespread resistance to them. When a drug is removed from use, the resistant bacteria gradually fall off.

What is the future of antibiotic drugs? There is a great divergence of opinion. Some feel it is too late to undo any of the damage, although we will probably not be wiped out by bacterial epidemics simply because we have improved our sanitation greatly since the early part of the century. Others feel that with the proper controls, the drugs can be made to last.

The outlook is generally bleak. Over the past decade there has been a slowing down in the rate of discovery of usable new antibiotics. Although "new" drugs are continually being found, these drugs are often chemical variants of known drugs and do not represent the major advances that penicillin, the tetracyclines and the synthetic penicillins did. According to Dr. Novick, "No major new class of antibiotics has been discovered in at least the last 10 years." Structurally and mechanically, the new drugs are more and more similar. Many of them are also more toxic to the patient's tissues.

Many see education and regulation as the most important and necessary weapons with which to fight resistance. Dr. Novick feels that antibiotics should be as strictly controlled as narcotics. He proposes that physicians prescribing the drugs should be required to indicate the diagnosis on the prescription form itself. Under such a system, the information could be stored in a computer for periodic review by authorities, such as a committee of infectious-disease physicians.

Although the American Medical Association and most of its members would probably respond unfavorably to such a proposal, Dr. Novick argues that "the howls of anguish that will be raised about interference with the 'right' to prescribe can be answered with the comment that the medical profession has totally failed to develop and enforce even minimum standards during the 30 years of antibiotic usage."

The Manic-Depressive Cycle

by Harold M. Schmeck, Jr.

New research is linking manic-depressive illness, one of the most important forms of human mental disorder, to biological clocks that fail to keep proper time. The studies are producing new concepts in treatment and strategies for using existing drugs.

Within every human being is a set of biological clocks whose subtle chemical ticking helps govern the normal daily rise and fall of temperature, the production of important hormones and other substances and such basic urges as sleep and hunger. Evidence compiled largely within the last few years links derangements of these biological rhythm-keepers with manic-depressive illness, a common disorder that can totally disable its victims.

This evidence, gathered by scientists at the National Institute of Mental Health, is already prompting new ideas about the treatment of depression and about the biological basis of this crippling affliction, which, in all its forms, may affect as many as seven in every 100 Americans at any given time. Every human being has ups and downs of mood, but depression severe enough to be classed as illness is far more

profound. The simplest daily tasks become impossible obstacles in the patients' minds. Some commit suicide in the grip of their depression. In about one-third of such patients, the depression alternates in a regular pattern with opposite emotions sometimes so extreme as to be equally disabling. Some of these cases of cyclical illness appear, in fact, to be aberrant forms of the normal monthly, seasonal or even annual rhythms of the human body, according to a recent publication by Drs. Frederick K. Goodwin and Thomas A. Wehr. Dr. Goodwin is chief of the clinical psychobiology branch of the institute. Dr. Wehr is chief of the clinical research unit in that branch.

The scientists have produced dramatic temporary improvement in some patients by depriving them of a single night's sleep, then moving their sleeping hours forward by several hours, thus evidently giving their biological clocks a nudge toward normalcy. In one patient, all symptoms of depression were erased for two weeks. The good effect returned for two weeks following another night's sleep-deprivation and further advancement of sleeping time. The ef-

97

Dr. Frederick K. Goodwin

Dr. Thomas A. Wehr

fect could not be repeated a third time, perhaps, Dr. Goodwin believes, because three such changes returned the rhythm to its original abnormal state.

Drugs May Speed Up Cycles

The new research also suggests that one important group of drugs, called the tricyclic antidepressants, speeds up the cycles of manic-depressive illness while lithium, also important in treating this form of illness, slows them down. These discoveries are helping scientists make better use of the drugs.

The link between human depressive illness and some derangement of biological rhythms has long been suspected because the illness itself is cyclic in nature. But scientists have lacked a way of properly demonstrating such effects. Two recent innovations have provided the means to do so. One, a device small enough to be worn on a patient's wrist, keeps track of the person's activity, day and night, for as long as nine days without replacement. It functions like a submarine or missile inertial guidance system, by recording every change in motion. The device was developed by Theodore Colburn, an engineer at the institute. When all the data are compiled by computer, it shows when the patient's peaks of activity came, when he or she was quiet, asleep and awake.

Computer Helps Analysis

Digested by computer, the pattern of a person's active and passive periods for a full year can be compressed onto one 8-by-11-inch sheet of paper. Data such as this have showed that many symptoms of the illness, previously thought to be random events, were actually biological rhythms, albeit abnormal ones. The second recent innovation was a reliable and accurate way of assaying the human body's production of the hormone melatonin, a chemical created by the pineal gland and known to be intimately involved in the regulation of biological clocks. The assay was devised by Dr. Alfred J. Lewy.

Helped by these two devices, scientists observed that about half of the manic-depressive

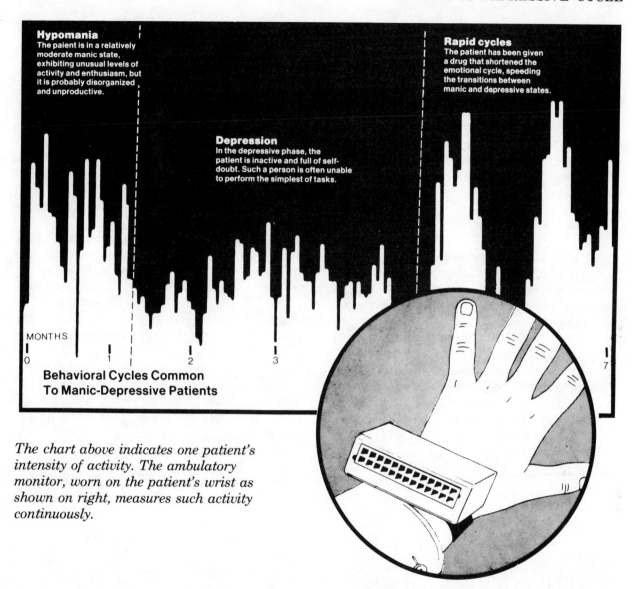

Hypomania
The paient is in a relatively moderate manic state, exhibiting unusual levels of activity and enthusiasm, but it is probably disorganized and unproductive.

Depression
In the depressive phase, the patient is inactive and full of self-doubt. Such a person is often unable to perform the simplest of tasks.

Rapid cycles
The patient has been given a drug that shortened the emotional cycle, speeding the transitions between manic and depressive states.

MONTHS
0   1   2   3   7

Behavioral Cycles Common To Manic-Depressive Patients

The chart above indicates one patient's intensity of activity. The ambulatory monitor, worn on the patient's wrist as shown on right, measures such activity continuously.

patients they were studying had biological rhythms that were drifting away from the normal 24-hour cycle dictated by terrestrial day and night. This same drifting has been observed in normal persons who have been isolated for long periods in closed environments such as caves, where the steadying signals of sunlight and darkness and other environmental clues are not present. "We were intrigued by the fact that a number of our patients were behaving as though they, too, were cut off from all environmental stimuli," Dr. Goodwin said in a recent interview. Before the activity monitor and the melatonin assay were developed, these shifts could not be detected. It had always been as-

sumed that the patients simply had difficulty sleeping when, in fact, their "normal" sleeping hours had been rearranged.

Other research has also showed evidence of problems with biological clocks. There appears to be a shift in the depressed patient's sleep cycle, so that dreaming sleep comes earlier in the night than normal. All such effects used to be thought of as random sleep disturbances, but the activity-monitor studies shows they were patterns that were cyclical but out of phase.

Like almost everything else that occurs in the brain, the underlying mechanisms involve chemistry. In a report to the American Psychiatric Association last year, the scientists at the

National Institute of Mental Health showed that melatonin production was greater in manic-depressive patients than in normal people. Even more important, in the scientists' view, was their evidence of a shift in the timing of the hormone's production. In normal people, the peak occurs just before dawn and ends abruptly when daylight comes. In manic patients, the peak came earlier in the night and began to diminish well before dawn.

Systems May Be in Conflict

All of this converging evidence has led to a new hypothesis to explain some forms of manic-depressive illness. It is known that the human body has several biological clocks. One system, for example, governs dreaming sleep, known to scientists as REM (for Rapid Eye Movement) sleep, and also controls the diurnal rise and fall of body temperature. Another biological clock system controls the nondreaming phase of sleep. In the depressive patients, it seemed that the clocks governing the two types of sleep were drifting away from each other, possibly because they were governed by different nerve-signal chemicals.

The hypothesis, as explained by Dr. Goodwin, is that the clocks governing different brain chemicals may get out of synchonization in a depressive patient so that two powerful chemicals that ought to counterbalance each other—one at a peak when the other is at a trough—might peak or drop simultaneously. Experiments in which rats are kept for long periods in conditions of abnormal light and other unusual conditions suggest that this kind of derangement can be induced in the animals.

The effect produced by such biological clock derangements, according to the scientists' new theory, may be more or less like the abnormal oscillations that can build up to destroy a suspension bridge when it is pounded by wind or other vibrations. What circumstances might produce such a biological oscillation in humans is unknown, a target of future research. Meanwhile, the studies have already opened new vistas of the functions and malfunctions of the brain and have suggested new ways of coping with one of the most puzzling and disabling disorders of the human mind.

Medical Technology: The New Revolution

by Laurence Cherry

If you have to go to the hospital 10 years from now, your visit may run something like this:

Past the inevitable receptionist, your street clothes exchanged for a shapeless hospital gown, you enter a small, antiseptic room. You take a seat and offer your arm to a rectangular machine. Painlessly the machine draws a blood sample and within seconds has analyzed it down to its smallest meaningful platelet. The information is flashed to a central computer deep within the hospital, where it is compared with previous readings to detect an infection anywhere in your body.

You move to an adjoining room and sit under a massive apparatus. Silently, your body is probed by X-rays or microwaves, while sensors inspect the surface of your skin. A thermogram will show areas of raised temperature, which can reveal incipient disease. Although you feel nothing, see nothing, the inner workings of your body are being deeply scrutinized. A developing gallstone, still barely larger than a grain of sand, is noted and appraised; like a tiny white clot lodged within a coronary artery or a polyp hidden in your nasal cavity, it may be harmless, but nevertheless deserves watching.

Within moments, a minutely detailed workup has been prepared by computer and sent to your doctor. It contains both diagnoses and suggested methods of treatment.

Medicine today is in the midst of a technological revolution, a transformation that is already changing the art of healing. New instruments and machines can already glimpse a 3-month-old fetus curled within its mother's womb, painlessly diagnose brain damage, help surgeons fuse damaged nerves and blood vessels.

And still other seemingly miraculous inventions are almost at hand. At Rockefeller University and New York Hospital, an experimental "artificial pancreas" can instantaneously measure glucose levels and adjust the amount of insulin fed into the bloodstreams of selected diabetic patients, preventing wild daily fluctuations in glucose levels. Experiments with sophisticated electronics at the University of Utah and New York's Columbia Presbyterian Medical Center have meant sight for the blind and hearing for the deaf. At the National Institutes of Health in Bethesda, various medical teams are refining a complicated technique used in chemistry called nuclear magnetic resonance

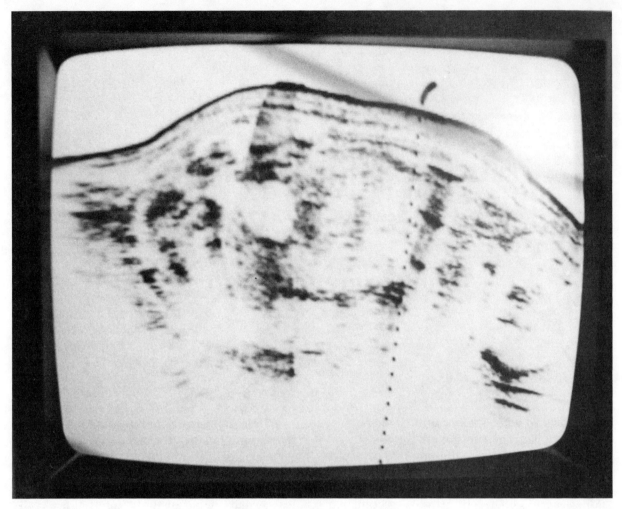

An ultrasonic photo of a fetus. The dots across the center are centimeter marks.

to track the chemistry of living cells. In the not very distant future they hope to be able to detect changes in heart muscle cells before a heart attack occurs and then quickly arrest them; they should also be able to detect early rejection of transplanted organs and take preventive action.

But along with this dramatic new technology and its apparent potential for solving many of our most perplexing medical problems, controversy has developed about its benefits and costs. Critics contend that the increasing use of machines is dehumanizing the practice of medicine and creating intolerable medical expenses as well as hidden medical dangers. In November, 1978, at the behest of top Congres-

sional leaders, a National Center for Health-Care Technology was established in Washington to take a closer look at the new technology. "Medical instrumentation has reached the point and expense where it must be closely scrutinized," says Dr. Seymour Perry, the acting director of the new center. "We know there have been truly important advances. Now we have to decide which of them are appropriate and which are not."

The Korean and Vietnam Wars both played a part in creating the new technology. Experimental physicists and mathematicians first employed to develop deadly new electronic gadgets for warfare (such as improved radar to track enemy missiles or infrared sensors to spot troop movements through nighttime jungles) began to look around for other areas in which to practice their skills. Advanced computers arrived on the scene in the early 1960's. By the early 1970's, the amalgamation of medicine and physics began to be known as bioengineering and departments of bioengineering cropped up in medical schools around the country.

In a small pastel room at New York Hospital, a 36-year-old woman, six months pregnant with her first child, lies on an examining table. While music plays in the background, a young technician swabs her belly with a thick gel, then holds a beige wandlike probe, not much longer than a toothbrush, directly over it.

Nearby, an image of the fetus in the mother's womb suddenly swims into view on the screen of what looks like a small portable television set. Though murky, the image is clear enough to show the baby curled within the womb, and, at the center, a smudge of pulsing gray, its rapidly beating heart.

"Is that my baby?" the woman excitedly asks, craning her neck for a better look at the screen.

"That's your baby's chest, and there's a foot," answers a radiologist standing next to the screen, snapping a lever that will record the view in still photos to be examined later. "He's lying with his head down."

"Is everything normal?"

"Everything looks fine."

Ultrasound is one of the most promising developments in the new field of bioengineering. Conventional X-rays reveal little about the organs deep within our anatomy; for example, until recently the only way to obtain truly accurate information about the heart was to insert a snakelike catheter through a vein in the arm and gradually work it into the chambers of the heart, a risky and sometimes even fatal procedure. But now with ultrasound a picture can be obtained of the organs of the body at work.

Ultrasound, using the same principle developed years ago to locate enemy submarines, employs ultrasonic waves. Sonar signals too high for humans to hear are bounced off the organs of the body and received by a tiny instrument that translates them into pictures. In patients with gallbladder disease—a leading cause of surgery in adults—ultrasound has now been refined

to the point where it can detect gallstones. It is also beginning to be employed to examine the prostate gland, malfunctions of which affect nearly half of all men over 50. "Nowadays, instead of going through time-consuming and uncomfortable tests, the patient goes straight to ultrasound," says Dr. Joseph P. Whalen, radiologist in chief at New York Hospital and professor of radiology at Cornell University Medical College. "It's a whole new dimension in diagnosis."

But probably the most widespread use of ultrasound has been in obstetrics, where it is now employed to monitor almost half of all pregnancies and deliveries. "In the first three months we can use ultrasound to determine if indeed the woman is pregnant," says Dr. Heidi Weissmann, a radiologist and ultrasound specialist at Montefiore Hospital and Medical Center. "Calculations and chemical tests are by no means always reliable." The probe can detect if the fetus is developing outside the womb, for example—a serious hazard to the mother's health.

Ultrasound has also made amniocentesis much safer. This procedure involves the insertion of a hollow needle into the amniotic cavity and the removal of some amniotic fluid. This contains cells sloughed off by the growing baby, cells that can be used to determine if it has certain genetic abnormalities. (In the case of a deformed or Mongoloid fetus, the mother might elect to have an abortion.) "A few years ago, before ultrasound, we used to have to stick the needle in without knowing exactly where," says Weissmann. "There was always the chance of jabbing it into some vital area. Now you can see where the head, heart, umbilical cord are."

The woman in her early 60's is rushed to Yale-New Haven Hospital, showing all the symptoms of a massive stroke. Her eyes are glazed, her speech slurred; she is unable to lift her right hand. On an impulse, the emergency-room doctor calls the hospital's radiology department. The woman is quickly wheeled to a well-lighted room dominated by a large, arching apparatus. She is placed on a special couch or "gantry" and slowly moved by conveyor belt into what looks like the hatch of a space capsule. A thin beam of X-rays makes a lateral sweep of her head, collecting more than 10,000

103

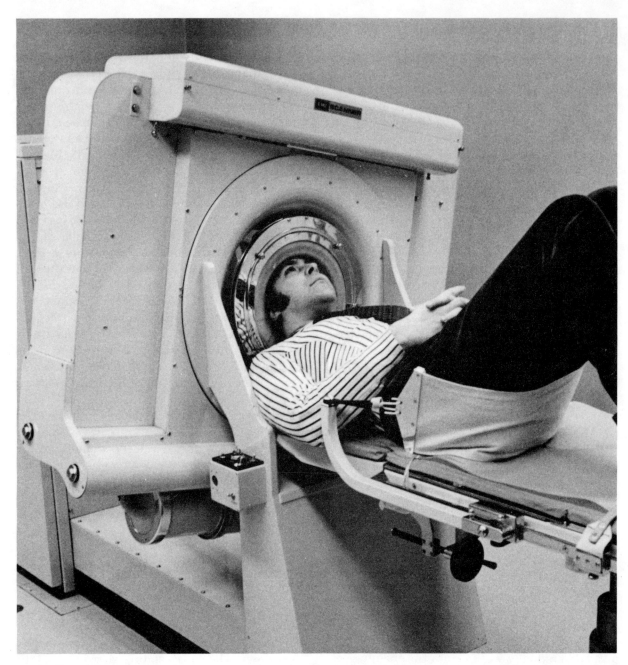

A CAT scanner can obtain a cross-section of a patient's body, thus improving diagnostic accuracy.

readings; it then rotates 10 degrees for another sweep. As the angle changes, a completely new set of data is collected and stored.

Across the way, in a darkened control room, a radiologist peers at the screen of a computer console, which provides a detailed outline of the woman's brain. The results of the scan indicate a dark gray circle on one of her pulsing cerebral lobes; the woman has not had a stroke, she has a brain tumor.

In a matter of hours the woman has surgery for what turns out to be a benign tumor. In a few weeks she is released from the hospital.

The Computerized Axial Tomography (CAT)

scanner is an imaging device closely allied to ultrasound. In fact, at some places the two have been combined in a single treatment unit. New York Hospital, for example, created the Department of Body Imaging for the machines. But unlike ultrasound, the CAT scanner uses a battery of X-rays to take a cross-sectional picture—a tomogram—of the patient's body. Then computers put the millions of bits of information together in a clear picture on a computer screen. "I think most physicians would agree that it's one of the most revolutionary advances in almost 70 years," says Dr. Whalen.

In many cases, the CAT scanner has already replaced other forms of diagnosis. Instead of having to inject air into the brain—a sometimes excruciating procedure called pneumoencephalography—doctors can now obtain an even clearer view of a suspected brain tumor with a CAT scanner. "Another example is cancer of the pancreas," says Dr. Whalen. "This is extremely difficult to diagnose without surgery. In the olden days—that is, five years ago—you might have had to put a catheter into the arteries of the pancreas and inject it with contrast agent. Now the patient can come in to one of our three scanners, spend possibly half an hour, and the only discomfort involved is having to hold his breath for a few seconds. Sometimes we've found inoperable cancer, but even then we've saved the patient needless additional suffering and expense."

But diagnosis is only one area in which the new medical technology has had a striking impact. Important gains have also been made in treatment.

For 32-year-old fireman James Spink, a pleasant afternoon has become a nightmare. While doing some carpentry work at home, his electric saw slipped from his grasp, slashing his left hand and severing his thumb. He is rushed to Montefiore Hospital in the Bronx, where his bleeding is stopped, but his thumb cannot be saved. Since Spink is left-handed, the loss of his thumb could mean the end of his 11-year career as a firefighter.

But plastic surgeons at Montefiore have a different idea. With Spink's eager permission, they use microsurgery—surgery conducted with the aid of high-powered microscopes—to remove the fireman's big toe, along with its attached blood

vessels, nerves and tendons, and transfer it to his hand to replace the missing thumb. With sutures almost invisible to the naked eye, blood vessels must be sewn together, nerves reattached so that the toe-become-thumb will have enough sensation to function.

Fourteen months later, James Spink returns to his job as hook-and-ladder man on Engine 46 with Ladder Company 27 in the Bronx, having passed the Fire Department's rigorous physical examinations. The remaining stump of his big toe gives him enough stability to walk, and his new thumb, while it looks a little shorter and stubbier than the original, works almost as well. "I didn't think I'd ever be able to work as a fireman again," says Spink. "Going back to work was the happiest moment of my life."

"Microsurgery is probably the most important thing to come along in surgery in decades," says Dr. Laurence LeWinn, assistant professor of surgery at New York Hospital-Cornell Medical Center. "It has opened up new vistas on just about everything."

The basic tools for this advance are microscopes capable of magnifying nerves and blood vessels up to 40 times. Usually operated by zoom pedals to make clumsy manipulation unnecessary, they are often connected to television screens so that other members of the operating team can see what the surgeon is doing. Almost as important are the instruments—from scissors with tiny blades to miniature forceps. Surgical thread is so thin that it is practically invisible to the naked eye. Used together, these have allowed specially trained surgeons to accomplish feats impossible a few years ago.

Within the past year, microsurgical cases have regularly made headlines. One that attracted particular interest was that of Renee Katz, a 17-year-old student and flutist at New York's High School of Music and Art. Last May, she was pushed by a stranger into the path of a subway train. She was taken to Bellevue Hospital with her severed hand, and surgeons there managed to reattach it in a long and grueling operation. When Renee Katz left the hospital in July, 1979, Bellevue doctors were hopeful that she might even be able to play the flute again.

The high success rate for reattachment is due in part to better understanding of the compli-

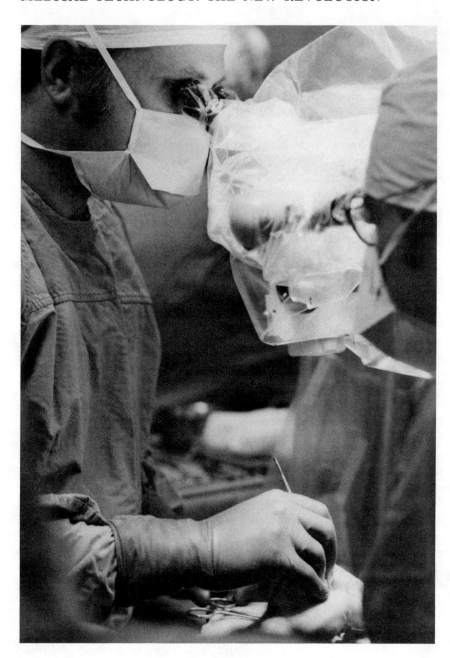

Dr. Berish Strauch, chief of the Plastic Reconstructive Surgery Service at Montefiore Hospital, looks through the microscope as he performs microsurgery on a patient's hand.

cated structure of nerves and how one can be grafted onto another that is partially damaged.

Microsurgery is also being used for such things as replacing a cancerous esophagus with a stretch of the patient's intestine, removal of tiny pituitary tumors that can turn children into ungainly giants, and restoring mobility to a partially paralyzed face by transferring nerves. But perhaps the most exciting use of microsurgery is in the prevention of strokes.

When the brain is cut off from the flow of blood by an obstruction in an artery, the result may be irreversible damage. "Stroke is by far the commonest serious disease of the nervous system and one of the most important health problems in the United States," says Dr. Jack M. Fein, associate professor of neurosurgery at the Albert Einstein College of Medicine. There are half a million new stroke victims every year; a third die within a month, while half of the rest become permanent invalids. "Contrary to what many people think, this is by no means entirely a geriatric problem," says Dr. Fein. "Several of our patients have been in their 30's, and probably the greatest number are in their 50's and early 60's. This terrible affliction cuts down people in the prime of life."

But before a major crippling stroke, a victim usually experiences brief "warning strokes" that can last anywhere from several minutes to a whole day. "The symptoms can range from numbness in one side of the body to difficulty in speaking or writing or even temporary blindness, depending on which part of the brain is affected," says Dr. Russel H. Patterson Jr., professor of surgery-neurosurgery at New York Hospital-Cornell Medical Center.

Not long ago, a 40-year-old executive was talking to a client when suddenly he began to use the wrong words (since blood was unable to reach the speech center of his brain). Within two minutes, his right side was paralyzed. Within an hour, however, the symptoms had passed. The next day, his doctor referred him to the Albert Einstein College of Medicine, where he was found to be an excellent candidate for an exciting new treatment made possible by microsurgery: a stroke-prevention operation.

First, a CAT scanner may determine the extent of permanent tissue damage; no operation can help those whose brains have already been massively, permanently affected. If the obstruction is in the brain, the surgeon drills a hole about the size of a silver dollar through the skull and, under the high magnification of the microscope, hooks one nearby artery to another, thus bypassing the obstruction.

Although only a few years old, the operation has already proved its effectiveness. The executive, who had two more warning strokes in quick succession while awaiting stroke-prevention surgery, has had no recurrence in the three years since. Out of one group of 400 high-risk patients of all ages studied for almost three years, only four of those who had the operation suffered strokes, in marked contrast to a control group, where almost half did. "I think this is going to have tremendous impact," says Dr. Fein. "Up until now, we had really no way of preventing this truly terrible affliction. Almost every family in this country has at least in some

way been affected by the day-to-day agony of a relative who has experienced a stroke—what one neurologist in Boston calls 'super death.' Now, at least with a large number of people, we can try to do something about it. In the future, this kind of surgery should greatly reduce the personal, social and economic toll of this dreaded disease."

Another experimental but promising area of the new medical technology is the use of complicated electronics to restore vision to the blind and hearing to the deaf.

Six years ago, a team of scientists at the University of Utah, working with other scientists at the University of Western Ontario, electronically stimulated the brains of blind volunteers in the cerebral area known as the visual cortex so that the volunteers "saw" letters of the alphabet.

An even more dramatic experiment took place five years ago. A 33-year-old man had been blinded 10 years earlier in a gunshot accident. When a television camera was connected to electrodes implanted on his brain, he was able to detect white horizontal and vertical lines on a dark background. "The experimental system functioned as a complete, though crude, artificial eye," says Dr. William H. Dobelle, director of the Utah project and currently both a member of the faculty at the University of Utah and head of the Division of Artificial Organs, Department of Surgery, at Columbia Presbyterian Medical Center in New York. In a later experiment, six electrodes on the man's brain were stimulated to form an image of letters of the Braille alphabet. With this stimulation, he was able to "read" phrases and short sentences, such as, "When the crow went into . . ." and "He had a cat and ball." "Without practice, the man—who was an extremely poor Braille reader—was able to read Braille at 30 characters per minute, or five times faster than he could using his finger tips," says Dr. Dobelle. In December, 1978, in New York, two new volunteers received implants, and so far the electrodes are functioning and they too seem to be able to visualize Braille letters.

But Dr. Dobelle and his collaborators are hoping that their system will do more than help the blind to read. Essentially, our eyes are like incredibly intricate cameras that catch light,

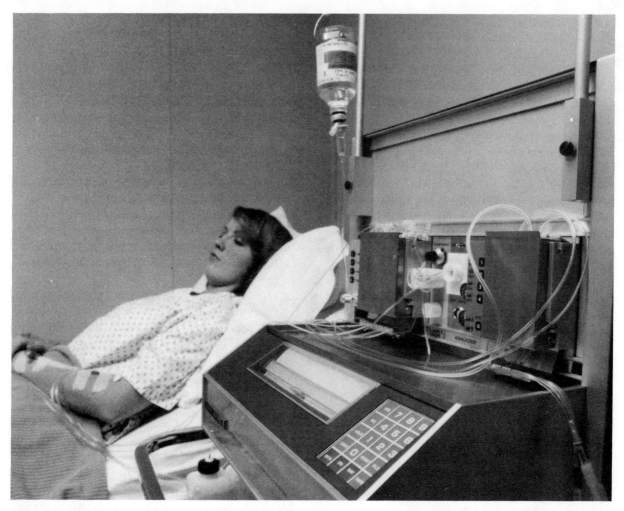

Patients that have used the "artificial pancreas" have been selected carefully, as the device, although promising, is still considered experimental.

transform it into electrical impulses, and then relay it to the visual cortex in the brain, where it is translated into the complex phenomenon called vision. "As far as we know now, there seems to be no reason why this can't be artificially duplicated," says Dr. Dobelle. He and his colleagues have already made plans for a special miniature television camera to be implanted in the eye of a volunteer and connected with wires to several hundred tiny electrodes on the brain. A CAT scanner will first be used to create an image of the volunteer's visual cortex, since the shape of each person's brain differs markedly; then the individually designed array of electrodes will be implanted, and the camera in the eye will transmit information about light pat-

terns to the brain—the artificial equivalent of vision. "From computer simulation studies we've done, we know that with anywhere from 250 to 500 electrodes you can start getting useful results," says Dr. Dobelle. Although he does not expect to restore normal vision completely, he nevertheless hopes that the blind will be able to read and, most important of all, to recognize people and things around them. "I hope we'll be able to give them the same sort of murky, black-and-white vision that you can see in the scratchy television pictures that early spacecraft sent back to earth," he says.

A related area in which Dr. Dobelle and his colleagues at Columbia and Utah are working intensively is artificial hearing. A quarter of a million Americans are totally deaf; one way to restore their hearing is to stimulate auditory nerve fibers electrically. Dr. Dobelle and his group have already implanted electrodes in the inner ears of a few volunteers—with encouraging results. One 47-year-old social worker, totally deaf for many years, was able to recognize such melodies as "Mary Had a Little Lamb," "Yankee Doodle" and "Twinkle, Twinkle, Little Star." "I believe society can be assured of the ultimate success of this research for the deaf, although of course many unforeseen obstacles doubtless remain," says Dr. Dobelle. "Naturally what they will hear is going to be pretty tinny. Walter Cronkite may sound like Donald Duck to these people, but the important thing is that they'll be able to recognize sounds and, above all, speech."

Dr. Dobelle is the first to admit that problems remain to be faced before that goal is realized. "The last thing we want is to have hordes of people lined up outside our hospital, hoping for help that we can't yet give them," he says. Vision and hearing are enormously complicated areas; nevertheless, on the basis of work already done, Dr. Dobelle is optimistic about the future. "I do really think that this is going to happen, that this technology is going to work," he says.

Other advances in medical technology also seem to hold promise for the future.

The "artificial pancreas," developed recently by Miles Laboratories, duplicates one of the main functions of the pancreas: it regulates changes in levels of blood glucose by injecting tiny amounts of insulin into the bloodstream. Still highly experimental, it is currently being tested at a few medical centers and has not yet received final F.D.A. approval.

Looking rather like a large stove on wheels, the machine is able both to monitor the glucose level in a diabetic patient and then, if it senses too much of a deviation, dole out tiny amounts of insulin for up to four days. The device has already aided several carefully selected diabetic women, who were helped through labor while attached to the machine. Doctors look forward to the day when smaller and more portable versions of the machine may help the country's hundreds of thousands of diabetics lead more normal lives.

A technique called nuclear magnetic resonance (N.M.R.) is also promising. Basically, the procedure involves putting groups of living cells in a strong magnetic field and then bombarding them with radio waves. A computer analyzes the amount of energy absorbed by different molecules within the cell to provide information about various events occurring within it. "Nuclear magnetic resonance allows us to see minute changes taking place within cells almost as they happen," says one researcher at the National Institutes of Health. "We can see all sorts of things that X-rays won't show—tracking several chemical reactions at the same time, for example." The technique is still too new and experimental for scientists to be willing to predict many of its potential uses. But several are hopeful about the new information it will give about the differences between normal and diseased cells—how a healthy cell turns into a dangerous, malignant one, for instance, as well as what kinds of treatment work best in either halting or reversing the process. "There's a lot of excitement," admits one scientist. "The living cell is where the action is, and N.M.R. offers one of the best ways of finding out exactly what's going on."

And yet, despite its promise, the new medical technology has come under increasingly sharp criticism. "Medical technologies are neither perfect nor risk-free," says Dr. Ivan L. Bennett Jr., provost/dean of the School of Medicine at New York University, who blames "the Marcus Welby syndrome" for the assumption that doctors—and the machines they use—can cure every case "in 30 or 60 minutes, less time out for commercials." The history of modern medicine is crowded with techniques that were loudly praised and then quietly discarded, from using X-ray machines in the 1940's to irradiate the thymus gland as a disease-prevention measure (but which, in fact, has caused increased risk of thyroid cancer) to the vogue for gastric freezing as a cure for ulcers in the 1960's, long since dismissed as either ineffective or downright harmful.

One much-discussed example of potential abuse is ultrasound. Although few deny the great benefits it can bring, several in the medical community consider it almost alarmingly over-used, particularly for fetal monitoring. All too often, they charge, technicians have mis-read images and imagined complications where none in fact existed; the result has been need-less, and potentially harmful, Caesarian sec-tions. "Although everyone agrees it's a great device, I think there's generally a greater sense of caution now," admits one New York radiolo-gist. "We do recognize that this technological advance can be misused, and that if you use a lot of ultrasound, you can cause abnormalities of fetal development."

More subtle risks may be involved in the over-use of medical technology, too. The pa-tient who spends more than a few days in the hospital may soon have the discouraging feeling that he is being treated by an array of ma-chines. This is particularly true of the patient in an intensive-care unit, where he is attached, day and night, to beeping, buzzing newly devel-oped electronic monitors. "One of the things that happens to many of these people is that they develop what psychiatrists call an 'I.C.U. psychosis,'" says Dr. Andrew A. Sorensen, asso-ciate professor of preventive medicine and com-munity health at the University of Rochester Medical School. "They just stop reacting and retreat into their own world. In these cases, there are unquestionably harmful effects associ-ated with medical technology."

Other critics predict these effects will become even more common. Despite their grudging re-spect for the healing potential of the new tech-nology, their vision of the future is not a splendid one, where the ailing can be promptly and painlessly cured by a host of beneficent machines. Instead, they foresee a time when doctors will be largely transformed into techni-cians, operating apparatuses the layman cannot hope to fathom. The gulf of suspicion between patients and their healers, already distressingly large, will grow even wider. The general practi-tioner, made newly important within the past 10 years by medical schools anxious to empha-size medicine's "human face," will be unable to compete with the sophisticated diagnostic ma-chines that only large hospitals can afford, and may well disappear. In this gloomy view of the future, the patient arriving at a hospital will not have a single doctor at all, but will simply be led, like a reluctant child, from one machine to the next, each manned by a detached and in-different staff. "I'm not even sure that—for many patients—this will mean better medicine," says one critic. "We're finding out more and more how important the psychological element is in healing. If the patient feels anxious, resent-ful, caught in an alien and hostile environment, for many the end result of that stress may be to negate whatever superior medical advantages the machines offer."

Moreover, some see the possibility of greater geographic imbalance in the availability of treatment than exist now. "There are already massive inequities in our national health-care system," says Dr. Andrew Sorensen. "Places like New York City, Chicago, San Francisco are very well served in some areas, but there are still many sections of the country, particularly rural ones, where the level of medical care is shockingly low." Since only the largest urban medical centers will be able to afford the expen-sive new technology, in the future the disparity between the privileged metropolis and medi-cally neglected small town is likely to grow rather than to diminish.

The overall price tag of the new technology has already stirred angry debate. "Health tech-nologies contribute enormously to the inflation-ary spiral," Senator Edward M. Kennedy, chairman of the Sub-committee on Health and Scientific Research, has recently said. "As much as 40 percent of the annual increase in the cost of a hospital day can be attributed to their use." Total medical costs have soared to $182 billion (from less than a quarter of that 10 years ago), while the cost to the average person of a one-day stay in the hospital has risen from $35 in 1963 to $195 today. The medical-technology industry, responsible for manufacturing the new devices, is now valued at over $7 billion in this country.

One of the favorite targets of critics has been the CAT scanner, which—at $750,000 per unit—is one of the most expensive medical machines ever manufactured. Some see hospitals' eager-ness for the device—what is called CAT fever—as a perfect illustration of what Dr. Ivan Ben-nett has dubbed "the technological impera-tive": the compulsive urge among hospitals to acquire the latest gadgetry in order to impress patients and the medical community. "If one hospital has it, another wants it," says one ex-

Dr. Ivan L. Bennett Jr.

pert. "But is it the patient who really benefits?"

President Carter himself recently criticized hospitals' attitudes and confessed that he had once shared them. Mr. Carter said he now realizes that when he was a member of the Sumter County (Ga.) Hospital Authority (along with his uncle, mother and brother), he had "ripped people off." "We were naturally inclined to buy a new machine whenever it became available," he admitted, "and then to require that every patient who came into the hospital submit a blood sample or some other aspect of their body to the machine for analysis, whether they needed it or not, in order to rapidly defray the cost of purchase of the machine."

The response of many doctors to the President's increasingly strident criticism of expensive medical machines has been swift—and angry. "The new devices have saved lives and relieved suffering in countless cases," says one. "How does the Government intend to reckon that up in dollars and cents?" Even before the CAT scanner became generally available five years ago, some point out, hospital costs were steadily rising. "Technology is being made the whipping boy by politicians looking for votes," insists one physician at a large New York medical center. "But waste has always been a problem in hospitals. How about all the millions of dollars spent on unnecessary linen and paper slippers for patients, all the piddling expenses that keep adding up?"

But in a time of soaring inflation and general retrenchment, the cost of the new technology seems to affront more than just politicians. The CAT scanner, admittedly, is super-expensive, but few of the other devices are cheap. An ultrasound unit, for example, costs up to $100,000. The usual defense offered by hospital officials, that older procedures—since they required more personnel—often cost more, is usually ignored or derided: The mood in Washington and elsewhere today is stern and unforgiving. The more than 200 health-systems agencies scattered through the country, responsible for approving large-scale hospital expenditures, have already begun to clamp the lid down. Only about 200 hospitals a year now have their requests for CAT scanners approved—a small fraction of those who apply. "One result of this in the corporate world is that some companies have begun to edge away from expensive technical research in the health area," says one executive with a large medical-equipment firm. Other companies have squelched plans to research improved versions of the CAT scanner. "Why should we invest $5 million in researching it if the Government won't let us sell it to customers?" says one official.

But few believe that a Government policy of strict across-the-board cost containment can really work without affecting health care. "The current system is ridiculous, but most plans around to change it aren't much better," says Dr. Murray Eden, chief of the Biomedical Engineering and Instrumentation Branch of the National Institutes of Health. "There's a great need for new direction and a settling of priorities. From a purely technological point of view, the prospects for the future are glittering, but

111

the drive to contain health-care costs will obviously have an effect. As consumers, most of us want, demand, better health care, but we are offended when we get the bill. Somewhere there has to be some clearer thinking about where we're going to spend our money."

In just such an attempt to introduce clear thinking into the technology debate, Congress last year created the National Center for Health-Care Technology, a part of the Department of Health, Education and Welfare. "We intend to assess the value and cost of various aspects of the new medical technology and tell the public, practicing physicians, medical centers and big third-party payers like Blue Cross-Blue Shield what we find," says Dr. Seymour Perry, the center's acting head. "We aim to act as a catalyst, primarily through consensus conferences held every few months or so about different devices and procedures. Our findings won't have the force of law, but they will have the prestige of prominent members of the medical community behind them. That will count for a lot more than if some bureaucrat in Washington has the final say."

Whether the center can truly help to settle the debate remains to be seen, but its establishment has been generally—if hardly lavishly—welcomed in the medical community. "Most of all we hope to influence attitudes," says Dr. Perry. "Americans have long had a love affair with technology. As a people, we are finally going to have to take a good hard look at our limited resources and see which of the new devices around should be allowed to survive and spread. Our aim should be to make sure that medical technology is our servant and never becomes our master."

Hope for Burn Victims

by Laurence Cherry

Burns are probably the most agonizing, as well as the most damaging, of all injuries. Not only do they scorch the body, they sear the mind as well. Years of psychotherapy are often required to ease the memory of the torment severely burned people suffer. Little wonder that many of the major religions picture the damned as burning throughout eternity.

Unfortunately, burns are not uncommon. Two and a half million Americans were burned in 1977 (a third of them children), almost a hundred thousand of them seriously enough to require hospitalization. Burns now rank as the main cause of death for those under 40, and the third leading cause of death for all age groups. Moreover, some experts believe the number of burn injuries is rising: The use of new synthetic (and less flame-resistant) building materials has increased the number of destructive fires; the growing popularity of electrical appliances of all kinds has resulted in more electrical burns, and the development of new caustic chemicals over the past several decades has meant more people burned both in factories and at home. "Although most people don't realize it, this is actu-

ally an epidemic," says Dr. Arnold Luterman, an attending burn specialist at the burn center at New York Hospital-Cornell Medical Center. "It can happen to me, to you, to anyone, at any time. And yet although the Government has spent billions on cancer research, on heart disease, until recently burn research was almost ignored."

But that lack of interest appears to be changing. Within the past few years, an entirely new medical specialty called "burn medicine" has come into being, with its own professional organization, the American Burn Association. This broad new discipline includes specially trained burn doctors, burn nurses, occupational therapists, physiotherapists, psychiatrists and social workers.

As a result, important progress in treating one of mankind's worst and most widespread afflictions has already been made. "It's no longer axiomatic, as it was only a few years ago," says Dr. Luterman, "that a badly burned patient has to die or become a cripple for life. Thanks to some very hard work and several extremely important breakthroughs, the picture's finally starting to alter."

The skin is the body's largest and one of its most complex organs. Spread out flat it would cover approximately 18 square feet, every inch of which includes about a yard of blood vessels, four yards of nerves, a hundred sweat glands and more than three million cells, constantly dying and being replaced. We need this elaborate natural spacesuit to navigate the many perils of life on planet Earth, for without it not only would we be prey to deadly bacteria, but we would quickly perish from the loss of body heat.

A burn is a breach in this vital natural barrier. A first-degree burn (such as a bad sunburn) reddens the skin; although painful, it poses no threat to life. A second-degree burn, far more painful and far more serious, destroys the top layers of the skin and can lead to permanent scarring. If not treated properly, a second-degree burn can turn into a third-degree one, most dangerous of all, in which all the layers of skin are destroyed and the skin cells can no longer replace themselves. Skin burned to the third degree is dead and useless tissue, a perfect breeding ground for virulent bacteria and an immediate danger to life. The American Burn Association defines a severely burned patient as anyone with second- and third-degree burns over 20 percent of the body, or even less among children, whose skin is very soft and tender, and the elderly, whose top layers of skin are worn off when the proteins that bind skin tissue together loosen in old age.

For centuries, the standard treatment for burns was simply to smear them with anything from grease to spider webs. "Ever since man first started getting burned, he concentrated on treating the external wound," says Dr. Irving Feller, president of the National Institute of Burn Medicine, a support and study foundation in Ann Arbor, Mich. "Very little was done to find out what was happening inside the patient's body." But, in fact, a serious burn is a major crisis for almost every organ in the body. The metabolic rate soars; the body's biochemical defenders rush to protect it against the inevitable invasion of harmful bacteria; vital fluids pour into the area around the burn, causing general dehydration elsewhere. In order to avert catastrophe, medical intervention must be

Dr. P. W. Curreri is a world authority on the treatment of burns and is one of the two doctors responsible for the establishment of the New York Hospital Burn Center.

sophisticated—and immediate.

Until 1960, the only place truly equipped to handle this kind of medical emergency was Brooke Army Medical Center in San Antonio, where many of today's leading burn doctors were trained. Burn victims elsewhere were usually treated by staff unfamiliar with serious burns—often with tragic results. Today there are more than a hundred burn units in hospitals around the country where victims can receive the intense attention they need. There are also 13 burn centers, more elaborate facilities with sophisticated equipment and a large team of burn specialists. New York Hospital's Burn Center, one of the largest burn treatment centers in the country for adults, was finally opened in December 1976, after years of campaigning by community leaders. Dr. G. T. Shires, chairman of the Department of Surgery at Cornell Medical Center and surgeon in chief of New York Hospital, was the prime mover in establishing the center. He and Dr. P.W. Curreri, director of New York Hospital's Burn

Center, are world authorities on the treatment of burns and the trauma, or shock, that accompanies them. In 1977, the center treated more than 200 major burn cases. Patients included not only residents of New York City—which has the largest number of fires and burn casualties in the country—but also victims from as far away as Norway and Ecuador. "For a truly serious burn case, I don't think there's any substitute for a burn center," says Dr. Luterman, who trained with a Brooke surgeon. "We have the highly trained staff and, as important, we have the equipment. We see too many referred patients who have wounds that weren't serious to begin with but became so because they didn't receive proper treatment." The New York Hospital Burn Center will eventually be expanded to almost double its present size, from 24 beds to 40. But the price of running a burn center is staggering: It costs $660 a day to treat a burn victim (as compared with $250 for other kinds of patients), and New York Hospital must raise

Dr. Arnold Luterman of the New York Hospital has stated, "It's no longer axiomatic ... that a badly burned patient has to die or become a cripple for life."

$4 million before it can enlarge its facilities.

A burn victim brought to a burn center after an accident is usually rushed to a tanking room, a large chamber filled with specially constructed troughlike tubs. There, his burns are gently bathed and also carefully assessed. "You can't tell at once how bad things are going to be," says one expert at the New York Hospital Burn Center. "There's a tremendous amount of swelling several hours after a burn. We recently admitted a man here who looked only slightly red when he first arrived, but 10 hours later his face had ballooned, and his tongue bulged out so much he couldn't talk and could hardly breathe." Sometimes large incisions have to be made to reduce pressure caused by the swelling. Any loose skin is also removed while the patient is in the tank, sometimes a painful process despite injections of morphine. "The first night I was there it was unbelievable," says Kevin, a 17-year-old Boston boy who climbed an electrified highway tower on a dare and was burned over nearly half his body. "I never thought pain could be so painful." But in fact, although the patient can hardly be expected to appreciate it, the pain is an encouraging sign, since it demonstrates nerves are still alive; there is no pain from a more dangerous third-degree burn, since all skin tissue, including pain receptors, has been destroyed.

Smoke inhalation is an immediate problem. The smoke from burning pinewood and acrylics can particularly damage the lungs, but smoke of all kinds can affect the tissues of the larynx and vocal cords, making them swell so enormously that the burn victim suffocates. If there are obvious signs of damage, the burn specialist inserts a tube down the throat to make breathing easier; otherwise the patient is checked constantly and a special fiber-optic bronchtoscope is used to inspect the larynx and air passages for signs of trouble.

Burn victims are often so dehydrated they quickly go into shock. "They need a tremendous amount of fluid, and they need it fast," says Dr. Luterman. During the first 24 hours, a salt solution called lactated Ringer's solution is fed them in large amounts intravenously. Meanwhile, masked, gowned and disinfected nurses coat the burns with such recently developed topical agents as Sulfamylon and Silvadene

Cream to destroy pathological bacteria. "These dressings are among the biggest breakthroughs we've had," says one expert. "Before, the severely burned patient just couldn't fight off the germs. That isn't true today." The burn victim is constantly monitored by a nurse in a sterilized room, while a thermal shield above his bed automatically prevents body heat from escaping and, if necessary, supplies warmth through heated coils.

One of the most important, and painful, parts of treatment soon follows. Second-degree burns are often only cleaned and dressed, and heal in about three weeks as new skin grows back. But many burn victims are not so lucky; their wounds are largely third-degree, made up of charred and useless flesh. An elementary principle of medicine is to get rid of dead skin, and to accomplish that, burn surgeons employ a delicately honed pneumatic scalpel, with a blade no more than one twenty-thousandth of an inch thick. The blood loss is great, so that only a small percentage of a large third-degree burn can be removed at any one time. "The surgeon really has to break the blood bank any time he does this sort of thing," says Dr. Luterman; 17-year-old Kevin, for example, required several dozen transfusions when his large burns were cut away at a Boston hospital. At New York Hospital's Burn Center and other places, burn specialists are experimenting with different types of miniature lasers; although more cumbersome and far more expensive than the pneumatic scalpels, their narrow beam of intense heat cuts away dead tissue with a minimum of blood loss.

After removing the burned skin, the exposed layers of muscle and fat must next be immediately covered. If only a small part of the body has been burned, skin grafts can be taken from untouched areas. Skin from the thigh, for example, can cover a burned shoulder. Even a small amount of skin can be greatly enlarged by putting it through a device called the Tanner mesher, which cuts the skin so that it can be expanded. But often burns are too extensive, and the patient is not able to wait for his second-degree burns to heal so that the new skin can be used for grafting areas completely charred. A substitute must somehow be quickly found.

For the past few years, the lowly pig, one of the few hairless mammals, has been a convenient source of temporary skin grafts. But although pig skin resembles human skin more than that of most mammals, it is still very different, and therefore quickly rejected by the burned victim's immune system. Human skin is far preferable, and the more closely it matches the patient's own tissue type, the more slowly the body will reject it—giving a burn victim's less injured flesh more time to heal. Skin grafts from unburned relatives have sometimes been used, but without good results. "A mother's or father's skin is often less like a child's than that of a complete stranger," says one expert. "So unless you get a graft from your identical twin, who's genetically the same as you, you aren't much better off."

The best solution at the moment is skin taken from a cadaver. A paper-thin layer of skin about four inches wide is removed from a donor's trunk and legs within 24 hours after death, chemically treated, and then slowly frozen to minus 180 degrees so that it can be stored in a "skin bank" for almost a year. The New York Hospital Burn Center opened the country's eighth skin bank in March, 1978. "At last we have a dependable source for our patients," says Dr. Luterman, who can recall frantic searches in the past for persons who had just died and could be used.

But a badly burned patient may need skin shavings from as many as three donors, so the skin bank needs at least 300 cadavers a year to aid all of its major burn cases. Meanwhile other researchers are at work developing alternatives. At the Shriners Burn Institute in Boston, a group headed by chief surgeon Dr. John F. Burke has been investigating possibilities for "synthetic skin." Although so far it's impossible to completely simulate living tissue, some of its functions can already be duplicated. Some burns, at least, can be sprayed with hydron, the material used in contact lenses. "It lets water through," says an expert, "and keeps out bacteria, two of the most important functions of our skin." Other researchers in Japan are working with callagen, the basic protein of skin, spinning large sheets of it to be put on a wound and to act in some ways like natural skin. "Within five or 10 years we're going to have an artificial skin that will not be very different from the real thing," says one investigator. "And that's the day we'll all shout hallelujah."

But even after grafting is completed, other problems remain for the burn victim. "A few years ago, burn patients after two or three weeks suddenly died of pneumonia or some wasting illness," says Dr. Luterman. "What actually was going on was that they were dying of malnutrition." A burn injury produces a tremendous demand for calories to heal it, a need that must be quickly met. Burn patients were encouraged to gorge themselves on steaks, milkshakes, omelettes—with disappointing results.

"The person with a severe burn has a very altered metabolism and needs to consume thousands of calories a day," says Dr. Luterman. "There's just no way he can manage to eat all that." So burn doctors now pump a nutritious potion directly into a patient's stomach, 24 hours a day. Most burn patients still eat three meals, but the mixture supplies their body with all the calories they need (sometimes 3,000 to 4,000 calories a day in the case of burned children). "I'd say this was one of our most important breakthroughs," says Dr. Luterman.

And so, attached to a host of monitoring ma-

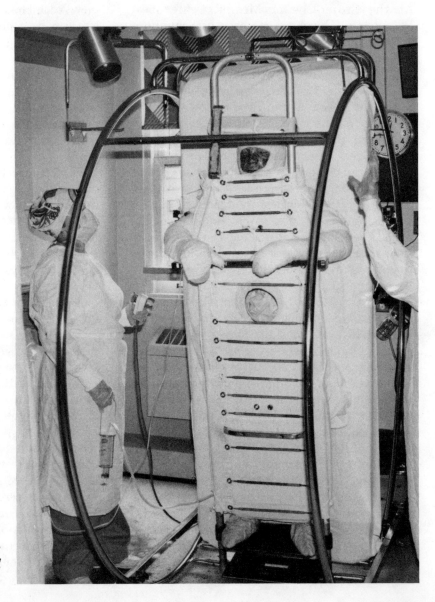

This circolectric bed is specially designed to turn patients, provide access to the wounds and prevent sustained pressure.

chines, the burn patient very gradually begins to recover. There are daily baths in the hydrotherapy tanks, where old dressings are removed and new ones put on. The rustle of sheets, even currents of air moving across exposed nerves, can lead to agonizing pain, and there is still more discomfort as the physiotherapists continually manipulate joints to prevent them from contracting (in the past, even after their wounds had healed, many burn victims were unable to move their arms, legs or fingers). Even improved technology—such as a cranelike machine that scoops the patient out of bed and onto a stretcher so gently he's hardly aware of being moved—obviously can't eliminate all pain. At the Crozer-Chester Medical Center near Philadelphia, burn experts have used hypnosis to try to check the patient's suffering; at other centers, biofeedback is sometimes used. But whether in pain or not, within two or three days the burn patient is usually strongly encouraged to get out of bed; within two or three weeks, to walk around the ward and to begin to take care of himself. But this kind of progress often leads to problems of another kind: When the burn patient somewhere catches sight of his reflection, it can be a devastating revelation. "Whatever psychological problems a patient had before he got burned are suddenly magnified," says one specialist. "For the first weeks, the patients are too sick to care and just happy to have survived. Then they realize what's happened to them."

Recently special pressure masks—including ones that cover the whole body—have been developed to exert constant force on wounds to eliminate much ugly scarring. "If treatment isn't handled right, the scarring afterward can look worse than the original burn," says one expert. But even so, the patient is often disfigured, at least until plastic surgery can be performed, usually months after the accident—and even then, without perfect results. Grafted skin contains no hair follicles, sweat glands or nerve endings, is less elastic and cosmetically less attractive. "Reconstructive surgery can work wonders, but not miracles," says a doctor at New York Hospital's Burn Center. "There's a girl on our ward right now who used to be a striking beauty. She was burned in an explosion and her appearance is very altered—she can't

close her eyelids entirely and there's going to be considerable scarring. Plastic surgery can eventually eliminate a lot of that, but let's face it: The girl is going to go back into a world that's very different from the one she left. People are going to stare at her, and some of them are going to be cruel. And, believe me, that young woman knows it—and she's terrified."

Most burn-center psychiatrists find themselves counseling members of their own team as well. Working with burn victims is probably one of the most demanding areas in medicine; the average length of service for a burn nurse is less than 10 months. "The turnover rate is *very* high," admits Janice Cuzzell, chief nurse at New York Hospital's Burn Center. "Not everyone can be a burn nurse. To some degree you have to disregard what you were taught in nursing school, to comfort and relieve pain, because in treating burn patients it's sometimes, unfortunately, necessary to inflict it. And it's also important that the burn nurse not be someone who's obsessively tidy, because a burn patient can't stay neat for very long." Some centers have set up special stress workshops for their burn nurses.

One highly controversial question in burn medicine is whether treatment of burns should always be attempted. No treatment at all means certain death, but in some particularly severe cases in which practically the entire body is charred, death is likely in a matter of days anyway.

At the burn center at Los Angeles Coty-University of Southern California Medical Center victims in this special category are allowed to make the decision about treatment themselves. Every year, several patients are admitted so badly burned that survival for more than a few days, no matter what drastic measures are attempted, seems unlikely. A member of the burn team then speaks to the patient, without family members present. "He tries to take the role of a compassionate friend who is willing to listen," says Dr. Bruce Zawacki, chief physician at the Los Angeles center. "Hands are often held, and the attempt is made to look deeply into the patient's eyes. After rapport has been established . . . we ask them whether or not they want full medical treatment."

Two sisters, for example, aged 68 and 70,

were involved in a car accident that burned more than 90 percent of their bodies. They were admitted to the Los Angeles Burn Center two hours later, and the burn team agreed that on the basis of national mortality statistics survival for women of their age and with their type of injury was "virtually unprecedented."

The women were interviewed separately. The younger sister immediately asked the doctor if she was likely to die. When he told her his true opinion, she replied matter-of-factly: "Well, I never dreamed that life would end like this, but since we all have to go sometime, I'd like to go quietly and comfortably." Her older sister, how- ever, denied that she was seriously injured. "I feel so good. Wouldn't I be hurting horribly if I were going to die?" she asked. The doctor explained to her that often patients feel no pain from third-degree burns, since all skin tissue has been destroyed. The woman at first refused to make any decision, but eventually refused full treatment. Her bed was placed next to her sister's so that they could see and touch each other easily. They discussed funeral arrangements and joked about the damage done to their hair. The hospital chaplain prayed with them; the younger sister died a few hours later, the older one the following day.

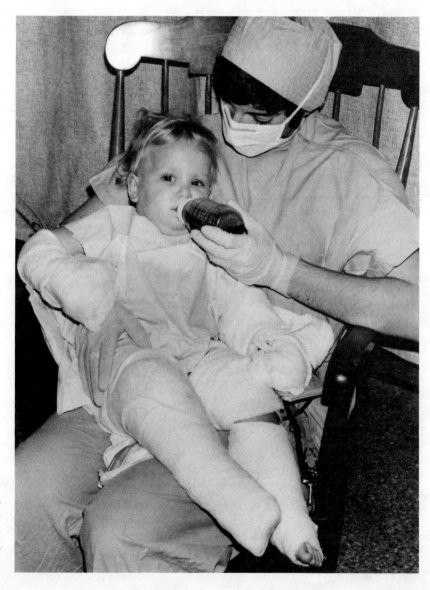

Emotional support, including a genuine interest and concern for the patient, is as essential to survival as treatment and medications.

National Burn Information Exchange
BURNED PATIENT SURVIVAL BY AGE GROUP
Percent Total Area Burned

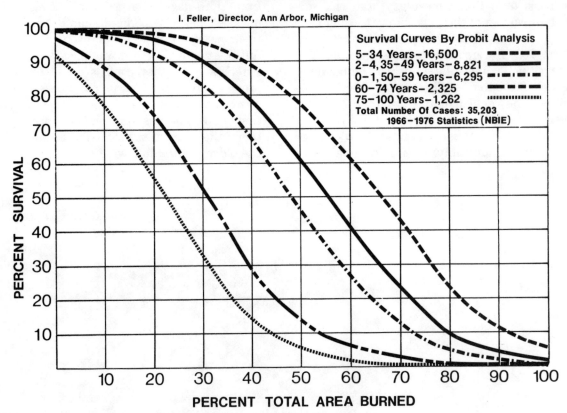

I. Feller, Director, Ann Arbor, Michigan

Survival Curves By Probit Analysis
5–34 Years – 16,500
2–4, 35–49 Years – 8,821
0–1, 50–59 Years – 6,295
60–74 Years – 2,325
75–100 Years – 1,262
Total Number Of Cases: 35,203
1966–1976 Statistics (NBIE)

Mortality analysis: Percent survival vs. age and total area burned. The chances for survival of a severe burn are affected by the patients age and the size of the total area burned as shown in this graph as well as past medical history, depth of burn, part of body burned, and concurrent injuries. This analysis was completed on 35,000 burn patients reported to The National Burn Information Exchange between 1966 and 1976. Through application of basic principles of medicine, continuous monitoring, and clinically-applicable research the odds for survival for the severely burned patient are improved everyday (The National Burn Information Exchange is a national data gathering registry located in Ann Arbor, Michigan. Through analysis of data such as this, we are able to recognize milestones in progress and plot our course toward better survival in the future).

This kind of choice is only offered to adult burn victims, since mortality statistics about burned children are considered too unreliable to use as guidelines. Last year, 24 adults were diagnosed on admission as having little or no chance of surviving: 21 of them chose not to undergo treatment.

But without wishing to be embroiled in public controversy, many burn doctors elsewhere are privately critical of the Los Angeles center's policy. "We don't give up on any burn patient, no matter what the statistics," says Dr. Luterman, of New York Hospital's burn center. "Who's to say that he or she might not be the first one to survive that kind of burn? In burn medicine, old truisms are disproved all the time." Moreover, many are skeptical that a newly admitted burn patient is really able to make a rational decision about treatment. "Death with dignity sounds great, but these people have just been in an accident and are in psychological shock," says one specialist. "Their decision would be based on how the burn doctor at their bedside phrased things. It just doesn't seem very palatable to me."

Hardly seriously considered a few years ago, the notion that burns can be prevented is becoming increasingly widespread. Not long ago, for example, the American Burn Association established a special Burn Prevention Committee. The committee coordinates many of its efforts with the National Fire Prevention and Control Administration, established by Congress in 1974, which has set the goal of reducing burn injuries by 50 percent within the next 10 to 15 years.

This massive, almost unprecedented campaign mostly relies on increasing public awareness about burns. Although obviously house fires, car accidents and chemical explosions can hardly be predicted, experts believe people can indeed safeguard themselves against their worst consequences. "Smoke detectors, for example, could reduce the loss of life from fires by over 40 percent," says an official of the administration. "We keep reminding people to install at least one in their homes. We also tell them they should plan and practice a home escape plan—once a fire has started, there are only seconds to get out." In its pamphlets, the administration recommends there be two exits to every room, and that a family test its escape plan before a real emergency.

In addition, the administration helps to coordinate more elaborate projects in special target cities. In 1974, for example, Boston was chosen as the site for Project Burn Prevention, an intensive public-education campaign. The city was selected partly because Massachusetts is one of the few states with a central burn registry (all burns covering more than 5 percent of the body must be reported, thus giving researchers detailed information about frequency and type of burns) and also because Boston has been a particularly burn-conscious city ever since the tragic fire of Nov. 28, 1942, when a local nightclub named the Coconut Grove suddenly erupted in flames. Terrified patrons stampeded the exits; the revolving door jammed, and almost 500 people died—one of the worst fires in American history.

For two years, the Project Burn Prevention team carried out expensive studies to determine how much Boston residents already knew about burns. "By and large, we found terrible ignorance, from children on up," says Elizabeth McLoughlin, project director. Few parents were aware, for example, that the skin of young children is particularly sensitive and that they can be scalded by bath water that adults find perfectly comfortable. Hardly any high school students knew that sticking a fork into a plugged-in toaster could cause an electrical burn, or that it's dangerous to touch an electrical fixture with wet hands and feet.

Throughout 1978, Boston residents have been bombarded with information about how to prevent burns and what first-aid measures to take if they occur. In a kind of vast municipal consciousness-raising, commercials were run on local TV stations; specialists appeared on Boston TV and radio shows; posters were put up in Boston subways and leaflets distributed; special burn-prevention classes were held in some schools, with evening meetings for adults. "We're still in the evaluation phase right now," says Miss McLoughlin. "We have our fingers crossed that it's made a real difference in the burn-injury figures. If it has—and we have good reason to hope so—the project will be extended nationwide."

One municipality that prefers not to wait is Oklahoma City. A Metropolitan Fire and Burn Prevention Council was set up there in 1977, a voluntary group including everyone from city merchants to doctors to firemen. "The response has been fantastic," says Phil Stout, the council's vice chairman. Special meetings have been held for city residents; the local newspaper not long ago ran a burn-prevention supplement; and a special burn-prevention school program has been begun.

As in Boston, those responsible for organizing the Oklahoma City program are still not sure whether or not their burn-education program has really worked in reducing the number of burn injuries. But like the Boston group, they continue their efforts because they are convinced, as a special task force of the Center for Disease Control put it in a recent report, that "burn injuries are uniquely severe—and entirely preventable."

Aging

by Harold M. Schmeck, Jr.

They were two men almost as different as life and death: one vigorous, erect, active in mind and body; the other stooped, shuffling and seemingly fading into extreme old age. Paradoxically, they had one thing in common. They were both 65 years old. This kind of disparity in the effects of increasing age on individuals has impressed, and often surprised, many scientists who are studying the complex biology of the aging process.

A group of 10-year-old children will not vary much from child to child, said Dr. Nathan Shock of the National Institute on Aging. There will be more variation among 20-year-olds. And with increasing age the variation also increases. "In an 80- or 90-year-old group the variance is just tremendous," said Dr. Shock, who, until three years ago, was head of an unusual Federal project called the Baltimore Longitudinal Study of Aging, that is tracing the aging process in several hundred men and women throughout their adult lives.

Scientific studies of aging have increased markedly in recent years for at least two reasons. First, the sophistication of modern techniques allows studies that were beyond

practical possibility a few years ago. Second, the average age of Americans is increasing, making the problems of aging more and more important to society.

Many of the aging trends that have been documented over the years in humans are discouraging. Muscle is replaced by fat. Physical strength ebbs. Nerve signals lose speed in transmission. Defenses against infection diminish. The size of the brain decreases, losing at least one tenth of its maximum weight. There is evidence that cells begin to lose their exquisite control over their own processes so that some substances present only in fetal life begin to be programmed again for production in aging cells where they have no business. Sometimes the aging body seems to forget how to recognize its own tissues so that internal battles take place; natural defenses turn against tissues of the body. Traces of metals are vital to human cells. With aging some cells begin to take up too much or too little metal or sometimes the wrong metals altogether.

Over the long haul such changes seem inexorable. Like more obvious effects such as graying hair and baldness, their underlying causes are

Average Decreases In Body Functions With Age

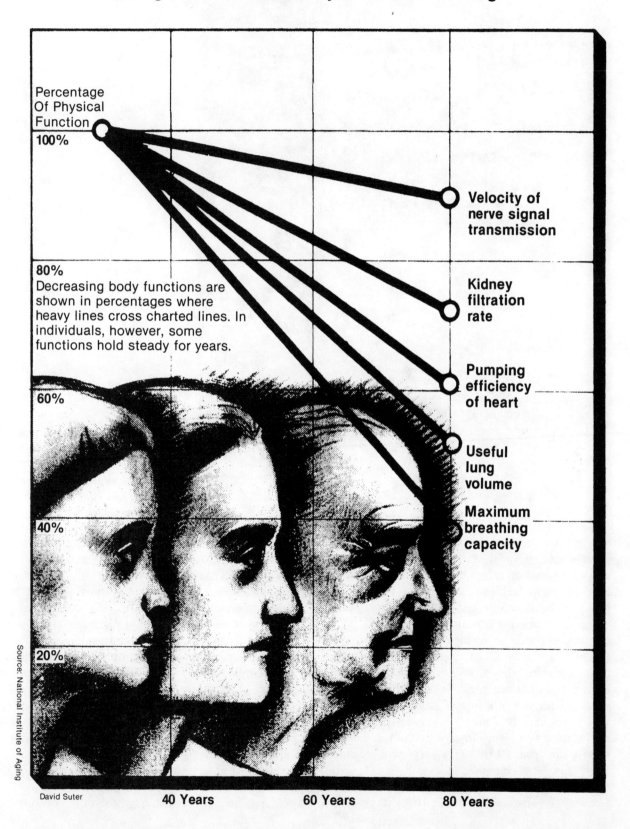

Percentage
Of Physical
Function
100%

80%
Decreasing body functions are
shown in percentages where
heavy lines cross charted lines. In
individuals, however, some
functions hold steady for years.

60%

40%

20%

Velocity of
nerve signal
transmission

Kidney
filtration
rate

Pumping
efficiency
of heart

Useful
lung
volume

Maximum
breathing
capacity

40 Years   60 Years   80 Years

David Suter

Source: National Institute of Aging

123

GERONTOLOGY
RESEARCH CENTER

NATIONAL INSTITUTES OF HEALTH

PUBLIC HEALTH SERVICE

DEPARTMENT OF HEALTH
EDUCATION AND WELFARE

Dr. Nathan W. Shock, who was head of the Baltimore Longitudinal Study of Aging, directed research at the unit for over 35 years.

still unknown. But the huge variation among individuals shows that the worst need not always be true and offers hope that ways may be found to help each individual make the most of the possibilities inherent in his or her genes. That is the operating philosophy of much of the current research on aging.

The Baltimore study began about 20 years ago, predating the current interest in research on aging, but it has provided an almost unique resource for many kinds of studies, behavioral and biological. It is now following a population of 650 men and 150 women, all volunteers, ranging in age from 20 to 103. Every two years for the younger members and every year for the older ones, the volunteers check in to the Baltimore City Hospital for about three days of in-

tensive physical and mental testing so that scientists can judge how each person is doing in the losing contest with time. The volunteers are not an average group by any means, but the study has compiled a wealth of valuable data and has already produced surprises.

It has long been assumed that, in physical and some behavioral terms, human life is a discouragingly steady downhill slope from about the age of 30 onward. Standard graphs based on studies of hundreds of persons of all ages show steady decline from the 30's in such things as hand-grip strength, kidney function, breathing capacity and heart output. Each declines at its own rate, but they all go in the same direction.

Accordingly, a group of 30-year-olds will outperform any comparable group of octogenari-

Dr. Richard C. Greulich, NIA Scientific Director, chats with Mrs. Grace Malakoff, one of the volunteer participants in the Baltimore Longitudinal Study of Aging, a long term study of individual age changes.

ans. For a group, there are indisputable decrements, or losses, in performance over the adult years. But recent findings of the longitudinal study have shown that individuals do not always behave like the hypothetical average person. Some persons simply do not decline in the simple straight-line fashion that the standard graphs show. For many years, some show no decline at all. The Baltimore study has documented this for two important measures of the ravages of time: kidney function and problem-solving ability. "There are some subjects 65 to 80 who are just not showing decrements within themselves," said Dr. Shock, "and that surprises me."

In fact, the study has found about a dozen people in whom the periodic tests show kidney function improving with age. Dr. Shock and his colleagues find it hard to believe this is really true, but it is abundantly clear that kidney function has at least been holding steady in these people, sometimes for many years.

On tests of problem-solving ability, too, some members of the study group seem to be at least holding their own against aging. These tend to be people for whom problem solving has been a way of life for years. Dr. Shock said the new behavioral evidence reinforces the truism that functions that are continually exercised are less likely to grow rusty even with age.

Many of the effects of aging—gray hair, loss in visual acuity, diminution of taste and smell sensitivity—have been obvious to humans ever since men and women began to live long enough to grow old, but the reasons for aging have never been obvious. There are at least a half dozen current theories of the biology of aging. There is no conclusive evidence to support any of them, but the theories give scientists provocative questions to ask through their research. In the late 1950's and early 1960's Drs. Leonard Hayflick and Paul Moorhead, then at the Wistar Institute in Philadelphia, discovered that normal human cells growing in tissue culture were not immortal, as some cancer cells appeared to be under like conditions, but would eventually degenerate and die after many generations of reproduction. This phenomenon has since been confirmed by many others. The circumstances vary somewhat with different kinds of cells, but generally it appears that such cells have a capacity to replicate themselves about 50 times and no more. Cells taken from older people replicate fewer times than those from the young. Perhaps these cells growing in laboratory flasks reflect a feature of a clock of aging at work. It is obvious today that this is not the whole story by any means, but the idea does suggest research possibilities.

For example, scientists of the National Institute of Aging have begun taking small skin samples from the men and women in the Baltimore longitudinal study and preserving them, frozen in tissue cultures. Ten or 20 years hence, said Dr. Richard C. Greulich, director of the institute's Gerontology Research Center in Baltimore, these cells can be revived from the deep freeze. Since they will have been in what amounts to suspended animation for the intervening decades they will come out of the freezer as youthful as when they were originally collected. Scientists will then be able to compare these young cells with the 20-years-older contemporary cells from the same person. It is like confronting a middle-aged person with him or herself in youth and may give new insights into the nature of aging. Since aging seems to affect many, perhaps all, of the tissues of the body, one theory holds that there may be some specific internal chemistry at work to produce such effects. What would happen, then, if the blood circulation of an old individual could be connected with one who was young?

Experiments to answer that question were proposed in a symposium volume, "The Biology of Aging," published in 1978 by Plenum Press for the American Institute of Biological Sciences. Dr. David E. Harrison of the Jackson Laboratory, Bar Harbor, Me., has since done the experiments he proposed in that volume. Using techniques of microsurgery, scientists at Jackson Laboratory made what amounted almost to Siamese twins of pairs of laboratory mice of the same inbred strain—one young, the other elderly by mouse standards, in each pair. It was possible that the young blood would give a spurt of youthfulness to the old member of the pair or that the old one would make the younger age more rapidly if there was some circulation factor in the aging process. In fact, said Dr. Harrison, neither effect took place and other scientists who have tried similar tests have had the same results. There was one demonstrable effect from Dr. Harrison's experiments. This was related to the animals' immune defense system, something that does at least partially circulate in the blood. The cross circulation did not help the older animal's immunological defenses, but it did produce defects in the young animal's system.

The scientist sees these results as a hint that not all systems and organs age from the same cause even in the same individual. Such results argue against the concept that some single key to the aging process exists and that scientists might someday find a way of turning it off.

Cells Survive Transplants

Related research suggests that some kinds of cells have a far greater potential for long life than others. This has been shown in experiments in which bone marrow cells have been transplanted from a young animal to an old animal and then transplanted again when the recipient died. Such transplants have outlasted several animals in succession before their function stopped. Furthermore, their eventual demise appears to have been caused more by the trauma of repeated transplantations than by an aging process, Dr. Harrison said.

Dr. Gunther L. Eichorn of the aging institute has studied the uptake of traces of metals by human tissues, research prompted in part by the fact that traces of some metals are essential

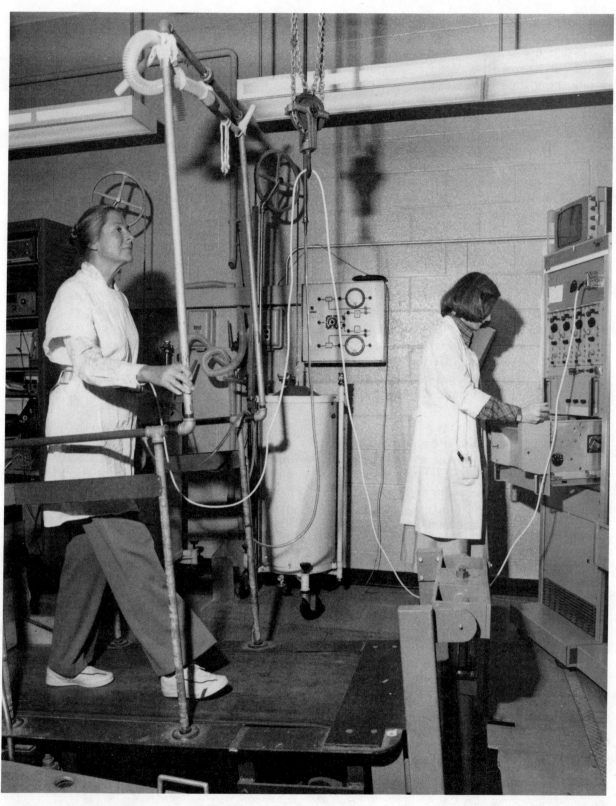

A technician helps administer an exercise electrocardiography test to a volunteer at the Gerontology Research Center.

127

to a cell's machinery for carrying out its genetic instructions and making the products normal to it. He and his colleagues, studying the chemistry of the lens of the human eye, have found significant changes with age in the amounts and identity of metals in the lens. Perhaps particularly significant, he believes, is a large increase in nickel content between childhood and old age. Nickel seems to have an adverse effect on the cell's precision in making its characteristic products. One hypothesis is that such a change might help explain the production errors that lead to cataracts in the eyes of the elderly.

One prominent theory advanced 15 years ago by Dr. Leslie Orgel of Stanford University attributes aging to an accumulation of errors in the manufacturing processes of cells, culminating at last in death. This theory has led Dr. Robert Loftfield of the University of New Mexico School of Medicine to do some of the first rigorous tests of the actual error rates of animal cells. He has found rates that are much lower than earlier calculations had suggested, indicating that living cells have highly perfected means of self-repair.

It is widely believed that aging has been an integral characteristic of life at least since the first multicelled plants and animals arose on earth. Even such incredibly long-lived species as sequoia and bristlecone pine may not be as close to immortality as is popularly imagined, according to Dr. Richard G. Cutler of the National Institute on Aging.

Living specimens have been dated at 3,000 to 4,000 years of age, he noted, but most of such a tree is a structure formed from the walls of dead cells. The living portion consists of only a thin layer of dividing cells located just inside the bark. Little of this is more than a year old at any time.

Current theories of aging include a wear-and-tear hypothesis in which body systems are viewed as simply wearing out over a lifetime and the theory that outside events such as radiation may produce cumulatively fatal damage.

One theory holds that senescence—the process of aging—is programmed into the genetics of the organisms. Perhaps the genes "selfishly" produce disposable bodies because this is the most economical way of perpetuating the genes themselves. This is a modern expression of the old idea that a chicken is only an egg's way of producing more and more eggs.

Most scientists involved in aging research see little prospect of ever halting the aging process altogether or even making major extensions to the probable maximum average human lifespan of slightly over 100 years. What they do hope research will achieve in time is a better quality of life for a much larger portion of the human lifespan so that fewer of the final years will be marred by physical and mental disability. It is this possibility that seems foreshadowed by the performance of some humans in circumventing far longer than the average the inexorable force of aging.

Penicillin

by Lawrence K. Altman

Although it kills guinea pigs and thus might never have been approved for use on humans if it were developed under modern regulations, penicillin, which revolutionized the practice of medicine when it was introduced in World War II, remains a "wonder drug" almost 40 years later, and its importance is still growing.

Almost overnight, the antibiotic tamed a host of infectious diseases that had killed and crippled since ancient times. It is still the drug of choice for a long list of infections—among them gonorrhea, syphilis, impetigo, "strep" throats, pneumococcal pneumonia, sinusitis, childbirth fever, lung abscesses and spinal meningitis.

Most experts believe that in the treatment of streptococcal infections penicillin, a natural substance produced by molds, has greatly reduced the incidence of rheumatic fever, once a common complication of streptococcal infections. Doctors have learned that penicillin can be given in almost unlimited doses without injuring the patient; some specialists say they prescribe it in amounts up to 20 million units a day—and sometimes in even larger doses—to treat the severest problems.

And the impact of penicillin has gone far beyond its usefulness in treating certain diseases. It was one of the few drugs discovered in a university laboratory. It took more than a decade to unlock the secret of preparing large amounts for commerical production, but then penicillin helped to make the drug industry a potent economic force. It ushered in a series of other "wonder drugs," and when chemical mastery of the molecule gave rise to semi-synthetic penicillins—derivatives created by chemically manipulating portions of the basic natural molecule—they became a symbol of modern therapeutics.

Many of the other so-called wonder drugs disappointed original boosters because their effects proved temporary or were offset by serious complications or toxic reactions that showed up only with long-term use.

The penicillin antibiotic family now includes at least 11 drugs that can treat a much wider range of infections than penicillin itself. And, although there is a wide range in costs, the members of the family are considered among the cheapest, least toxic and most effective drugs known, according to experts such as Dr.

129

H. Sherwood Lawrence, the chief of infectious diseases at New York University Medical School.

Penicillin's impact, beyond having been sustained in virtually all fields of medicine for almost four decades, continues to grow. Recently, a substance that is formed naturally in the body as a degradation product of penicillin was licensed for the treatment of cases of severe rheumatoid arthritis that do not respond to conventional measures. The substance, manufactured as a drug called penicillamine, has been used for several years in the treatment of two rare hereditary disorders called Wilson's Disease and cystinuria and has been prescribed in some poisonings to promote the excretion of heavy metals like lead and mercury. It is, however, much more toxic than penicillin.

Penicillin's special ability is that it affects only actively multiplying bacteria without harming human cells. In bacteria, it thwarts multiplication by preventing the formation of new cell walls. Other antibiotics, such as amphotericin, interfere with the biochemistry of human cells as much as that of offending organisms. The chief role of antibiotics is to prepare organisms for easier destruction by the body's immunological defense system, according to infectious-disease experts like Dr. Louis Weinstein of the Peter Bent Brigham Hospital in Boston.

Despite its huge impact, penicillin has had to overcome a series of obstacles since 1928, when it was accidentally discovered in a British laboratory by Sir Alexander Fleming. Although scientists had been searching in vain for a "magic bullet" since the late 19th century, the significance of Dr. Fleming's observations was not immediately appreciated. But the discovery of sulfa drugs in the 1930's renewed interest in "magic bullets," and the pressing needs of World War II led to the applied research that produced the first batches of penicillin.

Its value has since been threatened several times by the sudden appearance of strains of bacteria that were resistant to the antibiotic. For example, penicillin-resistant staphylococci caused infections in many hospitals beginning in the late 1950's. Soon Methicillin was marketed, becoming the first of a series of semi-synthetic penicillins that can treat staphylococci

Dr. H. Sherwood Lawrence states that penicillin and its derivatives are still most effective today.

resistant to penicillin itself. More recently, public health officials have been concerned about the discovery of penicillin-resistant strains of the bacteria that cause gonorrhea and pneumococcal pneumonia.

Still, the bulk of infections that doctors treat every day are caused by strains that succumb to penicillin therapy. In fact, Dr. Mercedes Albuerne of the Food and Drug Administration said, doctors each year write more than 80 million prescriptions for the penicillins, making them the most widely used class of antibiotics.

That situation markedly contrasts to the earliest days of penicillin therapy, when the antibiotic's developers could make just a few thousand units at a time from Fleming's original strain. Because the British lacked the apparatus to make penicillin during wartime, they grew the mold in bedpans. When doctors learned that penicillin was excreted unchanged in the urine, they recovered it from those under treatment, purified it and gave it to others. The first patient treated, an Oxford policeman who had streptococcal and staphylococcal infections, responded to penicillin therapy initially but died after the supply ran out, leading an Oxford professor to define penicillin as "a remarkable substance grown in bedpans and purified by passage through the Oxford Police Force."

The mass production of penicillin was accomplished in this country using fermentation techniques. To increase production for commercial purposes, scientists selected fast-growing strains, then irradiated them to produce faster-growing mutants. One of the best strains came from a mold on a cantaloupe.

Although penicillin is much less toxic than most other drugs, it can kill. Each year, experts estimate, a few hundred people die, chiefly through reactions that usually occur within minutes after an injection. Rashes and hives are less severe but more frequent manifestations of penicillin allergy. Dr. Weinstein estimates that 2 percent of the population is allergic to penicillin.

And humans are not the only species with a sometimes-violent reaction to the antibiotic. It

The late Sir Alexander Fleming, the discoverer of penicillin.

has been said that penicillin, if it were discovered today, would not pass the extensive animal research tests that are a prerequisite to marketing a drug because it kills guinea pigs. Just why it does so is a mystery. Scientific literature is filled with references to the variability of the phenomenon and, for the last 10 years, Dr. Lewis Thomas, president of the Memorial Sloan-Kettering Cancer Center, has been studying it in unpublished experiments in New York, in New Haven and in Edinburgh, Scotland. He said he had collected guinea pigs from breeders in different parts of the world and that they had been kept under identical climatic and housing conditions. For unknown reasons, Dr. Thomas said, penicillin is lethal for guinea pigs only in the winter, not during other seasons.

Like penicillin itself, the usefulness of penicillamine, the substance formed naturally in the body, in treating rare hereditary disorders was found accidentally. The discovery was made by a British scientist, Dr. John Walshe, who was working on problems of liver disease at the Boston City Hospital in the early 1950's. Through a series of observations and deductions, Dr. Walshe learned that penicillamine would promote the excretion of heavy metals from the body. He found that it worked in Wilson's Disease, in which a biochemical defect causes abnormally high amounts of copper to accumulate.

Another unplanned discovery was that penicillamine, which has no antibiotic properties and is much more toxic than penicillin, could be used in treating rheumatoid arthritis. That finding was made when Dr. Israeli A. Jaffe tried to determine the role of a substance called rheumatoid factor in patients with the disease. Because penicillamine was known to have an effect on rheumatoid factor in test tubes, Dr. Jaffe studied it on a few patients and learned that some of them showed beneficial effects. Further studies in Britain and this country have confirmed the findings.

Although many health officials remain concerned that the appearance of new penicillin-resistant strains of bacteria may herald serious problems for the antibiotic, others—among them, Dr. Weinstein—point out that it took more than 30 years for these strains to appear, so they are cautiously optimistic that penicillin will be the dominant antibiotic for many years.

The Elephant Seal

by Walter Sullivan

The elephant seal, once near extinction after hunters slaughtered it indiscriminately in the last century, has now become such a prolific breeder that it is colonizing the beaches of California. The reproductive success of the three-ton animals, which are now estimated to number 65,000, forces upon conservationists a difficult decision: Should a protected species brought back from near annihilation be allowed to proliferate indefinitely?

Originally, northern elephant seals by the thousands bred and were hunted for their oil on beaches from Point Reyes, north of San Francisco, to Cabo San Lázaro near the southern tip of Baja California. However, from 1884 to 1892, according to Dr. Burney J. LeBoeuf of the University of California at Santa Cruz, there is no record that a single elephant seal was seen anywhere.

Then, in 1892, specimen collectors for the Smithsonian Institution found eight of the huge animals on Isla de Guadalupe, which rises 4,800 feet from the Pacific Ocean west of Baja California. They killed all but one. While a few others were presumably at sea, the total number of survivors may not have exceeded 20 and the next generation may have been sired by only one or two dominant bulls.

That, according to Dr. LeBoeuf, was one of the most drastic "genetic bottlenecks" known. As a consequence, the thousands of northern elephant seals alive today appear almost as alike as identical twins. They therefore seem to lack the genetic diversity that might enable the species to cope with new diseases or other environmental changes. Dr. LeBoeuf fears that such genetic impoverishment may be faced by other species brought back from near extinction, such as the black-footed ferret, California condor, sea otter and California gray whale.

The northern elephant seal, weighing two to four tons and 16 feet long, is closely related to the slightly larger southern elephant seal, which inhabits the islands around Antarctica. It, too, was decimated by hunters of the last century, but apparently did not pass through so tight a genetic bottleneck and has retained more of its diversity.

The northern elephant seal began recovering initially because its sole rookery was too iso-

The elephantlike probiscus identifies the gender of this elephant seal as a male of the species.

lated to tempt hunters. When 264 of the animals were found on Guadalupe in 1922, Mexico outlawed a resumption of hunting, and the United States later followed suit.

The giant seals prefer islands but are confined to those with beaches, since they are too massive to climb onto rocks. In the 1970's, they have established themselves on two additional islands off California (Southeast Farallon Island off San Francisco and San Clemente off the town of that name) and two off Mexico's Baja California (Isla Natividad and Isla San Martin). Now, however, they have run out of islands within their habitat and in 1975, for the first time in this century, a female was observed to have given birth to a pup on the mainland—a beach 19 miles up the coast from here opposite Año Nuevo Island, whose beaches had become saturated with elephant seals.

Such is the rate of their population growth that last year about 100 pups were born on the mainland beach where five years ago there was but a single birth. Another 1,100 were born on the island. Some 570 adults occupied the mainland beach close to where Route 1, California's coastal highway, skirts the shore.

There are reports that elephant seals are already scouting the beaches at Point Reyes, the original northern limit of their range, but this could not be verified.

Dr. William Doyle, director of the university's Center for Coastal Marine Studies, foresees an increasing number of episodes in which Californians, awakened by deep bellowing, call the police to announce that "there is this monster outside my beach window—dying." Sooner or later, he fears, one of the huge animals will haul itself onto Route 1 in the dead of night "and some small foreign car will be demolished."

The massive animals hug the ground and often move so slowly they appear to be incapacitated. They can, nevertheless, inflict a severe bite and the bulls, in their battles for dominance of a harem, sometimes inflict fatal wounds on one another. It is the males that carry the elephantlike proboscis that gives the species its name. The seals are docile unless approached within eight to 10 feet—a characteristic that helped expedite their near annihilation. However, there has been concern that for this reason tourists might come dangerously close.

For more than a decade Dr. LeBoeuf has tagged or marked 12,000 of the animals at rookeries from Guadalupe to the Farallons. They are painted with long poles, to provide a margin of safety, or with paint pellets fired by a gun. He and his students also have studied the extraordinary milk production of the females. After conception, the female spends close to a year at sea, fattening on squid, octopus and fish. In about mid-December, she hauls out onto a beach, joins the harem of an imposing bull and six days later drops her single pup. For the next 28 days, the mother nurses her pup, which gains weight at a phenomenal rate. In those four weeks, it increases from 60 to 300 pounds. And for every pound it gains, the mother loses two, since she neither feeds nor drinks in this period.

By means of a suction device at the end of a long pole and other methods, milk samples have been collected and analyzed. The mean level of their fat content is 54.5 per cent, the highest found in any mammal, and the water content is only 32.8 per cent, the lowest known. The meager water content presumably helps the animal produce so large a volume of milk without drinking.

In the last four days of the nursing period, the mother mates with the bull, or an interloper, and then returns to the sea, leaving the pup to molt and learn to swim on its own. Life for a pup in the rookery is hazardous. They are often trampled and crushed in the efforts of the bulls to achieve high social rank and copulate. According to Dr. LeBoeuf, "Males are impervious to a pup's presence and neither its shrill cries nor its mother's aggressiveness persuades a two- to three-ton bull to move when he comes to rest on a pup."

Dr. LeBoeuf has found that 13 to 14 percent of the pups on Año Nuevo die before they are weaned. Some, when they become separated from their mothers, try to suckle other females. Often, in response, they are bitten or have their skulls crushed. Incited by the pups' squawking, five or six females may "mob" it with fatal results. However, a third of the mothers that lose their pups adopt another.

□

Before settlement of the West Coast, the elephant seal population on the mainland was kept down by such predators as grizzly bears and cougars. But such checks no longer exist. The giant seals have become a tourist attraction at Año Nuevo Point, where an estimated 245,000 visitors have come to see them in the first three years after their arrival. Sooner or later, however, a confrontation seems inevitable between elephant seals and such users of California's beaches as surfers, nudists and conventional bathers.

Creating the Energy-Efficient Society

by Anthony J. Parisi

Welcome to the efficient society.

Almost unnoticed, Americans have begun to save energy by wasting less. In the process, they have almost halted the growth in oil imports, lessened the drain on the dollar, deflected some inflationary forces, avoided a lot of pollution and eased the tension over such issues as nuclear power and strip mining. The nation remains in a difficult energy bind—there is absolutely no question about that—but these unheralded gains suggest that the country is, in fact, stumbling on a way out of that bind, one that is far less tortured and painful than many thoughtful people had feared. It is called energy efficiency.

"We are already on the road to solving our energy problem," says Vince Taylor, a physicist and economist who is a consultant to the Union of Concerned Scientists, an environmentalist group. "The path is really bright. The opportunities are enormous. Ten years from now we will look back and be amazed at how much energy we've been able to get along without—and without major changes in our life style."

To many, Taylor's words may sound like optimism run amok. But the facts he marshals are impressive. In a paper entitled "The Easy Path Energy Plan," which is fast making the rounds of the energy community, Taylor opposes the conventional view as held both in the United States and abroad—that America is the land of the free and the home of the gluttonous. He shows that in 1978 America consumed just 5 percent more energy than it did in 1973, even though the economy expanded more than 12 percent during those five years. By contrast, over the prior five-year period it took a 22 percent increase in energy consumption to fuel an economic expansion of 17 percent. If Americans had been as energy inefficient in 1978 as they were in 1973, the nation would have had to import half again as much oil as it did.

"The reason our energy problems appear so intractable to most people, even to supposed experts, is that attention has been focused entirely on the possibilities for expanding supplies," Taylor concludes. "Yet the more closely people have looked at these supposed solutions, the clearer it has become that this route will lead to no immediate answer." Meanwhile, conservation has been largely written off in official circles as back-to-the-woods romanticism. Or, worse, those wedded to the notion of infinitely expanding supplies equate conservation with sacrifice and burden. Yet sacrifice is something the efficient society tries to avoid. The need and desire to overcome human hardship were, after all, motivations for creating social organization in the first place.

There is now evidence to suggest that many Americans are realizing that they have a choice, in dealing with the energy crisis, between suffering and energy efficiency, and they are choosing efficiency. Public posturing aside, they largely ignore the 55-mile-per-hour speed limit and balk when told to bear 65 degrees in winter and 78 degrees in summer. Instead, they are driving smaller cars, insulating their homes, streamlining their industrial processes and designing their buildings to ward off the sun in summer and embrace it in winter.

America is beginning to capture energy once wasted, and people are discovering in the process that there are rewards beyond even the money this saves, much like the little thrills one gets from enjoying leftovers or finding a bargain. "There are a lot of subtle, intangible benefits," says Amory Lovins, of the Friends of the Earth, whose scholarly, almost poetic, papers have made him a kind of high lama of the energy-efficiency sect. "It makes you more flexible," he says. "It's good for the spirit."

It's also effective. Heating specialists have found that reducing the temperature of a poorly insulated home from 68 to 65 degrees will trim fuel consumption by only about 15 percent. Adding more insulation in the attic and other accessible places can cut consumption in half. With a comparable new home, thoroughly insulated, designed with such passive solar features as greenhouses to trap the sun's energy in winter and southerly overhangs to block it in summer, and perhaps fitted with a modern wood-burning stove instead of an anachronistic fireplace that literally sucks heat out of the room, a family can easily halve its fuel consumption yet again.

Driving slowly in a car that gets 15 miles a gallon helps a little; driving a car that gets 27.5

miles a gallon, the level mandated for 1985 models, helps a lot. Based only on the mileage standards already on the books—standards that many believe are too loose—the oil industry expects the demand for gasoline, which accounts for 40 percent of all the oil consumed in this country, to start dropping within a year. Some are already saying that we may never again use as much as we did in 1978.

New skyscrapers can provide all the comforts of buildings designed in the 1960's but with half the energy. Among other innovations, they recycle waste heat from computers, lights and even the occupants. Those precious B.T.U.'s used to be thrown away—even as the boilers below were devouring still more fuel to replace them.

In the industrial sector, where 40 percent of the nation's energy is consumed, the spectacular gains in energy efficiency have already crushed old canards. Despite repeated warnings from business quarters that zero energy growth might mean economic disaster, the nation's mills and factories actually used less energy last year than they did in 1973. Dow Chemical, for example, realized in the 60's that rapidly rising fuel costs were putting its Michigan plants at a competitive disadvantage to petrochemical complexes on the Gulf Coast, where energy was still considerably cheaper. In 1967, Dow, which alone devours .5 percent of all the energy consumed in the United States, launched an aggressive fuel-conservation program. Within a decade, it cut the amount of fuel needed to make a pound of product by 40 percent, principally by plugging steam leaks and keeping them plugged.

Some experts believe that industry will be able to get by on less energy in 10 years than it needs now, especially if the Government grants greater tax credits on investments that save energy. But even without such encouragement, advances are coming. The Union Carbide Corporation, for example, has started making polyethylene, a petrochemical mainstay, with a new process that uses only a fourth as much energy as the old.

All these gains are quietly adding up to a staggering sum. "Since 1973," says Lee Schipper, a staff scientist at Lawrence Berkeley Laboratory, "we have gotten more energy from

These aluminum beverage cans will be recycled at a saving of ninety-five percent of the energy needed to make aluminum from bauxite.

Solar water heaters are a standard feature of this housing development in California. Well insulated homes increase the viability of such systems.

efficiency improvements than from any form of supply—including oil imports."

Ironically, it was exactly these kinds of improvements that President Carter anticipated when he proposed his first, conservation-oriented energy plan three years ago. Congress, sensing public dissatisfaction, chopped it to bits. Now the President is back with a supply-oriented plan centered not on efficiency but on synthetic fuels. The benefits of energy efficiency are even more appealing today, however, than they were then.

These advantages tend to cluster in two areas: economics and the environment. The environmental appeal is obvious—energy recovered through efficiency improvements leaves few if any traces—but the economics are less apparent. The A.F.L.-C.I.O.'s George Meany and the leaders of the National Association for the Ad-

vancement of Colored People are among those who have opposed an all-out program for conservation and energy efficiency, and the essential thread of their objections is that it would somehow result in deprivation, especially for lower-income groups. Thus, some workers and minorities have formed a loose coalition with some industrialists who like to crow that the United States produced, not conserved, its way to greatness.

But this conventional faith in production and ever-expanding energy consumption as the means to achieving all social ends went awry as fuel costs started soaring in the early 70's. When that happened, it became cheaper to conserve than to produce. The challenge posed by the energy crisis is not how to get out of the bind for free—that's impossible—but how to get out the least costly way. As Amory Lovins puts it, "Conservation will not be cheap—just cheaper than not conserving." The key, he says, is capital: "These days, it takes less capital to save energy than to produce it. Society has only so much capital, and what you want to do is invest it in the most productive way possible. If we fail to do that, money will be drawn unnecessarily from other uses—including a lot of social programs that might have helped poor people." As far as jobs are concerned, the nature of some industries that are tied to energy conservation is such that they themselves become substantial employers. "A dollar spent on insulation creates more jobs than a dollar spent on shale oil," Lovins points out.

Viewed in this perspective, efficiency improvements begin to look like a steal compared to such big technology schemes as converting coal into gas and oil, the alternative that President Carter has advocated. By the latest estimates, commercial versions of these synthetic fuel plants would produce oil costing around $40 a barrel, a figure that has tripled in the last five years. By contrast, researchers at the University of California, who are developing housing efficiency standards for the Department of Energy, conclude that a national program to insulate the nation's existing homes would recover energy at a cost of between $10 and $20 a barrel. There would be no environmental disruption, and the savings would start pouring in right away, not 10 years from now. "For $1,500 to $2,000 dollars," says Arthur Rosenfeld, a University of California physicist, "we could retrofit the typical American home and cut energy consumption in half—in half."

Savings of this magnitude may be possible in the economy as a whole. Sweden and West Germany now consume 50 percent less energy for the same amount of heavy industrial production than the United States does. The situations are not precisely comparable but there is no fundamental reason why Americans, given time, cannot become at least 30 percent more efficient.

Roger Sant, director of the Energy Productivity Center of the Mellon Institute in Washington, D.C., has compiled a breakdown of what the country's energy picture might have looked like in 1978 if, magically, all energy services had been delivered, not by the expensive ways we have inherited, but by the cheapest, most efficient means possible. The findings, he says, are "fabulous": Oil consumption would have been 28 percent less; imports would have plunged from more than eight million barrels a day to barely four million; well over a third of all central power stations could have been eliminated, perhaps obviating the need for nuclear power; overall energy costs to the consumer would have dropped 17 percent.

Even before the first oil shock, in late 1973 and early 1974, energy efficiency had become the subject of considerable intellectual scrutiny. The Ford Foundation's controversial 1974 report "A Time to Choose," for example, warned that if the United States continued using energy at the going rate, supplies would have to swell an impossible 150 percent by the turn of the century. "Technical fixes" could hold energy growth to 50 percent, the report declared, with no appreciable impact on economic growth. And if the nation went all out, the study added, America could achieve zero energy growth early in the 21st century.

In business circles, the idea of zero energy growth went over like Copernicus in the house of Ptolemy. Traditionalists charged that the study was unsound and the studiers were incompetent. Yet today most projections for domestic energy consumption 20 years hence—even most industry projections—are closer to the foundation's zero-growth scenario than its technical-fix scenario. Some have gone beyond: early last year the President's Council on Environmental Quality issued a paper with the happy title "The Good News About Energy." It concluded that total energy use in the United States "need not increase greatly between now and the end of the century, perhaps by no more than 10 to 15 percent."

Last year, none other than the Harvard Business School, no stranger to business interests, endorsed the efficiency-first energy path. In a report entitled "Energy Future," it concludes: "The United States can use 30 or 40 percent less energy than it does, with virtually no penalty for the way Americans live—save that billions of dollars will be spared, save that the environment will be less strained, the air less polluted, the dollar under less pressure, save that the growing and alarming dependence on OPEC oil

Solar collectors form the roof of this waste treatment plant in Wilton, Maine, and supply heat to sludge digesters, enabling the production of methane gas. Thus a waste product generates an energy resource.

will be reduced, and Western society will be less likely to suffer internal and international tension."

As the Harvard study makes clear, there is another, more pragmatic reason for favoring efficiency. Except for the slow progress being made on solar and geothermal forms of energy, all other domestic energy sources either seem to be waning naturally or wallowing in an environmental muddle. And even solar enthusiasts, generally an impatient breed, concede that before society could truly switch to renewable sources, it must trim waste. "We should recognize," says Denis Hayes, director of the federally funded Solar Energy Research Institute, "that conservation is a precondition to a solar transition." Solar becomes a much more attractive option in an energy-tight home, for example.

Despite the sharply higher prices that oil and gas producers have enjoyed in recent years, the nation's proved reserves of oil have declined 28 percent since the record level reached in 1970; gas reserves have dropped 32 percent from their peak in 1967. The declines have come in spite of a near doubling in the number of wells drilled since 1971. Hoping to spur still more exploration (as well as to encourage more conservation), the Government is now phasing out price controls on both these fuels. Few experts think this move will do more than delay the long decline in these once-abundant hydrocarbons.

Coal production is rising, but slowly, and quality has been slipping. On a tonnage basis, Americans consumed only 9 percent more coal in 1978 than they did in 1973, and on an energy-content basis, the increase was less than 7 percent, because the growth has come mainly in low-quality Western coal. The energy from this additional tonnage did not even offset a fifth of what was lost from declining oil and gas production. Dreams of doubling or even tripling coal output by 1985 have long since faded. The supply of coal is there, but the demand is not, at least not on terms that the public finds acceptable. Although the United States has nearly a third of the world's coal, a series of concerns, mostly environmental, have restrained development at virtually every stage. The biggest: resistance to more strip mining; labor, safety and health problems in underground mines; and, most telling of all, air-pollution regulations where the extra coal would be burned. Converting coal into oil or gas, in addition to being very expensive, poses fresh environmental concerns that some think could prove even more troublesome.

Nuclear power, after a slow start, has grown rapidly in recent years and now provides close to 13 percent of all the electricity and nearly 4 percent of all the energy consumed in the United States. Long before the accident at Three Mile Island dropped a big question mark in the atom's path, however, new orders for nuclear power plants in this country succumbed to relentless environmental, safety and even economic pressures; orders have all but halted. Because of these pressures, the Harvard study concluded that nuclear power "could actually undergo an absolute decline within 10 years."

Some of the objections to nuclear power and other new energy projects could be overruled, of course. President Carter presumably had that in mind when he proposed an Energy Mobilization Board. Yet this tactic might mean only more and more confrontation.

"Carter described the problems as environmental red tape, but that is a fundamental misconception," Luther Gerlach, professor of anthropology at the University of Minnesota, insists. For 10 years Gerlach has studied what he calls the real "energy wars," the protests that have increasingly erupted around the country over new energy projects. He believes it is foolhardy to assume that these struggles are the handiwork of a small group of dissidents. "People say the Tellico Dam was stopped by the snail darter, but it wasn't," he says. "It was stopped by people who didn't want to lose their land and who seized on the Endangered Species Act as a way to prevent it from happening. We have devised a ritual for doing this sort of thing, and the ritual isn't the problem. In fact it

has helped keep these things from getting out of hand. Take it away," he warns, "and there will only be more direct conflict."

Denis Hayes of the Solar Energy Research Institute believes, as do others, that, in this sense, energy efficiency is not only the cheapest, cleanest and fastest way to go today but that it is also the most harmonious. Greater social harmony emerges as a kind of grand bonus. The alternative, as Amory Lovins has put it, is a highly managed society ruled by a "complex of warfare-welfare-industrial-communications-police bureaucracies with a technocratic ideology."

And yet, technology pervades the efficient economy. The difference is that it is servant, not icon. It may be as simple as a new formula for caulking or as complex as a microprocessor that improves auto mileage by automatically adjusting the carburetor's fuel-air mixture. But it is usually unobtrusive, which is why the sizable strides in efficiency already achieved in the American economy have gone largely unnoticed. America, perhaps more than any other nation, has liked its technology big. A crash program gave us synthetic rubber during World War II, so why can't a crash program give us synthetic fuel now? Economists, in their own way, often concur. When the price of a resource rises, they reason, technology's scope widens, marginal deposits eventually become economical and supplies expand. Why not now?

The answer is that high energy prices are having much more clout on the demand side of the equation than on the supply side. This is what happens when a resource base can no longer outpace consumption and begins to shrink from exhaustion, as domestic oil reserves seem to be doing right now. Technology is responding all right, but not so much in exploiting marginal resources as in finding ways to get by on less. Yankee ingenuity lives.

If—and that "if" is still very much warranted —the trend continues, the nation will wean itself from oil as other resources (more coal for a while, then solar) begin to shoulder the burden. In this event, oil prices will eventually taper off at some lofty level and oil will linger on as a highly expensive commodity reserved for only the most critical purposes. Just as whales outlived the importance of whale oil, petroleum de-

A silo fills a 110-car train with coal as it inches through the structure. It takes approximately two hours to load the train that never stops during loading, thereby increasing energy efficiency.

posits will outlast dominant use of petroleum.

All this might be taken for granted except that generations of Americans have enjoyed nearly a century of expanding energy supplies and shrinking energy prices. Americans have a certain mind-set toward supply, a bias imbedded not only in their thinking but in their customs, laws and institutions. The examples are endless: Federal subsidies for energy-development projects, tax depletion allowances, accelerated depreciation for power plants, write-offs for business fuel expenditures. By conservative count, the pricing subsidies alone may exceed $50 billion a year. Along the way, Americans seem to have lost the kind of energy sensibility that scarce supplies and high prices exact over time. Amory Lovins gives an illustration:

"Thirty years ago, refrigerators used to have motors that were close to 90 percent efficient. Today they're 60 percent or less, because as electricity prices fell, we skimped on the copper windings. We used to put the motor on the top, where it belongs; today it goes underneath, where it must use half its energy just to get rid of its own heat. The trim-line craze hit, so we skimped on insulation—remember when refrigerator walls used to be four inches thick? Besides that, we design them so that when we open the door the cold air falls out. We could make them horizontal, like supermarket freezers, or at least have individual compartments to keep some of the cold air in. Because we let the cold air out so freely, frost builds up quickly, so we put about 700 watts of heaters in most of our refrigerators to get rid of it. A lot of models also have strip heaters around the doors to keep the seals from sticking; a Teflon coating would do. Then to get rid of all this heat, we stick a radiator on the back, and let it heat up the house to give our air-conditioners something to work on. To top it off, we usually install the refrigerator next to another heat-generating appliance such as a stove or dishwasher, so when that goes on the refrigerator tends to go on, too."

To be sure, the Government now sets targets for energy efficiency in appliances. It has also tried to offset the subsidies for supplies that are by now tightly woven into the economy by offering tax credits for home insulation, for example. But habits acquired over decades are not easily discarded, and the deck clearly remains stacked against efficiency. "There just isn't any constituency for conservation, despite all its appeal," says Robert Stobaugh, the director of the Harvard Business School study. "That's why the Government has got to get behind it more than it has." He argues that the nation must devise a conservation system to compete directly with oil, gas and electricity, and suggests one way would be to get the utilities to coordinate energy-saving investments in homes, collecting half the money from the Government and half from the homeowner.

A few utilities have already moved in this direction. Northern California's Pacific Gas & Electric Company, one of the largest in the country, has for the last year and a half offered its customers loans of up to $500 for ceiling insulation—and the company says customers typically reduce their heating bills by 25 percent. That alone is almost enough to cover the payments on the five-year, 8 percent loans. The rather dramatic result is that with no money up front and only a modest monthly charge, customers can improve their home insulation, and, then, five years later, start pocketing at least a fourth of what they would have been paying for heat.

The company expects 10,000 customers to take advantage of the plan this year. That, it figures, will free enough energy next year to supply 970 average gas customers and 223 average electricity customers. "If we can put enough of these savings together," R. Michael Mertz,

manager of Pacific's energy and conservation services, says, "it will turn out to be a lot cheaper than building a new power plant."

In western Oregon, the Portland General Electric Company has taken the idea one small but psychologically important step further. It will pay contractors to install insulation, caulking, storm doors and whatever else it takes to reduce power consumption in the 90,000 or so electrically heated homes that the utility serves. Customers do not repay the interest-free loans until they sell their homes. Meanwhile, the money is included in the utility's rate base, where it earns the same return as the company's investments in power plants. This ground-breaking arrangement neutralizes management's natural inclination to expand the rate base by building a new plant even when money-saving alternatives abound. "I think this is one of the most exciting things happening," says Roger Sant of the Mellon energy center. "There's this attitude that we ought to keep the utilities out of it, and I think that's unwise."

The bicycle remains one of the most efficient forms of transport devised by man, and is being used increasingly by commuters.

143

More such imaginative approaches to improving energy efficiency in the residential sector are needed. With just a little enticement, industry already seems eager to grow more efficient on its own, because efficiency, in a future of high energy cost, will be the only road to profitability. Savings in the transportation field can also mount up quickly, because the national fleet of motor vehicles lasts six years on the average, meaning that mileage standards can be raised as warranted and can be broadly implemented within that time. Office buildings and homes stand for decades, however. Even if new construction becomes a model of energy thrift, can the country afford to ignore its existing housing stock? Within those structures lie "proved reserves" of energy that it has barely begun to tap. Tapping them will not be easy—

just easier than not tapping them. The costs will occasionally be steep, the conceptual barriers formidable, the politics exasperating. But the alternative is the inefficient society, which, we are finding, is a concept that has suddenly grown obsolete. "This country was built on inexpensive energy, and we had plenty of it domestically until the early 70's," says David Sternlight, chief economist for The Atlantic Richfield Company. "The situation has changed, and now that it has, we are beginning to change, too."

The heartening thing in all this is that the solution to the energy crisis, if one can hope that these beginnings really will be pursued, seems to be emerging in spite of ourselves. And there is, it turns out, a certain simple elegance to it all.

Tiny Town vs. Mining Giant

by Roger Neville Williams

Crested Butte sweeps its rocky ridge into the Colorado sky, high above the tiny hamlet which has taken its name. More than a butte, it is a 12,000-foot peak with a saw-toothed crest, a mini-Matterhorn challenged only by the supine Mount Emmons across the valley. The two mountains stand like bookends above the plain.

In between lies "The Butte," an ex-coal-mining town of 1,000 people, many from New York, California and Atlanta, who have trimmed out the old village in Disneyesque fuchsias and lavenders while adding stately Victorian buildings of their own. The entire town is a national historic site, almost entirely surrounded by National Forest land.

Three miles to the north is ex-Secretary of the Army Howard (Bo) Callaway's ski area, on the rim of the vast cirque edging the valley, where Bo and his brother built their condominium village. It is a tasteful, modern ski complex. Crested Butte and the ski mountain lie some 25 miles south of Aspen as the bullet flies, or 225 miles from Aspen by paved road and mountain pass.

The townsite is in a remote, enchanting setting at the end of the road in one of Colorado's last unspoiled valleys. Crested Butte lies at the end of the road of some people's lives as well, a last frontier now threatened by massive industrialism unlike anything Western Colorado has ever seen.

AMAX Inc., formerly American Metal Climax Inc., a giant mining corporation with more than $3 billion in assets, wants to construct a billion-dollar molybdenum mine two miles from town, and the urban refugees who have settled permanently in Crested Butte, and who see themselves as preservationists of the surrounding wilderness and of the historic landmark to which they have brought a renaissance, are not too happy about it.

When I drove up the 28 miles from the sleepy town of Gunnison, past the abandoned, lichen-covered homesteads, past the ranchers' proud turn-of-the-century homes, I was met at the plain of the North Valley by hundreds of poky Herefords coming down the road, prodded along by mounted cowboys in snow-covered

145

The town of Crested Butte is located across from Mount Emmons in one of Colorado's last unspoiled valleys.

146

chaps—a real cattle drive. This is the Old West, still mythic in its appeal, a tranquil region of range and mountains, relatively unscarred by its one compact Victorian mining town and scarcely marked by the recreation boom of the last 15 years.

In 1977, two miles from Main Street and 11,000 feet up on Mount Emmons (known to locals as "Red Lady Mountain"), prospectors for AMAX sank their core drills into what is thought to be the world's richest known deposit of molybdenum ore. Colorado has two other larger deposits, at Henderson near Berthoud Pass, and at Leadville, both being mined by AMAX's Climax Molybdenum Division, but neither ore body compares to that of Mount Emmons, which has been estimated to have a market value of $7 billion. Worldwide demand for the "gray gold" is rising at 7 percent a year, and Climax Molybdenum—which provides nearly half of the free world's supply—wants the Red Lady's moly.

In addition to the mine on the mountain, AMAX has proposed a mill and tailings pond (slime dump) of staggering proportions, all of it to be set down on surrounding National Forest and ranchland that has never known modern industrialization. The mine and mill would employ 1,300 people, cost as much as $1 billion, and require more than 2,000 construction workers during the building phase.

Of the 165 million tons of ore estimated, conservatively, to be inside Mount Emmons, 164 million tons of it would end up *outside* the mountain, on the surrounding land. There will be a tailings pond, a useless, caustic, chemical-laden sludge that's left after the moly concentrate has been extracted, covering 3,000 acres, 30 times the size of the town of Crested Butte. Gunnison County's total population, currently 11,000, would more than double over the next six years. Bumper stickers seen around town say: "DON'T CLIMAX IN THE BUTTE." All anyone can talk about in town is "the mine." Crested Butte is a town fighting to save itself.

So what is molybdenum, aside from being nearly unpronounceable? (It's been called "Molly Be Damned.") It is a silver-gray metallic element with a melting point of 4,730 degrees Fahrenheit that is used to alloy most steel products, to provide durability as well as resis-

tance to corrosion and severe temperatures. It lightens steel, while hardening it, and it is found in everything from tools and engine blocks to steam turbines, jet engines, pipelines and nuclear reactors.

Molybdenum has been used in armor plate and cannon since 1894. In 1905, a German company discovered the world's largest deposit at Climax Station, near the town of Leadville, Colo. The company, Metallgesellschaft, changed its name to American Metal Co. when World War I came along, but that didn't prevent the War Minerals Board from seizing its stock and placing it under the trusteeship of Henry Morgenthau and Andrew Mellon. A rival company, Climax Molybdenum, was then formed to provide moly for Allied war instruments. By World War II, molybdenum was the country's No. 1 strategic metal, and troops were garrisoned near Climax to guard the mine and mill from possible Axis sabotage.

When AMAX officials came to Crested Butte a year ago to announce their find, the last thing they expected to encounter in a tiny, rural community was a phalanx of resident New York lawyers, who, along with just about everyone else in town, want to keep the Butte and its surroundings as they found it.

There is New York University Law School graduate Myles Rademan, the town planner who came to the Butte six years ago and says: "You just can't imagine the size of this project, its magnitude. When you have 200 or 300 *million* tons of tailings, you're talking about a retaining wall the size of the Aswan Dam or bigger. Areas under consideration for tailings dumps are among the most beloved and beautiful parcels of land in the world. What we're dealing with here is the disemboweling of the West."

There is Gil Hersch, a former New Yorker who now owns and publishes the weekly Crested Butte Chronicle. He told me: "I'm opposed to the mine. We're killing our planet. I'm interested in the major paradigms in the world right now, between the traditional capitalistic outlook of more-makes-better, as opposed to the New Age culture which says we've got to live in harmony with nature. AMAX came in here with the statement that they were going to make this the first in a new generation of mines.

The Crested Butte ski area is located three miles north of the town on the rim of the vast cirque that edges the valley.

We asked, 'What is a new generation of mines?' Is it that it's just 15 years newer? Or is it the difference between the Industrial Revolution and the New Age Revolution?"

And there is County Commissioner David Leinsdorf, son of conductor Erich Leinsdorf. He was recently re-elected by playing David to the AMAX Goliath. He advocates a much smaller mining operation than AMAX envisions. A Columbia Law School graduate, ex-Nader Raider and former Justice Department attorney, he moved to the Butte in 1971 and became Colorado's youngest county commissioner in 1974, acceding to a post normally reserved for conservative, native-born ranchers.

The stakes are high: A $7 billion mineral deposit versus the priceless value of wilderness; technological progress and modern industrialization versus a ranching and resort economy; transient workers and "boom town" greed ver-sus a tiny, stable community practicing, for the most part, a kind of voluntary simplicity.

Recreation provides Gunnison County's chief income, as a million and a half campers, hikers, fishermen, back-packers, hunters, jeepers, and skiers visit Gunnison National Forest each year, and one might expect the resort industry to lead the fight to preserve the integrity of this region of unparalleled natural beauty. But that's not the case.

"I wish they'd found their moly somewhere else, but I'm not going to lie down in front of any trucks to stop AMAX. It's not my style," said Bo Callaway in his office overlooking his ski lifts. "I support the free-enterprise system, and I'm not comfortable telling a mining company when and where they can mine. If AMAX goes the extra mile and operates openly, I'll continue to work with them."

As President Ford's campaign manager,

before he resigned over the "Callaway Affair" and moved permanently to Crested Butte, Bo was the enemy of the area's environmentalists. He proposed a bigger ski area, on another mountain, and was accused by Myles Arber, the former editor of The Chronicle, NBC News and Senator Floyd Haskell, the Colorado Democrat, of using his Cabinet post in Washington to lever the required special-use permit from the Forest Service. He handed me a copy of Harper's with the July 1977 cover story absolving him of any wrongdoing, his sweet vindication.

Money is money, and $7 billion is sitting inside Mount Emmons. Already it has had its effect—just lying there: $75,000 condominiums now sell for $200,000 and Crested Butte lots, which brought $10,000 last year, are going for $25,000 today. Terry Hamlin, a former head of the ski patrol, ski-area marketing manager, real-estate agent and a Colorado native, is a case in point. The young, personable ex-ski bum is now manager of local affairs for AMAX. "A man on the way up," taunts Gil Hersch in The Chronicle. A shotgun blast shattered the windows of Mr. Hamlin's AMAX office in the fall of 1978, but he was away at the time.

Hamlin drove me up to the mine site on Mount Emmons, two miles above town on the Kebler Pass Road. Already, 135 men and women are employed here in "exploration," bearded young geologists examining core samples, miners cleaning out and shoring up the drifts (tunnels) of the abandoned Keystone Mine. The tunnels of the defunct lead-zinc mine happen to lie directly beneath the huge molybdenum ore body and are being used for exploratory core drilling.

In 1977, AMAX took the mine over from a Wyoming firm, fully aware that the mine's 100-year-old tailings dump had collapsed, polluting Coal Creek, Crested Butte's primary water supply. Under a Colorado Department of Health cease-and-desist order, AMAX had to spend $800,000 to clean up the previous mine owner's mess and stabilize the old tailings pond. Terry Hamlin handed me a colorful, 18-page AMAX brochure that promised to bring brown trout back to Coal Creek, concluding, "AMAX is committed to the people of Colorado to help maintain the air, water and natural environment that make the good life here what it is."

"Next summer we're building a $2 million water-treatment plant up here to completely end the Keystone drainage contamination of Coal Creek," Hamlin explained. "In the past, at the historic stage of the development of the West, mining companies were not concerned with the environment. But AMAX is. We have to be." It was a theme I was to hear again and again from AMAX officials.

But no one on the Town Council has bought AMAX's expensive public-relations arguments. "It seems highly unlikely that the mine and the town can be compatible, or that recreation and mining can be compatible," says William Mitchell, 35, Crested Butte's Mayor and chairman of the Town Council. "I'm very anxious about it. This is a national playground and it belongs to everyone. These are public lands. Those of us who've consciously given up conveniences and have adopted a harder way of life as a trade-off for the natural wonders surrounding us have become trustees of a magnificent wilderness."

Mayor Mitchell—he goes by his last name alone—has been using his "situation," as he calls it, to attract attention to Crested Butte's plight. After a 1971 motorcycle accident badly burned his body, hands and face (now restored by plastic surgery) and a subsequent airplane crash fractured his spine, Mayor Mitchell is now a paraplegic—in what he calls "the least wheel-chair accessible town in America," Mayor Mitchell says, "I'm way too selfish for self-pity. If I hadn't got burned up or been in a crash, I would not have enough money to be Mayor of Crested Butte, since the job pays only $25 a month and I'm at it full time." Mayor Mitchell's dynamism, charisma and tough leadership qualities, combined with his ex-radio announcer's voice, keep one from noticing his "situation."

"He's a one-man media event," says Myles Rademan, noting the national publicity afforded Crested Butte under such headlines as "Paralyzed Mayor Battles Mine Owners." When President Carter invited Mayor Mitchell to Washington to advise the President's Committee on Employment of the Handicapped, the Mayor dropped by the Interior Department to see Secretary Cecil Andrus, a man who, he notes, launched his career stopping a molybde-

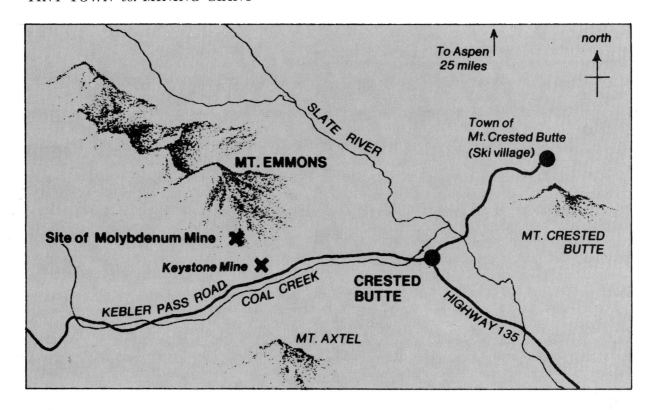

num mine at White Cloud, Idaho.

Mayor Mitchell confronts and confounds AMAX's media blitz (full-page ads in the local papers, a monthly sheet called The Moly News featuring columns by company executives, and a comic strip called "Miss Moly") with a tireless campaign of his own. In recent months, he has testified before the House Subcommittee of Mines and Mining, and has met with Paul Ehrlich, John Denver, Robert Redford, Jack Anderson and David Brower, president of Friends of the Earth. He once threatened to address an AMAX stockholders meeting, until AMAX chairman Pierre Gousseland and the then-president of the Climax Division, Jack Goth, invited him, along with Messrs. Leinsdorf, Callaway, Rademan and the Mayor of Gunnison, to visit the home office in Greenwich, Conn., last year.

"We can't give in to the divine right of ownership by mining companies," says Mayor Mitchell. "I'm fighting for every protection I can get for this valley. We can understand the value of Yellowstone and Yosemite—there are probably tons of mineral deposits in Yosemite and a decision was made in 1890 to preserve it— but what is the value of this valley? There have

been more than 1,500 mining claims filed in this county this year. What they want to do is make Gunnison County one large open pit mine."

In November 1978, Mitchell was unhappy to see Colorado's environmentalist Senator, Floyd Haskell, a Democrat, defeated by William Armstrong, a Republican Congressman. Armstrong had been listed by Environmental Action as one of Congress's "Dirty Dozen" for his sorry environmental voting record while a Congressman in an adjoining district. But Mayor Mitchell is heartened by the position of Democratic Governor Richard Lamm, who recently counseled him: "[AMAX's] admission price to this community is going to be very high."

The result of Mayor Mitchell's activism has been an enormous amount of unprecedented co-operation between a giant corporation and a small community. Despite a unanimous vote by the Town Council on Feb. 20 to oppose the mine, the Mayor knows that it is hard to stop a billion-dollar-a-year corporation from doing what it wants. Messrs. Leinsdorf, Rademan and Hersch, lawyers all, also know that the Mining Law of 1872 guarantees mining companies access to all mineral deposits under

150

public lands. And so they are fighting what the Mayor calls a "gentlemen's war."

I was unprepared for all this cooperation. I had half expected to find a local Monkey Wrench Gang loose in the woods, pouring Karo syrup into bulldozers, dynamiting construction sites, rolling boulders down on workers' pickups. In fact, there has been some of that: a D-7 Caterpillar was riddled with rifle bullets, gas tanks have been sugared, and there was the shotgun blast through Terry Hamlin's window. A resident of Ohio Creek, an area threatened by the proposed tailings pond, said at a public hearing that if AMAX came to his valley, he would oppose the company by force, if necessary. AMAX, meanwhile, proudly points out in The Moly News that its security guards remain unarmed. So far.

In an attempt to anticipate problems before they happen, Messrs. Leinsdorf, Rademan, Hersch, Callaway and Mitchell and a talented young planner for Gunnison County, Jim Kuziak, are attempting an untried and radical method of dealing with the massive mining operation. As Mr. Leinsdorf explained it: "I'm not as concerned with the environmental consequences as I am by the boom-town syndrome, the spin-off that comes from rapid industrialization and a high rate of growth: social and economic problems, unemployment, crime, drug abuse, alcoholism, child abuse, transient workers. So we're trying to see to it that the development that comes does not overwhelm us. It's called the Colorado Review Process, involving AMAX, the Forest Service, the Colorado Department of Natural Resources and the County."

The Colorado Review Process (C.R.P.) was devised for reviewing proposed ski-area development, but it has never been applied to min-

AMAX, Inc. wants to construct a billion-dollar molybdenum mine similar to their other installations.

The entire town of Crested Butte is a national historic site, almost entirely surrounded by National Forest land.

ing. The process addresses such problems as housing, transportation, schools, sewage, air pollution and environmental impact. The C.R.P. is the brainchild of Mr. Leinsdorf's old Columbia Law School classmate Harris Sherman, director of the State's Department of Natural Resources and a Lamm appointee. AMAX has signed an agreement with the Forest Service, Gunnison County and Mr. Sherman's agency to participate in the C.R.P. It is an important breakthrough in a state that has probably been the least progressive in the West on questions of land use planning and mining controls.

Mr. Leinsdorf led the fight three years ago to have the Board of Commissioners adopt the county's Land Use Resolution, one of the most innovative documents of its kind in the country. He also insisted that AMAX and the Forest Service participate in the C.R.P. Mr. Leinsdorf has taken on corporate giants before: He was a co-author of the book "Citibank" for Ralph Na-

der, a critical look at the First National City Corporation. When the Crested Butte delegation went to Greenwich to see AMAX's top executive officers, Mr. Leinsdorf opened the meeting by telling a story about his first job, in the Antitrust Division of the Justice Department.

"I was given a filing cabinet full of files on a possible restraint-of-trade and monopolistic-practices case," he began. "I was told to examine all the evidence and either bring charges against the company or close the case. That company was American Metal Climax. I was to see if a company which produced 70 percent of the molybdenum in the United States was engaging in unfair practices." As the executives tensed up, Mr. Leinsdorf laughed and added, "I found none and closed the case. But now, 10 years later, 2,000 miles west of New York City, I'm involved with AMAX once again. Which just goes to show, there really is no running away."

In addition to the mine on the mountain, AMAX, Inc. has proposed a mill and tailings pond (slime dump) of staggering proportions. This is the proposed tailings site at Carbon Creek.

Mr. Leinsdorf believes that it is possible to make the Mount Emmons mine a model project. He sees the joint public review as an opportunity to develop a new process that could apply to the whole spectrum of natural-resource development throughout the West: uranium, copper, shale oil, gas and coal. In that spirit, AMAX has contributed $100,000 to the Gunnison County Planning Department, toward a computerized planning system. But Mr. Leinsdorf also told me, "If AMAX is not willing to build the mine on a scale and a schedule that maximizes the benefits to the county, I'm prepared to fight them and vote no on their zoning-change permit. The only way to keep the tourist and ranching economy from being overwhelmed is to do it on a smaller scale."

At the first C.R.P. hearing at Gunnison High School in September, 1978, every opinion on the mine was heard in the long, emotionally intense and crowded meeting. AMAX officials listened and answered questions very carefully. AMAX

emphasized employment and taxes, while the local governments pointed to environmental degradation, social upheaval and irreparable harm to the tourist industry.

Although public sentiment at that particular meeting was predominantly antimine, a few retired Crested Butte miners spoke in favor of it, remembering the prosperous coal-mining days of the 30's and 40's. One Gunnison businessman said Crested Butte had an "obligation to humanity to supply molybdenum to the world." A native Crested Butte resident stood up and shouted, "I can't eat scenery!"

At AMAX's Climax Molybdenum Division offices in Denver, I spoke with Stanley Dempsey, AMAX's vice president for external affairs. A jovial, thoughtful man of 39, Mr. Dempsey has taken on the burden of getting the mine built. He has spent a great deal of time in the Butte, where he is respected for his candor and sincerity.

"I think we're lucky to come into a place like

Two of the historic buildings in Crested Butte are the Old City Hall (left) and the old Slogar Building (above) which currently houses a restaurant.

Gunnison County, where both the traditional community and the new-life-style community are very sophisticated. Despite a strong heritage against a lot of government control, the county has had the political will to pass a strong Land Use Resolution. Few places have that on the book yet. I'd rather have a lot of sophisticated enemies to work with than a bunch of dumb friends."

Stan Dempsey was in charge of environmental controls during the construction of the gigantic Henderson molybdenum mine, a project now hailed in the mining world, and by conservationists as well, as the most environmentally sound mine and milling operation in the world. "I don't worry about the physical impact, I think we can handle that," he says. "The growth-management issue is the challenge. That's why we really believe in open planning.

We realized that the public was not going to put up with the kind of mining that's been done in the past and we know that we have to solve the housing and transportation problems which are the principal constraints on mining."

AMAX, at Mr. Dempsey's suggestion, recently organized an educational "boom-town tour" for 36 town and county officials to see what was going on in other mining towns. AMAX picked up the entire tab—charter planes, hotels and meals—for the tour of six Colorado and Wyoming boom towns recently "impacted" by energy and mineral development, including the infamous Gillette, often described as an "aluminum ghetto." Myles Rademan called me when he got back; the trip had backfired somewhat. "What we saw out there was a real mind blower. It was frightening. We will have to take a quantum leap to avoid becoming like them."

Stan Dempsey does not try to defend AMAX's environmental record at its Climax operation near Leadville, America's second-largest hard-rock mine. Nor does AMAX's public-relations director, Terry Fitzsimmons, who represents the third-generation of a Leadville mining family—his grandfather worked for Horace Tabor (of "The Ballad of Baby Doe" fame). Mr. Fitzsimmons said, "At Mount Emmons we plan to build a mine in keeping with the values of today. When Climax was built, the last thing miners or anyone else cared about was the environment."

In the Butte, it's the *first* thing anyone thinks about, and the residents continue to worry about their mountain's collapsing. "Subsidence," mining men call it, and people in the Butte don't want Mount Emmons to "subside," to crack and slip and cave in, as Bartlett Mountain did at AMAX's moly-ore mine at Climax.

One particularly concerned Butte citizen is Susan Cottingham, 30, the chairman of the legal committee of the High Country Citizens Alliance. This 140-person group devoted to preserving the quality of life in the mountains is challenging the idea that mining is the highest and best use of the land.

The mine is not unstoppable, she told me. "AMAX has been stopped from doing projects in Wyoming and Tennessee. If a lot of aggressive and very intelligent people can't stop it

here, the West might as well roll over and die. The technological dream of a 'model mine' belies human nature. I like a lot of the AMAX front men, but I don't believe their promises. I guess I'm an environmental paranoid. But then just look at their record."

Gil Hersch, down at his cramped Chronicle office, did exactly that. He reprinted a devastating report by some Tennesseans that carefully documented AMAX's coal, zinc, lead and copper operations in six states. "[AMAX has] a record of noncompliance with the law and of disregard for local citizens," the report stated. "Moreover, AMAX has shown a pattern of aloof resistance toward public officials, employees or ordinary citizens who have called upon the company to match its image with its performance."

In Colorado, AMAX has fought all "severance tax" proposals (taxing minerals as they leave the ground)—even though the money would be allocated to "impact mitigation," something to which AMAX says it is dedicated.

Chuck Malick, 28, is president of the High Country Citizens Alliance. The leather-worker and shopkeeper came with his wife to Colorado eight years ago as part of "the hippie dream." Standing by a crackling Ashley stove in his barn-wood paneled living room, I asked him: "This was a mining town. What's wrong with its becoming a mining town again?"

"We're not against mining," he explained. "The Keystone Mine operated here until 1975 and employed about 50 people. I'd welcome several small mines. Our concern is that the public should have something to say about the management of resources on public lands, especially in a fragile area like this. What the nation is being asked to do in the West, by mining and energy corporations like AMAX, is to sacrifice our national playgrounds. The old adage that there's always someplace else to go is just not true anymore."

Then Mr. Malick added, "All this environmental stuff is not just flowers and trees. You kill the recreational trade and I'm out of a job. And right now there is no unemployment here, but in mining boom towns the unemployment figures are around 11 or 12 percent. We don't need that."

The High Country Citizens Alliance has been

A million and a half campers, hikers, fishermen, backpackers, hunters, jeepers and skiers visit Gunnison National Forest each year.

156

successful in persuading the Forest Service, which has traditionally been overly cooperative with mining and timber interests, to consider a "no-action alternative" in its environmental-impact statement—that is, no mine. The Forest Service also listened to the Alliance's and to County Planner Kuziak's objection to AMAX's plan to build two 16-by-16-foot drifts (tunnels) to the ore body; it persuaded AMAX to put the tunnels "on hold" for now. It is the company's first setback.

Newly appointed Crested Butte Councilman Kirk Jones, a hard-drinking construction worker, claims that he represents 85 percent of the town's residents when he says, "I'm a consequence of the 60's and I'm tired of hearing about Leinsdorf's 'model mine.' I say to hell with the mine. Let the moly stay there; it could be a national reserve. Maybe in 30 years they'll have the technology to take it out without making a mess."

Myles Rademan says, "We're talking about our home here. I see this as a community struggle, not as an environmental fight." Which is why he led a trip to see Orville Schell in Bolinas, Calif., in summer 1978 with Messrs. Mitchell, Kuziak, Leinsdorf and Terry Hamlin, the AMAX public-relations man. Mr. Schell's book "The Town That Fought to Save Itself" chronicles a small community's battles with developers for control of its charming Pacific Coast town; and it's a kind of bible in Crested Butte. Myles Rademan wanted the group to meet the author, who commiserated with them. "Here was another community refusing to accept every indignity thrust upon it," says Mr. Rademan.

However, as a town planner, Mr. Rademan believes cooperation with AMAX is the town's best defense. "We're in a position of having to optimize something we don't really want," he explains. "From a professional standpoint, it's exciting. This project could be a model for how you industrialize sensitive areas, as energy and mining companies seek to take over the West. We can set a new level of corporate responsibility."

Corporate responsibility notwithstanding, Stan Dempsey wants to build his mine. But he's not sure it's economically feasible for AMAX to do the project on a scale any smaller than originally proposed. After two years of studies and talk, the big company is beginning to dig in its heels as it attempts to meet an already delayed timetable for construction (work is scheduled to begin in 1981).

And the Crested Butte Town Council won't listen any longer to AMAX's plans for a mine and mill the size the company wants. They are standing fast, as they made clear in their resolution calling for "a stop to the proposed activity on the Mount Emmons project...until a real benefit to Gunnison County and the nation can be shown." When Mayor Mitchell gaveled the unanimous vote, the first time town officials went on record against the mine, 250 people attending the meeting whistled and cheered, as television cameras recorded the event.

□

The gentlemen's war is heating up. On Washington's Birthday, 1979, 30 members of the High Country Citizens Alliance ski-toured over the range to Aspen and held a street protest against AMAX. In early March, two commissioners from adjoining Pitkin County led a delegation from Aspen and cross-country skied back over the high-mountain route to Crested Butte, where they held a rally in opposition to the mine. It's not clear now what is going to happen to Gunnison County and the town of Crested Butte, but the people on the front lines in this fight to determine the future of some of our most beautiful Western lands know what they don't want. The lines are drawn in a battle that will be repeated in dozens of Crested Buttes throughout the country in the 1980's.

157

Love Canal, U.S.A.

by Michael H. Brown

In the years since Rachel Carson's "Silent Spring," a great national concern has arisen over air and water pollution. It now appears that pollution seeping into the earth itself has gone largely unnoticed and in some cases may be far more dangerous as a direct cause of cancer and other severe human illnesses. "Toxic chemical waste," says John E. Moss, who was chairman of the House Subcommittee on Oversight and Investigations before his retirement this month, "may be the sleeping giant of the decade." Not until the nightmare of the Love Canal unfolded in Niagara County, N.Y., did Americans become aware of the vast dangers of ground pollution. But the problem since then seems only to be worsening.

Each year, several hundred new chemical compounds are added to the 70,000 that already exist in America, and the wastes from their production—nearly 92 billion pounds a year—are often placed in makeshift underground storage sites. Federal officials now suspect that more than 800 such sites have the potential of becoming as dangerous as those at the Love Canal and some are probably already severely hazardous

to unsuspecting neighbors. The problem is how to find them and how to pay the enormous costs of cleaning them up before more tragedy results. So far, Federal, state and local governments have been, for the most part, reluctant to face the issue.

Sometime in the 1940's—no one knows or wants to remember just when—the Hooker Chemical Company, which is now a subsidiary of Occidental Petroleum, found an abandoned canal near Niagara Falls, and began dumping countless hundreds of 55-gallon drums there. In 1953, the canal was filled in and sold to the city for an elementary school and playground (the purchase price was a token $1), and modest single-family dwellings were built nearby. There were signs of trouble now and then—occasional collapses of earth where drums had rotted through, and skin rashes in children or dogs that romped on the field—but they were given little thought until the spring of 1978. By then, many of the homes were deteriorating rapidly and were found to be infiltrated by highly toxic chemicals that had percolated into the basements. The New York State Health Depart-

158

*This infra-red photo shows the ground pollution in the schoolyard
and backyards in the Love Canal area.*

ment investigated and discovered startling health problems: birth defects, miscarriages, epilepsy, liver abnormalities, sores, rectal bleeding, headaches—not to mention undiscovered but possible latent illnesses. In August, President Carter declared a Federal emergency. With that, the state began evacuating residents from the neighborhood along the Love Canal, as it is named after the unsuccessful entrepreneur, William Love, who built it in 1894. Two hundred homes were boarded up, the school was closed and the nation got a glimpse of what Senator Daniel Patrick Moynihan called "a peculiarly primitive poisoning of the atmosphere by a firm."

But it was clearly not so peculiar. Since then, new dumping grounds have been reported in several precarious places. Under a ball field near another elementary school in Niagara Falls health officials have found a landfill containing many of the same compounds; it was discovered because the ball field swelled and contracted like a bowl of gelatin when heavy equipment moved across it. Officials have discovered, too, that Hooker disposed of nearly four times the amount of chemicals present in the Love Canal several hundred feet west of the city's municipal water-treatment facility, and residues have been tracked inside water-intake pipelines. Across town, near Niagara University, a 16-acre

Hooker landfill containing such killers as Mirex, C-56 and lindane—essentially chemicals that were used in the manufacture of pest killers and plastics—has been found to be fouling a neighboring stream, Bloody Run Creek, which flows past drinking-water wells. About 80,000 tons of toxic waste are said to have been dumped there over the years.

Still worse, as the company recently acknowledged, Hooker buried up to 3,700 *tons* of trichlorophenol waste, which contains one of the world's most deadly chemicals, dioxin, at various sites in Niagara County between 1947 and 1972. Investigators immediately sought to determine whether dioxin had seeped out and, indeed, the substance was identified in small quantities within leachate taken from the periphery of the Love Canal, an indication that it may have begun to migrate. There are now believed to be an estimated 141 pounds of dioxin in the canal site—and as much as 2,000 pounds buried elsewhere in the county. The Love Canal is above the city's public water-supply intake on the Niagara River but a quarter of a mile away; the other sites are closer—in one case within 300 feet—but downstream of the intake. However, the Niagara flows into Lake Ontario, which Syracuse, Rochester, Toronto and several other communities make use of for water supply. Although health officials regard the dioxin discovery as alarming, they do not yet consider it a direct health threat because it is not known to have come into contact with humans or to have leached into water supplies. Academic chemists point out, however, that as little as *three ounces* of dioxin are enough to kill more than a million people. It was dioxin, 2 to 11 pounds of it, which was dispersed in Seveso, Italy, after an explosion at a trichlorophenol plant: Dead animals littered the streets, hundreds of people were treated for severe skin lesions and 1,000 acres had to be evacuated.

Two weeks ago, New York State health officials began to examine and conduct studies of residents and workers in the Niagara University area because of the dioxin concentrations. One local physician there expresses concern over an apparently high rate of respiratory ailments, and union officials say that workers in industries alongside the landfill are suffering from emphysema, cancer and skin rashes. Cats

have lost fur and teeth after playing near Bloody Run; some young goats have died after grazing on its banks, and the creek is devoid of all aquatic life.

So far, there are at least 15 dumps in Niagara County alone that have been discovered to contain toxic chemicals. But no one in the county, or anywhere else in the country, is sure exactly where underground dumpsites are. Of the thousands of covered pits suspected of containing toxic wastes in the United States, the U.S. Environmental Protection Agency says it is a fair estimate that as many as 838 are, or could become, serious health hazards. But the machinery to carry out the kind of monitoring and inspecting now being done in Niagara County does not generally exist elsewhere. And the

A young Love Canal resident sits dejectedly by a fenced off area considered to be dangerous by the New York State Health Department.

E.P.A., internal memorandums reveal, has not been eager to set it up because of the extraordinary expense and political problems that would inevitably present themselves. In fact, one regional official was reprimanded for trying to get the type of action that must be taken to guard against another Love Canal.

In at least one known case there are symptoms disturbingly similar. Just 400 feet from a residential area in Elkton, Md., is a disposal area that, according to E.P.A. files, was used both by the Galaxy Chemical Company and by a suspected, unidentified midnight hauler. Residents have complained of sore throats, respiratory problems and headaches, all reminiscent of the early days of trouble at the Love Canal. One local doctor contends that the cancer death rate in the area is 30 times greater than elsewhere in the county, though his report is the subject of much controversy. So far, no evidence of direct human contact with leachate is known to have occurred there, as it did at Niagara Falls; nor have residents demanded evacuation.

In Rehoboth, Mass., 1,000 cubic yards of resins left over from a solvent redistilling process were ordered removed from a dumpsite that the owner had placed within 10 feet of his own house. In Lowell, Mass., some 15,000 drums and 43 tanks of assorted toxic wastes are at present being removed from a site within 200 yards of homes, and chemicals leaking from the drums are appearing in sewers and a nearby river.

Authorities in Michigan claim that the beleaguered Hooker Company has dumped C-56 into sandy soil, contaminating public wells, which have been closed off, and polluting White Lake, near Montague; the state is trying to force the company into a $200 million cleanup. Hooker has also been involved in lawsuits filed by maimed workers in Hopewell, Va., who became sterile and lost their memories after exposure to Kepone, a pesticide that Allied Chemical and Hooker jointly made and packaged.

The U.S. Comptroller General, at the request of Congress, has mapped out stretches through much of the East, Texas and Louisiana and parts of Oregon, Washington and California as regions with the greatest potential for trouble. "Texans are only now becoming concerned about solid-waste disposal," says Doris Ebner,

environmental manager for the Houston-Galveston Area Council. "What will happen is that there will be some disaster to make a flash." But serious ground investigations are still not given a top priority.

□

The tendency not to connect health problems with ground pollution has certainly been widespread. In the past, ground pollution was not a major concern in Niagara Falls, either. Because that city is relatively small and has a cheap source of hydroelectricity for chemical firms, most of its people have lived their whole lives on top of or near the hidden strains and goo of industrial pollution. Children near the chemical dumpsites often played with phosphorescent rocks, which would explode brilliantly when they were thrown against concrete. Dirt on the old canal had turned white, yellow, red, blue and black; rocks were orangish; and cesspools of caustic sludge gushed from several locations. These manifestations were viewed more as a matter of esthetics than as a health problem.

But indiscriminate dumping, dumping whatever wherever, has been a national way of life. Though American manufacturers of plastics, pesticides, herbicides and other products that produce huge amounts of toxic wastes are beginning to deposit them in centralized landfill sites—which may insure a closer inspection—the common practice has been to dispose of residues and forget about them. This has been true of private individuals as well, from independent haulers to local farmers.

Farmlands, because they make for nicely isolated dumping grounds, have posed special problems. In 1974, a 100-square-mile pastureland around Darrow and Geismar, La., was found to be contaminated with hexachlorobenzene (HCB), which was produced by the volatilization of wastes dumped into pits. HCB, a byproduct of the manufacture of carbon tetrachloride and perchloroethylene, causes liver deterioration, convulsions and death. During a routine sampling of beef fat by the U.S. Department of Agriculture as part of the Meat and Poultry Inspection Program, 1.5 parts per million of HCB was tracked in the meat of a steer belonging to W. I. Duplessis of Darrow. Further samplings showed that cattle were carrying the same toxin. Soil and vegetation were likewise tainted. The dumps were covered with plastic and dirt, and 30,000 cattle were ordered destroyed. The cattle were fed special diets instead of being slaughtered, however, and moved away from the area; their levels receded to an "acceptable" point, and only 27 were deemed unmarketable and killed. No one can be sure how many cattle, grazing near dumpsites elsewhere, have made it to the dinner table undetected.

Several years ago in Perham, Minn., 11 persons suffered arsenic poisoning from leaching grasshopper bait. Those struck with contamination worked for a building contractor who drilled a well 20 feet from where bait had been

buried by a farmer 30 years before. Severe neuropathy cost one of the employees the use of his legs for six months.

Much of past dumping has been plainly illegal. New Jersey, one of the most industrialized states and one whose cancer rate has been found to be substantially higher than the national average, has been a favorite spot for midnight haulers, or "scavengers," paid to cart off wastes and unload them in swamps, sewers, pits or abandoned wells to avoid paying for disposal at approved sites. In Coventry, R.I., officials found an illegal and highly toxic dump on a pig farm owned by a convicted gambler. It contained one suspected cancer-causing agent, carbon tetrachloride, and another compound that

Chemical wastes are not always disposed of properly, causing health hazards for future generations.

New York State Department of Health researchers testing the soil in the Love Canal area.

will ignite at 80 degrees Fahrenheit.

More blatant violators have been known simply to loosen tank-truck valves and get rid of contaminants along roadways in the dark of night. The owner of a New York company that reprocesses electrical transformers is currently on trial on charges of deliberately spilling out polychlorinated biphenyls (PCB's) from his truck onto 270 miles of a highway in North Carolina, and 700 residents of the Warrenton, N.C., area recently protested a state plan to create a new dump there for some 40,000 cubic yards of the tainted soil.

In other instances, dangerous conditions have been brought about more innocently. In Missouri, dioxin was discharged into waste oil and the oil was later sprayed on three race tracks and a farm road to control dust. Some 63 appaloosa and quarter horses, 6 dogs, 12 cats and

a large number of birds died as a result. A child who frequently played on the dirt road was rushed to the hospital with severe bladder pains and urinary bleeding.

Ground pollution's greatest threat is to the national drinking supply. More than 100 million Americans depend upon ground water as the major source of life's most vital fluid. Springs and wells, as opposed to rivers and lakes fed by running streams, are the main drinking reservoirs in 32 states. Florida's population, for example, is 91 percent dependent on ground water. Pouring tons of chemicals into the earth can be comparable, in an indirect way, to disposing of poisonous wastes upstream from a municipal river intake.

Chemical landfills never lie dormant. When water penetrates buried wastes, it removes soluble components, producing a grossly polluted

163

liquid leachate that extends out from the dump. Therein resides the danger. Leaching can continue, at any given site, for more than 100 years, picking up dangerous, stable materials and spreading them around a surprisingly large area. E.P.A.'s Office of Solid Waste has guessed that the average landfill site, about 17 acres in size, produces 4.6 million gallons of leachate a year if there are 10 inches of rainfall. In the spring of 1978, the Comptroller General reported that a *billion* gallons of ground water had been polluted near an Islip, L.I., landfill. A contaminated aquifer that was a mile long and 1,300 feet wide spoiled some drinking-water wells, which had to be sealed off and the homes connected to another source. In humid regions, where rainfall exceeds evaporation, the problem is most acute: The more water in the ground, the more leaching occurs.

Several years ago the Union Carbide Corporation contracted with an independent hauler to remove an unknown number of drums from its Bound Brook, N.J., facility. Inside were wash solvents and residues from organic chemical and plastics manufacture. Instead of going to the Dover Township landfill, much of the waste was dumped on a former chicken farm in the Pleasant Plains section of Dover. Mr. and Mrs. Samuel Reich had leased the land to Nicholas Fernicola on the assumption, according to case files, that he was in the drum-salvaging business. When the Reichs smelled pungent odors emanating from the property, they investigated the land and found thousands of containers, both buried and strewn about the surface. Additional drums were discovered in a wooded area near the Winding River, four miles away. The drums were hauled away under court order, but the damage had been done. Sufficient quantities of chemicals had already entered the environment, and early in 1974 residents of the area began tasting and smelling strange things in their water. Dover's Board of Health, in emergency action, passed an ordinance forbidding the use of 148 wells and ordering that they be permanently sealed. Although there were no documented cases of illness as a result, it is difficult to determine how many residents had consumed potentially harmful substances before the odors were noted. Equally difficult is determining where and how far the leachate traveled.

The Government itself has been the cause of serious ground-water contamination. Sloppy storage at the Rocky Mountain Arsenal, formerly an Army production center for chemical-warfare agents, led to the contamination of 30 square miles of shallow aquifer near Denver and, in turn, to the abandonment of 64 wells used for drinking water and irrigation. Waterfowl in the area died, and poisoned soil turned sugar beets and pasture grasses a sickly yellow. An estimated $78 million will be needed to complete the proposed cleanup, but there is no way of recovering the chemicals that have already escaped. One irrigation well that shows traces of contamination is only a mile south of the city of Brighton's public well field. The arsenal dug an injection well 12,045 feet deep for immediate disposal, but such facilities do little to insure against long-range migration; as it turned out, the well caused earth tremors and had to be closed.

In 1976, President Ford signed into law the Resource Conservation and Recovery Act. It may become an important piece of legislation, if the E.P.A. decides to implement it. This new law provides for a hazardous-waste regulatory program, control of open dumping, an inventory of disposal sites, and grants and programs for communities to set up solid-waste management systems. The passage of that law was provoked by the fact that toxic-waste disposal not only has gone unwatched, but is indeed increasing at an alarming rate. The chief reason for the increase is, paradoxically, the imposition of air and water pollution regulations that have stepped up the practice of burying materials in the ground. Issuance of new disposal regulations was supposed to have been made within 18 months of the President's signature, but today the E.P.A. is predicting that they will not be ready before 1980.

Spurred by the Love Canal crisis, Representative Moss's House subcommittee met last fall to determine what was happening to the law. It was a discouraging hearing. Hugh B. Kaufman, an E.P.A. official assigned to look for landfill problems, told the Congressmen that the agency's policy has been to avoid finding such situations. "There were no guidelines in this memorandum [on landfills] for the regional office to alert the public to the potential dangers," Kaufman testified. "In fact, the memo further instructed the regions not to find new problem sites because they might be required to provide this information to Congress and the public." On July 16, according to Mr. Kaufman, Steffen Plehn, head of E.P.A.'s Office of Solid Waste, told him to stop looking for imminent hazards. Mr. Plehn admitted that Mr. Kaufman's statement was essentially true, but the reason, he said, was that jurisdiction for such matters was being defined under the agency's enforcement division while his unit was culling a "data base." The problem, according to Mr. Plehn, was bureaucratic.

As long ago as April 20, 1978, and more than three months before officials recognized the Love Canal as an emergency, Mr. Kaufman

Special precautions must be taken for disposing of hazardous materials such as pesticide containers to prevent future Love Canal-type contamination.

wrote John P. Lehman, E.P.A.'s Hazardous Waste Management Division director, and said it was "imperative" that dumpsites across the country be cleaned up immediately. "We are receiving reports that, for the most part, the state of hazardous-waste management in the U.S. is as bad or worse than it was when Congress passed [the Resource Conservation and Recovery Act]," Mr. Kaufman wrote, "I recommend that we shift our policy emphasis and not close our eyes to the fact that hazardous-waste facilities located in many states are presenting hazards to the public." Neither E.P.A. officials nor regional offices paid much attention to that advice. When Mr. Lehman warned E.P.A.'s regional office for Ohio that a chemical facility in Akron might be an "imminent hazard" (it appeared to be leaking chemicals into drinking wells), the office sent back a pointed note reprimanding him for "loosely" using the term "imminent hazard" and stating that the region's Air and Hazardous Material Division did "not intend to send any person from this office out to inspect the facility at this time." At about the same time, Mr. Plehn wrote Mr. Lehman a memorandum suggesting that he "put a hold on all imminent-hazard efforts."

But the agency cannot be held as the sole culprit. Its large volume of responsibilities—from car emissions to microwaves—is an awesome task. And it often gets little help from state, county and city agencies. The Niagara County health department and the city government did not consider the Love Canal situation an emergency, for example, and, in fact, played down the problem, and the New York State Department of Environmental Conservation did little in the way of investigation. Not until the state Department of Health stepped in was the matter regarded as urgent.

Much of the randomness with which chemical companies have chosen their dumping grounds over the years will no doubt continue until the Resource Conservation and Recovery Act is implemented. Even then the problem will not go away. There is simply no such thing as a totally secure, self-contained landfill, a fact even those in the business admit. "There is no proof a landfill, 100 years from now, won't leach," says Paul Chenard, president of SCA Chemical Waste Services Inc. He says disposal methods have been improved. Pits can be lined with a special plastic. Waste-disposal firms can excavate on clay-based soil, compact the ground, install standpipes to pump out leachate, and slope the final cover to minimize rain infiltration. But the state of the art is new and no one issues guarantees. Many environmentalists feel that only when there is "cradle-to-death" legislation demanding that wastes be rendered innocuous before disposal will the problem be under control, and there are no signs of that happening in the near future.

□

An E.P.A. memorandum has listed more than 32,254 storage, treatment and disposal sites, both on and off industrial premises, as existing in the nation. In an earlier breakdown, California ranked first, with 2,985; Pennsylvania, New York, Ohio and Texas were not far behind. Those statistics, officials emphasize, refer only to *known* sites. And even at the known sites the quality of the treatment is questionable. One estimate is that less than 7 percent of the 92 billion pounds of chemical waste generated each year receives proper disposal. After working in Niagara Falls for several months, Dr. David Axelrod, New York State Health Commissioner, says the overall problems of improper disposal and treatment "are incredibly immense." The Hooker Company—which contends that it did not know the possible dangers and was simply disposing of wastes as everyone else did—is already faced with claims against it in excess of $2 billion, and citizens' demands upon the state are only just beginning. New discoveries of dioxin are prompting new demonstrations, new arrests of demonstrators and new requests for evacuation and relocation. Patricia Pino, whose home in Niagara Falls is now unmarketable, was one of those arrested. "We request a reprieve from death row," she telegraphed Gov. Hugh Carey. "We are innocent of any crime." Her two children have liver abnormalities, and she has learned that she herself has cancer.

Cancer Safety

by William E. Burrows

Sometimes a simple question put by a layman can get to the heart of a complex scientific problem more surely than expert interrogation. So it was at the New York Academy of Sciences' International Conference on Public Control of Environmental Health Hazards in 1978. Peter A. A. Berle, then New York State's Environmental Conservation Commissioner, had just unveiled a plan for dredging heavily contaminated "hot spots" along the upper Hudson River of 340,000 pounds of the PCB's that had been dumped into the waterway by the General Electric Company. A succession of health officials, scientists and corporate representatives rose to question Mr. Berle about the details of removing the PCB's (polychlorinated biphenyls—heat-resistant chemicals used for insulating transformers and capacitors), which have been shown to cause birth defects, reproductive failure and cancer in animals, and are strongly suspected of being carcinogenic to man.

When her turn came, Carolyn Cunningham, the head of the Conservation Advisory Council for Rye, N.Y., whose "Tuesday Only" tag indicated her limited status at the meeting, stepped to the microphone and asked a question so elementary that none of the experts in the room would have dreamed of raising it. Yet the answer to it continues to elude and confound them all: "The acceptable level for PCB's has been set at 5 parts per million. Is that level safe?"

Mr. Berle deferred to Leo Hetling, then his director of pure-waters research, who answered: "That's like asking how many cigarettes can one safely smoke. The Food and Drug Administration considers it safe for eating fish."

Mrs. Cunningham was not satisfied with Mr. Hetling's evasive reply. But his smoking analogy amounted to the plain truth. No one knows exactly how many PCB's the human body can safely assimilate, so setting "acceptable" levels for them, as well as for thousands of other dangerous chemicals, including saccharin, is scientifically absurd.

Saccharin, in fact, is currently the object of a bitter controversy over whether it should be banned in the United States, as it is in Canada. Repeated laboratory tests have showed that the artificial sweetener causes cancer in animals and almost without question can do the same in humans. While acknowledging that saccharin can be lethal, a National Academy of Sciences panel recommended to Congress that the additive be restricted but not banned entirely, since it is considered necessary for those who must restrict their sugar intake. There were 12 vigorous dissenters among the 37 panel members, however. Some of them went so far as to contend that there is really no scientific basis for setting human risk levels for carcinogens and that dividing additives into risk categories is, therefore, senseless. Meanwhile, the House Subcommittee on Health and the Environment scheduled hearings on saccharin amid what was one of the fiercest lobbying battles in memory.

Levels of acceptability—the doses of chemicals and radiation people may safely absorb—are becoming critically important now that so many cancers are thought to be environmentally caused. And since most cancer-causing chemicals have long latency periods, the real effects of the petrochemical explosion of the 40's, 50's and 60's are only just beginning to be felt. An estimated 400,000 Americans will die of cancer this year and it is thought that 20 percent of all Americans now living—perhaps one out of every five reading this—are going to die of some form of cancer unless something is done about it, and quickly.

Yet none of the public-health officials who set acceptable levels for the thousands of chemicals we eat, drink and breathe can be absolutely sure that those levels adequately protect the public from serious illness or deadly disease. Any dose of a toxin, however low, involves some risk. But trying to calculate the precise degree of risk is incredibly difficult.

To make matters worse, the entire level-setting process takes place in a regulatory morass involving several Federal agencies and a dozen laws (each of which is to some extent vague, inconsistent or contradictory), state and local agencies, the courts, Congress, business interests, environmentalists, "independent" testing laboratories, the National Academy of Sciences, hospitals and universities, a legion of lobbyists, and a growing number of health functionaries on virtually all levels of government. The result is pandemonium.

In the end, economic, not scientific, factors frequently prevail. Often these are incorporated

into law. The Toxic Substances Control Act, for example, stipulates that health risks be balanced against economic factors and other "public impacts." It is the scientists and statisticians, however, on whom we must depend to apply data from cellular and animal experiments in an effort to figure out how much of which poison, individually and in combination, the human body can tolerate. But E. Cuyler Hammond, a vice president of the American Cancer Society and an expert statistician, says that the process, though seemingly sound, is basically "by guess and by God."

Yet industrialists, lawyers, politicians and economists in essence take these numbers, imprecise as they are, and present the public with difficult choices: How much of these poisons are you willing to live with? If you don't swallow a little poison every day—a level we agree is acceptable—you will be thrown out of work and the country will go to the dogs. The strong suggestion is that eating, drinking and breathing a certain amount of toxins is the inevitable price of progress. We are, in effect, being conditioned to accept man-made poisons in our air, food and water as being normal.

The vast majority of people, however, never think of challenging these choices until a Love Canal starts bubbling under their feet or a James River is closed to fishing. Then they react with outrage; not because it happens, but because it happens to them.

Lawyers play key roles in level setting because the process is not so much an ongoing clash of opposing scientific truths as one between conflicting social and economic priorities. Regulatory agencies have a real fear of being sued by industry, according to Dr. Sidney Wolfe, a physician who was on the staff of the National Institutes of Health before becoming director of Ralph Nader's Health Research Group in Washington. "In order to keep the agency out of court, they act only when they have the most open-and-shut case," he claims. "When we go into a hearing, we not only see lawyers from industry, but Wall Street analysts, too. There's big money at stake."

□

What's acceptable and what isn't is most often associated with something called cost-

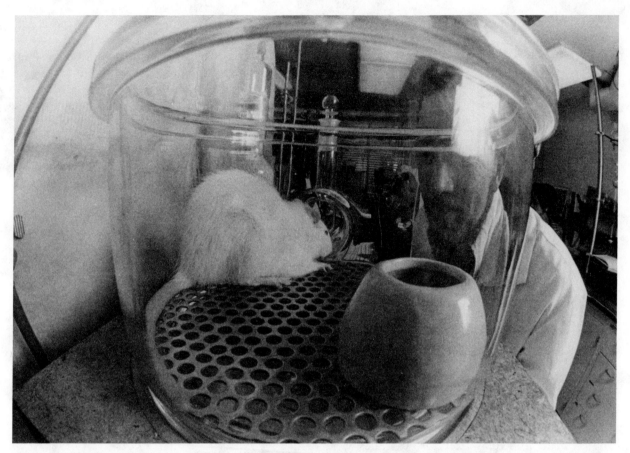

Repeated laboratory tests have shown that Saccharin causes cancer in animals.

benefit, or risk-benefit, analysis. Deceptively simple in theory, it weighs pluses and minuses. The benefits of, say, asbestos are added: fire-resistant homes, schools and offices, plus jobs for asbestos workers, and their combined effect on the economy. The minuses are also totaled: the sharply increasing numbers of people dying from lung cancer, and the cost of caring for the ill and supporting the survivors.

If benefits clearly outweigh costs, it is full speed ahead. If costs far outweigh benefits, the product either never sees the light of day or, if already on the market, is canceled. There are generally no clear-cut imbalances, however, so some level thought to be acceptable is invented.

This raises a fundamental question: To whom, exactly, is the level acceptable? When a newscaster says that "the quality of air today is acceptable," to whom is he or she referring? What is acceptable to the taxi driver who must earn a living with his automobile is not necessa-

rily acceptable to the asthmatic breathing the fumes—except at the moment when the asthmatic, having a seizure, needs the taxi in order to get to a hospital; then the taxi and its wake of noxious vapors become eminently acceptable to driver and passenger alike.

Although corporate lawyers and economists, as well as many in the public sector, maintain that it is perfectly fair to make production decisions and set acceptable levels after a careful weighing of all likely costs and benefits, others are beginning to challenge the concept on two grounds.

First, cost-benefit tries to equate what is economically, let alone morally, unequatable: kilowatt-hours of electricity produced by a nuclear power plant versus the number of cancer deaths caused by a slow radiation leak at the site where the spent fuel is stored, for example. This kind of equation makes no sense unless we can decide how many kilowatt-hours of electricity a human life is worth.

Second, those who pay the costs and those who derive the benefits are not necessarily the same. Men who dig coal pay a heavy cost in terms of cave-ins, poisoned air and black lung, yet their monetary benefit is not commensurate with those risks.

Before a meaningful scientific basis can be established for setting truly acceptable levels, a deeply important question needs to be answered: Exactly how much of a given substance does it take to cause a human cell to turn cancerous? If no one knows, then every person who believes that there is some magic formula that constitutes a boundary between safety and death is seriously misguided. If there are boundaries, they stand not so much between health and illness as between profit and loss.

The vast majority of those in cancer research think that environmentally caused cancer is the result of something called a dose-response relationship. This means that there is most likely some kind of direct relationship between the amount of the cancer-causing chemical a person is exposed to and the length of time it takes to contract the disease. A dose-response chart would have a line going from zero to maximum dose, with the risk accelerating and the time span shortening in proportion to the increasing dose.

The big question, though, is this: At precisely what point along that line will someone contract cancer? Given the fact that individuals vary, that there are long latency periods for most cancer-causing substances, and that combinations of chemicals are undoubtedly worse than the simple sum of their elements, it becomes impossible to pick a point on that line and say with certainty that it represents the start of a malignancy. That is what Leo Hetling meant when he asked about the number of cigarettes that can be safely smoked. No cigarette can be safely smoked, but it is impossible to tell which of the thousands upon thousands will be the one that begins the process of wild cellular growth that is cancer.

There are currently two principal ways in which scientists try to determine what causes cancer and how much of it is too much: studying groups of humans and testing animals. Neither method is wholly satisfactory. Epide-

miology compares groups that are exposed to certain kinds of chemicals and radiation with control groups that are not exposed. It has some serious shortcomings, however. For one thing, it is impossible to isolate people, like laboratory animals, for most or all of their lives, so it is impossible to know about everything they eat, drink and breathe. Further, the cause and effect relationship in epidemiological studies is often weak. Asbestos workers *do* have a higher percentage of lung cancer than does the general public, but that does not necessarily mean the asbestos causes the cancer; it may mean that asbestos fibers in the lungs trigger something else that causes the cancer. Finally, epidemiologists are hampered by usually small groups, individual resistance to participation and, in a society as mobile as this one, the difficulty of access to good records.

Animal experiments, generally with rodents, have for the most part been very effective in determining whether a given chemical is carcinogenic. But there are many scientists who argue that applying such data to humans, which is called extrapolation, can be misleading. "There

"There is no reason to believe that what causes cancer in animals will do it in human beings and vice versa," says Dr. Irving J. Selikoff.

We depend on scientists and statisticians, such as E. Cuyler Hammond of the American Cancer Society to apply data from experiments and tell us which poisons the human body can tolerate.

is no reason to believe that what causes cancer in animals will do it in human beings, and vice versa," says Dr. Irving J. Selikoff, director of the Environmental Sciences Laboratory in the Mount Sinai School of Medicine in New York. "If you can't extrapolate from a mouse to a rat, how can you do it from a mouse to a man?" he asks. Dr. Selikoff does not question the value of animal experiments, but only maintains that biological systems and responses vary even between different species of rodents, so precise relationships between rodents and humans are just that much more difficult to establish. Furthermore, a typical animal experiment involves 100 or fewer test animals, yet it costs upward of $250,000.

Since the regulatory agencies are not funded to perform anywhere near the number of necessary experiments (there are about 35,000 different pesticide formulations alone), the chemical manufacturers, themselves, incredibly, assume that responsibility. Testing is either done in-house or, more often, is farmed out to "independent" laboratories. In that chemical and drug companies are in business to sell their wares, not to see them squelched in laboratories for being dangerous to human health, it is not too far fetched to suggest that these labs give their clients' concoctions every reasonable doubt.

In mid-1977, the Environmental Protection Agency and the Food and Drug Administration began joint audits of 100 laboratories. Only three, Industrial Bio-Test Laboratories of Northbrook, Ill., and two other labs doing far less testing, have been found to have deficiencies, according to Fred T. Arnold, chief regulatory analyst for pesticides at the E.P.A. And deficiences, he adds, are not necessarily deliberately caused. Until the aftermath of that audit, Industrial Bio-Test was one of the biggest of

171

the "independents" and did about 4,300 pesticide tests for such companies as American Cyanamid, Chevron, Ciba-Geigy, Dow, Gulf, 3M, Monsanto, Shell and Velsicol, plus the United States Department of Agriculture and the F.D.A. itself.

According to Mr. Arnold, his agency has no direct authority to regulate laboratories, but it can require that manufacturers undertake "stringent" testing of pesticides by whatever means are necessary. If the tests are judged inadequate or distorted, the E.P.A. can order them repeated, which is what is now happening in the Industrial Bio-Test case. But, Mr. Arnold says, what with redosing and reanalyzing, it will be two years before the various toxicity levels are fully determined. Meanwhile, some of the 123 pesticides in question, among them several of the most heavily used in the world, remain in mass production.

□

Toxic chemicals, including those that can cause cancer, are supposed to be regulated directly by four Federal agencies:

The Environmental Protection Agency, the largest of the regulators, which is responsible for protecting the overall environment.

The Food and Drug Administration, operating under the Department of Health, Education and Welfare, which is responsible for drugs, food, cosmetics, medical devices, television sets and microwave ovens.

The Consumer Product Safety Commission, an independent agency, which monitors such consumer items as children's clothing, patching compound, and aerosol sprays.

The Occupational Safety and Health Administration (OSHA), part of the Department of Labor, which tries to control "hazards in the work-place," from asbestos particles in the air to the number of fire exits.

Although these agencies are required by law to do the actual regulating, they are merely the most visible part of a much larger mechanism. In addition to coming from industry and universities, many of the data used for decision making come from the National Cancer Institute, the National Institute of Environmental Health Science and the National Institute for Occupational Safety and Health. Then there are all of the other agencies, large and small, with primary responsibilities elsewhere which nonetheless become involved in toxic substances research and regulation.

In August 1977, the four main regulatory agencies spawned something called the Interagency Regulatory Liaison Group (I.R.L.G.), which is supposed to facilitate cooperation among them. An I.R.L.G. risk-assessment group announced in February, 1979, that it had come up with methods for deciding whether something is carcinogenic and, if so, on the extent of the risk it poses. The report was then submitted for peer review and public comment.

□

The situation has been so confused that when the E.P.A. recently asked the National Academy of Sciences to evaluate two pesticides—heptachlor and chlordane—one academy committee came up with a risk assessment, while another reported that it hadn't enough information to do so with reliability. The discrepancy came less from disagreement over the validity of extrapolating animal test data than from ambiguities in the law.

What is acceptable and what is not is terribly complicated by the 12 laws, each of which came out of a different Congressional committee, under which the four major agencies function. The Clean Air Act, Water Pollution Control Act, Safe Drinking Water Act and Federal Insecticide, Fungicide and Rodenticide Act, all administered by the E.P.A., permit cost-benefit analysis for setting acceptable levels, but do not require it. The Food, Drug and Cosmetic Act (F.D.C.A.), demands cost-benefit analysis in some instances and prohibits it in others. The F.D.C.A.'s controversial "Delaney clause" forbids carcinogenic additives from being put into food, but since PCB's (as one example) are environmental rather than an additive, they are not covered by the clause.

The elasticity of the Clean Air Act is likely to have prompted Charles L. Schultze, chairman of the Council of Economic Advisers, to warn E.P.A. Administrator Douglas Costle that his agency's broad new proposals to control air pollution would "impose substantially higher costs on business than is necessary." The E.P.A.,

A group of asbestos workers demonstrated for a medical clause in their contract to protect them against job related diseases.

bending to such pressure, weakened a proposed smog regulation for the first time in its history. More recently, a memorandum from Mr. Schultze and Alfred E. Kahn, the President's chief adviser on inflation, said that E.P.A.'s pending water-pollution regulations could be "prohibitively expensive" and that the whole program should be re-examined to relate the costs to the benefits. Here, laid bare, is the nub of the antiregulatory argument and the basis for most of the courtroom action: Following all of the rules and regulations is economically crippling and dangerously inflationary.

It is Mr. Schultze's use of the word "necessary" in the air-pollution warning that would send economists and ecologists going for one another's throats. How necessary is clean air and how clean should it be in order to be acceptable? What if requirements for super-duper clean air so constrict business that companies collapse and thousands are thrown out of work?

Would those unemployed workers rather have perfect air, inflation and no jobs, or not-so-perfect air, a healthy economy and work? This is the essence of industry's argument.

Although existing law stipulates that 5 parts per million is the allowable level in fish, as Leon Hetling told Carolyn Cunningham, the F.D.A. in fact proposed in April 1977 to lower that level to 2 parts per million, as Canada had already done. As required by law, the proposal appeared in the Federal Register. Interested parties were given 30 days to file objections and request a hearing.

Robert G. Martin, assistant vice president of the Sport Fishing Institute, an organization representing the multibillion-dollar sport-fishing industry, maintains that he has yet to see studies "implicating PCB's with human health. You really can't be against public health," he says, "but I find it difficult to see where human health has been involved." In checking his files,

Mr. Martin adds, "I could find no reference to the institute officially commenting on a proposal to lower allowable limits of PCB's from 5 to 2 parts per million." F.D.A. records, however, tell a different story. They show that Gilbert C. Radonski, executive secretary of the institute, sent a letter to the agency on May 23, 1977, which said that it "has not been demonstrated that an eminent health hazard exists that would justify a reduction in the total of PCB's in fish from 5 parts per million to 2 parts per million." The letter also called for more research on PCB's and for the issuance of "guidelines" on the best ways to prepare and cook fish contaminated by the chemicals. (The institute's motto is: "The Quality of Fishing Reflects the Quality of Living.")

Other fishing organizations, such as the Midwest Federated Fisheries Council and the National Fisheries Institute, and even the New York State Legislature, came out for delaying a lowering of the PCB tolerance level in fish "pending further studies on the drastic and possibly tragic economic implications any change would instigate." This position prompted one member of the New York PCB Settlement Advisory Committee to say privately, "What they want, at bottom, is a body count [before they believe that PCB's are carcinogenic to humans]." Meanwhile, the proposal to drop the PCB level, a classic victim of cost-benefit analysis, seems economically unacceptable and is now in limbo.

After years of notable victories by environmentalists, the economics-versus-ecology battle looks as though it is beginning to tilt the other way, in part because of persistent inflation and also because of an equally persistent mistrust of big government and its sluggish and meddling bureaucracy. Some observers even sense a growing backlash among citizens who feel that good old American enterprise is choking to death on hopelessly snarled red tape and ridiculous regulations. They feel, and with some justification, that they are overregulated and underprotected. (Given the President's announcement that OSHA was eliminating 928 "unnecessary" regulations, this sentiment seems at least partly shared by the Administration.)

But because of the long latency period, it is vital to work now to prevent as much cancer as possible in the year 2000, warns Dr. Irving Selikoff of Mount Sinai. "How much risk can you live with? That's the nature of the debate over the word 'acceptable,' and it must be decided by society, not by scientists."

There are about 100,000 known natural chemical entities, 1 to 5 percent of which are thought to be carcinogenic, according to Dr. W. Gary Flamm, a toxicologist in the Food and Drug Administration's Bureau of Foods. So, what do toxicologists eat?

"Everything," he says. "My philosophy is to spread the risk. If I ate one thing [in excess] I'd be in trouble."

Most grains, including corn, and peanuts develop a mold called *Aspergillus flavus* which, in turn, produces aflatoxin B, a known carcinogen. Peanut butter contains an almost infinitesimal level of aflatoxin B, says Dr. Flamm. But he adds, "This doesn't mean that you shouldn't eat peanut butter. All it means is that you'd be smart not to eat peanut butter, or anything else, exclusively."

A Family Miracle

by D. H. Melhem

An ordinary scene on a public tennis court in East Hampton: two parents with their children, playing doubles. Yet, as part of the foursome last summer, I knew we were somehow extraordinary. Most remarkable was the powerful right-hand swing of my former husband as he deftly placed the ball. His grip was secure. He ran confidently. There was no sign of paralysis, and when he spoke to our son who was using his new, birthday tennis racket, no stammer could be heard. I knew it was a very special moment, my daughter beside me, everyone in full sunlight, enjoying the game with a man reclaimed for living. Nearly six years before, a major stroke had left him paralyzed, speechless and then aphasic (afflicted with a major speech disorder). The stroke had come shortly after our divorce became final, yet we struggled together for the next two years to exceed the limited goals set by doctors, nurses, therapists and even family; we aimed for my husband's *complete* recovery.

The summer of our separation, I wrote my master's thesis. After a long hiatus, I had re-sumed my studies in contemporary American literature and was working toward my Ph.D. at the City University of New York. A year later, I had completed all course requirements and exams and was preparing for Ph.D. orals, which were scheduled for December. It was the last mountain before the Everest of the dissertation. My first book of poems was to be published in the fall.

On the last Saturday of September 1972, my teen-age son, Gregory, rushed home from a visit with his father, exclaiming, "Dad is acting funny." I telephoned; there was no answer. We sped to the apartment and found my husband, Chester, prone on the floor, wearing his robe and pajamas, dressed as our son had left him. He seemed to be sleeping peacefully, his head cradled in his left arm. I fell beside him and begged him to speak. He opened his eyes, regarding me with a fierce intensity. He opened his mouth to utter "Ah—ah—ah—" and closed it. The silent words lay frozen in his gaze. I did not realize that the right arm stretched at his side had become paralyzed. When he closed his eyes,

This action photo shows Chester restored to a full life and enjoying a vigorous game of tennis.

I rushed to the phone.

I called the police and an ambulance arrived. Within minutes, Chester was being wheeled on a stretcher into a hospital emergency room. As he lay waiting to be examined, I held his right hand. I was terrified that he might be comatose, or even dying.

"Do you hear me?" I implored. "Lift a finger if you do."

He opened his eyes and moved the fingers of his left hand. His expression seemed quite serene.

"Fine," I said. "You're going to be all right."

His face moved strangely and I realized he was trying to smile. Feeling myself about to weep, I kissed his hand.

"Your husband has suffered a stroke," the doctor said, as Chester, now asleep, reappeared from the emergency room. "We'll have to put him into intensive care." It was about 6:00 A.M. The doctor advised us to go home; the X-ray results would not be ready until late in the afternoon. Gregory and I clung to each other in the cab on the way home.

It was a massive stroke. The left side of the brain was affected, causing speech loss and paralysis on the right side. I asked the doctor how long it would take for recovery, expecting a convalescence of weeks or months. He looked at me pityingly.

"This is a major stroke," he said. "There could be another one; that's what we have to watch for now. Recovery is a very individual matter—we can't promise anything. Months—maybe years."

The words began to register. As I gazed at the good, familiar face in the bed, seeing the vulnerability of that proud frame, the facts of divorce and my new, barely won independence slipped away. The children drew closer, trying to find comfort in our solidarity against disaster. As generously sustaining as they were—how

176

they had comforted me in my grief over my mother's death three years earlier!—they looked at me with trust, full of children's faith in a parent's power over fate.

I remember the silence, Chester's eyes trying to communicate, the first faint signs of movement on his right side. And the initial utterance of that strangely nasal voice articulating a word which I recognized as my name.

From the beginning, with his first gesture in the emergency room, I felt that he could recover fully, and I told him so as soon as he could be made aware of it. My daughter, Dana, and son, Gregory, believed it, too. It became our mutual faith.

The immediate crisis passed. I received the papers announcing that our divorce had become final. My publisher delivered the first copies of my book, "Notes on 94th Street." And Chester was moved from intensive care to a comfortable room that he shared with another patient. He could look out at a courtyard, hospital buildings, the city. I remember the marvel of seeing him stand again about two weeks later, of his first steps using a walker. His speech, however, was nearly unintelligible. He would become frustrated, knowing that even though I might understand, his voice was strange and his words were distorted. Gradually, a more terrible realization grew: His speech was reflecting a serious disorder that would grossly impair his reading. He had been severely stricken with aphasia.

Therein lay a dreadful irony. A "master teacher" of remedial reading for many years was now afflicted with a reading disability worse than that of his high-school pupils. He saw letters and words inverted; he would see one thing and say another. Furthermore, he could not count or do the simplest arithmetic; he had to learn, like a child, that one and one made two and that there were five pennies in a nickel.

It was frightening for us to observe how much damage had been done to what had been considered primarily localized cerebral functions. We did not then know what research has now verified: that other areas of the brain are also involved in learning and locution. We have since learned that control of these capacities is far more generalized than had been assumed. Thus, if one area is affected, others may compensate.

As Chester began to communicate, I understood that most of his errors involved a highly developed intelligence. His brain was functioning on a plane of poetic metaphor. The doctor, for example, at times became the "chairman of the board" or the "president of the corporation," "nurse" became "waitress," by what might be classified in linguistics as "in-class substitution." Any unafflicted person could experience this, like recalling a cherry tree as a crab apple. Phrases were often poetically compressed. He would read "books offered for sale" as "your offers" or he might read "resort" as "hotel." At times, humor combined with infirmity. Seven weeks after the stroke, his nurse dictated to Chester the sentence, "I shall be going home soon." In response, Chester scrawled, "I don't recommend coming here." Though he couldn't always express things clearly, we accepted his patterns and backed the effort. His motivation was critical.

Knowing his interests, I was able to personalize his treatment. He loved art; I found a book of paintings with large titles which he would try to read. While frustration would sometimes overwhelm him, he enjoyed the reproductions and wanted to determine the names of the paintings. I bought an unlined, spiral notebook and made an alphabet, with letters for him to copy each day. I wrote numbers. I uttered words and phrases for him to repeat. He used colored Pentels to write and made a wonderful drawing of a pot of flowers. We discovered that a blackboard was especially useful; Chester could erase whatever he wanted to rewrite. The doctors soon became very interested in what we were doing; one said I was "inventing" helpful supplementary treatment.

Two weeks after the stroke, Chester made a circle of five dots with his affected right hand. The physiotherapist wanted him to train his left hand to write; but I, aware of the psychological strain involved in changing handedness, insisted that he be encouraged to develop his right, especially since its dexterity was returning. The lessons were nearly perpetual; even Gregory, and Dana, when she was home from college, became his teachers. Sometimes he tired of the nagging, the pressure to continue. But we knew that if we relented, if the seductive lethargy were ever to be given rein, we would all be lost.

The speech therapist thought my expectations were unrealistic; doctors and therapists seemed to turn mute when I suggested that Chester would teach again. I remember being appalled by the handbook they gave me, entitled "Caring for the Stroke Patient." It advised the family of a stroke patient to expect a *minimum* from their charge at home. The booklet almost seemed to encourage treating the patient like a handicapped child or a house pet.

Three weeks after the stroke, Chester said, "Words surround me. They are there." Adrift in that turbulent verbal sea, he would snatch at one, then another as they swirled past and floated beyond him. In a poem, I expressed the predicament: "You seek a word/ metaphors merge at their edges."

□

At the same time, I was waging a private battle—to hold fast to a dream (as in Langston Hughes's poem), my dream of taking orals and advancing to doctoral candidacy. I would rise at 6 A.M., breakfast, study, see Gregory off to school, study. Then I would rush to the hospital, day after day for 54 days. Gregory visited Chester every afternoon; Dana returned on weekends. Since we all helped with the reading and writing and there was so much to be done, there was no time for self-pity, even though I was falling farther and farther behind in my work.

It was not easy for a son and daughter to hear their father stammer over simple words and read them incorrectly, substituting phantom images, yet they accepted his difficulty, so that every correct syllable and word became a small victory, a group achievement. Like a picture that had been crudely erased, we were tracing, bit by bit, original lines and contours, reclaiming their vivid arrangements, remaking the work of art which is a maturely detailed human being. "The Child is father of the Man," as Wordsworth tells us. The children were, indeed, fathering the man, and we all were content with the rainbow of recovery.

After a stroke, major gains are made within six months; then the rate of recovery tapers off. For this reason, daily physiotherapy is begun as soon and as intensively as possible. There were massages and thermal applications, pulley exercises for the paralyzed hand and arm, bicycle workouts for the leg. Eventually, Chester could manage some of the exercises by himself. In addition, his private nurses were given lists of exercises which he was to continue in his room. Plastic clay was constantly in his fingers, or else balls of rubber and wool. He was encouraged to do as much as possible toward feeding and dressing himself. We always assured Chester that he was doing better and we *believed* that he was.

□

In early November, the doctors recommended an archarteriogram to determine both the cause of his stroke and whether another stroke was likely. Because it is a somewhat hazardous procedure, we had to sign for it, as if for major surgery. The results of the test showed that the two carotid arteries leading to his brain were badly clogged by cholesterol deposits, an undetected accumulation of many years. The left one, which had caused the stroke, seemed nearly closed. The right was 97 percent occluded, high up, and might cause a stroke in the near future. As a result, the two vertebral arteries (posterior) were enlarged, having developed over the years to carry the major circulatory load.

I called in consulting opinions, chiefly that of one particular specialist who concurred that immediate surgery was indicated to remove the cholesterol deposits. Responsibility weighed heavily, but the decision was made to go ahead with two separate operations, a week apart. We became curiously elated. Something wonderful might happen. We still believed in miracles.

□

It was now more than a month after the stroke. Chester was copying letters painfully but with their distinguishing characters in his notebook; he was beginning to read numbers; his recent memory was returning. One night, after we had worked on having him read back letters and numbers he had written, he read the date "1923." The four numbers, correctly identified in their order, were a marvel. Carefully and distinctly, he observed, "I am very impressed by the procedure of this night." We both knew that he meant "progress," but the substitution of "procedure" seemed elegant. All those words in coherent sequence. Beautiful words in that dear, strange voice. I wanted to cry.

Words: those floating, elusive symbols which did not always correspond or cohere. We were intrigued by Chester's notion that letters of the alphabet were shaped "in the hand"—that he was having difficulty writing legibly because, he said, the neural impulses in his hand were weak. I took notes on our conversations in my own notebook. His answers to my questions were often striking. In one exchange, he described his own progress:

Q: What do you feel when you can't express what you are trying to say?

A: Whenever I feel as well as I do—I am coming to another criterion. People who have stayed alive at that point have settled there. The rest, a very small number of people, have gone on to gain more and more, and less and less.

Chester himself suggested one question. The complexity and poetically symbolic nature of his response amazed me. His question was: "How are these impressions related to the whole condition?"

And he answered himself: "In the whole case —at the beginning, there seems to be a powerful residual meaning to the whole of life. It made it much more meaningful. Consequently, it made it much more meaningless as new transparent pressures began to mount, to keep the traditions for conditions to remain the same. I think the real aspect of life is coldness."

He spoke metaphorically of "a gray decrease into the future darkness."

In the same notebook there are drawings made by Gregory to illustrate words or concepts for his father: stick figures—"This is a man"; numbers; stock-market quotations; scientific cartoon drawings. Everywhere the necessary, tedious, frustrating repetition, repetition, repetition. That was the path to relearning.

It was Presidential election time; I went to the Board of Elections to get Chester an absentee ballot. I remember watching his right hand move laboriously across the ballot to form letters, barely legible, but letters, nonetheless. He was signing his name.

The day of the first surgery, I went down with Chester to the "O.R." floor, that place of life and death and renewal. The operation was not lengthy. The doctor came to the room to tell us that he had made only an exploratory incision. The left artery was completely closed. There was no blood circulating through it. Any opening or clearing might flood the brain, causing a lethal stroke. The second operation would be crucial.

There was simply not enough blood from the rear arteries to support normal functioning. And if something happened to them? I tried to mask my fear. We consented to the next archarteriogram and the next operation.

How to face it? The children were staunch. Faith, like the very bone and marrow of the soul, was being put into the caldron of our lives. Dana and Gregory looked to me for the kind of strength they, too, must show. Examples lay for me in my own mother and her mother. There was always a design of things that *ought* to be done and of who must do them. While duty was sometimes onerous, it made for clarity of purpose. Impulse, casualness, "doing one's thing" were egoistic luxuries in a large family, where many individual needs had to be considered.

The Second Operation. Life seemed a recurrence of dreadful occasions. Dana, Gregory and I marked time in the waiting room as the evening grew dark and cold. Hours passed. At last the call came from the operating room.

"It's over and he's fine!" Chester's dedicated nurse told us excitedly. "He was talking to me very clearly. I've never seen anything like it—all these machines going. They're washing out the artery—they really did it this time. The doctors tested him and he was answering them. He's just fine!"

The children and I were jubilant. It had all been worthwhile—the tests, the anxiety, the effort. Dana and Gregory hugged me. Their father, the one who had been resourceful in play, verbal, intelligent, strong—this man was being returned to them in vigor and fluency.

The doctor appeared, very pleased and confident. "It went very well. There's nothing to worry about now." The small surgeon looked suddenly enormous. His hands glowed with an aura of gold. He had opened an artery leading

Their ordeal over, the family enjoys a joke.

to the brain; he had held the power and fragility of a human life in his fingers.

And so it was over. We wanted to see and hear the magic. But the possibility we had clung to—that the surgery might retrieve the speech, mobility and dexterity all at once—this was not to be. Chester was fine, indeed, hopeful, in good spirits—but we could discern no remarkable changes. It would be the same round of exercise, speech therapy, manual training and repetition, repetition, as before. We had enjoyed our share of miracles.

Soon it was time to think of his going home. Strangely, yet easily, the old dependencies were resumed. He wanted to go back to my apartment. So we went, and I nursed him. It soon became clear I could not take my December orals—only a few weeks away. I thought of my mother, who had sacrificed her creative impulses and given up her own ambitions in order to serve her family—husband, siblings, her mother, me. I reluctantly wrote to my orals committee to postpone the examination.

Thanksgiving eve, 1972. We threw ourselves into a marathon of preparations. Turkey, yams,

American bread stuffing and Greco-Lebanese chestnut dressing, Dana's cranberry sauce, Gregory's mincemeat for one of my pies, and creamed onions, their father's favorite vegetable. It was a joyful time; Chester would be home tomorrow.

Thanksgiving: Homecoming. Joy and anxiety. The responsibility suddenly awesome. Chester's circulation was not yet fully adjusted. He was not to rise suddenly, but to get up in stages; not to stand too quickly after lying down. He needed help with bathing and dressing; his low-cholesterol diet and prescriptions were to be strictly supervised. I had informed myself on nutrition and health foods; I learned to add lecithin to my cooking, to use polyunsaturated fats and oils. The accumulated cholesterol deposits could be reduced; in many cases, diet could actually repair, as well as retard, the damage.

As we left for the hospital to get Chester, even our dog, Homer, seemed excited. It was all so quick—a few goodbyes to the hospital staff and we were downstairs. Chester looked at the busy street. The traffic gave him sudden pleasure and he smiled, a little crookedly.

We were on our way home, past welcoming neighbors and doorman, up to the familiar door, and into the apartment. He looked around, walking slowly from room to room, and finally said, "It looks nice."

I sat with him in the living room, talking for a few minutes, then went to the kitchen. Pots were on the stove; the children bustled about; the turkey was in the oven. We started peeling chestnuts. Suddenly, there was a crashing thud. We ran to the hall bathroom and found Chester collapsed on the floor. I held him, screaming for him to speak. I dashed cold water in his face. It seemed as if we could not be lucky again—as if, like some human doll coming apart after repair, he would not revive. It was too much to bear. I shouted wildly at the doctor on the telephone.

"He's dying! He just got home! Why did you discharge him? Come right away!"

The doctor assured me that the patient would survive, that it was just all the excitement. And Chester *was* reviving. In a few minutes we helped him downstairs and sat him in a chair until we could get a cab. Back, back to the hospital emergency room. The nightmare was recurring.

"He's all right," the doctor pronounced, saying he could go home. We all returned to Thanksgiving.

At night I would listen for his breathing. I became an even lighter sleeper than I had been as a mother; his faintest stirrings awakened me. On the second night, he got up to go to the bathroom and collapsed again. The doctor surmised that he had gotten up too quickly, the symptom would pass. We were like two people crawling from a train wreck, one physically whole, struggling against anxiety, the other limping, stammering in a strange voice while managing a slightly crooked smile.

We worked hard. Over and over: words, numbers, calculations, reading, conversing, speaking into a tape recorder and playing it back. Each mealtime became an hour of study, three hours a day. Questions. Talk about current events, cultural matters, family. Talk. Talk. Talk.

And physical exercise. And nearly daily visits to doctors and therapists. Everything new became momentous. The first walk unaccompanied—a block to 95th Street. Crossing a street alone. Walking without a cane. Each accomplishment reinforcing the last. There were occasional doubts, backward slips, plateaus. Yet improvement, ever more slowly, did come. We were racing against time.

Finally, Chester could enter a taxi, utter the destination and go to see his analyst by himself or go to the hospital for occupational and physiotherapy. I tucked index cards into his pockets in case he might need help, cards with his name and address, doctor's name and hospital, and the information, "I have suffered a stroke. Please take me to—Hospital." Impersonal tags, but they gave us a sense of security.

Little by little the symptoms faded. There was no longer any limp; his facial paralysis had vanished; his patient's higher pitched, nasal voice was giving way to its former rich timbre. The stammering was nearly gone. He was writing legibly with his right hand; he read what he saw on the page—the aphasia had receded. He took a driver-refresher course and passed it.

He attended a meeting at the psychoanalytic institute where he had been studying, to show his analyst that he could meet the challenge, three months after his stroke. He tried to take notes on the proceedings, then gave up. But it was a major step toward regaining his place, his concept of himself in the world.

We started talking about the fall semester. I had postponed my orals again, but I was anxious to get back to work. Chester had to take a physical at the Board of Education before he could return to his high-school teaching. This was another hurdle—the most important, in many ways. He wanted to regain his professional life. To him, resumption meant being restored as a man.

☐

And so, after a summer in the country, we took the subway to Brooklyn for the test, a journey into past and future. There it was at last, the old building, its gray facade masking Chester's fate. I thought of the beautiful belt he had made for me in occupational therapy: small, brown loops of leather, which he had linked together over many weeks with painstaking care, a belt I still wear with pride. I remember how he gave it to me with a shy sort of delight. The kindly therapists were very pleased with the belt, also, but with a subtle difference: as if this might be accepted as a pinnacle of achievement. Eventually, they, too, were carried along by the current of our faith and their patient's remarkable progress.

Chester was thoroughly examined and questioned by the board's doctors. He wrote his name, the end-product of how many words, phrases, sentences that had been dictated to him every day, of how many symbols copied, over and over. I waited prayerfully. So much effort, so much good work by so many people—doctors, nurses, therapists, family—it could not have been in vain.

"I passed," he said simply, with a big smile. "It's O.K."

I hugged him, the champion.

The rest is continuity and struggle. Facing his remedial-reading classes, embarrassed over occasional lapses and difficulty with spelling—these challenges themselves refined the recovery. But Chester's students were especially motivated by his example. He resumed working for a year, then took early retirement to seek another kind of fulfillment in voluntary clinical work.

At home, therapies went on less intensively. Occupational and speech exercises were no longer needed. Finally, the surgeon told him, "You don't have to come back anymore." It was accomplished.

For me, orals still lay ahead. I prepared a new dissertation prospectus, having changed my subject to that of an admired woman poet, Gwendolyn Brooks. Then, in May 1974, I met with my orals committee, and my own triumph, small in the context of our lives, but significant, nevertheless, was achieved.

Although resumption of the marriage was not to be, the friendship could not be severed. I was a woman who had come to terms not only with her immediate family situation, but, in another sense, with that altruistic part of herself, an aspect of the mother she had emulated. On the tennis court last summer, an image came to me —my husband and I, many winters ago, at a lake we knew and loved:

A Winter Lake*

Someone who loved you
    young
holds youth in you
with remembering eyes
    retains
the point ingeminate
that proud season

I see past whiskers and
    slackening skin
the set mouth and its
    mischief
to the cold high sun of a
    winter's day
over a lake of skaters
    how we dared

the thin edge
    but in the end
did not advance too far

and though we were not
    timid or
thought not that we were
we did not   test then
our singleness   but
    went together
an exchange of hands and
    blades
toward the chill, indefinite
    air

*©1977 by D. H. Melham. Reprinted by permission of *The Smith.*

Animal Experiments

by Patricia Curtis

The professor was late leaving the medical school because he'd had to review papers by his third-year students in experimental surgery. It was well after 11 when he wearily drove his car into the garage. The house was dark except for a hall light left on for him. His wife and youngsters were already asleep, he realized, and the professor suddenly felt lonely as he fit his key in the lock. But even as he pushed open the door, Sabrina was there to welcome him. She was always waiting for him, lying on the rug just inside the door.

The little dog leaped up ecstatically, wagging her tail and licking the professor's hand. The professor stroked her affectionately. She flopped on her back and grinned at him as he tickled her chest and belly; then she jumped to her feet and danced around his legs as he walked into the kitchen to get something to eat. Sabrina's exuberant joy at his return never failed to cheer him.

Early next morning, the professor drove back to the medical school and entered the laboratory. He noticed that a dog on which one of his students had operated the previous afternoon still had an endotracheal tube in its throat and obviously had not received pain medication. He must be more strict in his orders, he thought to himself. Another dog had bled through its bandages and lay silently in a pool of blood. Sloppy work, the professor thought—must speak to that student. None of the dogs made any sounds, because new arrivals at the laboratory were always subjected to an operation called a ventriculocordectomy that destroyed their vocal cords so that no barks or howls disturbed people in the medical school and surrounding buildings.

The professor looked over the animals that would be used that day by his surgery students. He came across a new female dog that had just been delivered by the dealer. Badly frightened, she whined and wagged her tail ingratiatingly as he paused in front of her cage. The professor felt a stab. The small dog bore an amazing resemblance to Sabrina. Quickly he walked away. Nevertheless, he made a note to remind himself to give orders for her vocal cords to be destroyed and for her to be conditioned for experimental surgery.

American researchers sacrifice approximately 64 million animals annually. Some 400,000 dogs, 200,000 cats, 33,000 apes and monkeys, thousands of horses, ponies, calves, sheep, goats and pigs, and millions of rabbits, hamsters, guinea pigs, birds, rats and mice are used every year in experiments that often involve intense suffering. The research establishment has generally insisted that live animals provide the only reliable tests for drugs, chemicals and cosmetics that will be used by people. Researchers also believe that animal experiments are necessary in the search for cures for human illnesses and defects. There is no question that many important medical discoveries, from polio vaccine to the physiology of the stress response, have indeed been made through the use of animals. Thus universities, medical and scientific institutions, pharmaceutical companies, cosmetics manufacturers and the military have always taken for granted their right to use animals in almost any way they see fit.

But increasing numbers of scientists are beginning to ask themselves some hard ethical questions and to re-evaluate their routine use of painful testing tools such as electric shock, stomach tubes, hot plates, restraining boxes and radiation devices. A new debate has arisen over whether all such experiments are worth the suffering they entail.

Strongly opposing curtailment of animal experimentation are groups such as the National Society for Medical Research, which insists that any such reduction would jeopardize public safety and scientific progress. The N.S.M.R. was formed to resist what it considers the threat of Government regulation of animal research and to refute the charges of humane societies. Many scientists, however, although they firmly believe that some animal research is necessary, no longer endorse such an absolutist approach to the issue.

"Some knowledge can be obtained at too high a price," writes British physiologist Dr. D. H. Smyth in his recent book "Alternatives to Animal Experiments."

"The lives and suffering of animals must surely count for something," says Jeremy J. Stone, director of the Washington-based Federation of American Scientists, which has devoted an entire newsletter to a discussion of the rights

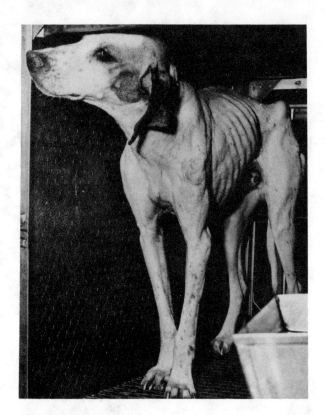

This emaciated dog is part of a laboratory experiment.

of animals.

According to physiologist Dr. F. Barbara Orlans of the National Institutes of Health, "Within the scientific community there's a growing concern for animals that has not yet had a forum." Dr. Orlans is president of the newly formed Scientists' Center for Animal Welfare, which hopes to raise the level of awareness on the part of fellow scientists and the public about avoidable suffering inflicted on lab animals, wildlife and animals raised for meat. "We will try to be a voice of reason. We can perhaps be a link between scientists and the humane organizations," Dr. Orlans explains. "We hope also to provide solid factual data on which animal-protection decisions can be based."

Another link between researchers and humane organizations is a new committee comprising more than 400 doctors and scientists that has been formed by Friends of Animals, a national animal-welfare group. Headed by eight M.D.'s, the committee is making a survey of

Federally funded animal-research projects. Friends of Animals hopes that the study will expose not only needless atrocities performed on animals, but also boondoggles involving taxpayers' money.

One reason scientists are no longer so indifferent to the suffering they inflict on animals is the discoveries that science itself has made. We now know that many animals feel, think, reason, communicate, have sophisticated social systems and even, on occasion, behave altruistically toward each other. Communication by sign language with higher primates, demonstrations of the intelligence of dolphins and whales, observations of the complex societies of wolves and other animals, and many other investigations have narrowed the gap between ourselves and the rest of the animal kingdom, making it more difficult to rationalize inhumane experiments. Dr. Dallas Pratt, author of "Painful Experiments on Animals," points out that "among the rats and mice, the computers and oscilloscopes, there is Koko"—referring to the young gorilla whom a California primatologist has taught a

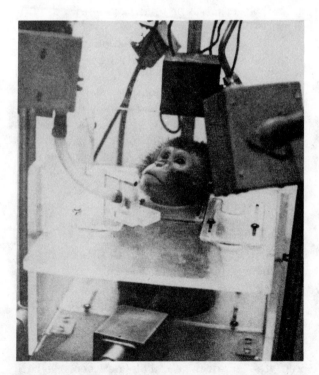

This monkey has been placed in a restraining chair and is being subjected to electrical shocks.

working vocabulary of 375 words and concepts in sign language and who has even learned to take snapshots with a Polaroid camera. It's hard not to feel squeamish about subjecting animals to inhumane experiments when they possess almost human intelligence.

The thinking of researchers is also beginning to be affected by the growing movement for animal rights. The rising concern for the welfare of animals is seen by some people as a natural extension of contemporary movements promoting civil rights, women's rights, homosexual rights, human rights and children's rights. Public interest in preserving endangered species is based first on an increasing awareness of the complexity and fragility of ecosystems, and second on the notion, still much debated, that any species of plant or animal, from the lowly snail darter to the blue whale, has the right to continue to exist. From here it is only a short logical step to the belief that animals have the right to exist without suffering unnecessarily.

Near the top of the list of animal-welfare activists' causes is putting an end to inhumane experiments on laboratory animals. In Great Britain, where a vigorous antivivisection movement has existed for more than a century, a clandestine group called the Animal Liberation Front conducts commando-style raids on laboratories, liberating animals and sabotaging research equipment. A.L.F. members have also been known to slash tires and pour sugar in the gas tanks of trucks used by animal dealers who supply labs. To be sure, this group of zealots hasn't made much of a dent in England's vast research community, but it does appeal to a gut reaction on the part of many Britons against animal research.

Animal-rights activists are not merely sentimental do-gooders and pet-lovers. They have mounted a philosophical attack on the traditional Western attitude toward animals, branding it as "speciesist" (like racist or sexist), a term derived from the word "speciesism," coined by psychologist and author Dr. Richard Ryder. The Australian philosopher Peter Singer, in his influential 1975 book "Animal Liberation," argued that the "speciesist" rationalization, "Human beings come first," is usually used by people who do nothing for either human or nonhuman animals. And he pointed out the parallels between the oppression of blacks, women and animals: Such oppression is usually rationalized on the grounds that the oppressed group is inferior.

In 1977, when outraged antivivisectionists heard about some highly unpleasant electric-shock and burn experiments conducted on young pigs in Denmark, they wasted no time in pointing out the irony that the tests were being conducted by Amnesty International, the human-rights organization. Amnesty International was attempting to prove that human prisoners could be tortured without leaving any marks, and pigs were used because of the similarity of their skin to ours. (The tests were subsequently discontinued.)

Paradoxically, the public tends to be "speciesist" in its reaction to animal experimentation: For many people, a test is permissible when it inflicts pain on a "lower" animal like a hamster, but not when the victim is a dog. When it was discovered in the summer of 1976 that the American Museum of Natural History was damaging the brains of cats and running painful sex experiments on them, hundreds of people picketed in protest. The museum's Animal Behavior Department defended itself on the grounds that the research was intended to gain a better understanding of human sexual responses. Animal-rights groups, scientists among them, were not convinced of the necessity of the tests, which came to an end only when the chief researcher retired. But the protesters made no stir about the pigeons, doves and rats that suffered in the same laboratory.

If United States Army researchers had used guinea pigs instead of beagles when they tried out a poison gas, they probably would not have provoked the public outcry that resulted in the curtailment of their funding in 1974. When a few Avon saleswomen quit their jobs in 1978 after reading about painful eye-makeup tests the company conducts on rabbits, they did not complain about the thousands of guinea pigs and rats Avon routinely puts to death in acute-toxicity tests.

It is not known whether any single vertebrate species is more or less immune to pain than another. A neat line cannot be drawn across the evolutionary scale dividing the sensitive from the insensitive. Yet the suffering of laboratory rats and mice is regarded as trivial by scientists and the public alike. These rodents have the dubious honor of being our No. 1 experimental animals, composing possibly 75 percent of America's total lab-animal population. As Russell Baker once wrote, "This is no time to be a mouse."

Rats and mice are specifically excluded from a Federal law designed to give some protection to laboratory animals. The Animal Welfare Act, passed in 1966 and amended in 1970, is administered by the Department of Agriculture and covers only about 4 percent of laboratory animals. Animal advocates worked hard for the bill, which sets some standards for the housing of animals in laboratories and at the dealers' facilities from which many of them are obtained. But the law places no restrictions on the kinds of experiments to which animals may be subjected. It does indicate that pain-relieving drugs should be used on the few types of animals it covers—but it includes a loophole so as not to inhibit researchers unduly. If a scientist claims that pain is a necessary part of an experiment, anesthetics or analgesics may be withheld.

One standard test conducted on rats by drug companies is called the "writhing test" because of the agonized way the animals react to irritants injected into their abdomens. Paradoxically, this test assesses the efficacy of pain-killers, which are administered only after the rats show signs of acute suffering.

Equally common are psychological experiments in "learned helplessness" that have been conducted on rats, dogs and other kinds of animals. In some of these tests, caged animals are given painful electric shocks until they learn certain maneuvers to obtain their food. As they become adept at avoiding the shocks, the researchers keep changing the rules so that the animals have to keep learning more and more ways to avoid shocks. Ultimately no way remains to escape, and the animals simply give up and lie on the floors of their cages, passively receiving shock after shock. Researchers have attempted to draw parallels between "learned helplessness" and depression in human beings, but some critics have difficulty perceiving their

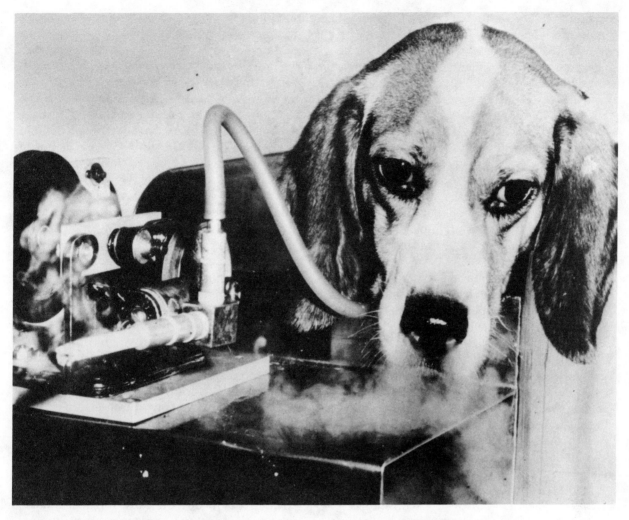

A dog being forced to inhale cigarette smoke through a tube inserted into his windpipe.

necessity. "What more are we going to learn about human depression by continuing to produce immobility in animals?" asks former animal experimenter Dr. Roger Ulrich, now a research professor of psychology at Western Michigan University.

Electric shock is widely used on many different kinds of animals in various types of research. In one experiment typical of a series that has been under way since 1966 at the Armed Forces Radiobiology Research Institute in Bethesda, Md., 10 rhesus monkeys were starved for 18 hours and then "encouraged" with electric prods to run rapidly on treadmills. This went on for several weeks before the monkeys were subjected to 4,600 rads of gamma-neutron radiation. Then they were retested on the treadmills for six hours, and subsequently for two hours each day until they died. Mean survival time for the vomiting, incapacitated monkeys was recorded in A.F.F.R.I.'s report as 37 hours. Dogs have been used in similar experiments, whose purpose is to get an idea of the effects of radiation on human endurance.

Now A.F.F.R.I. and other American research facilities are having to look for new sources of monkeys. In March 1978, the Government of India banned further export of rhesus monkeys to the United States. The native population was dwindling and Prime Minister Morarji R. Desai cited violations of a previous agreement that restricted the use of rhesus monkeys to medical research under humane conditions. "There is no difference between cruelty to animals and cruelty to human beings," the ascetic Prime Minister stated. The International Primate Protection League, a four-year-old watchdog group whose members include many scientists and especially primatologists (Jane Goodall, for one), had spread word in the Indian press that American scientists were using rhesus monkeys in grisly trauma experiments. According to the Primate Protection League, these tests included dipping monkeys in boiling water at the University of Kansas, shooting them in the face with high-powered rifles at the University of Chicago, and slamming them in the stomach with a cannon-impactor traveling at a speed of 70 miles per hour at the University of Michigan.

"I feel justified in stating that fully 80 percent of the experiments involving rhesus monkeys are either unnecessary, represent useless duplication of previous work, or could utilize nonanimal alternatives," wrote Illinois Wesleyan University biologist Dr. John E. McArdle, a specialist in primate functional anatomy, in a letter to Prime Minister Desai, who so far has held firm despite pressure from the American scientific community to rescind the ban. In the meantime, researchers are making do with non-Indian rhesus monkeys and a close relative, the crab-eating macaque.

One of the arguments in favor of animal tests is that under the controlled circumstances of the experimental laboratory they are likely to be objective and consistent. But the results of the same tests conducted on the same kinds of animals often differ from one laboratory to the next. When 25 cooperating companies, including Avon, Revlon and American Cyanamid, conducted a comprehensive study of eye- and skin-irritation tests using rabbits, the results varied widely. The study concluded that these tests "should not be recommended as standard procedures in any new regulations" because they yielded "unreliable results."

One of these tests, the Draize Ophthalmic Irritancy Test, is used to evaluate the effect upon the eyes of household and aerosol products, shampoos and eye makeup. Rabbits are used because their eyes do not have effective tear glands and thus cannot easily flush away or dissolve irritants. The animals are pinioned in stocks and their eyes are exposed to a substance until inflammation, ulceration or gross damage occurs.

Many investigators concede that the data provided by such experiments are often inconsistent and that the stresses caused by crowded cages, callous treatment, pain and fear can affect animals' metabolisms and thus confuse test results. "Since there is hardly a single organ or biochemical system in the body that is not affected by stress," says Dr. Harold Hillman, a British physiologist, "it is almost certainly the main reason for the wide variation reported among animals on whom painful experiments have been done."

Very often, different species respond differently to substances or situations. The rationale for many animal tests is that they predict human reactions, but thalidomide, for example, did not produce deformities in the fetuses of dogs, cats, monkeys and hamsters. On the other hand, insulin has been proved harmful to rabbits and mice although it saves human lives.

Researchers are becoming increasingly dubious about the efficacy of the LD/50, a test for acute toxicity that consists of force-feeding a group of animals a specific substance until half of them die, ostensibly providing a quantitative measure of how poisonous the substance is. In "Painful Experiments on Animals," Dr. Pratt asks what we learn from forcing hair dye or face powder into a dog or rat through a stomach tube until its internal organs rupture.

One small victory for animal-welfare activists that was hailed by many American scientists was the 1975 Canadian ban on the use of vertebrate animals by students participating in science fairs. Children had been awarded prizes for attempting heart-transplant surgery on unanesthetized rabbits, amputating the feet of lizards, performing Caesarean operations on pregnant mice, bleeding dogs into a state of shock and blinding pigeons. Remarking that such "experiments" were a distortion of the spirit of research, science-fair officials ruled out all such projects except observations of the normal living patterns of wild or domestic animals.

In this country, the search for adequate substitutes for laboratory animals was officially launched in the summer of 1977, when the American Fund for Alternatives to Animal Research made its first grant—$12,500 to a biology

These rabbits have been placed in a restraining box so that the effect on the eyes of certain drugs and cosmetics can be tested.

professor at Whitman College in Walla Walla, Wash. The award to Dr. Earl William Fleck will help finance his development of a test substituting one-celled organisms called tetrahymena for animals in screening substances for teratogens, agents that can cause birth defects. It is expected that the test, if and when perfected, will be cheaper, quicker, more accurate and certainly more humane than putting thousands of pregnant animals to death.

According to veterinarian Thurman Grafton, executive director of the National Society for Medical Research, people who talk about alternatives to animals are creating false hopes. "These new technologies can only be adjuncts to the use of animals," he claims. "While they serve a purpose in furnishing clues as to what direction a type of research might take, you will always ultimately need an intact animal with all its living complications and interchanging biochemical functions to properly assay a drug."

"Not so," says Ethel Thurston, administrator of the American Fund for Alternatives. "Enough progress has already been made to indicate that certain techniques can completely replace animals."

Several of these techniques have been developed over the last five years in Great Britain, where the Lord Dowding Fund for Humane Research has given grants totaling more than $400,000 to dozens of scientists engaged in research aimed at finding experimental substitutes for animals. Dowding is financing several developmental studies of the Ames Test, a promising technique invented by a Berkeley biochemistry professor, Dr. Bruce Ames, that uses salmonella bacteria rather than animals to determine the carcinogenic properties of chemicals. (It was the Ames Test that recently revealed the possible carcinogenic dangers of certain hair dyes.) Another Dowding Fund recipient, research physician Dr. John C. Petricciani, now with the Food and Drug Administration, has devised a method of assessing how tumors grow by inoculating the tumor cells into skin from 9-day-old chicken embryos instead of into living animals.

Animal tests are frequently replaced by other methods discovered and developed by scientists like Dr. Ames who are not trying to avoid the use of animals per se but are simply searching for simpler and more cost-efficient ways to achieve their goals, Dr. Hans Stich, a Canadian cancer researcher, for example, has devised a new test for detecting carcinogenicity in chemicals; it uses human cells, takes one week and costs only about $260. The traditional method, using rats and mice, takes three years and costs approximately $150,000.

In addition to egg embryos, bacteria and simple organisms, possible substitutes for animals include tissue cultures, human and other mammal cells grown in test tubes, and organ banks. Preserved human corneas, for instance, might be used to spare rabbits the agony of the Draize test. Computers could also play a role if researchers used them fully to analyze experimental data, predict the properties of new drugs, and test theoretical data. Computers can even be programmed to simulate living processes. Mechanical models and audio-visual aids can and do substitute for animals as teaching instruments. Simulated human models could provide valid information in car-crash tests.

In the winter of 1977/78, Representative Robert F. Drinan, Democrat of Massachusetts, introduced a bill authorizing the Department of Health, Education and Welfare to fund projects aimed at discovering research methods that would reduce both the numbers of animals used in laboratories and the suffering to which they are subjected.

Meanwhile, medical and military research and an unending stream of new pharmaceutical, cosmetic and household products are resulting in an ever-increasing use of animals in the laboratory.

The most recent and thorough exploration of alternatives is Dr. D. H. Smyth's book "Alternatives to Animal Experiments," which examines every option and weighs its pros and cons. He concludes that there is certainly reason to hope that the numbers of laboratory animals can be drastically reduced, but also warns that it is unlikely a complete phasing out of animal experimentation will happen soon. "By the time we can produce complete alternatives to living tissue," Dr. Smyth writes, "we will not need those alternatives because we will already understand how living tissues work."

Still, Dr. Smyth asks, "Does this mean we can perpetrate any cruelty on animals to satisfy scientific curiosity in the hope that it will one day be useful? To me it certainly does not.... Everyone has a right to decide that certain procedures are unacceptable."

Richard Ryder calls animal experimenters to task for trying to have it both ways: Researchers defend their work scientifically on the basis of the *similarities* between human beings and animals, but defend it morally on the basis of the *differences*.

And there's the rub: The differences aren't as reassuringly clear-cut as they once were. We now know that some animals have a more highly developed intelligence than some human beings—infants, for example, or the retarded and the senile. Dr. Ryder asks, "If we were to be discovered by some more intelligent creatures in the universe, would they be justified in experimenting on us?"

Smallpox Is Not Dead

by William Stockton

We take off our watches, bracelets, rings and other personal possessions, and my host, Dr. James Nakano, locks them away. We walk down a hall from his cluttered office to an unmarked wooden door. He unlocks it.

Inside is a tiny dressing room equipped with a toilet, sink, hooks on the wall and several lockers. We strip naked and don green surgical pants and pullover tops and put on disposable green surgical caps, taking care to cover ears and hair.

We step barefoot through the shower (without using it) and go through an unlocked door to an air lock outside the laboratory. It is all slightly unnerving, claustrophobic.

Yet there is no disputing the necessity for these precautions. Tragic events in England last summer leave no doubt about how dangerous to mankind smallpox research can be.

On Sept. 1, 1978, Dr. Henry Bedson, 49, a renowned microbiologist and smallpox authority at Birmingham University in England, entered the potting shed outside his home and cut his throat. His wife, Ann, was talking on the phone and she watched from a window as her husband

disappeared into the shed. The couple had been about to do some gardening. When she went in search of him a few minutes later, she found him in a pool of blood on the potting-shed floor. An ambulance rushed him to a hospital, but he died five days later.

Dr. Bedson's suicide and my presence in the smallpox laboratory at the Federal Government's Center for Disease Control (C.D.C.) in Atlanta were related because of the two other events that preceded the scientist's death:

In August 1977, a team of World Health Organization (W.H.O.) scientists working in Merka, Somalia, diagnosed a case of smallpox in a cook named Ali Maaow Maalin. He was isolated, and the 161 people who had been in recent contact with him were searched out and vaccinated. Health teams then fanned out in search of the contacts of Ali's contacts, examining every case of chicken pox and skin rash they could find. No more smallpox was discovered, and by mid-1978 W.H.O. officials were declaring ly solved.

The second thing I think about is that Dr. Lane is, at least in part, right. Because people

191

that mankind probably had seen its last case of smallpox. The ancient scourge that had killed millions since the dawn of civilization would soon be officially eradicated.

But just a year later, a medical photographer at Birmingham University—Janet Parker, 40, who worked one floor above Henry Bedson's lab —became ill. Thinking she had influenza, she stayed home from work, but a rash appeared and her symptoms worsened. She entered a Birmingham hospital on the afternoon of Aug. 24, and doctors, working far into the night, reached the astonishing diagnosis: She had contracted smallpox—the disease that was thought no longer to exist.

Janet Parker was hurriedly moved to a special isolation hospital. She died of smallpox on Sept. 11. Three days later, her mother, Hilda Whitcomb, 70, was diagnosed as having smallpox; she, too, was placed in isolation, and eventually recovered. Another 300 people were quarantined and vaccinated before the emergency was declared over.

Dr. Bedson's laboratory was studying smallpox virus. The virus escaped, probably through a leaky inspection port on a duct carrying cables and wiring. Janet Parker worked in a room directly above another leaky port in the duct. The laboratory was subsequently found to have been shockingly mismanaged. Only luck prevented a major outbreak in Birmingham of a particularly virulent strain of smallpox. "I am sorry to have misplaced the trust which so many of my friends and colleagues placed in my work . . . ," Dr. Bedson said in a note he left. "I realize this act is the least sensible I have done, but it may, I hope in the end, allow [my family] to get some peace."

These events cast in sharp relief a difficult problem that science and mankind never has had to face before: If an ancient, deadly and historically feared disease is at last eradicated through the marvels of modern medicine, should the laboratory stocks of the virus that caused it be kept for important related research? Nine laboratories, three in the United States, are known to have retained smallpox virus. What steps are being taken so that none will escape again in the distant future, as it did in Birmingham, conceivably causing a major epidemic in a population that by then may have

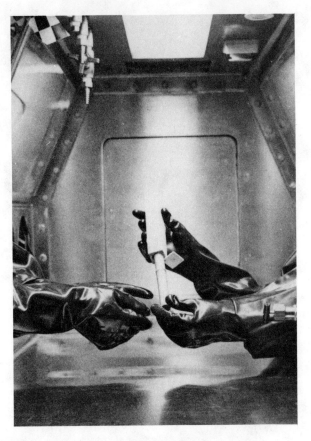

Hands are inserted into gloves in order to remove specimens from the cabinet.

lost its immunity, a population treated by doctors who may have all but forgotten the disease? And how reliable are these precautions?

The air lock outside the smallpox laboratory at the Atlanta center—which is the only place in the United States where the smallpox virus is being studied—is bathed with ultraviolet light until we enter. The light is shut off automatically by the opening of the door from the shower so that we won't be exposed to the radiation. We step to a cabinet—also lighted ultravioletly—and select pairs of old tennis shoes for our bare feet. My shoes have no laces and flop.

Several weeks before my tour, I had been vaccinated against smallpox. The day I arrived at the center, a member of the public-information staff escorted me along a covered catwalk joining the main building with the laboratories handling dangerous materials. On the steel door to

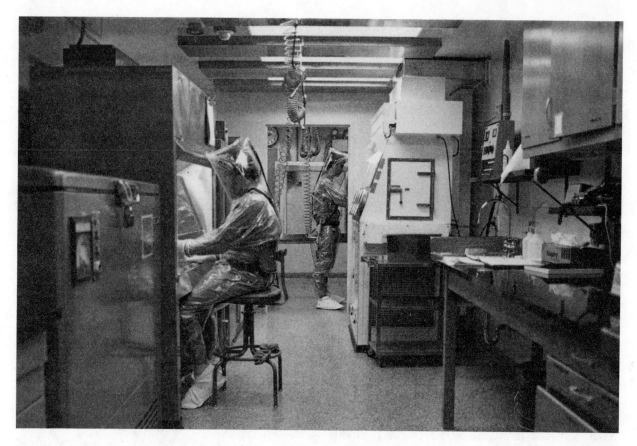

Special protective suits are required for working in the Maximum Containment Laboratory at the Center for Disease Control.

Dr. Nakano's floor was a yellow warning forbidding entry to anyone who has not received a smallpox immunization within three years. I was told by various people at the lab that the sign is commonly ignored. Surprisingly, the door to the smallpox floor was unlocked, and the hall leading into the building was deserted. No guard challenged us. No bell rang. Our passage wasn't monitored on closed-circuit television. No one was aware of our entry until we turned a corner at the end of the hall and stepped into Dr. Nakano's windowless office, where he and I talked for about an hour before we headed for the lab.

I am reassured by the lock on the dressing-room door. (The British inquiry had found that Dr. Bedson's lab often was unlocked, often even unattended.)

"Are we ready?" Dr. Nakano says, inspecting my outfit and moving toward the smallpox-lab-

oratory door. "O.K., here we go," he says, stepping in.

The research at the Atlanta lab had its beginnings in 1796 when an English country physician named Edward Jenner found that if a person was deliberately infected with cowpox, which caused only a mild illness, he would be immune from smallpox. Although the practice of vaccinating people with cowpox spread quickly to other countries, smallpox maintained its hold on most of the world until the 20th century. Even after immunization against it became widespread in the industrialized nations, the majority of third-world nations continued to suffer from it, at least until 1967, when an intensified international campaign was launched.

Most infectious diseases, even if they are wiped out, will return again because the responsible agent—usually a virus—can live naturally

193

in some animal and emerge to reinfect humans. But smallpox has no known animal host. If the last smallpox viral particle can be killed in the last case of human smallpox, then the virus is gone forever, most scientists believe, although there are several "maybes" attached to this possibility.

By 1977, smallpox remained only in the Horn of Africa, among parts of Ethiopia, Somalia and Kenya. Finally, only the nomadic tribes of the region were infected and now, with the treatment of Ali Maaow Maalin and his contacts and with the containment of the virus in Birmingham, smallpox does indeed seem vanquished. The World Health Organization won't officially declare it so for a year, however, to make certain it finds nothing more. To encourage reporting, a $1,000 bounty is offered to any person who brings in a smallpox case.

Yet most smallpox experts believe that stocks of smallpox virus should be saved, and they base their argument on the possibility that the disease might somehow recur or some new form develop. There are several ways this might happen, none of which experts believe are likely. One involves the chance that viral particles might be lying dormant in someone who once had smallpox and survived. Other viruses are known to act in this way. But as yet there has never been a known smallpox case in a smallpox-free country, such as the United States, whose source couldn't be accounted for. The source has always been traced either to a traveler from an infected area or to a laboratory where an accident occurred. No outbreak has ever been attributed to the virus spontaneously arising in someone who had the disease years before.

The most worrisome, remote, possibility is that animal pox—diseases that are characterized by viral skin eruption and frequently other deeper complications—might somehow be altered through natural or man-made events and become smallpox. There are a number of known animal poxes—monkeypox, raccoonpox, cowpox and so on. Monkeypox causes the most concern because three dozen humans are known to have caught monkeypox from handling monkeys. There is no evidence that those people passed the disease on to another human. Worrisome, too, is whitepox, a little-understood form of skin eruption in animals. No case of whitepox in humans is known, but since the whitepox virus can't be distinguished from smallpox virus, a case might go undetected. No one is willing to rule out the possibility that whitepox could be a close relative of smallpox, waiting for something to trigger its appearance in humans.

Fears about monkeypox and whitepox are the most persuasive reasons why smallpox virus stores in laboratories should be kept. The handful of scientists around the world who work with smallpox have ambitious plans to study it and the animal poxes further. They are seeking definitive answers about whether the animal diseases could affect humans, perhaps even becoming infectious from human to human and, in effect, replacing smallpox. They contend they need smallpox virus to carry out the experiments.

In fact, Dr. Bedson's laboratory in Birmingham was working on such problems. A method had been developed to differentiate one virus from another by analyzing the proteins found in the coat of each virus particle. The work has been halted now, of course, and the laboratory closed.

Dr. Michael Lane, who is the head of the Center for Disease Control's smallpox eradication unit and is not involved in smallpox-virus research, is a lonely scientific voice advocating the eventual destruction of virus stores. "There's no question that for the next two or three years we should keep the virus as we complete the search for any remaining smallpox cases in the world," he says. "But very shortly after we reach that point, I think the virus should be destroyed. I'm not sure I see the theoretical benefits of keeping this little lump of genetic material available forever."

Smallpox vaccine is made not from smallpox virus, but from a harmless relative, vaccinia virus. Smallpox virus won't be needed if vaccine manufacture must be resumed someday. Dr. Lane contends that vaccinia virus is sufficient within the laboratory to diagnose the presence of smallpox, if a suspected case should ever arise. Stores of the animal-pox viruses would not be destroyed, so they would be available to test whether a suspicious case had an animal origin. Dr. Lane, who argues that laboratory workers could do without smallpox virus itself and not have their future work greatly affected, insists that "we need a lot more open scientific debate on the question."

The World Health Organization hopes to reduce the number of laboratories holding smallpox virus to just four by 1980. As of January 1979, there were eight, in addition to Atlanta's: the U.S. Army Medical Research Institute of Infectious Diseases at Fort Detrick, Md.; the American Type Culture Collection, Rockville, Md.; the Research Institute for Viral Preparations, Moscow; St. Mary's Hospital Medical, London; *Institut für Schiffs-und-Tropenkrankheiten,* Hamburg; *Rijks Instituut voor de Volksgezondheid,* the Netherlands; the National Institute of Virology, South Africa, and the Institute for the Control of Drugs and Biological Products, Peking.

The Atlanta center, St. Mary's Hospital in London and the Russian laboratory are three likely permanent sites. Until December, the Chinese were an unknown quantity. But when the Global Commission for the Eradication of Smallpox met in Geneva, China sent a brief report, saying simply that the virus exists in one laboratory in Peking. Nothing is as yet known about the safety or sophistication with which the smallpox virus is handled, or about plans to save or destroy the virus. There has been speculation that, during the Cultural Revolution in the 60's, some smallpox samples may have become lost in freezers of various laboratories as scientists and technicians were swept up by the Red Guards.

Lost or hidden vials remain a worldwide concern. The accurate reporting of laboratories "has to be on a good-faith basis," says Dr. Donald A. Henderson, former head of the W.H.O. eradication program in Geneva and now dean of the School of Hygiene and Public Health at the Johns Hopkins University in Baltimore. "There is no way that we can go through every deep freeze in the world and look at each vial."

Officials at the Atlanta center recently sought to persuade the Defense Department and the American Type Culture Collection, a private scientific group, to transfer all the virus there. Neither group is at present conducting smallpox experiments; both were reluctant at first to comply, but have now agreed. The Defense Department was assured that it could go to At-lanta and perform experiments if necessary. And the Rockville, Md., scientists were assured that they would be consulted before any decision was made to destroy smallpox stores.

It will probably be some time before the virus is consolidated within one institution. The Atlanta center plans to keep a backup supply in a storage unit being built several miles away in case a storage freezer fails, for example, and destroys the primary specimens. However, the bulk of the nation's store of the virulent virus will be retained in Dr. Nakano's laboratory.

As I stand in the lab itself, my feeling of claustrophobia intensifies. It is a room about the size of a large living room, with a smaller room to the side. The humming overhead is from the air-filtration system. Work tables and shelves line the walls. Beside the door are two large padlocked freezers that contain smallpox samples. And at the other end of the room are biological safety cabinets, where the smallpox is examined and worked with through the use of large built-in rubber gloves; a worker inserts his or her hands into the gloves to manipulate equipment inside.

I peer around, looking for some of the safety shortcomings that Dr. Nakano has frankly acknowledged exist. He has told me that, after a smallpox laboratory accident in Great Britain in 1966, he "decided to set up the safest laboratory possible. I knew that if anything ever happened with smallpox in the United States, everyone would point the finger at the C.D.C. So I toured the labs in Europe to see how they were doing it, and then tried to make this lab even better. We used 1966 standards. The standards have become more rigid since then and we've done our best to keep up."

Dr. Nakano has shown me a set of World Health Organization recommendations. Conforming with these, the lab has negative air pressure inside so that, if any cracks in walls and openings aren't sealed, air will not leak out but instead will be drawn in; the outside air lock through which we entered and will leave; showers for use each time anyone leaves; special air filters to take out contaminated material from air circulating through the closed "glove box" cabinets; its own sterilizing equipment; a system for decontaminating lavatory effluent.

"But there are some weak points," Dr.

Nakano says. Air drawn into the room is not filtered, for example, so a failure of the air-circulation system could cause a backflow, sweeping contaminated air backward through the ducts and out of the lab. Difficulties have been encountered in sealing cracks in the walls, ceilings and floors.

Dr. Nakano is quick to point out, however, that authorization has been received to build a new $1 million smallpox lab in another part of the building, incorporating all the safety and technology improvements made available since 1966. It is expected to be completed by the end of the year.

At the safety cabinets, Dr. Nakano shows me how air drawn in from the room passes through them and then through high-density filters to take out any contamination before being discharged from the lab. The cabinets are filled with a mist of a sterilizing substance to kill any remaining smallpox virus once an experiment is finished.

We inspect the room's two sinks. The one closest to the work area has its drain plugged. Liquids poured into it are collected in a bucket underneath. The contents are sterilized and then poured down the other sink, which connects to the sewer.

"Here's an example of where we have a potential human-factor problem, where someone could make a mistake," Dr. Nakano says, pointing at the second sink. "Everyone is trained never to pour anything down this sink unless it has been treated first. But someone could forget. Our new lab will take care of this particular problem."

Only one person, Denise Brown, is working in the lab, as is often the case. She sits at one of the work tables, dressed as we are, preparing material for study under an electron microscope in another part of the building. "It takes a special kind of person to work in here alone with all these safety procedures and the like day after day and not make a mistake," he says.

The technician laughs. "That's for sure," she says. "But I like it in here by myself. You get a lot more work done. Not all that yakking with everybody all day long."

She usually takes a morning break and a lunch break. Each time she leaves the lab, she must leave her surgical clothes on the laboratory side of the shower, take a complete shower with soap, and change into street clothes.

"Even with all this containment we have to have people trained to come in here every day, do their work and leave without ever causing a problem," Dr. Nakano says.

"You sure do," she echoes.

"There are many, many little details," he says. "When you take the shower you must always be sure to blow your nose thoroughly. You may have breathed in something in the air and it has lodged in your nose. Then, outside, you sneeze and contaminate something. Isn't that right?" he asks, smiling.

She makes a face.

One wall of the laboratory has a large window looking out into the hall through which visitors pass just after entering the building. Dr. Nakano sees me looking at it. "You need the window so you can see into the laboratory when someone is working alone, in case there is an accident," he explains. But someone could always break into the lab by smashing the window, he adds.

It is time to go. We say goodbye to Denise Brown and step back into the air lock.

Until 10 or 15 years ago, many scientists working with dangerous viruses and bacteria had a cavalier attitude about the risks. A prevailing belief in some laboratories was that workers should be exposed to the agent under study so they would catch it and become immune, obvious exceptions being the highly dangerous organisms that produce frequently fatal diseases.

Smallpox in the lab was often treated casually. In Britain years ago, one famous smallpox scientist kept live smallpox material in an envelope on a shelf in his office. It was routine to conduct experiments on open benches with no protective equipment. And only last month, the shocking findings of a British Government panel that investigated the Bedson affair were leaked to the press. The inquiry found that Dr. Bedson's laboratory's containment procedures were woefully inadequate, marked by carelessness and failure to follow prescribed procedures; that since 1975, when he was appointed head of Birmingham University's microbiology department, he had spent little time in the laboratory, turning its operation over to a research fellow who had never been formally trained in containment procedures; that the laboratory's workload had increased as much as tenfold in recent months in a mad rush to complete research before the lab was to be closed at the end of 1978; that he was less than frank about some of his laboratory's procedures and even lied to safety inspectors about some operations. He was a member of various official groups that were supposed to oversee his facility's safety, but the groups had found nothing wrong in his lab.

It is difficult to measure just how frequently laboratory infections occur throughout the world. Unusual infections are reported in the scientific literature, but many others considered "routine" are not. In a study completed in 1975, Dr. Robert M. Pike at the University of Texas Southwestern Medical School in Dallas tried assessing the number of known worldwide laboratory infections. He identified 3,900 (2,500 in the United States) that caused at least 164 deaths among laboratory workers in the past several decades since the advent of modern scientific research. The study identified 18 infections involving smallpox; 10 of the victims in the United States died. Dr. Pike found that 18 percent of the infections were caused by known accidents, which means that, in 82 percent of the infections, the route of exposure to the infectious agent remained a mystery.

In 10 cases the infection was the result of an apparent suicide attempt. In seven cases someone tried deliberately to harm another person. Two persons were infected for experimental reasons, a procedure which would not now be permitted in view of changing medical ethics. Dr. Pike also reported a case in Japan in 1966 of a disturbed bacteriologist's deliberately spreading typhoid organisms in food, causing 44 cases of typhoid fever.

The Center for Disease Control has developed a reputation as one of the most careful of the world's laboratories that study dangerous organisms. It has handled all the most deadly infectious agents known to mankind and has never had a fatality. But early in 1977 the laboratory was badly shaken when two workers contracted Rocky Mountain spotted fever and died. One man was a warehouseman, the other was involved with collecting waste material and

sterilizing glassware. Neither was studying the disease. Clearly, Rocky Mountain spotted fever had escaped the rooms where it was being studied. A breakdown in safety procedures almost certainly was responsible.

Shocked C.D.C. officials launched a massive investigation not only of how the Rocky Mountain spotted fever had escaped, but also of the center's overall safety procedures. The final report, published at the end of 1977, is hard-hitting, surprisingly so since it represents a Government institution investigating itself.

The report's authors found deficient safety practices to be widespread at the institution. Buildings housing laboratories that study dangerous organisms were often "inherently unsafe for much of the work being performed in them." Biological safety cabinets often malfunctioned. As an economy measure, fans that forced air through the cabinets were turned off each day at 4:30 P.M., causing a backflow which could sweep contaminated air into the rooms and halls of a building if some worker was still performing an experiment. Many laboratories working with highly infectious agents did not have their own sterilizing equipment for glassware. This meant that contaminated glassware was carried through halls and stacked in racks—sometimes near elevators—to await sterilization in central autoclaves. Packages containing Class 4 infectious agents—the most dangerous—had been unpacked in a main laboratory before being taken into the maximum containment laboratory. A "disturbingly high frequency" of unreported laboratory-acquired infections was found. The safety study revealed that 124 infections were acquired by center employees through 1976, in either laboratory or field work. None of these involved smallpox.

Despite the shortcomings revealed by the study, the center is generally regarded as being as safe as any laboratory in the world and safer than most. "Many of our facilities were built almost 20 years ago when some of the organisms we study now hadn't even been discovered," says Dr. John Richardson, the head of the Federal institution's biosafety office. "Safety procedures evolve with time. New equipment and new procedures are developed and we become more sensitive to the added need for safety. The important thing is to make certain we continue learning and stay alert."

When I asked about the ease with which I had entered the building where the smallpox laboratory is located, Dr. Richardson said that the center plans to install special locks on all that building's exterior doors. The locks will open only with coded magnetic cards.

Back in the air lock, Dr. Nakano and I step out of our shoes, onto the cold tile floor, and place them in the sterilizing cabinet. He remains in the air lock while I enter the shower room. Nothing that has been on the laboratory or "dirty" side of the shower must pass through to the clean side except a thoroughly scrubbed and naked body.

So I strip off the surgical garb and place it on a rack beneath an ultraviolet lamp and get in the shower. I soap myself thoroughly, but do not wash my hair because it has been covered. I shout at Dr. Nakano that I am finished and step into the "clean" dressing room. He follows me into the shower. Back in his office, I retrieve my valuables and sign a logbook where the name and address of every visitor in the lab is recorded. "If I begin to feel ill in a couple of weeks, I'll give you a call," I say jokingly.

"Call me immediately," he replies without a smile.

Walking along the catwalk and then down the halls of the main building, I am struck by two things. The first is that, although the center prides itself on an open atmosphere—employees aren't required to wear badges; visitors can roam all the halls unquestioned—I find myself hoping that, if bureaucratic problems are slowing installation of the magnetic card locks on those exterior doors, the problems are quickly solved.

The second thing I think about is that Dr. Lane is, at least in part, right. Because people are people, regardless of how safe laboratories handling smallpox become, human error almost certainly will release smallpox virus into the en-

vironment sooner or later. In the "worst case" situation, as many scientists generally perceive it, several thousand people might contract the disease before urgent efforts to vaccinate and surround the outbreak could take effect. And despite all that medicine has to offer, there is no cure for smallpox, which has a fatality rate of about 25 percent in its most virulent form, called variola major, the variety that killed Janet Parker.

I have found the atmosphere in the laboratory is oppressive. The attention to detail, the complicated entrance and exit procedures and the solitude when one is locked in do require a special personality. And there is always the chance that repetition eventually will breed indifference, even contempt. Smallpox virus, like radiation, is something you can't see. Nothing reminds you each time you enter or leave the room that you are dealing with a dangerous organism. Mental alertness is the only answer.

"You can provide the best facilities and the best equipment, but the bottom line is how well the people are trained and how closely the laboratory's immediate supervisor monitors everything on a day-to-day basis," biosafety officer Dr. Richardson says to me later. "Everyone needs someone looking over his shoulder, looking for problems, ways to improve. But beyond that, I'm not sure we have an answer, in the end, to the human factor."

It is almost noon, so I go down to the main building's ground floor and join the long line filing into the cafeteria. Just as I reach the steam tables and stare down at the food, contemplating my entree selection, I suddenly remember something that causes my stomach to jump. A cold feeling settles over me. I want to glance over my shoulder to see if James Nakano is hurrying after me, ordering me back to the dressing room outside his laboratory.

I have forgotten to blow my nose in the shower. I have completely forgotten.

Opting for Suicide

by Edward M. Brecher

No doubt, many people who face a lingering death—from cancer, say, or some other disease—contemplate suicide. But by the time they are ready to take action, it is often already too late. Closely monitored by family and caretakers, they lack access to any effective means of suicide. They may also be physically or mentally incapacitated. Their last-minute, improvised suicide attempts are quite likely to end in failure, humiliation and, perhaps, additional pain. This is the case history of a patient who firmly believes in advance planning. I am that patient.

I received a diagnosis of cancer of the colon, and a recommendation for prompt surgery, on June 17, 1978, shortly before my 67th birthday. As every prudent person should, I had given some thought during the preceding years to the advisability of suicide in such a contingency, and I thought further about it following my cancer diagnosis. As matters turned out, suicide proved unnecessary in my case, but I regard my suicide planning as a durable asset, a resource upon which I can draw should the occasion arise in the future.

I first began to think about the problem in October 1961. My wife and I and our 15-year-old son were hiking through New England's glorious autumnal foliage near our home when our aged German shepherd, Rufty, suffered a heart attack and lay writhing in the leaves, clearly in great pain. I hurried home and phoned a veterinarian, who arrived quite promptly. We found Rufty cradled in my son's arms.

"As soon as this convulsion is over," the veterinarian said, "I'll put Rufty out of her pain."

"No, don't wait," my son replied. "Do it right now."

The veterinarian extracted a syringe from his black bag, inserted it in a vein, and pushed the plunger. Rufty relaxed, and a moment later it was over. That moment was fraught with emotion. I looked straight at my son and blurted out what was in my heart:

"I hope someone will be as kind to me when my turn comes."

A few years later, the father of a friend of mine received the same kindness. The old man lay terminally ill on his sickbed late one night,

Edward M. Brecher

surrounded by half a dozen members of his family. The 75-year-old physician who had attended them all, and had delivered several of them, was sent for. He arrived, examined the patient briefly, then filled his syringe and gave an injection.

"Is that to ease the pain?" someone asked.

"No, that was to ease the passing," the physician said. My friend likes to tell the story as an example of how fortunate his New England village was to have a horse-and-buggy doctor as recently as the 1960's.

My late wife, Ruth Brecher, who was also my collaborator as a writer, developed inoperable cancer in 1965 and died after a 19-month illness. Her care was managed at home, in accordance with her personal wishes, including adequate doses of morphine and sedatives as often as she requested them. I was deeply grateful to the physician who abided by her desires—but I resolved to follow a different course if I myself were ever in a similar situation.

I was vividly reminded of these earlier matters in 1975, when the newspapers carried accounts of the deaths of Dr. and Mrs. Henry P. Van Dusen. Dr. Van Dusen, an eminent theologian, was for many years president of the Union Theological Seminary in New York. Years before their death, he and his wife had entered into a suicide pact, resolving to depart from life —voluntarily and together—at an appropriate time. When Dr. Van Dusen was 77 and his wife 80, they agreed that the time had come. Together they swallowed what they assumed were adequate doses of sleeping medication. Mrs. Van Dusen died the next day; but Dr. Van Dusen was taken to a nursing home, where he lived on for 15 days. He had failed in what was probably the most important action of his entire life.

Even so, the Van Dusens were fortunate. Many of those who attempt suicide are discovered, rushed by ambulance to the nearest hospital, and subjected to stomach pumping or other demeaning and painful emergency procedures. These are often, alas, successful.

Among those moved by the Van Dusen episode, and by even more harrowing accounts of botched suicides and successful resuscitations, was a California psychiatrist. He wrote a letter to the editor of Psychiatric News proposing a "Hemlock Society" that would "dedicate itself to providing information and personal counseling to those giving serious consideration to suicide." I promptly wrote him requesting membership in the society, but it was never formed.

"I regret to say that my own interest in this project waned," the psychiatrist subsequently wrote me. "It immediately became apparent to me that, if I pursued the matter in this community, I would be identified as 'the prosuicide psychiatrist,' or something equally controversial. . . . Also, the local district attorney's office . . . advised me that I and all persons in a 'Hemlock Society' would be subject to prosecution if we were seen in any way as 'aiding and abetting a suicide.' Consequently, I had to move other projects higher on the priority system.

"I continue to believe that there are a large number of thoughtful and concerned people who would support such a movement if certain others provided the leadership."

The basic principle of such an organization, it seems to me, can be simply and clearly stated: Nobody who doesn't want to die of cancer, or of any other disease, should have to die of that disease. Alternative modes of death should be available.

I had more important business than suicide planning, however, during the period immediately following my own cancer diagnosis. My first need, as I saw it, was to determine whether I could continue to enjoy life—or whether a cancer diagnosis in itself was enough to sour the weeks and months ahead. Accordingly, two days after the diagnosis I took off (as previously scheduled) for a human-sexuality workshop on Cape Breton Island in Nova Scotia.

My two weeks there were among the richest and most rewarding of my life, in a dramatic setting, surrounded by exciting people, dealing with fascinating subject matter, and even including what I have always considered the ultimate of life's enjoyments—a full-fledged falling-in-love experience. Far from souring life, the cancer in my colon added a unique zest to those two weeks.

On my return home, I consulted with my three grown sons, all of whom were nearby. They, like me, vividly remembered their mother's last 19 months.

"Whatever happens," I assured each of them, "I am not going to die of cancer." All three fully understood my meaning, and were unreservedly supportive.

The question of whether to accept or refuse cancer surgery came next in my thinking. This is perhaps the most important decision cancer patients must make; yet few of them give it even a moment's consideration. They simply do what they are told to do. I think the medical profession is at fault in this respect. The surgical option is too often presented to the patient as if it were not an option at all but a foregone conclusion. Many patients, indeed, are "given the rush act" so that they won't have time to think things through. Thus, at the very beginning of their careers as patients, cancer victims are deprived of an invaluable privilege of the human condition: the opportunity to plot their own course. Once they let others make that crucial decision for them, they are already reduced to a dependent status.

When a cancer patient does weigh the options, however, it immediately becomes apparent that refusing surgery is utterly irrational if the only alternative is to let nature take its course and to die miserably after a protracted period of suffering. A feasible alternative to surgery must be available if the choice is to have any meaning. That feasible alternative, I believe, is to enjoy life to the full as long as possible and then to terminate it in your own way at a moment of your own choosing. Accordingly, before I could decide whether or not to accept surgery, I had to make sure that suicide was an available option. I devoted my next two weeks to "suicide shopping."

Since guns, knives, dangling from ropes and jumping from high places are not my style, I soon narrowed my alternatives to three: an overdose of sleeping medication, intravenous injection of a rapid poison such as cyanide or nicotine, and carbon monoxide (automobile exhaust).

I was doubtful about carbon monoxide because of the Federal air-pollution regulations designed to curb automobile exhaust gases; but an engineer friend of mine assured me that there is still plenty of carbon monoxide in the exhaust from even a 1978-model car. It just takes a bit longer to be effective.

A physician friend of mine was also helpful. He offered to write a prescription for a month's sleeping medication, cautioning me that it should be taken under circumstances which would prevent my being discovered while still alive and having my stomach pumped.

The offer of sleeping medication is a traditional ploy used by some physicians to retain control of suicide-prone patients. The offer makes it almost certain that the patient will return for the prescription before taking action—and the physician, instead of supplying the medication, can then institute appropriate antisuicide measures. I was confident, however, that in my case the offer was made in good faith.

It was at about this point that I made a most

welcome discovery about attitudes toward suicide. In all, I discussed my plans very frankly with nine women and men. Eight of them, including my three sons, were fully supportive. The ninth, while not in agreement, made no effort to dissuade me. Attitudes toward suicide among civilized people, I concluded, are rapidly changing, although the change has not yet been publicly noted.

Another welcome discovery followed. I had always thought of suicide as an inevitably lonely experience—best performed, perhaps, deep in the woods near my home or in some distant motel room. I was therefore deeply moved when a young registered nurse who was very close to me said: "Let me be with you and give you the injection. I love you and I'd consider it a privilege."

A woman my own age made a similar suggestion—that I come to her island in the Caribbean, where I would be surrounded by affection.

I was even more moved when one of my sons approached me with another suggestion. He reminded me that many years earlier, when his mother and I used to read out loud to the children each night after dinner, we had read them Plato's account of the death of Socrates, describing Socrates surrounded by his intimate friends and enjoying their company to the full until the moment came for him to drink the hemlock.

"I have two requests," my son continued.

"First, I don't want you just to disappear. I want to be able to say goodbye. Don't go off to a meeting somewhere and not come back.

"Second, when you are considering alternatives, I wish you'd consider the Socratic alternative—inviting in the friends you really want to be with for a last evening or even a weekend."

My first reaction was one of shocked amusement. How could I possibly decide whom to invite to such an occasion? And think of the distress of those who were not invited! Surely that would be the ultimate snub. I reached no decision then on whether or not to follow the Socratic precedent, and I still have not, but I have decided I will not be alone.

By the end of my two-week suicide shopping period, I felt confident that I could rely on any of the three courses mentioned above, and that I could count on the support of those near and dear to me. I was ready for the decision about surgery. I chose to accept it. Actually, I chose a modified form of conservative surgery and found a surgeon who agreed. The hospital consent form was altered to eliminate the patient's traditional consent to "any other procedures which may prove necessary." But that is another story. Fortunately, the surgery was successful, and I now expect to die of a heart attack like any other self-respecting, cigarette-smoking, beef-eating, 67-year-old American male.

□

I have given some thought also to the ethical problem of accepting the help of others or of involving others in my planning—since aiding and abetting a suicide might result in their being prosecuted for murder.

Quite simply, the risk of being charged with murder would certainly not deter me from aiding someone I love if I deemed it appropriate. I would want to be sure, of course, that this was a considered decision rather than a momentary whim on the part of the person seeking my help. And the circumstances would have to be such that I understood and approved the decision. My decision to help would be easier to reach if I felt in addition that I would behave similarly in like circumstances. Since I am prepared to help others close to me despite the risk to me, I see no ethical objection to my accepting the help of others, despite the risk to them.

As a practical matter, the risk of prosecution is small if plans are prudently laid and skillfully executed. This is particularly true in terminal cases; for even if by mischance the facts become known, only an exceptionally strict prosecutor would willingly prosecute for murder someone whose only offense was helping a dying friend in dire need. Such prosecutors, I trust, will sooner or later—let us hope sooner—vanish from our society. Until then, prudence and caution should of course be exercised, both by those planning suicide and by those assisting them.

Even when prosecutors do intrude, juries have a way of demonstrating their sympathy and human concern. Among many cases, I need only cite that of George Zygmaniak of Monmouth County, N.J., who broke his neck in a motorcycle accident in 1973. Paralyzed from the neck down, he begged his brother to help him die. Four days after the accident, George's brother killed him with a shotgun. Following a widely publicized trial for murder, the brother was acquitted by a jury. Acquittal in a murder trial, it should be remembered, can be handed down only by a unanimous jury of 12 individuals.

My own plans, incidentally, took account of the possibility that I might at some point—following a stroke, for example—be unable to give consent or take action myself. Those close to me agreed that, in that event, my present request for help would be taken as a continuing request.

It is unfortunate that each patient must do his own suicide shopping without even the most rudimentary guidelines from the medical profession. Most practicing physicians are themselves poorly versed in the advantages and disadvantages of various forms of voluntary life-termination available to laymen. Thus, all of us, quite unnecessarily, run the risk of suffering the fate of Dr. Van Dusen, or even worse.

As a modest first step, I suggest the preparation and widespread distribution of a pamphlet for laymen entitled "How Not to Commit Suicide," designed to warn against inadequate and inappropriate measures. If readers learn incidentally about some of the preferable ways, so

much the better. I would like to write such a pamphlet, but I have not found a physician knowledgeable in such matters who is prepared to collaborate. A recent book—"Common-Sense Suicide" by Doris Portwood, published by Dodd, Mead—is clear-eyed and honest, but is not a "how-to" guide.

I think it is high time that those who think as I do about suicide "come out of the closet." I am confident that even a modest band of women and men prepared to speak out frankly on the suicide issue can have a healthy impact on suicide law and on public attitudes toward suicide. My own experience indicates that coming out of the suicide closet can be a rewarding rather than a harrowing venture.

The suicide routes available and acceptable to me depended, obviously, on my personal tastes and preferences and on the particular people who are close to me. Others must lay their plans in the light of their own circumstances and resources. Many people, moreover, have deep religious, ethical or emotional objections to suicide by any means at all. But for a large and, I believe, growing portion of society who deem suicide vastly preferable to prolonged and unnecessary suffering, I strongly recommend advance planning. And the planning should be done years in advance of the occasion, so that the available alternatives can be unhurriedly explored and prudently weighed.

Life With Father

by Glenn Collins

For in the baby lies the future of the world:
Mother must hold the baby close so that the
baby knows that it is his world;
Father must take him to the highest hill so
that he can see what his world is like. —MAYAN
INDIAN PROVERB

The tiny white room on the ground floor of the
John Enders Research Building is only a block
away from the quiet green quadrangle of the
Harvard Medical School. The plate on the door
reads "RESEARCH LABORATORY I," and the room
is a jumble of television cameras, tape decks
and video cables. There are, however, some unexpected items: boxes of Kimbies are stacked
under a table; atop the table, a container of
Wet Ones Moist Towelettes, and next to the
Wet Ones, propped in a sturdy aluminum seat,
a 96-day-old baby named Eddie. He is intently
studying James, his father, standing before him.
Two television cameras are capturing these moments on half-inch magnetic tape.

"Bet you're glad to see me!" says James, smiling. "Were you good with Mommy? You know,
I missed you, all day. . . ." As he talks to his son,
he taps him, tickles him, and smiles, his eye-
brows moving in a language of their own. Eddie
arches forward in his jumpsuit, kicks his feet in
their little red socks, coos and giggles. After exactly two minutes, James leaves the room. The
cameras observe Eddie for another 30 seconds,
and then they are turned off.

Although a pediatrician on the staff of the
Child Development Unit of Children's Hospital
Medical Center in Boston will later play back
the tape, James and young Eddie aren't patients: They are participants in one aspect of
current research on fathering. Investigators will
play back the tape at one-seventh speed, and
will conduct a microanalysis of the facial expressions of James and Eddie, recording their
vocalizations and their body movements on
matching graphs. This information will be used
to create a sawtooth chart that plots a father's
typical interaction with a child; its signature is
distinctive, different from the characteristic
pattern of a mother's interaction.

Near Princeton, N.J., a father holds open the
front door and waits with his wife and two children as a team of researchers hefts a videotape

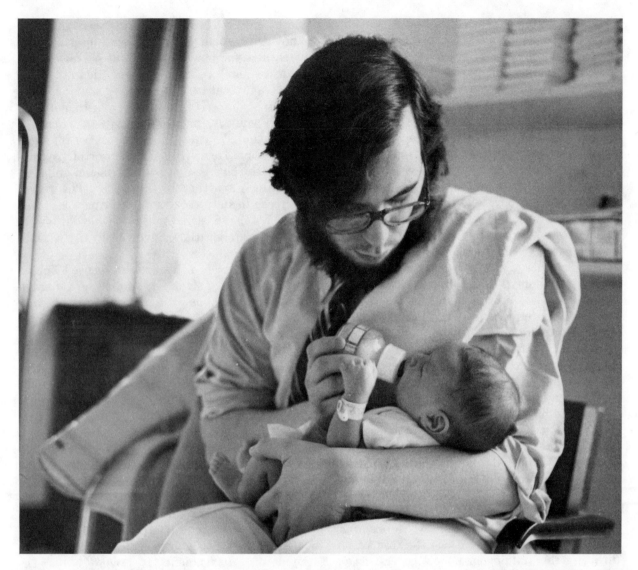

There is evidence that fathers can become as adept as mothers are at nursing and caring for young children, suggesting that the father's role is based more on culture and less on biology than previously assumed.

camera and assorted television equipment into his house. It is just about dinnertime, and the investigators, from the Infant Laboratory at the Educational Testing Service, ask the parents where they normally eat their evening meal. "Tonight, in the dining room," says the father. The E.T.S. technicians start the camera running, and leave the house.

Tentatively, the parents call their children to dinner. The 3-year-old waves at the television eye. The 6-year-old sticks out his tongue. The father seems a bit unnerved. They start eating,

and, before any of them might have expected, they forget about the technological presence in the dining room. After dinner, the E.T.S. researchers return for their equipment; later they analyze the behavior they view on the tape.

After studying 50 families, the E.T.S. investigators can generalize about what they have seen. Fathers talk more to their sons than they do to their daughters. Children talk less to fathers than to mothers, or to each other. And fathers, in their dinner behavior, tend to ask questions.

In a laboratory at the University of Wisconsin, a father sits in an easy chair four feet away from a television monitor. He is about to see something unpleasant, but he doesn't know it. Electrodes from an eight-channel polygraph recorder—a lie-detector—have been attached to his index and middle fingers, and a rubber cuff has been inflated on his left bicep; his heart rate, skin conductance and blood pressure are being monitored. Soon the television screen glows with a six-minute videotape of a 5-month-old baby boy. The infant looks around gravely and makes a sound; then he squirms, and soon he begins to cry. Loudly. Insistently. Interminably. Even though the baby on the screen isn't his, the father feels ever more uncomfortable under the assault; he moves, tenses, his heart rate rises and his blood pressure soars. Later, after testing 148 subjects, the investigators are able to report that there is no physiological difference between the reaction of a father or a mother to the sight of a squalling baby. To both, it is equally distressing.

Research examining what fathers do and how they do it has been booming in recent years. Not all of it employs computer analyses and electronic bric-a-brac. Much of it involves nothing more complicated than placing a trained observer in a room with a father who is playing with, or talking about, his child.

The impact of all this father-watching is beginning to be felt in courts of law, in hospitals and in universities, which face the task of redirecting the training of a new generation of doctors, pediatricians, psychotherapists, health-care professionals and teachers. "Our whole society has had the notion that a biological bond between mother and child made fathers less able, less interested and less important than mothers in caring for children," says James A. Levine, a Wellesley College researcher. "Courts have based decisions on that notion, therapists have treated patients on the basis of it, and men and women have made life choices because of it."

In fact, 44 percent of the mothers of children under the age of 6 in this country are working, only 24 percent of existing families are traditional nuclear families, and the "two-paycheck" marriage is the norm for nearly half of all two-parent families in America. In the changing society reflected by these statistics, the new knowledge about fathering has important implications for how children will be raised and educated, and will help to shape the kind of nation we inhabit in the 1980's.

Fathers haven't always been a fashionable research subject for social scientists. "When I started out 17 years ago, there just wasn't much data," says Henry Biller, professor of psychology at the University of Rhode Island and a pioneering researcher in the field. "The recent increase in data collection on fathers is amazing. We have something of a revolution in thinking among those involved in early childhood development."

In past decades, researchers focused on the father as a role model, or studied him inferentially: by examining the impact of his *absence*, in families where the father had died, divorced or gone to war. Fathers have also long had a place in psychoanalytic theory, becoming important in the Oedipal stage, when the son competes with him for the mother.

Social-development theorists viewed the mother-infant relationship as unique, vastly more important than subsequent relationships; it was even termed the prototype for all close relationships. In 1958 and then again in 1969, John Bowlby, the British psychiatrist, published his elegant and influential theories of attachment, a word that is usually defined by behaviorists as the preference for, or desire to be close to, a specific person. "But the real synonym for 'attachment' is 'love,'" says Dr. Michael Lewis, a developmental psychologist at the Educational Testing Service. Bowlby, drawing on the animal-study work of ethologists and the parental-deprivation observations of cognitive psychologists, suggested that there was an evolutionary advantage to a unique bond between mother and infant; he reasoned that this bond was an imperative of the very growth and development of the species.

Subsequently, many researchers investigated the mother-child interaction, revealing the nature of the infant's early relationship with its caretaker. However, fathers weren't even present in most of the studies. "A major reason that fathers were ignored was that fathers were inaccessible," says E. Mavis Hetherington, a University of Virginia psychology professor who has studied family-related questions for 25 years. "To observe fathers you have to work at night and on the weekends, and not many researchers like to do that."

Studies of humans and of nonhuman primates began to suggest that infants had strong attachments to persons who had little to do with their caretaking and physical gratification; nor were these relationships necessarily derived from the child's bond with its mother. In a classic study, primatologist Harry Harlow demonstrated that the attachment process was not limited to a feeding context. Investigators also showed that the actual amount of time an infant and his mother spent together was a poor predictor of the success of their relationship. Consequently, a child's tie to its mother continues to be viewed as crucially important; however, its exclusivity and uniqueness have been challenged. The new research emphasizes the complexity of an infant's social world.

Researchers have now identified some of the ways in which fathers are important to children. Henry Biller sums up the findings: "The presence and availability of fathers to kids is critical to their knowledge of social reality, their ability to relate to male figures, to their self-concepts, their acceptance of their own sexuality, their feeling of security. Fathers are important in the first years of life, and important throughout a child's development." Frank A. Pedersen of the National Institute of Child Health and Human Development has also demonstrated that mothers can perform better in their parenting roles when fathers provide emotional support.

Researchers from a number of disciplines using ingenious new methods now suggest that the father-infant relationship is not what we thought it was; that, for example, there are few significant differences in the way children attach to fathers and to mothers; that fathers can be as protective, giving and stimulating as mothers; that men have at least the potential to be as good at taking care of children as women are; and that the characteristic interplay of father and infant, when scrutinized minutely, is distinctive in many fascinating ways. The new fathering research offers fresh insights about the "distant" father and about fathers' roles across disparate cultures; it reveals that fathers have been ignored in research and in medical practice in curious and interesting ways; and it offers a synthesis of the relationship between fathers, children, families and society.

James Herzog, M.D., a psychiatrist who teaches at Harvard, says this of the new findings: "We're in what I call the post-competency phase now. We don't need to prove that fathers 'can do it, too.' The question now is, what is the specific role of the male parent, and what is the difference between being a father and being a mother?"

In 1970 a Harvard Ph.D. candidate named Milton Kotelchuck began a study of fathers that created a stir when it was presented in Philadelphia at the 1973 meeting of the Society for Research in Child Development. Kotelchuck, now director of health statistics and research for the Commonwealth of Massachusetts, had set up a classic "separation-protest" situation—a test of attachment—in studying the reactions of 144 infants when their fathers and mothers walked out of a playroom and left them with a stranger. Previous studies had observed the effects of a mother's departure on her child; Kotelchuck was able to determine that infants were just as upset when a father left them.

In four other studies, Kotelchuck and his associates found few significant differences in the way the infants attached to fathers and to mothers. They demonstrated that, in fact, children have extended social worlds and can attach equally well to siblings, peers and other figures.

Michael E. Lamb, research scientist at the University of Michigan's Center for Human Growth and Development, has carried on his investigations—including the crying-baby experiment described earlier—at Michigan, the University of Wisconsin at Madison, and at Yale, and was the editor of an influential 1976 anthology, "The Role of the Father in Child Development." His first key study of attachment appeared in 1975; in it, 7- and 8-month-old boys and girls and their parents were viewed in the home setting. An observer dictated a detailed account of the behavior he saw into a tape recorder. That narrative was then analyzed by applying 10 measures of attachment and affiliation: whether the baby "Smiles," "Vocalizes," "Looks," "Laughs," "Approaches," "Is in proximity," "Reaches to," "Touches," "Seeks to be held" or "Fusses to." Lamb and his co-workers found that no preferences were evident for one parent over the other among these infants, at the age when they should, according to Bowlby's theory, be forming their first attachments.

Lamb and his colleagues reported that when mothers held their infants, it was primarily for things like changing, feeding or bathing; fathers mostly held their children to play with them, and initiated a greater number of physical and idiosyncratic games than mothers did. This paternal play tended to be boisterous and physically stimulating. Furthermore, boys were held longer than girls by their fathers; fathers start showing a preference for boys at one year of age and this preference increases thereafter.

Currently, Lamb and his associates are studying 100 families from the time of pregnancy until their children attain the age of 18 months. The sample includes families where there are working wives; also represented are a few fathers who are primarily responsible for infant care. In Sweden, for the past six months, they have been observing role-sharing fathers and both mothers and fathers who have primary responsibility for child care.

If Michael Lamb has tended to focus on the child in his work, Ross D. Parke, professor of psychology at the University of Illinois at Champaign-Urbana, has centered his research on fathers themselves. In a 1972 study that is a classic in the literature of fathering, Parke and his colleagues haunted a hospital maternity ward in Madison, Wis., and observed the behavior of both middle-class and lower-class parents of newborn babies. They found, most strikingly, that fathers and mothers differed little in how much they interacted with their children. Fathers touched, looked at, talked to, rocked and kissed their children as much as their mothers did. The study suggested that they were as protective, giving and stimulating as the mothers were—even when the fathers were alone with their babies.

In later work, Parke and his collaborators measured the amount of milk that was left over in a baby's bottle after feeding time; infants consumed virtually the same amount of milk whether fathers or mothers did the feeding. They found that fathers were equally competent in correctly reading subtle changes in infants' behavior and acting on them; fathers reacted to such infant distress signals as spitting up, sneezing and coughing just as quickly and appropriately as mothers did. Parke asserted that men had at least the potential to be as good at caretaking as women. However, fathers tended to leave child care to their wives when both parents were present.

In the last few years, Parke, Douglas Sawin of the University of Texas and their collaborators have conducted two major studies involving 120 families. They observed family interactions, and used high-speed electronic "event recorders" with 10-button keyboards and solid-state memories to tap out four-digit codes that recorded behaviors as they saw them. Although there are very few differences in *quality* between mothers' and fathers' interactions with their children, one observed disparity is that fathers are more likely to touch and vocalize to first-born sons than to daughters, or to later-born children.

Eddie and James, whose close encounter began this article, were participants in a continuing investigation of children's early learning abilities and communication patterns at the Child Development Unit of Children's Hospital Medical Center in Boston. Originally, father-infant and mother-infant pairs were videotaped periodically during the first six months of babies' lives. The unit's newer work involves the father-mother-infant triad.

In Laboratory I, where young Eddie became something of an intramural television celebrity among social scientists, the research continues. Infants are placed in an alcove created by a blue-flowered curtain, and are taped with father or mother. These laboratory situations, though artificial, place the maximum communicative demand on the parent and child, the researchers say; they bring out the kinds of intense play situations that normally occur only during brief periods during an ordinary day.

Two trained observers play back the videotapes of these sessions and perform a "microbehavioral analysis" of the interaction of both the parent and the baby. The researchers

William Alberts holds his daughter Amy in the air and receives a smile.

assign numerical scores that rate such facial expressions as frowns, pouts and smiles; sounds like gurgles or coos; motions of hands and feet, and even eye movements. Ultimately, the observers note clusters of these behaviors and chart them during each second of elapsed time over the entire interaction.

Graphs of fathers' and mothers' behavior show distinctive patterns. In all of the families studied by the Child Development Unit, the chart of the mother's interaction is more modulated, enveloping, secure and controlled. The dialogue with the father is more playful, exciting and physical. Father displays more rapid shifts from the peaks of involvement to the valleys of minimal attention.

There are other characteristic differences: Mothers play more verbal games with infants, so-called "turn-taking" dialogues that are composed of bursts of talking or cooing that last four to eight seconds, and are interrupted by three- to four-second pauses. Fathers tend to play more physical games with infants; they touch their babies in rhythmic tapping patterns or circular motions.

To provide conceptual models for the way babies interact with adults, the Boston researchers have employed the theories of cybernetics, the discipline that studies the control and regulation of communication processes in animals and machines. Researchers have broken with the traditional lexicon of rat psychology, and talk about the "interlocking feedback of mutually regulated systems" and "homeostatic balances between attention and nonattention." The baby, in its reciprocal interaction with an adult, modifies its behavior in response to the feedback it is receiving. Infants, they say, seem to display periods of rapt attention followed by recovery intervals, in an internally regulated

In the filming room, Dr. Michael W. Yogman videotapes William and Amy Alberts through a one-way mirror.

cycle that maintains the balance of the infant's heart, lung and other physiological systems.

"It's important to say that father doesn't offer some qualitatively better kind of stimulation; it's just different," says T. Berry Brazelton, M.D., director of the Child Development Unit, a pioneer in the study of family interactions. "Mother has more of a tendency to teach the baby about inner control, and about how to keep the homeostatic system going; she then builds her stimulation on top of that system in a very smooth, regulated sort of way. The father adds a different dimension, a sort of play dimension, an excitement dimension, teaching the baby about some of the ups and downs—and also teaching the baby another very important thing: how to get *back* in control."

There are also interesting similarities in infants' relationships with both parents, says Michael Yogman, M.D., the pediatrician who videotaped James and Eddie and who has specialized in the study of fathers at the Child Development Unit since 1974. "With both parents," he says, "we see that behavior is mutually regulated and reciprocal, that there is a meshing of behaviors."

Dr. Brazelton says that "there's no question that a father is essential to children's development. Our work shows that babies have this very rich characteristic model of reaction to at least three different people—to father, to mother and to strangers. It shows me that the baby is looking for richness, that he's looking for at least two different interactants to learn about the world." For Dr. Brazelton, to whom Mayan Indians told the saying that preceded this article, its poetry is exceedingly descriptive.

"It seems to me," says Dr. Brazelton, "that the baby very carefully sets separate tracks for each of the two parents—which, to me, means that the baby wants different kinds of people as parents for his own needs. Perhaps the baby is bringing out differences that are critical to him as well as to them."

The Boston researchers plan to explore the later development of the paternal and maternal dialogues with children. They also hope to refine their procedures to the point where they may be useful as a diagnostic tool for practitioners.

Fathers are being studied from other perspectives. Although psychiatric clinicians, those who see patients, had always noted that the father played an important role in the psychological development of children, as late as 1973 the psychoanalytic literature bemoaned the lack of theorizing about the father's role during the first two years of life.

Building on Margaret Mahler's ideas on the successive stages of an infant's "psychological birth," psychoanalyst Ernst Abelin and others focused on the father's role in helping infants separate from mothers.

Some behavioral psychologists can't take the efforts of the psychoanalytic theorists very seriously, since the data for such work are often derived from the study of a single patient who may be going through the process of becoming a father, or coping with the difficulties of parenthood. "It's better to observe what's going on," says Alison Clarke-Stewart, a University of Chicago psychologist. "It's not distorted by retrospective recollection or the perceptions of the person who's being studied."

Psychoanalysts reply that the observational method is limited. "How people behave is highly determined by their fantasies, conflicts and unconscious processes," says Dr. Herzog. "These are the causes of the behavior that others observe. I have nothing against documenting this behavior, but we need to look at the inner life, too."

Part of that inner life is a well-documented clinical phenomenon, the so-called "womb-envy"—the envy of women's capacity to give birth—among some expectant fathers and even among male children. Perhaps a societal counterpart of this is the "couvade" phenomenon that anthropologists have noted in many cultures, where men undergo elaborate rites of passage paralleling their wives' pregnancies and birth-giving.

"We know that the time of pregnancy and becoming a father is extremely important to men, a crucial and stressful time," says Alan R. Gurwitt, M.D., a psychiatrist, analyst and associate clinical professor at the Yale Child Study Center. "Yet the astounding thing in this society is that the father has come to be a subject of ridicule—there is no end to the cartoon and movie stereotypes portraying the expectant father, and fathers in general, as bumbling fools."

He says there is still a tendency to ignore fathers on the part of obstetricians, pediatricians, nurses and even child psychiatrists. "This failure to involve fathers even in the treatment of their children runs very deeply," says John Munder Ross, a Manhattan psychotherapist and clinical assistant professor at Downstate Medical Center, who is coediting an anthology of the new psychoanalytic views of fathering. "It may have to do with the relations of clinical workers to their own fathers. There seems to be an awful lot of stereotyping of fathers as 'absent and ineffectual,' or 'tyrannical and sadistic.'"

To the psychoanalysts, the process that is fathering continues. "The middle-aged father frequently finds himself in a painful situation," says Stanley Cath, M.D., a psychoanalyst and associate clinical professor at Tufts Medical School. "His adolescent children may be rebellious and challenging to him; he himself may be trying to separate from his own father, who may be aged or dying; and the grandfather himself may be looking for support" as he faces the debilitation of old age. "Of course, a man can be the father to his children, and also the father to his parents," says Dr. Cath. "We rediscover the father, and the definition of fathering, throughout our lifespan."

As a social phenomenon, the evolution of fathering in man and various primate precursors is a matter of sheer conjecture. Paleontology provides little data on social interaction. Some cultural historians have tried to make inferences from the study of recent "primitive" societies, by which they mean complex societies that have not received the blessings of technology.

Margaret Mead's famous 1930 study of the

Professor Henry Biller

Manus people of New Guinea reported that, at the age of a year, children were given from the mother's care into the father's. He would play with the baby, feed it, bathe it, and take it to bed with him at night.

Fathers in the Thonga tribe in South Africa, observed during the last century, were ritually prevented from having almost anything to do with infants until the babies were 3 months old. However, fathers in the Lesu culture of Melanesia commonly took care of babies while their wives were busy cooking or gardening. And among the Kung bushmen in northwestern Botswana today, fathers have a great deal of contact with children, holding and fondling even young infants.

In analyses of all known cultures, anthropologists have suggested that, in about two-thirds of societies, wives and children accord the paterfamilias deference, that husbands exert authority over their wives and that most cultures

trace descent through the father's line. In non-industrial cultures, these analyses suggest, fathers generally play a small role in relating to young children. In other words, the similarities of men's roles outweigh the fascinating differences that may exist.

Male figures—though not necessarily fathers —are involved in child care in most cultures. Just how involved is another question. Applying a measurement called the Barry and Paxson Father-Infant Proximity Scale, researchers Mary Maxwell West and Melvin J. Konner at Harvard University found that social and cultural conditions are related to the level of involvement of fathers with their children, and suggest that there is the potential among males for caring for their young if other conditions encourage it. West and Konner found that fathers observed in cultures with monogamous nuclear families were generally involved parents. So were fathers in "gathering" societies—the form of society that existed during 98 percent of human history. They suggest that distant fathering is associated with warrior cultures ("hunting" societies) and with societies where men's agricultural or military activities take precedence.

Of course, the political and economic equivalents of warfare exist in modern industrial cultures, and it can be debated how much they affect males' involvement in fathering. There is conjecture that the tradition of the Roman paterfamilias had some influence on current patterns, as well as the Christian concept of the Old Testament God. The few attempts at compiling histories of fathering show the Industrial Revolution to be a major disrupter of family life as it existed when many fathers were tradesmen or farmers working in the presence of their children.

The cross-cultural evidence shows clearly that the father has been many things in many societies; it suggests that, if the culture allows, fathering can be whatever fathers want to make of it.

Is there any answer to the question posed earlier by Dr. James Herzog: Is fathering the same as mothering? And, if not, is one parenting style superior to the other?

"You don't want to imply from these studies that people are interchangeable," says Alan

Sroufe, a University of Minnesota child-development professor who is doing studies of attachment there. "Sure," he says, "an infant can attach to a woman or a man. But women have natural advantages in parenting. It's not just nursing—for example, mothers lactate as soon as a baby cries. But mothers also have the experience of carrying the baby for nine months, and if the business of attachment comes from sensitivity to being tuned into a baby, mothers have the advantage."

"But there is a crucial distinction to be made here," says Milton Kotelchuck. "Yes, pregnancy and lactation can make it easier for a mother to attach to a child. But the essential thing is that infants don't know that they are supposed to relate more to the mother than to the father."

"It is my speculation—and I want to emphasize that word," says Michael Lamb, "that we will find that biological differences are very small, and that they are exaggerated and magnified by the rituals and the roles that societies build around those distinctions. But are these differences genetic? My answer is 'Yes, but'— where the *but* is more important than the *yes*.

"Aside from the question of genetics," he says, "there is good evidence to believe that mothers and fathers can be equally effective as parents. They just have different styles. Perhaps it's really not fathering or mothering—it's parenting."

One researcher attempting to synthesize the relationship between child, family and society is Michael Lewis, director and senior scientist at the Institute for the Study of Exceptional Children at the Infant Laboratory of the Educational Testing Service. (It was his investigators who conducted the videotaped observations of Princeton fathers at dinner.) Lewis holds that different people—mothers, fathers, peers, siblings, grandparents, uncles, aunts and other relatives—serve the child's needs in different cultures in different ways: "I am saying that a father's role is cultural and historic rather than biological and evolutionary."

"There's no good data on any of this," Lewis says, "but my impression is that, to an extent in the general culture, fathers are defining their functions in new ways—the 'new fathering' we hear about." He adds that "we haven't assessed the basic question of values here yet, and that's

what we need to do. If the cultural matrix is changing, is it assisting the values of our culture?"

To an extent, society has legitimized the needs of parenting men. "In a sense, fathers have come out of the closet," says Mavis Hetherington. "They feel more comfortable about being parents, and are more actively fighting for their rights." Recent revolutionary changes in the way society views men are now treated by the media as commonplace: men's improved position in child-custody cases or men's right to single-parent adoptions in most states.

Nevertheless, it is James Levine's hunch that women are more aware of the issue of fatherhood than men are. "I think it is becoming more of a question for women as more of them are working outside the home. Women make demands on men to parent in a way that fits in with their new concepts of how they will live their lives," says Levine, a research associate at the Wellesley College Center for Research on Women who wrote an influential 1976 book on male parenting options, "Who Will Raise the Children?"

However, Levine says, "the biggest push for change is coming from the economic pressures— the necessity for both parents to work. I think the bottom line in all of this is the economic situation of women."

Michael Lamb believes that "it's a depressingly small number" of fathers who take on a large share of all that is involved in bringing up a child. He does not view the recent research about fathers' abilities as a new panacea. "But," he says, "I think we must realize that, in general, the average male won't be better than the average female as a caretaker. Yes, babies can attach to father. But that isn't to say that they won't be closest to the primary caretaker, which is usually mother."

Says Levine, "Where we really miss the boat is when we say the male role is changing, and cite as evidence the fact that men are changing diapers, bottle feeding, etcetera." The truly important part, Levine feels, involves a man's sense of emotional responsibility: "It's not just the taking *care* of kids, but it's who carries around that inner *sense* of caring, that extra dimension of emotional connection."

It is possible that there will be competition in

parenting. "At this point," says Dr. Brazelton, "everyone is goading men on to do more, but the second that men get good at it, and really enjoy nurturing, it may cause problems that'll have to be faced. Fathers who are taking an equally nurturant role may threaten some mothers."

For Levine, looking ahead, the most interesting question is, "research for what?" It seems to him that the next step, theoretically and practically, is to give some guidance to medical and mental-health practitioners: "The most interesting area for research has to do with total family interaction, the family systems perspective."

Virtually all of the father-watchers are wary, however, of being prescriptive—of saying that fathers should parent in a specific, more "nurturant" way.

"The crucial impact of the new research," says Douglas Sawin, "should be that a father's role ought to be an optional choice—and that, with a little support and training and education, they can be primary parents—but only if they want to be. For they have the basic competence and warmth and nurturance abilities. Whether they implement them or not is their decision."

Pet Therapy

by Patricia Curtis

As young, bearded Bill Powell rolls into his room in his electric wheelchair, his roommate, Crystal, quickly leaps into his lap. Mr. Powell is a quadriplegic. Crystal is a capuchin monkey.

The animal has been trained to do for her owner some of the everyday chores that most of us take for granted—turning a key in a door, turning on the light, fetching a book, taking a record from its sleeve and putting it on the turntable.

When he was a junior in college studying engineering, Mr. Powell was in a motorcycle accident that left him paralyzed in both legs and one arm; he has slight movement in the other arm but not in the fingers. He switched from engineering to computer work, obtained a master's degree, and now works as a programmer at Tufts New England Medical Center across the street from the Boston hotel where he lives. An attendant helps him dress in the morning and assists him to bed at night. Crystal provides daily companionship and increasingly adds to his independence.

Crystal was jointly trained by Mr. Powell and Dr. Mary Joan Willard, a psychologist in the rehabilitation department at Tufts New England. Working on a fellowship in neuropsychology, she realized that mechanical and electronic devices available to people who had lost the full use of their limbs because of spinal-cord injuries, multiple sclerosis or cerebral palsy were limited.

"With their marvelous agility, manual dexterity and intelligence, monkeys have an intriguing potential for acting as an extension of the handicapped person's body," states Dr. Willard, who uses the behavior modification techniques she learned as a research assistant to B. F. Skinner, the pioneering behavioral theorist. With the help of a professional animal trainer, the young psychologist set to work with two 2 1/2-year-old female capuchins, "organ grinders' monkeys."

Capuchins are very timid; Dr. Willard spent some two hours a day for a period of eight months or so socializing them. Then, the task-oriented training for serving quadriplegics took 30 minutes two or three times a day for another six months or more. Dr. Willard reinforces desired behavior with food and praise.

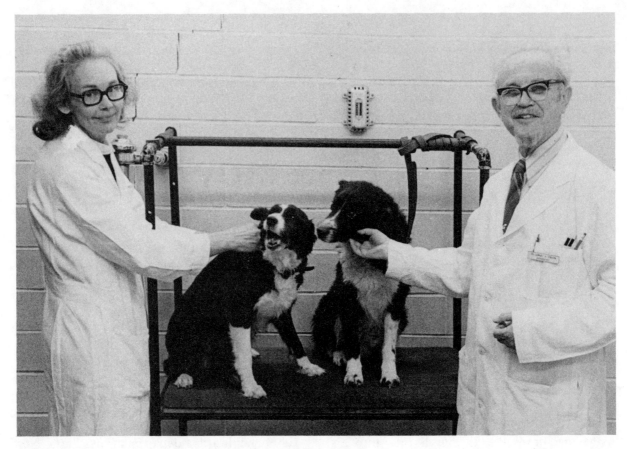

Psychobiologists Dr. Samuel A. Corson and Elizabeth O'Leary Corson with their pet therapists, collies Nell and Ned.

"I would like to see this work advanced," says Mr. Powell. "It would be a way to give disabled people the opportunity to break out of their social cages."

"Now that Bill has given us the chance to try out this project, we can assess its possibilities," Dr. Willard adds. "Bill was already remarkably independent in that he lives alone and holds down a full-time job. Crystal is a help to him, there's no question about that, but we can see that a monkey could make an even greater difference to someone who is housebound."

Dr. Willard and Mr. Powell think that Crystal will be able to perform everything expected of her as soon as some necessary equipment is installed. Eventually she will be able to unlock and open the door for him from inside the apartment. With a pellet dispenser attached to his chair, Mr. Powell will be able to reward Crystal when she performs well, and a light-

weight optical pointer—using a laser beam—will illuminate what he wishes her to fetch for him. With these, Crystal will increase his self-sufficiency and comfort greatly.

"If only capuchins could cook," says Bill Powell.

The use of animals to aid the handicapped has a precedent familiar to all by now—guide dogs for the blind. The first large-scale project of training dogs for this purpose began with The Seeing Eye Inc. 50 years ago.

Today the training of animals as aides to disabled people is a burgeoning business, attracting professionals and volunteers. Universities and research facilities from coast to coast are beginning to explore the potential of monkeys, dogs, cats and even horses as helpers in the process of treating the physically handicapped and aged.

Animals are also being used increasingly in

the treatment of mental illness. In July, 1979, the first national seminar on Pet Facilitated Therapy was held in California for professionals in the field. Sponsored by the Association for Pet Facilitated Therapy in San Francisco, an organization that trains assistance dogs of all kinds, the seminar will include psychiatrists, psychologists, social workers, veterinarians, teachers and other professionals involved in either human health or animal behavior.

A program for training hearing-ear dogs for the deaf originated about four years ago at the American Humane Association in Denver under the direction of an able dog trainer named Agnes McGrath. So far, only a few other places train hearing-ear dogs, and all of them have more requests for dogs than they can fill. Representative Fred Richmond, Democrat of Brooklyn, has introduced a bill to provide funds to further the training of these animals. There are about 13 million hearing-impaired persons in the United States, almost two million of whom are profoundly deaf. (Only the profoundly deaf are eligible for the American Humane Association program.)

A hearing-ear dog is taught to respond to such significant household sounds as a doorbell, smoke alarm, baby crying, teakettle singing or alarm clock. The animal will run between the sounds and its owner until the person responds. In the case of an alarm clock going off, the dog will jump on the bed and rouse its owner—and keep poking, jumping or licking until a deep sleeper is fully awake. On the street, the dog will react to any loud noise—a car horn, a siren, a shout.

At the Newbury Junior College division in Holliston, Mass., the hearing-ear-dog program is a favorite project of the school's vice president, Donald P. MacMunn, who introduced it into the curriculum. Under the no-nonsense instruction of Gloria Place, program director in kennel management, students at this vocational college can learn to become professional hearing-ear-dog trainers.

Dogs for the Holliston program are donated to the school or are hand-picked at a shelter for their intelligence, health, trainability, disposition and emotional stability. They must be at least 6 months and no more than 4 years old, and small dogs are preferred over large ones be-

cause they are more suitable for apartment living. Their preliminary training is simple obedience, including responding to silent hand signals for "sit," "come," "get off," "lie down," "get up" and the like. These dogs are not supposed to excel at following verbal commands but at discriminating sounds and acting upon them appropriately.

Some specialized training may be included, depending on the future owner's needs. "Our objective is not merely a trained dog, but a dog that serves a person," says Mrs. Place.

In Queens, N.Y., Wendy Heines, a young housewife, is the deaf owner of a golden retriever named Honey, who was selected for her by professional dog trainer Warren Eckstein of Master Dog Training in Oceanside, N.Y. While Honey has not received the intensive training that the dogs in Holliston's program do, he alerts his owner to some of the simple signals she needs to respond to at home—especially the cries of her 6-month-old son, Joshua.

"Honey behaves completely differently when he is telling me that Josh is crying from when somebody's at the door," says Mrs. Heines. "When Joshua needs me, Honey will come and put his paw in my lap or look steadily at me and cock his head. 'Aren't you going to go to him?' he seems to be saying."

At the Kanoza Nursing Home in Haverhill, Mass., a little black dog named Daffney doesn't have to do anything to earn her keep but be herself. Daffney was rescued from the Massachusetts S.P.C.A. shelter by representatives of the American Humane Education Society (A.H.E.S.) and the Junior League of Boston to participate in their program—pet therapy for the elderly. It places resident pets in nursing homes around the state to cheer and divert the elderly residents.

Daffney caused a stir even before she arrived at Kanoza. "Our Pet Is Coming!" read a handmade sign in a recreation room one day last December, and all hands gathered to await her arrival.

"This dog has never caused a problem or required any effort. She just slipped into the routine the minute she got here," says administrator Jon Guarino. "She has created harmony. Patients who didn't speak to each other before now do. Everybody gathers around

Phil Arkow of the Pike's Peak Region Humane Society regularly brings his Pet-Mobile to area nursing homes.

Daffney and talks, including some formerly withdrawn and lonely people. Even the staff seems more caring."

Counterparts of Daffney reside in several other custodial homes in Massachusetts, thanks to the efforts of the A.H.E.S., the Junior League, and the M.S.P.C.A., which share the work and costs of placement, health needs, follow-up care, instruction and the like. Missy, a cat, quickly became the darling of residents and staff alike in a rest home in Barnstable, Mass.; her presence was so therapeutic that the home soon adopted a second cat.

The concept of pets in custodial homes and mental hospitals is far more than a means of keeping residents entertained. It is taken seriously by many professionals in the care of the elderly and disabled, including psychobiologists such as Samuel A. Corson and Elizabeth O'Leary Corson of Ohio State University and

Boris Levinson, a psychologist formerly of Yeshiva University, N.Y., who pioneered in the field of pet-facilitated psychotherapy.

Under the Corsons' direction, a study was made in 1975 of the impact of dogs on elderly and disabled residents of Castle Nursing Homes in Millersburg, Ohio. The effects of the dogs were remarkable. Some patients who had not done so got out of bed so they could walk the dogs around. Some who neglected themselves and were self-pitying became more cheerful and self-reliant in response to the dogs. One brain-damaged, antisocial patient who was believed to be deaf and mute took one look at the dog brought to him and spoke his first words in 26 years: "You brought that dog," said he, and from then on continued to improve, both verbally and socially.

"The dogs acted as effective socializing catalysts and helped to improve the overall morale of the institution. They created a community out of individuals, many of whom were separated, detached, unhappy and self-pitying," wrote the Corsons in a report on this work in Current Psychiatric Therapies.

In another study by the Corsons, this one of 50 hospitalized psychiatric patients, 47 improved with pet-facilitated psychotherapy (P.F.P.). These were patients for whom other available therapeutic methods had failed, patients who were withdrawn and uncommunicative. The Corsons stress that P.F.P. is not a substitute for other forms of therapy, but an adjunct to facilitate the resocialization process. The essence of P.F.P. is the introduction of a non-threatening, loving pet to serve as a catalytic vehicle between the therapist and the patient. Its success is based on the proposition that many patients may accept the love of an animal before they can accept love from, and give love to, a human being. Dogs become, in the Corsons' words, "feeling-heart dogs."

Dr. Aaron H. Katcher, a psychiatrist at the University of Pennsylvania School of Medicine, uses P.F.P. He points out that although there are many known instances of the success and usefulness of P.F.P., there have been no controlled studies of it. But he cites a controlled study of a different kind of patient for whom pets played an important role. In this study, 91 cardiac patients were followed after they were released from a hospital coronary-care unit. The patients who went home to pets recovered or survived far better than those who did not. Whether the reason was that the pets gave needed love and companionship, provided a reason to live, or simply made a certain amount of exercise necessary, the results seem to confirm the belief that pets can be beneficial to health.

Pet animals are not the only ones that can help the health and well-being of handicapped people. At a riding academy in Boxford, Mass., 26-year-old Alice Weeks rolls her wheelchair up beside a large calm white horse, pulls herself to her feet, and brushes his neck and shoulders. Riding instructors Elizabeth Eckerson and Amanda Carey make no allowances—Miss Weeks has to do a good job of grooming the horse. Finally they are satisfied and boost her into the saddle. Their pupil, who is severely crippled with cerebral palsy, rides off at a trot,

posting very well.

"When Alice started riding here two and a half years ago, she couldn't push her own wheelchair, couldn't raise her arms and certainly couldn't stand even with help," explains Marjorie Kittredge, director of Windrush Farm Therapeutic Equitation. "She lived at home with her parents. Now she shares an apartment with another woman and works at the hospital where she also gets physical therapy."

"When I first came here to ride, I was really scared," says Miss Weeks. "Being on a horse felt weird. But now, it's thrilling, it's fun. And riding has made a big difference in my balancing ability."

Cantering beautifully in the ring with Alice Weeks is Mary Lou Barry, whose neck is in a brace. Miss Barry, a registered nurse, had been a true outdoorswoman—a skier and a backpack-

It has been found that pets in nursing homes cheer and divert the elderly residents.

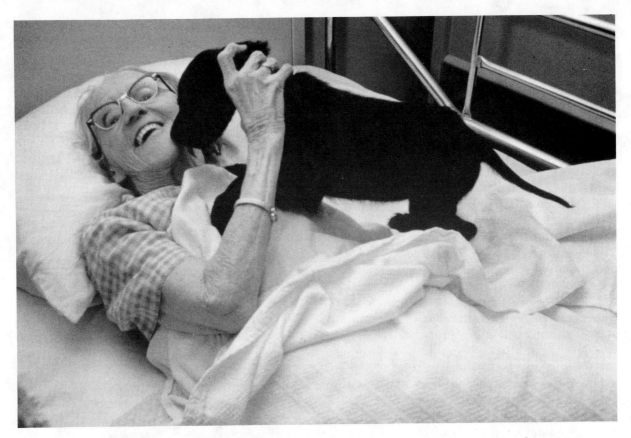

Doctors have found that patients have become more self reliant in response to pet therapy.

er—when she ruptured disks in her neck and developed thoracic outlet syndrome, a pinched brachial nerve. Complicated surgery had left her with her diaphragm permanently paralyzed on one side.

"When I met Mrs. Kittredge and she suggested riding, my orthopedist was skeptical, but I was ready to try anything to get better, and we agreed I couldn't be much worse," she relates. "At first, I got out of breath just grooming the horse. Now I ride once or twice a week, and I'm stronger, in better shape all over. But it's the mental uplift that's so tremendous. I thought I had lost forever my ability to enjoy the outdoors. Now I go on trail rides—I can even take low jumps. I'm a different person."

Martha Biery, who teaches therapeutic horsemanship to physically and mentally handicapped people at the Melmark Home near Philadelphia, believes her pupils benefit both physically and emotionally.

"Because the rider's body is constantly moving, readjusting to the motion of the horse," she explains, "this stimulates the vestibular part of the brain, which regulates balancing. Especially with people in wheelchairs, muscles stimulated in riding are getting sensations they never get otherwise and are sending signals to the brain. These riders get permanent benefits. Even the profoundly retarded, who at first are dead weight on the horses, improve."

At the Cheff Center for the Handicapped in Augusta, Mich., some 800 palsied, blind, legless, spastic or mentally retarded persons have, over the last ten years, benefited from the patience of Cheff's 30 sweet-tempered horses and a stream of teachers under the direction of Lida McCowan who trained in England, where riding for the handicapped originated in the early 1950's. Lida McCowan and Marjorie Kittredge both stress the importance in their field of North American Riding for the Handicapped, which is trying to professionalize and standardize the training, and which accredits both instructors and centers. The Cheff Center and a few of the other 100-odd therapeutic riding centers in the U.S. and Canada teach and accredit teachers. To qualify for accreditation, an instructor must be proficient in such subjects as physical therapy, orthopedics, horsemanship, horse care and stable management. Centers must qualify according to stiff standards of program and safety.

Weekly at Windrush Farm a group of emotionally disturbed young people between the ages of 6 and 18 charges into the barn where, aided by volunteers and supervised by Mrs. Kittredge and her staff, they brush, groom and saddle the horses and then, one at a time, are taught to perform tricks and gymnastics on the standing horses. Once these are mastered, the youngsters ride.

"The horses capture and hold the youngsters' attention, which for some of them is a novel experience in itself," Mrs. Kittredge points out. "Also, they overcome fear, develop self-control and taste the thrill of managing an awesome animal. Many of these kids have become dulled by continual failure. When they succeed with a horse, the therapeutic effect is magnified."

Starting with this theory, Green Chimneys, a resident school in Brewster, N.Y., for emotionally disturbed children, has established a true working farm. The 80-odd youngsters who are sent to this place for a maximum stay of two years are engaged in not only horse care and horseback riding, but the raising of cows, sheep, pigs, goats, ducks, chickens—the works.

A tough-looking 12-year-old energetically and competently shovels manure in the stall of a very pregnant cow.

"If she has her calf, I won't go home this weekend," he announces, running his hand fondly over the animal's bulging side. "Leave her? No way."

The farm functions as an important part of the special education and therapy these disabled children receive. It is believed that the animals, from the powerful horses down to the littlest ducklings and lambs, help the youngsters become more responsible, self-controlled and socialized.

Mother's Milk

by Robin Marantz Henig

The Williston Park Community Pool in Mineola, N.Y., had no doubt been the scene of more daring displays of flesh than Barbara Damon's. Mrs. Damon, wearing a one-piece bathing suit and draped in a towel, was breast-feeding her 2-month-old son, Michael, when the lifeguard confronted her, saying she was offending the other sunbathers. "He told me that I could nurse my baby in the restroom," Mrs. Damon said. "I said that the bathroom was not an appropriate place to nurse the baby."

Because Mrs. Damon continued to nurse Michael in public, the pool manager canceled her family's membership. The incident, brought to national attention by a suit the Damons filed in 1978, highlighted the dilemma facing many new mothers today, whether the benefits of breast-feeding warrant the extra effort it takes to nurse a child in contemporary America.

The number of women choosing to breast-feed has grown dramatically in recent years. According to a study made by a formula manufacturer, in 1971 the proportion of new mothers who left the hospital breast-feeding their babies was 23 percent; by 1977, the proportion had grown to 43 percent, and it's still climbing. The message of academic pediatricians and nutritionists has finally sunk in: Mother's milk is usually far superior to infant formula for a developing child.

However, even in the face of mounting evidence showing the benefits of breast-feeding both to mother and child, the decision to nurse may be a difficult one for the modern woman to make. Nursing is inconvenient, especially for the woman who works. The recent case of Linda Eaton, an Iowa City, Iowa, firefighter, exemplifies the problem. Mrs. Eaton was suspended from her job because she breast-fed her son while on 24-hour shifts. She nursed him during her "personal time," time male firefighters use to shower, eat, sleep or play cards. According to the city manager, she was suspended for refusal to follow orders. During a nationally televised news show before her suspension, Mrs. Eaton was shown nursing when the 'fire alarm sounded. She handed her baby over to his baby sitter, smiled at the cameras, and was the first person on the fire truck.

Other considerations that may complicate a woman's decision to nurse are hospital obstetrical procedures—which often interfere with suc-

Mrs. Eaton and her son.

Iowa City firefighter Linda Eaton was suspended for breast-feeding while on duty.

cessful nursing by sedating the mother during delivery and by separating her from her baby during its first days of life—and environmental pollution, which can make nursing dangerous, since some toxins may accumulate in breast milk. The woman's decision may also be influenced by her social status, educational level and economic standing.

□

Breast-feeding does not necessarily come naturally—even in the world of nature. Zoologists have found that chimpanzees need the instruction of other female chimps before they can successfully nurse their young. Interference in social groupings among animals—such as separation of a mother goat from her kid and the other goats during the first hour after birth—can hamper an animal's ability to nurse.

In humans, production of milk begins as a signal of the infant's need. As the baby sucks at the breast, the nerves of the mother's nipple send a message to the hypothalamus, an endocrine gland at the back of the brain. The pituitary gland, in turn, releases two hormones—oxytocin and prolactin. Oxytocin, the same hormone that doctors give to induce labor, stimulates contraction of the small saclike cells behind the areola, the dark area encircling the nipple. This forces the milk from the glandular tissue of the breast through the nipple, and initiates the flow of milk. At the same time, prolactin, the other hormone released by the pituitary, stimulates the production of milk through its action on the milk glands in the breast.

Almost anything can interrupt this delicate process. One study, conducted in early 1948 by Drs. Niles and Michael Newton in Philadelphia, showed that a woman who had nursed successfully for seven months could be so distracted by a tickle, a splash of ice water or a tricky mathematical problem that her milk flow virtually stopped. Dr. Mavis Gunther, a British pediatrician, found that even ideas could interfere with the flow of milk. Watching women using a breast pump to empty their breasts because their infants were too sick to nurse, Dr. Gunther said she could see the ebb and flow of the milk supply change with the topic of conversation.

There are also social and psychological obstacles. If a woman believes that for some reason she cannot breast-feed, she may think herself into a physiological state in which she cannot. But the fact remains that almost all women who want to breast-feed can. Small-breasted women can nurse as well as large-breasted women, since it's the amount of glandular tissue, not fat tissue, in the breast that determines the ability to produce milk. Large-breasted women won't increase their breast size by nursing; pregnancy, not nursing, is what accounts for the change in shape and texture of the breasts of women. Certain breast conditions associated with problems during nursing—such as mastitis, blocked milk ducts, breast engorgement or sore and cracked nipples—can usually be overcome with some simple techniques. And once an adequate milk supply has been established—usually after one month or so of frequent feedings at the infant's demand—most doctors agree that a daily bottle can be given in the mother's absence without interfering with milk flow, milk production, or the unique immunological protection afforded by human milk.

"Human milk is for human infants; cow's milk is for calves," said the late Dr. Paul Gyorgy, who spent more than 50 years studying the difference. As scientists discover more and more components of mother's milk, evidence mounts that the liquid contains just about everything an infant needs, not only for growth and nutrition but for coping with the harsh realities of life outside the womb.

□

Studies comparing the health of breast-fed and bottle-fed babies show that infants who nurse are less likely to have respiratory infections, allergies, diarrhea, gastrointestinal infections, eczema, ear infections and iron-deficiency anemia.

This is not to say that bottle-fed babies are unhealthy. As researchers learn more about what's in mother's milk, industrial scientists are able more closely to mimic it in new, "humanized" infant formula preparations. But even formula manufacturers agree that infant formula will always be second best. Among the compounds found uniquely in human milk are lipase, an enzyme that metabolizes fat; taurine, an amino acid involved in bile acid metabolism that may also help transmit nerve impulses in the brain; lysosome, an enzyme that fights bacteria; and lactoferrin, a protein that deprives certain bacteria, most often staphylococcus and *E. coli*, of the iron they need to survive. Breast milk also contains white cells that are better able to absorb bacteria than white cells found in blood. These cells, or macrophages, are transferred directly to the infant, and they engulf and kill any bacteria with which they come in contact. And the particular qualities of human milk—its low phosphate, low protein and high lactose content—create an acidic environment in the infant's alimentary canal that stimulates the growth of the so-called friendly bacteria and inhibits the growth of bacteria that could be harmful.

Some scientists think the immune protections provided through breast milk may last far beyond the weaning stage. At the Harvard School of Public Health, Drs. Isabelle Valadian and Robert B. Reed are following up a study initiated nearly 50 years ago on child health, growth and maturation, in Boston. A preliminary report indicates that adults who had participated in the study are today less likely to develop allergic reactions, such as eczema, rhinitis and asthma, if, as babies, they were breast-fed for at least six months.

Other components of breast milk also help to make for a healthier baby—and, perhaps, a healthier adult. Valadian and Reed of Harvard found that 30-year-olds who were breast-fed up to the age of 6 months have significantly lower serum cholesterol levels than adults who were breast-fed for two months or less. The difference may be due to the higher concentration of cholesterol in human milk than in cow's milk, a concentration some scientists believe may induce cholesterol-metabolizing enzymes to develop and lead to more efficient use of cholesterol in later life.

Mother's milk is, of course, not perfect. Some environmental pollutants have been shown to collect in breast milk, particularly such fat-soluble toxins as the agricultural chemicals DDT and PCB. DDT has been banned in this country, but harmful chemicals still persist in the waterways and food sources of some regions. In a recent policy statement, the American Academy of Pediatrics, which favors breast-feeding, cautioned women who are in high-risk occupations or live in areas where the chance of exposure is great, to have their breast milk analyzed for toxins before they begin nursing.

"Many compounds and drugs are also found in human milk," notes Dr. William Weil, chairman of the department of human development at Michigan State University, who testified before a Senate committee in 1977 about the hazards of contaminated mother's milk. "Many medications—anticonvulsants, antibiotics, sedatives—appear in breast milk, but by and large they are found in low quantities that are not considered disadvantageous to the child. Still, their presence could set up allergies and sensitivities to the drugs in later life."

The American Academy of Pediatrics has also recommended that nursing women refrain from taking specific drugs that might harm their infants: antithyroid compounds, antimetabolites, anticoagulants and cathartics. Some pediatricians tell nursing women to stay off the Pill, which interferes with the process of lactation. And they encourage moderation—or, if possible, abstinence—in smoking cigarettes and drinking coffee and alcohol.

□

If mother's milk is so good for her child—providing immunological protection, good nutrition, and possibly prevention of future problems like obesity, allergies, cavities and maybe even coronary artery disease—why isn't every young mother breast-feeding?

One reason is that many women simply do not know about the advantages. Doctors are reluctant to suggest breast-feeding, for they fear stirring up feelings of guilt and failure if the patient chooses the bottle. From a doctor's perspective, bottle feeding is easier. "The obstetrician's definition of a 'successful outcome' for his patient—the woman—is an uncomplicated delivery and an easy postpartum recovery," says Dr. Myron Winick, director of the Institute of Human Nutrition at Columbia University. "And the postpartum course is greatly simplified when the woman bottle feeds." The pediatrician, too, is apt to prefer treating a bottle-fed baby, Dr. Winick says, in

that he knows exactly how many ounces per day of exactly what formula the infant is getting.

By not advocating a specific feeding method, a doctor may be helping the woman to choose the one with which she is most comfortable, and a happy, relaxed mother feeding her child infant formula is better than a nervous mother trying to feed him breast milk. On the other hand, women may be making decisions about infant feeding without adequate information.

The women who are leading the movement back to nursing are those who have sources of information other than their obstetricians: better-educated, higher-income women who read books and magazines, attend natural childbirth classes, and tend to have the personal and social resources needed to make their own decisions. Among studies of young women in the university communities of Boston and East Lansing, Mich., where the women or their husbands were graduate students or faculty members, the proportion of breast-feeders was found to be about 75 percent. And in a poll of alumnae of Swarthmore College, nine out of 10 respondents had breast-fed.

□

Breast-feeding also has a connection to income. In Alabama, the proportion of middle-class mothers who breast-feed is twice that of lower-class mothers, and these figures are confirmed in other scattered surveys. Poorer women, who tend to have fewer sources of information and more problems to cope with, rely on the bottle because it is practical. With a bottle, anyone—grandmother, baby sitter, older child, father—can feed the baby.

Obstetric procedures in most modern hospitals, especially the larger, understaffed public hospitals serving many of the poor, tend to work against the ability to breast-feed. The first days after birth are crucial to building up both an adequate milk supply and a comfortable relationship between mother and child. But most hospitals separate the mother from her infant for all but feeding time, and feedings are scheduled at four-hour intervals—even though a breast-fed baby needs to nurse every two or two-and-a-half hours in the first few days.

Dr. Myron Winick, director of the Institute of Human Nutrition at Columbia University says, "We haven't adjusted our society to the needs of the breast-feeding woman who works."

When a woman is heavily sedated during childbirth, it may be days before her infant is alert enough to suck vigorously at the breast. In 1961, pediatrician Dr. T. Berry Brazelton at Children's Hospital Medical Center in Boston found that heavy medication with barbiturates during delivery impaired the success of breast-feeding for as long as five or six days. On the first day after birth, 65 percent of lightly medicated mothers had "effective" feedings, compared to just 30 percent of heavily medicated mothers.

Once a woman goes home with her baby, breast-feeding becomes even more traumatic. The new mother is frequently unable to tell if her child is getting enough milk. Added to this natural uncertainty are the problems a nursing woman encounters when dealing with the outside world—especially if she is a working woman.

"We haven't adjusted our society to the needs of the breast-feeding woman who works," says Dr. Winick of Columbia. "How do you breast-feed if you're working in an office or a factory? We're just not geared for that, and we haven't yet said as a society that the advantages are so great that we have to make special provisions for it."

With some ingenuity, breast-feeding and employment *can* mix. Working women can be taught to pump their milk by hand during the time they're away from home, to keep milk production stimulated. The milk may either be kept for the next day's feeding or the baby may be fed formula while the mother is away from home.

The frenetic pace of life today seems out of step with the measured, tranquil image of breast-feeding. What woman has time to nurse her baby five or six times a day, 20 or 25 minutes a feeding? Yet women who have nursed successfully, even the busiest among them, say they wouldn't miss the experience for the world. Not only is breast-feeding surprisingly convenient, they say—no bottles to clean, no formula to warm up, no equipment to tote—but it is fun: a sensual, satisfying experience that women look forward to as a haven in a hectic day.

The mother also benefits physically from the process. Hormones involved in milk production and lactation help shrink the uterus, utilize the fat deposits of pregnancy, prolong the postpartum period of infertility, and may even have a tranquilizing effect. Sex researchers William Masters and Virginia Johnson found that women who breast-feed resume an active sex life more quickly after delivery than do women who bottle-feed, and may in fact reach levels of excitement that exceed their prepregnancy states. Several investigators have also noted a decreased incidence of breast cancer among women who breast-feed, but confounding factors, such as the woman's age at childbirth and the number of children she has, make such findings difficult to interpret.

To allow women to savor this unique aspect of mothering, though, will take a reexamination of our society's values and priorities. Work schedules for new mothers will have to become more flexible to allow for longer lunch hours and more frequent breaks; feelings about the sight of bare breasts and nursing infants will have to be placed in perspective; information about the best way to breast-feed, and signs to assure a mother that her infant is being well fed, will have to be transmitted more effectively through obstetricians, pediatricians, nurses and even informal gatherings of nursing women. Only then will large numbers of women be able to experience that special kind of maternal pride. "The greatest part of breast-feeding," says Dr. Marvin Cornblath, a pediatrician at the National Institute of Child Health and Human Development in Bethesda, Md., "is when a mother comes in with her healthy, thriving baby and says, 'Look at that kid! Look how much he's grown since he was born! And all that came from me.'"

BIOLOGY

Inbred Mice

by Jane E. Brody

As Anna Stanley went about her chores one afternoon at the Jackson Laboratory in Bar Harbor, Maine—cleaning the mouse cages, replenishing the food and water—she spotted a deformed baby mouse in a 5-day-old litter of laboratory mice. The tiny creature had been born with no hind legs and a deformed front leg.

The discovery caused quite a stir in the animal room because Jackson Lab, which has just celebrated its 50th anniversary, is the repository for 70 percent of the world's known mouse mutants and the largest collection of inbred mice. Mutations that spontaneously occurred at the lab have given the world's researchers genetic models of such human illnesses as diabetes, obesity, muscular dystrophy, inherited anemias, leukemia and breast cancer.

With these animals, scientists can perform experiments that would be impossible or unethical to do in human beings. And, by incorporating the mutations into inbred strains of mice that are genetic carbon copies of one another, scientists can study the effects of single genes unconfused by the enormous genetic variability of ordinary animals and people.

The discovery wasn't the first anomalous mouse Anna Stanley, who is 59, has found during her 12 years at Jackson Laboratory, where three million descendants of the common house mouse are born each year. In years past, she has found among these inbred mice, which represent the world's most valuable tool for biological and medical research, a hairless dwarf, a mouse that danced in tight circles and one with a corkscrew tail. Jackson scientists examine each oddball mouse discovered in a new litter and decide whether to attempt to breed it in order to determine if the defect is caused by a genetic mutation. In the case of the hairless dwarf and the dancing mouse, both oddities were shown to be caused by genetic defects and the descendants of these mice—bred to pass the defect from generation to generation—are now being studied for hormonal and balance disturbances that may reveal new information about similar disturbances in humans.

If Jackson Laboratory follows its normal Tuesday routine, the mouse Anna Stanley

229

Inherited anemias, and the potential of marrow transplants to cure some forms of anemia as well as some forms of cancer, are the specialty of Dr. Seldon Bernstein.

A mouse mother from DBA inbred strain of mice watches over her young. The DBA inbred strain, the oldest in the world, has been inbred since 1909.

Anna Stanley goes about her work caring for and checking thousands of mice each week. Animal caretakers are trained to be alert for possible new mutations.

found will be transferred to the laboratory's mutant mouse stocks room. Although this mouse may not have a genetically caused deformity, the scientists here will try to find out by attempting repeated inbreeding of its offspring. If the defect is genetically caused—and the answer could take several years to determine—then biomedical scientists could have a new animal "model" that might aid research into the causes of human birth defects.

"We use inbred strains because they're a clean, pure test system," Priscilla Lane, a Jackson geneticist, explained. "We know that the effects we observe are due to the particular thing we're studying, whether it's a chemical carcinogen or environmental hazard or drug treat-

ment." This greatly reduces the number of animals needed to recognize an effect. If all the animals in a study are genetically different, it's harder to tell what caused what.

The late Dr. Clarence C. Little, who founded the laboratory in 1929, developed the first strain of inbred mice, called DBA. These mice are genetically prone to noise-induced epileptic seizures and breast cancers. He needed the genetically identical animals to carry out his cancer studies, in which he transplanted tumors from one animal to another. The transplants would be rejected as foreign unless the animals were identical twins, so he created in effect an endless family of such twins. Dr. Little, who initially had to "sell" the scientific community on the value of using inbred experimental animals, used to compare the special mice to pure chemicals. He suggested to his fellow scientists that just as they would not do chemical studies with undefined mixtures or impure substances, they should not try to do biological studies with unknown and variable mixtures of genes.

Dr. Seldon E. Bernstein, one of 35 staff scientists, notes that the mouse's value to research is further enhanced by its short reproductive cycle. It breeds at 50 to 60 days of age and produces a litter 20 days later, repeating the feat two or three times a year. "More generations of mice have lived since 1929 than of people since the human species evolved," Dr. Bernstein observed.

The mouse and the rat are highly unusual in their ability to inbreed. A new inbred strain of mouse takes about seven years to develop, a task that involves matings between brothers and sisters for 20 successive generations. At that point, it has been calculated, 99.999 percent of the genes in each animal are identical to those of its siblings.

An inbred strain of rabbit took the laboratory 35 years to produce. Other animals, including people, suffer from "inbreeding degeneration" when repeatedly mated with brothers and sisters. They become sickly and eventually fail to reproduce at all.

Breeding is only a small part of the work at Jackson lab. Most of the staff scientists seek answers to human ailments that may be found among the mutant strains. Dr. Bernstein, for example, has figured out how to cure a genetically caused anemia in mice that mimics a rare human anemia called Blackfan-Diamond disease. He found that the mouse disease was caused by a defect in the bone marrow cells that produce red blood cells. The mouse can be cured by a transfusion or bone marrow transplant of these so-called stem cells. The studies suggest possible treatments for human anemias that may be caused by environmental agents such as drugs or radiation. Based on his studies, Dr. Bernstein has concluded that persons who work with radiation or toxic chemicals should have small amounts of bone marrow put in a "bank" as a medical insurance policy.

In the island resort town of Bar Harbor, where fog- and tourist-filled summer days yield to cold and lonely winters, the mouse has become the most important year-round resident. It is treated accordingly. Housed in rooms that are environmentally constant, the cages and bedding of pine and cedar shavings are changed weekly. They are fed made-to-order sterilized feed, and their air is changed 10 times an hour.

All who enter the animal rooms must remove street clothes and don carefully laundered "mouse suits." To further reduce the possibility of disastrous epidemics, the cages are covered by filters that prevent infectious organisms from traveling from cage to cage. Caretakers are trained to spot not only possible new mutants but any animal that may appear even a little bit sick. All suspected of harboring disease are sent with their cage mates to a health inspector for examination and quarantine.

The precious animals, stacked seven cages high, occupy a total of 72,000 square feet, and a typical mouse room is 1,500 square feet, comparable to the floor space in an average three-bedroom house. The nonprofit laboratory sells two-thirds of the mice it raises to researchers in every state and many foreign countries. Prices range from $2 each for the stripped-down model of a normal inbred mouse that breeds easily to $20.60 each for the difficult-to-breed mouse with muscular dystrophy.

The dystrophic mouse, among other Jackson mutants with counterparts to severe human ailments, does not reproduce itself. To create one, geneticists mate two normal mice that are carriers of the gene for dystrophy. One quarter of their offspring will have the double dose of the dystrophy gene and show the symptoms of the muscle-wasting disease.

To improve the reproductive odds, the scientists can transplant the ovaries from a dystrophic mouse into a normal female of the same inbred strain. When mated with a carrier male, this female will produce half her offspring with dystrophy. In another approach, the female with the ovarian transplants can be artificially inseminated with semen from a dystrophic male, resulting in 100 percent dystrophic offspring.

Even if no one is in the immediate market for a dystrophic mouse, the lab has to keep the mutant gene going for future use. This requires continual breeding of known carriers of the dystrophy gene, a time- and space-consuming enterprise. Therefore, lab scientists have begun to look into the feasibility of storing desired genes by freezing embryos that harbor them. When a particular gene is needed for research, the embryo is defrosted and transplanted into a foster mother to nurture until weaning.

Dr. George D. Snell, retired senior scientist of the laboratory, believes the value of the inbred mouse will continue to grow, especially with the mushrooming need to test chemicals and contaminants for their ability to cause toxic effects and genetic damage. The growing interest in transplantation of organs is a further stimulus, the mouse having already guided much of the current understanding of tissue incompatibility between unrelated persons.

Plant-Animal Interaction

by Jane E. Brody

The thermometer on the ground next to us read 152 degrees Fahrenheit as we lay on our bellies in the midafternoon desert sun, trying to unravel the social structure of a newly discovered species of seed-harvesting ant. But the ants were not so foolish as their two-legged observers. With one or two exceptions, they waited out the scorching heat in the relatively cool tunnels of their huge underground nest.

Then, about an hour after nightfall when the temperature of the sandy topsoil dropped to a more comfortable 90 degrees, the pace of activity picked up. We counted the workers that carried in the tiny seeds that the ants store and live on, and we counted the workers that carried out the chaff, which litters the desert floor. Unseen below ground, other workers separated the seed from the chaff.

Winged forms—believed to be males and females ready for mating—also appeared with increasing frequency as the night wore on. And occasionally there emerged a "major worker," twice the size of the others, to clear a nest opening of accumulated debris. At 10:30 P.M., necks aching from our flashlight vigil, we called it

quits, although the ants undoubtedly worked on through the cool of the star-ridden night.

This study, one of many to cross the frontiers of desert science, is part of an ambitious effort to unravel the complex relationships between the plants and animals that make the unforgiving environment of Baja's Central Desert their home. Through periodic sojourns during the last several years, researchers from Idaho have discovered in the Baja desert more than a dozen animal species new to science, including a bivalve crustacean that lives in desert rainwater pools, various beetles and ants, and a new genus of a quarter-inch-long pseudoscorpion.

They have also discovered new associations between plants and animals. For example, the top of the barrel cactus was found to have nectar factories outside its flowers; stinging ants feed on the nectar and in return are believed to protect the cactus fruits from being eaten by bugs before the plant can seed itself.

Some 800 miles to the north, near Reno, a similar project proceeds in the Great Basin Desert of Nevada, the last major area of the contiguous United States to be explored. The

233

harshness of this shrubby, treeless and parched terrain tested the mettle of gold- and silver-hungry miners and pioneer families who in the mid-1800's sought their fortunes in California. The wagon trails across the desert are littered with the bones of oxen that succumbed to starvation and dehydration in the dry heat, or that perished in the sudden flash floods, sandstorms or snow storms for which this area is infamous.

Both projects are being funded by a private organization called Earthwatch of Belmont, Mass., and aided by volunteers from 16 to 65 who pay for the privilege of participating in field research. Although the Nevada and Baja studies are both basic research projects, their findings are expected to help guide human incursions into the desert, enabling man to mine the desert's resources with minimal disturbances to its delicate balance of life.

Contrary to popular impressions of the desert as a barren, lifeless, inhospitable wasteland, these studies have shown that a field guide's worth of plants and animals share one of the world's most fragile ecosystems. While not "teeming" with the colorfully obvious life-forms that are found in a tropical rain forest, the desert is host to a surprisingly large number of species that observers can easily find if they stop to look. Through evolution and survival of the fittest, each has found some way to cope with the deprivations of the desert, the primary one being lack of water. The Baja desert receives an average of four inches of rainfall a year, supplemented by early morning dew. The Great Basin areas under study get perhaps five inches of precipitation, but little or no dew.

Not much is known about the ecology of the desert because the environment challenges the tolerance of human observers and because funding organizations have been as unimpressed with this "nonproductive" land as the average citizen. Quick in-and-out collecting trips are not enough. To study interrelationships between plants and animals, researchers must spend weeks or longer in one spot, importing all food and water from home or resupplying from scattered small towns.

Patricia and Hamilton Vreeland of the University of Nevada at Reno said that the desert they are studying is a hotbed of geothermal energy and mineral resources waiting to be tapped, located in the nation's fastest growing state. "It's not a pristine environment untouched by humanity, and it doesn't house unique species that we know of," Mr. Vreeland noted. "We're trying to collect baseline data from which one can evaluate the effects of further human intrusions," he continued. "We're not idealistic ecologists who say the area must be preserved as is just because it's here. We recognize the need for trade-offs. But we think one should know the costs of development before it's too late."

Just the effect of human visitors and their dune buggies can be devastating to the desert. The thin layer of desert soil is protected from erosion by a fine crust composed of fungi, algae and mosses. When this crust is broken by a wheel or foot, the soil can easily erode, bringing an end to the desert's ability to support life. Mr. Vreeland continued, "The desert is fragile because, compared to a Maine forest, it houses a limited number of species." A disturbance in one can bring an end to another. Also, his co-worker Tom Lugaski added, "You can go out and do a lot of damage in a short time, and then it takes a very long time to undo that damage."

In the Baja, the desert workday begins at 5:30 A.M., when the sky lightens but before the scorching sun rises. Animal traps are checked, their inhabitants carefully measured and recorded and then released. Birds and bats caught in fine nets are similarly measured and stuffed for further study. Using hoola hoops to mark the study areas, an accounting is made of the plants, animal droppings and human litter found along the right-of-way cut five years ago for Baja's transpeninsular highway, a two-lane, shoulderless road with frequent washouts and more and bigger potholes than all of New York City's streets put together.

Despite its condition, the road has brought tourists to this otherwise inaccessible desert; on one evening, the research team counted several dozen recreational vehicles passing through, carrying people and objects that could disrupt this fragile environment.

After a break for breakfast at 8:30, work resumes until lunch, after which the heat—100-plus in the shade, 150 on the sunny ground—usually precludes physically taxing work until dusk. The hot afternoons are a time for napping

Small nectar factories discovered on the barrel cactus attract at least eleven different ant species. The ants collect nectar from the cactus and in return may discourage plant-eating insects from feeding on the cactus.

Expedition leader William H. Clark and the author check the height of a cardon cactus. Large cardon specimens can hold a half-ton of water.

in the shade of the desert's huge granite boulders, reading under the parachute that serves as a parasol over the campsite, pinning insects or stuffing animals. Later, the researchers take advantage of the evening cool, excavating ant nests, tracking down scorpions with a black light that causes them to luminesce bright green on the otherwise dark desert floor, hunting long-horned beetles that feed only at night.

"There are three basic ways to adapt to the desert," explained Dr. Robert Bratz of the College of Idaho, a longtime student of the Mexican desert who co-ordinated the Baja expedition directed by William H. Clark. "You learn how to get more water, you reduce the loss of water or you store water." Animals like coyotes and birds can travel to the desert's in-

frequent water holes. But small mammals must make do with what water happens to be nearby. The wood rat, for example, chews its way into the watery chambers of the massive cardón cactus, which then forms a thick scar tissue over the wood rat tunnels to protect itself from further dehydration. The cardón resembles Arizona's saguaro and, along with a bizarre-looking woody plant called the boojum, dominates the Baja desert landscape.

Other rodents stay underground during the heat of day, emerging only at night to gather food. The fleshy roots and tubers of many desert plants keep some desert animals supplied with water. Jackrabbits and cottontails seek their meals at dawn and dusk. Lizards and snakes have scaly skins and insects have outer

235

skeletons that keep water loss to a minimum. Even then, few are to be seen when the sun is high in the sky. Mr. Lugaski explained that the lizard partly controls its body temperature by changing color. It starts out dark-skinned in the morning; then as the temperature rises, pigmented structures in the skin close up and the skin lightens to reflect more heat. With nightfall, the skin again turns dark.

Perhaps the best-adapted desert mammal, Dr. Bratz noted, is the kangaroo rat (really a mouse), which can survive in adult life entirely on dry seeds. It excretes only solid wastes and can derive all the water it needs from the metabolic breakdown of fats and carbohydrates in the seeds. This long-tailed rodent, along with the smaller pocket mouse, cleaned the campsite of crumbs every night.

Plants have a somewhat harder time in the desert, since they are destined to stay where they happen to germinate. The cactus is nature's answer to water conservation. Its leaves are reduced to spines and it makes food through photosynthesis in its thick green stem. The innards of the cactus contain gelatin-like substances that attract and hold water—up to half a ton in the big cardóns, which are accordion-pleated for easy expansion when nature provides a surfeit of water. Most cactuses sport a massive network of surface roots, which act as catchbasins to retain every drop of available rainfall.

The boojum, named for the mystical thing in Lewis Carroll's "The Hunting of the Snark," is in essence a water tower—a woody, tapering cylinder filled with a bitter liquid. This tree, which is not a cactus and grows naturally only in the Baja Peninsula, resembles an upside-down carrot, with short scraggly branches extending from the trunk. Its close relative, the ocotillo, also known as coach whip or monkey tail cactus, leafs out only after a rain and photosynthesizes for a while; then the leaves drop off when the environment dries up again.

Other plants, like the mesquite, a bush-like tree under which Mexican cattle often seek relief from the sun, put down very deep taproots to reach the desert water table, perhaps 200 feet below the sandy surface. The seeds of many desert plants are coated with chemical inhibitors; they can germinate only when rain washes the chemical off. Then it is a rush through the life cycle—from sprout to bloom to fruit—before the water supply is exhausted.

Patricia Vreeland said that during the first Earthwatch expedition into the Great Basin Desert in June 1976, four inches of snow (representing half that area's average annual precipitation) collapsed several tents and turned the parched hillsides into rivers and the desiccated valleys into impassable mudholes. But a week later, the desert was a blaze of color as desert annuals cashed in on the unexpected windfall of water.

As Dr. Bratz pointed out: "There are no seasons, as such, in the desert. The desert blooms whenever it happens to rain." This fact makes desert study a rather chancy enterprise, since one never knows for sure which plants and animals will be available for study. "We always start out with far more projects in mind than we could possibly do in the allotted time because all aren't going to be available," Mr. Clark said. "Just because a certain plant is *supposed* to flower in June doesn't mean it will, and then the insect that feeds on it won't be there for study." He added that a field biologist "also has to be prepared for the unexpected—for example, the opportunity to study a plant or animal that just happens to be around when you are." It is this kind of unpredictability that distinguishes field from laboratory research. In the lab, Mr. Clark said, everything can be carefully controlled—"you come in in the morning, find a blue bottle on the table, mix it with the pink bottle and get orange."

In the desert that the Vreelands and Mr. Lugaski study, there are no notable cactuses or succulents as in the Baja. Here, foot-high silvery-green shrubs mark the lowlands—mostly sagebrush and shadscale along with spiny hopsage, rabbit brush, three-winged salt brush and tumbleweed (an imported species). Short evergreens—piñon pine and juniper—dot the cooler mountain slopes.

Yet the Great Basin Desert abounds with animal life—lizards, rabbits, squirrels, birds, desert mice and rats, and snakes, including the fierce panamint rattler as well as the more timid Great Basin rattler. A pair of great horned owls is nesting this year at one former Earthwatch site, and judging from the bones beneath their rock cliff, they dine well on small rodents and rabbits.

ARCHEOLOGY

The Ebla Ruins

by Boyce Rensberger

From the remains in Syria of the 4,500-year-old lost Kingdom of Ebla, scholars are reconstructing scenes from the early stages of civilization suggesting that mankind's first cities may have been far more like those of today than most people imagine. Some experts suggest that Ebla is proving to be among the greatest archeological finds of the century, and excavations at its site have disclosed a wealth of artifacts that provide new knowledge of artistic and technological achievement in the world's earliest civilizations. Of significance for science is evidence of the ways in which large urban centers and complex political and economic networks were first formed.

The site has also yielded thousands of inscribed clay tablets that some biblical scholars believe rival the Dead Sea Scrolls in authenticating and adding to knowledge of life in biblical and prebiblical times.

Some 2,500 years before the birth of Jesus—1,800 years before the rise of classical Greece—Ebla was a large and thriving commercial, administrative and intellectual center with economic and political institutions that sound remarkably familiar: For example, records discovered in the palace archive disclose the following details about the ancient civilization:

• The king of Ebla was elected for a seven-year term and shared power with a council of elders. Kings who lost re-election bids retired on government pensions.

• Ebla hosted international academic conferences, proceedings of which have been found in the palace archives. Professors from other nations came to Ebla to teach.

• Ebla dominated so many other cities politically and economically that it appears to have been the hub of the largest network of urban areas in its day. Among its many trading partners were Sodom and Gomorrah, cities whose historical reality had been doubted until now.

• The city of Ebla, the kingdom's capital, had about 30,000 residents, of whom 11,700 were civil servants. Many others were employed in government-owned textile and metal-working industries. The entire kingdom may have had a population of 260,000.

• Ebla maintained an academy in which students, many from other kingdoms, were trained in the cuneiform system of writing. In records of the academy, scholars have traced the career of one beginning student who eventually rose to the top of the kingdom's administrative hierarchy.

Until Ebla's discovery was announced in 1976, scholars knew of only two other civilizations of comparable sophistication and age, Sumer and Egypt. Ebla, in what had been considered a wasteland between the two, is now known to have had political and economic relations with both. One theory is that Ebla began as a distant outpost of the early Sumerian culture, which arose around 3100 B.C., then rapidly developed into an independent civilization. There is evidence, however, that the acropolis at Ebla was occupied as long ago as 3500 B.C.

The ruins of Ebla were discovered by Paolo Matthiae, a University of Rome archeologist who has been in charge of a dig on the site since 1964. Not until 1968 was there a hint that the site was that of Ebla, whose existence had long been inferred from Mesopotamian literature. At the time, most experts had no idea that Ebla was as important as it now seems to have been. That finding followed the excavation, from 1974 through 1976, of the palace archive.

More artistically impressive artifacts have come from other sites, but nothing comes close to the volume of written material found at Ebla. Some 15,000 clay tablets or fragments have been recovered. This is four times the writing known from all other archeological sites of the period. To decipher the tablets, Professor Matthiae called in Giovanni Pettinato, an Italian epigrapher, or specialist in interpreting inscriptions, who knew Sumerian cuneiform and who deciphered the new language on the tablets, now called Eblaite and recognized as the oldest known Semitic language.

The findings include a variety of documents ranging from literary texts, the contents of which have not been reported, to expense accounts of traveling diplomats and invoices for goods shipped and received. Professor Pettinato has also found a number of lists of such things as kings, gods, professions (more than 60 are included), plants, minerals, birds, mammals, fish, personal names, conjugations of verbs and even a list of beers, one of which was called Ebla. There are Sumerian-Eblaite dictionaries running to more than 3,000 words.

Shortly after the significance of the archive was recognized, Professors Matthiae and Pettinato began to disagree over a number of matters, from the precise dating of the tablets to who was receiving or deserving more publicity. According to an authoritative report in the journal Biblical Archaeology Review, the feud reached such proportions that the two scholars did not speak to one another for months, and Professor Matthiae appointed an international committee of 10 experts to take over the deciphering of the tablets—a monumental task that is expected to last for many years. The discord reportedly reached a point where the President of Italy called both men in and demanded that they put aside their differences. Professor Pettinato has since agreed to serve on the committee.

By far the most controversial findings to date have been the names on various tablets that bear uncanny similarity to biblical names. Although the tablets are believed to have been written some 1,500 years before the days of David and Solomon, they mention people by the names of Ab-ra-mu (Abram would be the Old Testament version), E-sa-um (Esau), Mi-ki-ilu (Michael), Da-'u-dum (David), Ish-ma-ilum (Ishmael) and Ish-ra-ilu (Israel).

The Ebla tablets also list five towns that are strikingly similar in name to the relatives of Abraham given in Genesis. The towns are Phaliga, Sarugi, Til-Turakhi, Nakhur and Haran. Abraham's relatives are named in the Bible as Peleg, Serug, Terah, Nahor and Haran. Biblical scholars have generally thought Abraham lived around 1800 B.C.

Yet another strange parallel with the Bible is a list of five towns (Sodom, Gomorrah, Admah, Zeboiim, and Bela, also called Zoar). Both the Ebla tablets and Genesis, written more than a

A general view of the excavation site at Ebla.

thousand years later, give the same list in the same order. In the Bible, Sodom and Gomorrah, often assumed to be allegorical, are destroyed for their wickedness. In the Ebla tablets, they are thriving commercial centers. The tablets also contain a poetic account of the creation of the world that is much like the Genesis story. And there is an Eblaite tale of a great flood that destroyed the world, an account similar to the flood stories of both the Bible and Sumerian poetry.

Professor Pettinato also believes he has found evidence that the god Ya, a contraction of the Hebrew god Yahweh, was among some 500 deities recognized at Ebla. He has suggested that Ya eventually rose in theological prominence to become the single deity recognized by the Hebrews. Other epigraphers note that translating the critical syllable as "ya" is but one of two possibilities for a certain cuneiform symbol. The other would leave no evidence for Ya at Ebla.

In any case, many biblical scholars believe that the world documented on the Ebla tablets was the cultural background from which the ancient Hebrews emerged. Some suggest the tablets may even prove as useful in assessing the Old Testament as have the Dead Sea Scrolls. The suggestion, however poorly founded, that the early Jews may have been Syrians, or vice versa, has proven so disquieting, given the mood of Arab-Israeli relations, that Biblical connections have been de-emphasized in recent reports on Ebla.

Of perhaps greater scientific significance is the evidence Ebla provides for the ways in which large urban centers and complex political and economic networks were first formed. Before the emergence of Ebla and its contemporaries, Sumer and Egypt, people everywhere lived either as hunters and gatherers, as nomadic pastoralists or as simple farmers and fishermen gathered into small villages. But it is clear from the few Ebla tablets that have been translated, that, throughout what is now a desert, there was a network of surprisingly large and prosperous cities engaged in complex trade and political relationships. There must also have been the ecological resources necessary to sustain the cities.

The first book on Ebla to appear in the United States is "Ebla: A Revelation in Archaeology," by Chaim Bermant, a British writer, and Michael Weitzman, an authority on ancient Near Eastern languages at University College, London. The book, published by Times Books, contains most of the findings to date and includes chapters on early Mesopotamian history and on the reading of cuneiform.

Today the region around Ebla is a treeless desert with only a wide mound where the great city once stood. (It was destroyed and rebuilt three times before its final destruction by the Hittites around 1650 B.C.) The ruins of Ebla cover about 140 acres, only a tiny portion of which has been excavated. It is assumed that digging and discovery will continue for generations.

'Space-Age' Archeology

by Franklin Folsom

About 90 miles northeast of Gallup, N.M., just south of the Four Corners where Utah, Colorado, Arizona and New Mexico meet, massive stone ruins of ancient, pre-Columbian cities silently emerge from the valley floor of Chaco Canyon. With tall sandstone cliffs as a backdrop, the vacant, remote settlements are a lonely reminder of a vanished but evidently sophisticated civilization that flourished here between A.D. 900 and 1300—and then mysteriously disappeared.

Archeologists have long been fascinated by Chaco Canyon and its mysterious inhabitants, called the Anasazi, or Ancient Ones, by the Navajos, who came to this area centuries later. Only in the last few years, however, have archeologists begun to unlock some of Chaco Canyon's secrets—through the efforts of a multidisciplinary scientific team that has adapted the advances of space-age technology to the study of ancient man. They are part of a revolution going on in the quiet world of archeology, a "new archeology" that involves a complex mixture of electronic equipment, contributions from far-flung scientific specialties and a good deal of hypothesizing.

At Chaco, a 32-square-mile national monument where the National Park Service is now in the last year of an intense 10-year archeological study, the new archeology has resulted in a surprising new yet coherent theory explaining how the Anasazi lived in this barren plateau country and why they may have abandoned their dramatic stone cities.

The Anasazi were an ingenious, vigorous, adaptable people whose highly developed society prospered despite an exceedingly inhospitable—if spectacular—environment. They are best known for their elaborately built stone towns. The most famous, Pueblo Bonito (Beautiful Village) is probably the largest prehistoric architectural complex in the United States. It housed about 1,000 people in a vast structure of 800 spacious rooms stretching over three acres. Shaped like an amphitheater, this oversized "apartment house" rose four and five stories high, with rooms arranged in a terraced semicircle around a central plaza. Ringing the plaza were circular ceremonial rooms, called kivas.

Anasazi society appears to have been complex and well organized. The master builders who designed Pueblo Bonito built twelve other huge,

Pueblo Bonito, seen here from the air.

walled-in complexes in the Chaco area, as well as 2,300 smaller sites. In addition, Anasazi "engineers" surveyed and then constructed more than 250 miles of wide, straight roads to link their communities to each other and to the outside world.

Well established in the canyon by A.D. 500, Anasazi farmers built dams and irrigation canals to water the corn, squash and beans they managed to grow in this desertlike country—and they providently stockpiled their crops against drought years. They hunted rabbit, deer, antelope and big horn sheep for food. Artisans wove yucca plant fibers into sturdy sandals and baskets, made cotton into clothing, and fashioned feathers and fur into winter ponchos.

Their pottery was skillfully shaped and painted. Chaco's masonry was an art in itself: Pueblo Bonito's beautifully veneered walls rival those of the Aztec culture in Mesoamerica and the Inca culture in South America. The Anasazi even imported foreign goods: copper bells, macaws and parrots from Mexico, raw turquoise from mines in central New Mexico and Olivella shells from the Gulf of California.

Who were the Anasazi, those clever people who flourished for hundreds of years in the canyon, then abandoned their cities in the 13th century?

Explorers and archeologists have asked that question ever since a certain Lieut. James H. Simpson discovered the canyon in 1849 on a military expedition exploring the area west of Santa Fe. William Henry Jackson, the dogged photographer of the old Southwest, took pictures of the canyon as early as 1877. And archeological excavation of the site has been going on for 80 years, with expeditions by the American

242

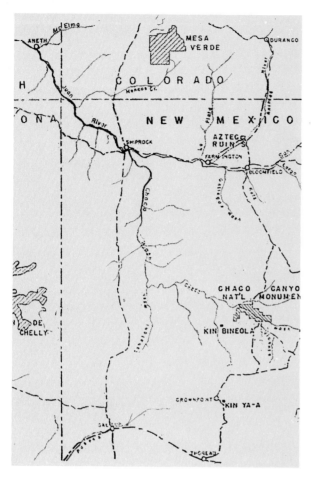

Location of Chaco Canyon National Monument in New Meixco.

Museum of Natural History (1896–99) and the National Geographic Society (1921–27). Even Charles Lindbergh, an aerial photography enthusiast, shot the canyon in 1929, bragging: "From my ship, I can find one undiscovered ruin for every one that has been located from the ground!"

The National Park Service Study, which got under way in 1970, is concerned with a broader range of questions concerning the overall Anasazi adaptations than were previous investigations. These questions include those concerned with the relationship of the people and their environment, their social organization, the sources for their raw materials, their technology, etc. Four years ago, Dr. W. James Judge, a 43-year-old "new" archeologist, succeeded Dr. Robert H. Lister as chief of the $200,000-per-year project. Dr. Judge oversees 10 full-time

archeologists in the year-round effort that involves summers of photographing, surveying, measuring, testing and excavating at the site itself and winters of inventorying (nowadays by computer), scientific analysis and evaluation of the data recovered from the site. For each day in the field, Dr. Judge's archeologists spend three days in labs at the Chaco Center on the Albuquerque campus of the University of New Mexico, 170 miles southeast of the canyon.

Dr. Judge takes an interdisciplinary approach; his team includes experts in architecture and masonry, geology and biology, fossils and bones, ceramics and stone artifacts. He hires other scientific specialists for help on specific problems and works closely with other National Park Service archeologists at the Remote Sensing Center on the same campus. They help Dr. Judge find sites, roads, even garden plots, by means of remote-recording instruments, such as cameras or scanning devices in satellites, planes and tethered balloons. They have devised new techniques for studying aerial photographs on electronic monitors that let them "see" ruins in the canyon that cannot be seen by the naked eye either on the ground or in a conventional photograph.

The work of these archeologists is breaking new ground. Unlike a traditional archeologist, who used to singlehandedly direct groups of unskilled laborers to scour a site for "goodies" to send home to museums, a new archeologist looks for information rather than objects. He discourages treasure hunts and heedless excavations. The Park Service calls this "conservation archeology." As Dr. Judge explains it: "We're careful about excavations now, because we destroy our own and future archeologists' data banks as we excavate. The more we dig, the more we destroy, so it behooves us to destroy as little as possible from the site."

The new archeologist is primarily interested in human behavior—how ancient people lived, how they related to each other, how the climate, plants and animals shaped men's lives. His approach is to "design a research problem" on some aspect of prehistoric human behavior and then plan an excavation to recover data relevant to the problem.

To illustrate his deductive approach to problems posed by Chaco Canyon, Dr. Judge

243

formulated a typical (and deceptively simple) question: "How did the Anasazi cope with Chaco Canyon's particularly harsh climate?"

"To answer this," says Dr. Judge, "we must first ask what the character of that environment was *then*. When we've answered that, we can ask how man adapted to it, what his subsistence strategy was."

The climate in Chaco Canyon today is brutal: 30 degrees below 0 in winter, with a considerable amount of snow; at least 90 degrees in summer, with highs reaching 120 degrees. But was it as severe 1,000 years ago? Dr. Judge's team employed some dendrochronologists, experts in tree-ring dating, to provide the answer. Over the past 50 years, dendrochronologists have charted the growth rings of certain Southwestern firs and pines, documenting the patterns of the past 2,000 years. These growth-ring charts also reveal rainfall levels, since trees have wider rings—or more growth—in wetter years.

Archeologists have estimated that there may have been as many as 75,000 Ponderosa pine and Douglas fir trees cut for construction at Chaco. Dendrochronologists studied the cross-sections of the ceiling beams in various Chaco buildings and matched their ring patterns with those of New Mexico's master charts to determine when they were cut down. Allowing for possible stockpiling or reuse of beams, they calculated that Pueblo Bonito was built between 920 and 1060. They then compared Chaco's tree rings with modern samples and concluded that rainfall has not decreased in the Chaco area over the intervening years.

This conclusion was then verified by geologists who studied layers of soil, particularly the alluvial deposits in Chaco Canyon's deeply cut arroyos (streambeds), and found little variation in moisture levels, and by palynologists, who determined from the ancient pollens preserved at Chaco that the vegetation hasn't changed.

If the climate has not changed, then, how did the Chacoans adapt to it? Dr. Judge projected another hypothesis: "If the population increased over time, we can assume their adapting mechanisms were successful."

The number of ancient community sites in the Chaco Canyon has been established: There are at least twelve large complexes like Pueblo

A multi-storied building in Pueblo Bonito.

Bonito and 2,300 lesser sites. But it was necessary to date the various sites and compare the numbers built in various periods to see if building had increased from one period to the next.

Dating of sites could be done by a number of methods: Carbon 14 analysis of construction materials, tree-ring dating where roof beams still existed, masonry and pottery style analysis and a new technique called archeomagnetic dating.

Derived from geophysics, archeomagnetism is based on the fact that the location of the north magnetic pole has shifted significantly during the course of the past milleniums. These "wanderings" have been charted as far back as A.D. 300. Knowing that the iron particles in clay line up with the magnetic pole and that, once clay is fired, its iron particles are locked in the direction of the magnetic field at that time, the

Anasazi masons constructed Pueblo Bonito's rooms like railroad flats, with centered doorways and walls beautifully veneered with blocks of dressed sandstone.

archeologists realized they could date Chaco's fire pits.

First, they recorded the precise location of the present magnetic pole at the site of an ancient fire pit. Then they sent a sample of the clay pit to labs at the University of Oklahoma, where technicians applied a sensitive magnetometer to the sample to discover the original orientation of its iron particles. Then, by comparing the position of the pole as indicated by the sample with that of the historical master chart, geophysicists were able to date the exact year a hearth was first used.

Using these techniques in combination, Dr. Judge's team was able to better determine which sites were contemporary in any given time period. From this and other information, they were able to estimate that there were about 1,600 Anasazi in Chaco by 700; 3,200 by

900; and 5,600 by 1100. They then see a dropoff to about 1,000 by the mid-1200's. By 1275, Chaco's buildings were no longer occupied.

With this evidence of the steady population growth over the course of four centuries, Dr. Judge went on to the next question: "What kinds of social mechanisms would be involved in promoting such an increase?" Part of the answer seems clear: As Chacoan society became more complex, there was more division of labor. This seems to be borne out by the increasing refinement of pottery, masonry, tools and ornaments, leading archeologists to suspect that such products were made by specialists.

Still, the question arises how Chaco's semi-desert soil and limited rainfall could support enough farming to feed several thousand people by the mid-1100's. Dr. Judge's archeological team focused on this problem and came to some

245

Aerial view of Pueblo Alto, another village complex of the Anasazi.

surprising conclusions. Using a variety of remote-sensing techniques, they mapped the canyon's arable land and located the areas where corn, squash and beans were cultivated. By calculating the yield per acre, they concluded that Chaco's crops were not sufficient to feed such a large population.

Could there have been additional crops? The palynologists were consulted and their answer was "No." Did the Chacoans increase their hunting? No, say bone experts, who have studied Chaco's trash mounds (the equivalent of a gold mine for an archeologist). They found the bones of rabbit, bighorn sheep, deer and antelope in the mounds, but there were not enough bones to indicate that meat was a major part of the Anasazi diet.

Dr. Judge's theory, evolved from many discussions with his colleagues, is that the Chacoans must have gone outside the canyon for the necessities that would permit growth.

He points, first of all, to Chaco's "imported goods": macaws and parrots, turquoise, copper bells, shells from the Gulf of California. Ornithologists who long ago studied the remains of scarlet and green macaws found at Chaco had determined that the birds were from Mexico. There is no natural turquoise in the Chaco basin; the nearest deposit of the mineral is at Cerillos, N.M., about 125 miles away. Geochemists in labs in Brookhaven, L.I., were sent turquoise beads from Chaco to test. They discovered that the beads have the same trace elements as Cerillos turquoise.

Then Chaco Center's petrologist, Helene Warren, who does microscopic analysis of the composition of rocks, analyzed the crushed rock used as temper in Chaco's pottery. She found

An excavated room (above) at
Pueblo Alto.

Excavation in progress;
(right) clearing off a floor and
taking notes.

An excavation team at work in Pueblo Alto.

A stone box with the door removed.

Pottery from Chaco Canyon National Monument (opposite page). Left to right, back row: Red wide mouth jar, Mug, Water/Storage jar, Duck Pot, Canteen. Front row: Pitcher, Three ladles, Trilobate bowl, Bowl.

that little of it came from the rock deposits in Chaco Canyon. This is quite startling, because pots and shards found at Chaco have distinct, recognizable styles; they are either painted in a controlled hachured style, black on white, or are plain, with a textured surface almost like corrugated cardboard.

Local artisans, says Dr. Judge, made handsome and serviceable vessels; however, at least during certain time periods, they made a relatively small percentage of the pottery actually used in the canyon. The rest came from potters some 15 to 75 miles away. The same is true of many of the stone tools used at Chaco.

Logical deduction from these facts led Dr. Judge and the others to put together an explanatory "model" of the "Chacoan phenomenon."

"Developments in Chaco from A.D. 900 to 1200 were probably unique," Dr. Judge says. "Society in the canyon flourished just *because*

it was so lacking in material resources. The very poverty of the land seems to have stimulated Chacoans to adopt a different method of survival. They made their unlikely habitat into a trade and distribution center, possibly using the imported turquoise, which they fashioned into beads and other ornaments, as the medium of exchange." Tens of thousands of those beads have been found in Chaco's ruins. Those curious "apartment houses"—the complexes like Pueblo Bonito—may have been reserved for travelers attending Chaco trade fairs.

"Small caretaker groups could have maintained the sites," Dr. Judge believes. "The specialists also stayed put, among them administrators and priests. Possibly there were year-round masons, whose skills account for the unique stone walls of Pueblo Bonito. More to the point, artisans must have been employed in making articles exchanged for imported goods—

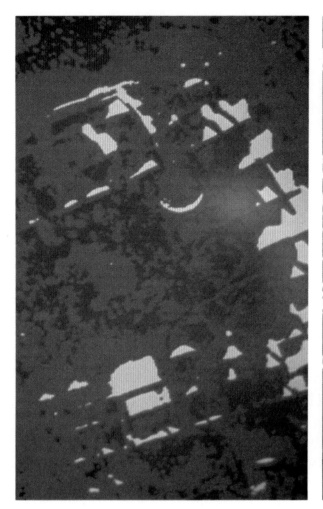

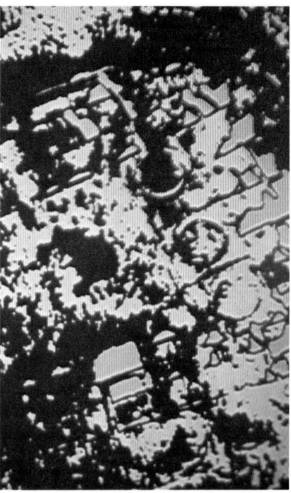

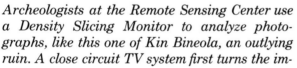

Archeologists at the Remote Sensing Center use a Density Slicing Monitor to analyze photographs, like this one of Kin Bineola, an outlying ruin. A close circuit TV system first turns the im- *age into black and white. Then a technician uses a density slicer to assign a different color to each shade of gray, or density band. By manipulating colors, a technician can discover new patterns or*

for birds and bells brought all the way from Mexico."

Clearly Chaco's inhabitants enjoyed prosperity for several years. But why, then, did they abandon their cities? Again, Dr. Judge has a theory. "My own view is that the Chacoans developed to a point where they could extract the maximum amount of energy available to them in the San Juan basin [the northwestern corner of New Mexico]—by extracting first the limited resources in the canyon and then those in the whole basin. That seems to have been the limit of their expansion.

"By the 12th century, they were straining their environment too much, given the sophisti-

cated economics and social system they had. Whereas they seemed to have been able to recover from earlier droughts [for example, by stockpiling corn], there may have been such severe environmental deterioration in the droughts of the late 1100's and mid-1200's, as shown by dendrochronologists, that they couldn't cope; it put their systems under too much stress. Their adapting mechanisms failed and they were forced to leave the canyon."

Verification for Dr. Judge's working hypothesis has been sought elsewhere, particularly at the remote-sensing labs on the same campus.

Under the direction of Dr. Thomas Lyons, an archeologist and geologist, an interdisciplinary

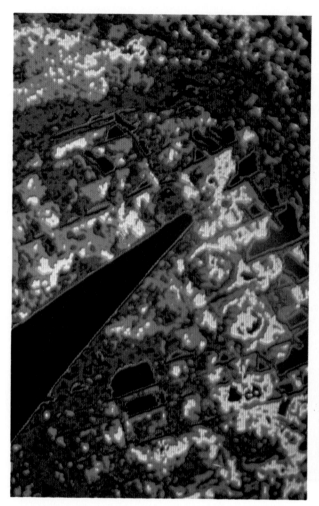

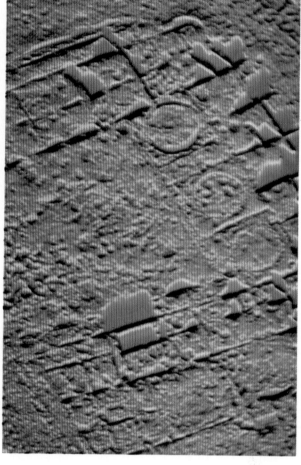

anomalies in the terrain that may turn out, upon later field inspection, to be a ruin.

Photograph at right has been processed by a second device, an edge enhancer, which isolates

lines barely visible in an untreated photograph. The enhancer has helped archaeologists to discover and then map the Chacoan's extensive road network.

team of 10 scientists works with sophisticated closed-circuit television systems to analyze thousands of black-and-white, color and infrared aerial photographs of Chaco furnished them by the United States Geological Survey, the Soil Conservation Service, N.A.S.A. and other governmental agencies, as well as by private engineering firms.

They usually begin with what they call "eyeball interpretation" of aerial photographs, using a stereoscope, a highly refined (and extremely useful) version of that favorite Victorian party-pleaser, the stereopticon. The stereoscope provides a three-dimensional impression of terrain, showing walls, for example, that could not be

seen on a single aerial photograph. This information is then transferred onto maps which help archeologists locate new sites.

For more refined photo interpretation, the sensing team goes to three electronic machines that are used with a closed-circuit television system. The most useful one, called an edge enhancer, electronically accentuates all lines that appear in an aerial photograph—lines not noticeable in a plain picture. This makes a largely obscured road or even a slight fault in a cliff stand out boldly on the television screen.

The edge enhancer has helped Dr. Lyons and his staff locate and then map many miles of "new" prehistoric roads throughout the Chaco

An aerial view of Kin Bineola, a small ruin.

area. Once the roads were mapped, archeologists checked them out on the ground. They discovered, to their astonishment, more than 250 miles of "highways"—most of them unpaved, some with sandstone flagging, some as wide as 30 feet, with curbs and retaining walls.

"These were not trails but engineered roads," Dr. Lyons says. "The people who built them laid them out in straight lines. When they came to a cliff or ledge, they surmounted it by cutting stairways or constructing masonry ramps. They built walkways across the bottoms of ravines. The roads exhibit a high degree of engineering and construction skills."

And where did the roads lead? To other Anasazi settlements in the canyon and to what Dr. Lyons calls "resource areas"—places where the Chacoans could cut down pine logs for roof

beams or collect rocks to shape into stone tools. And they hauled these back to their homes without wheeled vehicles or any beasts of burden. "With the heavy concentration of Anasazi population, local resources were no doubt reduced and depleted, thus forcing the Chaco people to exploit an ever-widening area," Dr. Lyons says, confirming Dr. Judge's conclusions.

Evidence of long distance trade from non-Chacoan areas are indicated by such items as the remains of garfish that occurred prehistorically in the Rio Grande to the east and south; turkeys that were apparently brought in from adjacent highlands to the east and west; and marine shell fragments which indicate trade from the Gulf of California. The mechanisms of transfer are not yet completely understood; however, over the final portion of the trip the items were carried on the Chacoan roads—some of which extend for as much as 30 miles away from the canyon.

A second machine is the density-slicing monitor, which lets Lyons's staff use the closed-circuit system to turn photographs first into black-and-white screen images, and then into 32 "density bands," or shades of gray. Each density band is then arbitrarily assigned a different color, giving the picture a rainbow effect (stone ruins can be made purple and vegetation orange, for example). As an archeologist changes the colors on the monitor, he can see "new" patterns in the terrain.

In one case, the density-slicing monitor re-vealed several straight lines less than half a mile from Pueblo Bonito. They seemed to be dividing up segments of an area the size of a football field. A later field inspection revealed they were berms (dirt ledges) dividing an ancient garden plot into several 50- by 60-foot sections with irrigation canals. They had discovered a garden that hadn't been cultivated since 1200.

The staff uses a third device, the perspective monitor, to "rotate" (electronically) an aerial screen image to give it a "false" or electronically created relief, making it appear three-dimensional. The perspective monitor is used not only to discover new sites but also to study the configuration of known structures—the shapes and

Kim Ya'a, an outlying ruin, seen from the air, in an edge enhanced photograph. A prehistoric road passes to the east of the ruin; it is the dark line which enters the top of the photo (i.e. from the north), bends obliquely next to the ruin and leaves to the southwest (at the lower left corner of the photo).

dimensions of rooms. This helps archeologists determine what certain rooms may have been used for—storage, living, ceremonies—*before* they begin to excavate them.

Another remote-sensing device is the thermal infrared scanner. Operated from an airplane, it can record differences in ground temperatures as minute as 1/4 degree centigrade. This enables an archeologist to detect buried walls, for example, because stone radiates more heat than soil, or a spring, because moist soil radiates more heat than parched, undisturbed soil.

Some time ago, a curious white area turned up on one scanner image and sent archeologists quickly into the field, to a site about 10 miles from Pueblo Bonito. There they found a 3-by-5-foot-high rim of earth sticking out from the bottom of a mesa, beneath an arroyo, or dry steam bed. The neck was filled with ancient pot sherds and construction materials, built up like a dam. Below the dam was a vast rectangular area covered with silted soil.

The Chacoans apparently dammed the arroyo to trap the water whenever a rare rainstorm occurred. When the small dam had filled, its water would flood the field, bringing with it fertilizing, nutrient-filled silt swept down from the mesa top by the rushing water.

□

Remote sensing technology, while still new, is a promising tool that will become even more useful as it is refined to the archeologist's needs. Used in conjunction with the scientific sleuthing of Dr. Judge's new archeologists, it provides important additional data to help in the substantiation (or refutation) of such hypotheses as the Chacoan trading-center theory.

Chaco Canyon, of course, is only one of dozens of major sites currently being excavated throughout the United States. A sense of very real urgency animates archeologists today. They are alarmed at the rapid destruction of sites—primarily by pot hunters—but also by what they call "land-modifying activities"—i.e, the building of dams, highways and power plants. Charles R. McGimsey 3d, author of "Public Archeology," warned in 1972 that most archeological sites in this country would be destroyed by the year 2000.

McGimsey's and other archeologists' concern has had some effect, over the years promoting the passage of a number of Federal and state laws that help to protect archeological sites, including the 1974 Archeological and Historical Preservation Act. It allows all Federal agencies to spend up to 1 percent of the money allocated for a project on archeological surveys, excavation and preservation.

Support for such work by the Government (and private business) helps to explain why archeology is a growth industry. A century ago there were almost no fully professional archeologists in this country. Now there are about 3,000 fully qualified, full-time North American archeologists. Government agencies that employ archeologists, or contract them, include the Bureau of Land Management (103 on staff), the Forest Service, National Park Service, Soil Conservation Service and the Department of Defense. And, of course, there are several thousand serious amateur archeologists who continue to discover new sites as well as assist on digs. The volume of archeological activity in this country is astonishing and includes the study of historical as well as prehistorical sites.

Supported by increasing popular interest, with laws and funds to aid them, archeologists are becoming more technically sophisticated and more clever about enlisting the services of other scientists. They are not afraid of new technology or methodology. If they can't solve every mystery, they are daring to hypothesize on the basis of what they do know and to speculate why we human beings have become what we are. The new archeologist knows that it is the technology this country developed for space exploration that is going to answer his questions about ancient man on earth.

The Biggest Dinosaur

by Bayard Webster

A Utah paleontologist, digging in an ancient dry river bed on a windswept Colorado mesa, has found bones of the biggest dinosaur that has yet been discovered—a huge animal that he estimates would have been able to look into a top-floor window of a five- or six-story building. The creature had a 40-foot-long neck, was about 80 feet long and probably weighed 80 tons. It was approximately 50 to 60 feet tall, or about the height of the obelisk in Central Park.

Dr. James A. Jensen, the paleontologist, identified the relic as having come from a species of Brachiosaurus, a genus in the sauropod family of long-necked herbivorous dinosaurs. Dr. Jensen, who is curator of the Earth Sciences Museum at Brigham Young University in Provo, Utah, believes the creature may have been the largest animal that ever walked the earth.

He based his conclusions on the fact that the first bone uncovered, a scapula, or shoulder blade, was nine feet long. A scapula of such huge size, he calculated, must have come from a creature with correspondingly gigantic proportions. Eight years ago, near the same site, the scientist found a scapula of a different dinosaur that was nearly eight feet long. At the time, dinosaur experts agreed that that animal was probably the largest known.

But last year, scrabbling around in the rocky soil of the mesa, located in a remote section of southwest Colorado, he and his crew uncovered what resembled a giant dog biscuit. It was the scapula of a dinosaur. Quickly identifying it as having come from one of the Brachiosaurids, the largest of the dinosaur families, Dr. Jensen calculated that the length of the scapula indicated that the animal's leg bones alone must have been 20 feet tall. He also determined that the bone had come from a species of Brachiosaurus different from the type that had had the eight-foot shoulder blade.

In a telephone interview, Dr. Jensen pointed out that Brachiosaurids were the largest known dinosaurs and lived in the late Jurassic period some 140 million years ago. They have been described by dinosaur historians as having been gentle plant-eaters that walked on four legs with their necks held upright like a giraffe's as they browsed the high limbs of trees. The tallest giraffes reach a height of about 20 feet.

The fossil site, (top, left) literally a burial ground of bones, is situated high above the Eskalante Valley. The river has since carved its way 2,000 feet below the old river bed being explored.

Dr. James A. Jensen (bottom, left) wearing the safari hat, and two assistants cast the scapula of "Ultrasaurus" in a plaster mold.

Dr. Jensen checks the condition of the plaster mold (top, right).

The crane (bottom, right) perched on the flatbed truck was designed by Dr. Jensen to lift excavated fossils and plaster castings from their resting place without damaging them.

Dr. Jensen (above) displays the shoulder blade of the biggest dinosaur to two crewpeople from a Japanese television network.

The television crew measures the scapula (top, right) to demonstrate the enormous size of the dinosaur fossil.

Driving a tractor along the bluff, Dr. Jensen recreates his finding of the biggest dinosaur (bottom, right). The tractor is also used to cover the site until the excavation team returns, to protect future finds from damage.

Dr. Jensen, who is known as "Dinosaur Jim" to his fellow paleontologists, has again attracted scientists to a problem that has been puzzling them for years. Those who study the physiology of both living and extinct animals have long wondered how blood reaches the heads of animals so tall as dinosaurs and giraffes. "They want to know what kind of heart a dinosaur could have had that could pump a column of blood 70 or 80 feet high," he said. "A giraffe has a four-chambered heart and we think most dinosaurs had two-chambered hearts. But I'm going to leave that problem to the paleophysiologists," he added.

"I think the main significance of this finding is that it may eventually help scientists find out how these animals could pump blood that high off the ground," he said. "Their heads were the highest of any animals and tremendous blood pressure must have been needed. We might someday learn something about human physiology from them."

Paradoxically, the huge Brachiosaurids had tiny brains that manipulated their front legs and jaws. They are believed to have had a second small brain on their spinal cord near the

pelvis that provided the impulses to move their tails and rear legs. The largest assembled skeleton of one is on display in the Berlin Museum in Germany. The animal, discovered in Africa, was 42 feet tall. Dr. Jensen's discovery, when completely assembled, would also dwarf the two large dinosaurs that are on exhibit in the fourth-floor dinosaur halls of New York's American Museum of Natural History. There, visitors are greeted with lifelike facsimiles of a plant-eating brontosaurus that is more than 60 feet long and a smaller carnivorous tyrannosaurus rex.

The Utah scientist said that his latest find has been nicknamed "ultrasaurus" but "it may take years before we can dig out all of its fossilized remains, positively classify it and christen it with a formal scientific name." In the scientific method of naming newly discovered species, the discoverer has the privilege of selecting the species name. "I don't know yet what that will be," Dr. Jensen said.

He planned to halt the painstaking work of uncovering the remainder of the dinosaur's bones by mid-August, 1979, so that his team could transport the relics that had been unearthed back to his vertebrate laboratory on the Brigham Young campus 300 miles away, where they could be examined and classified. Dr. Jensen plans to return each year to the Colorado dig, perched on a quarry-like shelf of the tree-studded mesa that lies high above the Escalante Valley on the western slope of the Rocky Mountains. Millions of years ago it was a river bed in which the bones of hundreds of ancient animals had collected.

Over the last 10 years Dr. Jensen has dug up the remains of dozens of previously undiscovered extinct animals, including many types of new dinosaurs at the Colorado dig. He is credited with having found and identified many species of fossilized birds, crocodiles, turtles, and mammals and other amphibians, as well as dinosaurs. "I think the mesa has produced the greatest number of fossil animals in this hemisphere," he said.

Rival Anthropologists

by Boyce Rensberger

Last February two well-known anthropologists challenged each other in what could become a wide-ranging debate over whether a finding was indeed a new species of pre-human being ancestral to all other known forms of human and human-like creatures. Richard Leakey, the Kenya anthropologist, is challenging the announcement by two American scientists that they had discovered such a new species. Dr. Donald C. Johanson, one of the Americans, appeared with Mr. Leakey at a symposium in Pittsburgh on human evolution and vigorously defended his interpretation.

The difference between the two views has implications beyond the details. If Dr. Johanson is correct, it would mean that the human species emerged from more primitive ancestors more recently, perhaps only two million years ago. On the other hand, if Mr. Leakey is correct, mankind appeared on the scene so long ago—more than four million years—that there is no clear evidence of a fossil form that could have been ancestral to human beings.

Although honest differences of opinion are common enough in all sciences, there were over-

tones of a confrontation between the two anthropologists, each of whom leads a major fossil-hunting expedition in eastern Africa. The two men have often been viewed as rivals.

Although the two lines of argument turn on fine points of interpretation, they provide an unusual glimpse of the ways in which anthropologists think about their fossils to forge new insights about human origins.

The controversy, one of the liveliest in paleoanthropology in some years, is likely to continue for some time. It has been 16 years since the last new species of human ancestor was formally named, and the debate over the validity of that name has not completely died down yet. At issue this time was the announcement by Dr. Johanson, a curator at the Cleveland Museum of Natural History, and Dr. Tim White of the University of California at Berkeley, that a large collection of fossil bones found in Ethiopia and Tanzania all represent a previously unrecognized form of human ancestor. They named the new species, which lived between three million and four million years ago, Australopithecus afarensis.

261

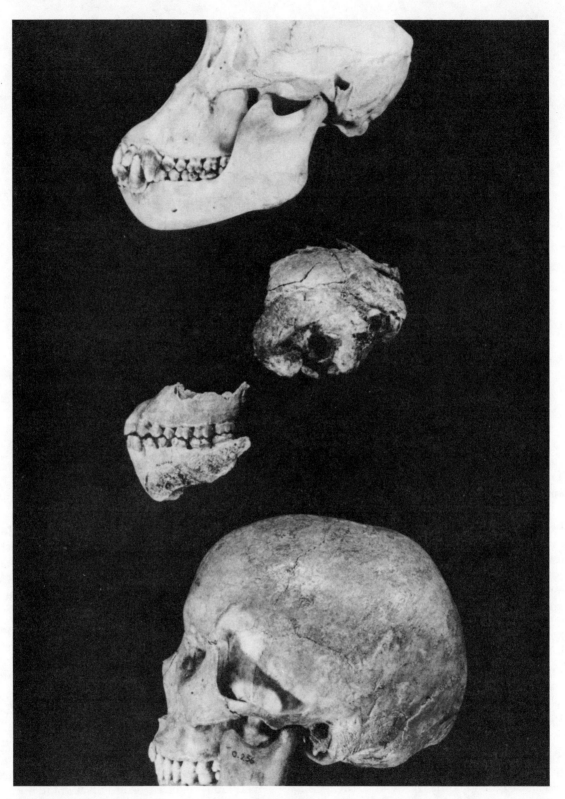

The fossil remains of the "Afar ape-man" (center) bear a striking resemblance in its jaws and cranium with those of a modern chimpanzee (top). They bear little similarity to the skull of modern man (bottom).

Preliminary interpretations had suggested the bones were from two species, an unusually ancient form of homo, or true human being, and Australopithecus africanus, a human-like species known from other discoveries, that eventually died out. After more detailed analysis, Dr. Johanson and Dr. White revised this opinion and concluded that even though there was a fair degree of variation in certain features of the fossils, they all represented one new species. They attributed the variation to differences between the sexes. In many primates, males and females differ substantially in skeletal anatomy.

Challenging this view, Mr. Leakey said that the variations in the bones was too great to attribute to sex differences. "I think Don was right the first time," he said. "They're sampling two different populations, homo and Australopithecus."

"No way," Dr. Johanson said in a separate interview. "The entire range of variation is represented at the 333 site where we've got at least 13 individuals all together." The 333 site is one of many Dr. Johanson has excavated in the Afar region of Ethiopia for which the new species is named. The site has yielded the remains of at least 13 individuals who, Dr. Johanson believes, were all killed in a single catastrophe of unknown cause. He suspects all 13 were members of a family who were, perhaps, caught in a flash flood. If true, this would mean that whatever differences the bones show would have to have been within the range of natural variation of a single species.

However, others have challenged the catastrophe theory on the ground that there is no good evidence of any such event having taken place. It is well established from other fossil sites that bones of several species that were once scattered can be gathered into small areas by streams. It is also known that leopards drag their prey to central locations where the bones may remain.

To support his challenge, Mr. Leakey also said his colleagues had discovered some new fossils in Kenya that were of similar age to Dr. Johanson's fossils but that they did not resemble the newly named species. This, he said, showed that the new species was not the only human-like creature living at the time. It, therefore, could not have been the common ancestor of all later forms, as Dr. Johanson has asserted. Mr. Leakey declined to discuss the new fossils in detail until he had published a formal report in a scientific journal. In an interview, however, he said they consisted of eight isolated teeth. "The material I've got is very insignificant but there's enough to challenge Don with," he said. "It gives me the right to offer my opinion."

Dr. Johanson said that although he has not had an opportunity to examine the teeth in detail, he did not think they were distinctive enough to say whether they were different from those of the new species he has named. He said the teeth could well belong to the same new species.

Although Mr. Leakey alluded to the difference of opinion in a news interview last February, he reserved more specific comment for the Pittsburgh symposium, which was co-sponsored by the Foundation for Research into the Origin of Man and the Carnegie Museum of Natural History.

One of the reasons for the differing opinions is the fact that new fossils of human ancestors commonly display a number of features, some of which resemble those thought to characterize one previously recognized species, and others of which may resemble features of a separate species. In Dr. Johanson's view it is this very combination of features in the Ethiopian and Tanzanian fossils that suggest the new, relatively ancient species was the common ancestor of the two lineages recognized in later times, Homo and later forms of Australopithecus.

He argued that it would be logical to expect such a combination of features in a species that was in evolutionary transition. If an evolutionary divergence is under way, he said, some members of the population evolving in one direction would have a higher frequency of traits typical of later forms appearing in that lineage. At the same time, other members of the transitional species, evolving into a second lineage, would show more features typical of the second lineage. Earlier in the transition, before the single species had diverged very far, all specimens should resemble one another more closely than they would after the divergence was well under way. Because of the fortuitous way in which fossils are found, it is difficult to know whether one is sampling the evolutionary divergence

263

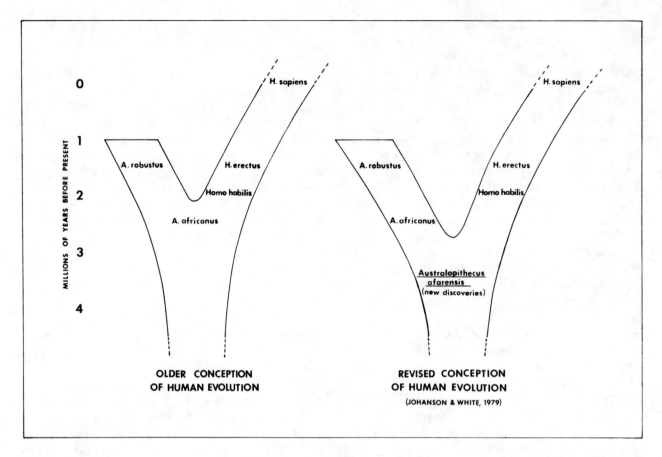

Two theories of human evolution.

early in its progress or later.

Both scientists agreed that the best way to resolve their difference was to study existing fossils more carefully and to search for additional remains of human ancestors that would fill the gaps in the evolutionary sequence. "After all," Mr. Leakey said, "it doesn't really matter what we call this or that specimen. What matters is that we have the fossils."

One of the gaps in the fossil evidence is the period between two million and three million years ago, a period from which few fossils have been recovered. There is general agreement that from two million years ago onward there were at least two lineages of human-like creatures, Homo and Australopithecus. Mr. Leakey argues that the two lineages were already in existence between three million and four million years ago. Dr. Johanson sees only one lineage at that time.

A much bigger gap in the fossil sequence is the period between four million years ago and 12 million years ago. Although nothing is known of what happened then, there are fossils of possibly ancestral forms that lived just before this gap. These fossils, called Ramapithecus, have been found in Africa and parts of Europe and Asia. At one time, argued Dr. David Pilbeam, a Yale University anthropologist and discoverer of many of the fossils, they represented a very early ancestor of the lineages that later became human.

Dr. Pilbeam, also participating in the symposium, said he is now not so sure Ramapithecus was ancestral to human beings. He said that he had found new fossils of the species that invalidate earlier conclusions. "Although Ramapithecus is still the best available candidate for a hominid ancestor," he said, using a term that covers several human-like lineages, "it isn't a very good candidate."

Richard Leakey: The Challenger

It is no longer necessary to identify Richard Leakey as the son of Louis and Mary Leakey, the pioneering Kenyan anthropologists. In the eight years since his father died and his mother withdrew to her camp at Olduvai Gorge in Tanzania, the young anthropologist has emerged as one of the best-known figures in science today. The 35-year-old native Kenyan was leader of a team that discovered some of the most spectacular fossils of human ancestors ever found, the cover subject of Time magazine's top-selling issue of 1977, co-author of two best-selling books. He has become one of the few scientists whose public lectures consistently draw huge, paying crowds of both eager students and established scholars. While he has succeeded as an anthropologist in his own right, Richard Leakey remains very much a blend of his parents. Those who know the family say he combines the strong-will and showman's flair of his father with the caution and respect for careful scientific analysis of his mother.

The combination has made Richard Leakey probably the most envied and most resented member of the small group of researchers privileged to have access to the fossil record of human evolution. As director of the National Museums of Kenya, Mr. Leakey exercises close control over who is permitted to conduct research in the country.

Richard Erskine Frere Leakey was born in Nairobi on Dec. 19, 1944, the second of Louis and Mary's three sons. "I would never describe it as a close family," Richard Leakey said a few years ago. Anthropology always took precedence over a conventional family life, he recalled. Determined to avoid his father's field, young Richard became a safari guide. But he soon tired of the business and decided to explore a little-known lake on the Kenya-Tanzania border. Obviously heir to what has been called Leakey's Luck, he found a fossil jaw of an extinct form of near-human being.

Succumbing to fossil fever, Mr. Leakey at first sought a degree in anthropology in London but ran out of money before starting and returned to Kenya to learn the subject first-hand. He had, of course, already had more experience in the field than most graduate anthropologists. He has never been to a university, Mr. Leakey likes to say, except to lecture.

Exploration at Lake Turkana

Since 1968, Richard Leakey has headed a team of scientists exploring the eastern shore of Kenya's remote Lake Turkana, far from his parents' province at Olduvai Gorge. Hundreds of bones of ancestral forms of human and pre-human beings have been discovered. The most famous, found in 1972, remains known as 1470, the unexpectedly large-brained skull named for its catalog number.

In recent years Richard Leakey has seldom spent more than weekends at his Lake Turkana base camp. In his stead much of the scientific leadership is exercised by Glynn Isaac, an archeologist at the University of California at Berkeley. Field operations are managed largely by Kamoya Kimeu, who has personally found many of the fossils for which Mr. Leakey is famous. "As I get older my interests continue to broaden," he once said. "I'm interested in Kenyan affairs and international affairs and I would hope that I am able to make contributions in these areas. But, I'm sure I'll always be interested in human evolution. After all, our past, as a species, may help guide us in the future."

Richard Leakey.

Dr. Donald Johanson (left) and Dr. Tim White (right), displaying some of the fossil fragments they uncovered. The fragments are over three million years old.

The Afar region of Ethiopia (right), site of the controversial fossil finds.

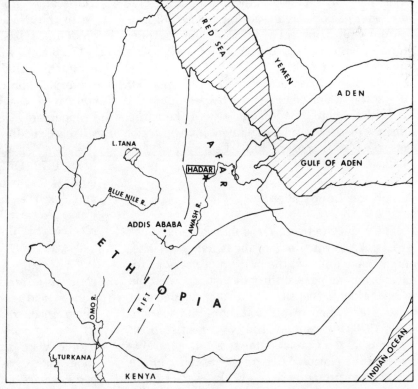

Donald Johnson: Lucky Professional

After decades at center stage in the dramatic search for human origins, the Leakeys have recently been forced to share star billing with Donald C. Johanson, a 35-year-old American anthropologist. With good fortune that rivals what has been called Leakey's Luck, Dr. Johanson and his colleagues have produced, from the Afar region of Ethiopia, a steady stream of major fossil discoveries over the last five years.

In 1973, for example, on his first full-fledged expedition to the Afar, Dr. Johanson's first find of a fossil from a human ancestor was a knee joint. That fossil, 3.3 million years of age, is the oldest known anatomical evidence of upright posture and locomotion. In 1974 he found the most nearly complete skeleton of a human ancestor, a small female known as Lucy. In 1975 and 1976, Dr. Johanson announced discovery of a cluster of bones representing at least 13 individuals, all apparently part of one extended family, who may have been killed in a single, unknown catastrophe.

When hostilities broke out in Ethiopia, Dr. Johanson deferred any new expeditions and turned to more detailed analyses of the earlier discoveries. This led to the new interpretation of the fossils that Richard Leakey has challenged.

Accord on Cooperation

The rivalry between Dr. Johanson and Richard Leakey, which began about five years ago, might have followed the pattern of previous relations among paleoanthropologists and become a bitter feud. Instead, the two men, peers in age, agreed to cooperate and share information.

In 1976, for example, the two scientists held an unusual joint news conference under the auspices of the National Geographic Society, long a backer and promoter of the Leakeys and now of Dr. Johanson as well. "For the first time," Mr. Leakey said then, "we have a trust between rival groups working on the evolution of man." It remains to be seen what effect the new clash over Dr. Johanson's views will have on that trust.

Donald Carl Johanson was born in Chicago in June 1943. He earned a bachelor's degree in anthropology from the University of Illinois in 1966 and began graduate studies at the University of Chicago under F. Clark Howell, the eminent paleoanthropologist who is now at the University of California at Berkeley. From 1970 through 1972, Dr. Johanson worked with Dr. Howell in a major fossil-hunting expedition in the Omo valley of Ethiopia. Eager to stake out a fossil claim for himself, the young anthropologist teamed up with Maurice Taieb, a geologist with the National Center for Scientific Research in Paris.

Dr. Taieb, who had worked in Ethiopia, had a hunch that the Afar region might be rich in preserved bones. A preliminary survey in 1972 confirmed the hunch. The American and the Frenchman formed the International Afar Research Expedition, the enterprise that produced the string of discoveries.

By 1972, Dr. Johanson had joined the Cleveland Museum of Natural History as a curator and became an adjunct professor at nearby Case Western Reserve University. In 1973 he received his doctorate from the University of Chicago.

"It's really amazing how the public has become interested in human evolution," Dr. Johanson said recently. He added that he had just given a lecture on his work at Indiana University to a packed auditorium from which many people were turned away. "The last time I spoke there," he recalled, "there were maybe 30 people there. It's really become a hot subject."

1979 Nobel Prizes in Science

Chemistry and Physics
by Malcolm W. Browne

The Research

Chemical research as down-to-earth as arthritis medicine and a theory of physics so profound as to affect man's perception of existence were both honored by Nobel Prizes. The chemistry and physics prizes, each worth approximately $190,000, in addition to the valuable gold medals themselves, were shared among three Americans, a Pakistani and a West German.

The chemistry prize was won by Herbert C. Brown of Purdue University and Georg Wittig of Heidelberg University, and the physics prize was awarded jointly to Steven Weinberg and Sheldon L. Glashow of Harvard University, and Abdus Salam, who works at universities in London and Trieste, Italy.

The two chemistry prize winners were honored for developing a group of substances capable of facilitating otherwise very difficult chemical reactions. This discovery has made possible the mass production of hundreds of important pharmaceuticals and industrial chemicals that would have been prohibitively expensive otherwise, including the arthritis medicine hydrocortisone.

While such practical applications have no part in the work of the physics prize recipients, many scientists regard their work as fundamental to understanding nature.

Although Drs. Weinberg, Glashow and Salam always worked separately, they were honored for their complementary research on a theory known to colleagues for the past decade as the Weinberg-Salam Theory of Weak Interactions. The theory is regarded by most scientists as a major step toward the goal of finding a unifying thread holding together the four fundamental forces of nature. Two of these forces, gravitation and electromagnetism, had been known for many centuries. The two others were discovered only after science began investigating the atom, since they operate only within an environment as small as an atomic nucleus. One is known as the strong force, or, to use a phrase preferred by physicists, the strong interaction, which holds atomic nuclei together. The other force, the weak interaction, causes radioactive decay in certain kinds of atomic nuclei.

Many scientists, including Albert Einstein, sought a system of mathematical equations that could explain all four interactions as separate manifestations of a single underlying principle of nature. While these attempts have defied complete solution, the Nobel award recognized that there was now general acceptance of a principle, developed by the three physics prize winners, unifying the weak and electromagnetic interactions.

Working separately, Dr. Weinberg, 46 years old, and Dr. Salam, 53, developed a system of equations known as a "gauge theory." Gauge theories are based on the mathematical equivalents of telescopes and microscopes, serving to change the scale of one frame of reference so as to compare it with a completely different frame of reference. In this case, the two different frames of reference were electromagnetism, which operates between large, easily observed objects, and the weak interaction, which is a nuclear force.

Among other things, the Weinberg-Salam theory states that weak interactions involve a flow of "neutral current" in an atomic nucleus. The neutral current is somewhat analogous to an electromagnetic current but does not carry any electrical charge. It relates to beta decay, a kind of radiation known since 1896, in which negative or positive electrons are ejected from the nuclei of radioactive atoms as they break apart. Having developed their gauge theory, Drs. Weinberg and Salam were dependent on the work of a number of other investigators to fill in the necessary mathematics needed to equate theory with reality. Furthermore, predictions made by their theory had to be confirmed by experiments.

One of the difficulties of the Weinberg-Salam theory was resolved by the practical work of the 46-year-old Dr. Glashow, the third winner of the physics prize. In the early 1960's, Murray Gell-Mann of the California Institute of Technology introduced the quark theory, which stated that all the large fundamental particles of nature, including protons, neutrons and mesons, are made up of combinations of still more fundamental particles named quarks. Three basic types of quarks, known as up quarks, down quarks and strange quarks were known at the time Drs. Weinberg and Salam announced their theory. But one aspect of their theory could not be explained by these three quarks alone.

The research conducted by Dr. Glashow on a new type of quark known as the "charmed quark" overcame this seeming difficulty in the Weinberg-Salam theory.

Experiments in Europe and the United States in 1972 and 1973 effectively confirmed the existence of neutral current predicted by the theory, and in 1978, scientists working with Stanford University's linear particle accelerator capped the confirmation of the theory with an experiment hailed by high-energy physicists throughout the world. In the Stanford experiment, electrons were hurled at atomic nuclei and examined as they rebounded. Electrons may spin either in a left-handed or right-handed direction, and it could be expected that there would be equal numbers of left-handed and right-handed electrons rebounding from nuclear collisions.

But the Weinberg-Salam theory predicted that because of the weak nuclear force, there would be a slight but significant difference in the number of right-handed and left-handed electrons emerging from the collisions. This effect, known as "parity violation," was actually found in the Stanford experiment.

Although the Weinberg-Salam theory is not regarded as absolutely proved, the Stanford experiment lent it such weight that few if any scientists challenge the main outline of the theory at this point.

The chemistry prize grew out of efforts that spanned much of the careers of the recipients. In Germany Dr. Wittig, who is 82, based the main body of his work on compounds of phosphorus, while his American cowinner, Dr. Brown, 67, worked primarily with compounds of boron. But both had a common aim. Many complicated molecules are extremely difficult to join, but the chemical linking of two or more large molecules is often vital to industrial processes, including the manufacture of pharmaceuticals.

A breakthrough in chemical technique permitting the comparatively easy joining of certain large molecules was the result of the work of Drs. Wittig and Brown. The compounds they have developed serve as temporary chemical links holding these large molecules together until permanent chemical joints are inserted to replace them.

The "links" used by Dr. Brown are known as boranes—compounds of boron and hy-

270

drogen that readily join with many of the large molecules on which life is based. Dr. Wittig uses chains of carbon, hydrogen and phosphorus atoms in somewhat the same way. These links have facilitated large-scale manufacture of many pharmaceuticals and a compound of uranium developed during World War II by Dr. Brown as a possible way of refining fuel for atomic bombs. "There are many interesting applications," he said in an interview. "I feel that we have uncovered a new continent, just beginning to explore its mountain ranges and valleys. But it will take another generation of chemists to fully explore and apply this new chemistry of boron hydrides and organoboranes."

Several of the winners said they had not been very surprised to learn of their awards, while one, Dr. Brown, who was on a business trip to New Jersey, said: "If I'd known I'd have stayed home to be with my wife, who's also a chemist." All the new laureates, who were selected by the Nobel Committee of the Swedish Academy, were deluged with congratulatory telephone calls and visits from friends and colleagues.

The Nobel Prizes, which have been awarded since 1901, were established by the will of Alfred Nobel, the Swedish chemist and industrialist who invented dynamite. Nobel, who died in 1896, stipulated that there should be only three categories of science in which prizes would be awarded: physics, chemistry and medicine. The two other prizes are for literature and peace. The Nobel Memorial Prize in Economic Science was established by the Central Bank of Sweden in 1968 as a memorial to Nobel.

Nobel has been criticized for his failure to recognize other branches of science, notably mathematics and astronomy. To remedy this, leading mathematicians created the Field Medal, which is regarded by mathematicians as roughly equal in prestige to the Nobel Prize.

Apart from its cash value, the Nobel Prize has become especially valuable to American scientists. Although the financing of scientific research has increased, the cost of research is growing so rapidly that many scientists find themselves constantly forced to justify their work to obtain renewed research grants. A Nobel Prize winner is among the few normally exempt from this requirement.

Sheldon L. Glashow

At 10 A.M. one morning, Dr. Glashow, his hair tousled and his grin broad, walked into his undergraduate course in particle physics at Harvard University and apologized to his students. "I told them I had to cancel the class and explain particle physics to the press," he said. He left the lecture hall to the accompaniment of applause.

Like the other native New Yorker who shared the 1979 Nobel physics prize with him, Dr. Glashow began the pursuit of his scientific bent at the Bronx High School of Science where he and Dr. Steven Weinberg were classmates. The two, though always operating independently of each other, were also classmates at Cornell, after which their careers diverged before they eventually found themselves on the physics faculty at Harvard.

After graduating from Cornell in 1954, Dr. Glashow got his master's degree in physics the following year and his Ph.D. in 1958, both at Harvard. Before coming to Harvard he was a

Professor Sheldon Glashow

271

research fellow at the California Institute of Technology, a National Science Foundation fellow from 1955 to 1960 and was awarded the J.R. Oppenheimer Memorial Prize for physics in 1977.

The tall, 46-year-old professor had heard rumors that he had been nominated for a Nobel prize but said "I didn't take it too seriously. But now I'm terribly proud and it's exciting." A resident of Brookline, Mass., married and the father of four children, he has been a Harvard professor since 1967.

In addition to many other honors, Dr. Glashow is known at the Bronx High School of Science for winning a Westinghouse Science Talent Search prize as a senior in 1950 when he prepared an exhibit on the principles of physics.

Steven Weinberg

In a volume entitled "The First Three Minutes," a book for the layman on the origin of the universe, Dr. Weinberg wrote a few years ago:

Professor Steven Weinberg

"The more the universe seems comprehensible, the more it also seems pointless." But assessing the work that won him a Nobel, he said that what he and those who share the physics award had found out was "a practical application, if you like, that people understand what makes the world tick. It's a deepening understanding of nature."

Like Dr. Glashow, the 46-year-old, red-haired, New York-born scientist began to follow the physics research trail in the Bronx High School of Science and graduated from Cornell in 1954. He did his postgraduate work at the Copenhagen Institute for Theoretical Physics from 1954 to 1955 and received his doctoral degree in 1957 from Princeton University. After stints at the University of California at Berkeley and the Massachusetts Institute of Technology, he joined the Harvard physics faculty in 1973.

Married for 25 years, he has one daughter and lives in Boston. In addition to "The First Three Minutes," he has written a more scholarly work, "Gravitation and Cosmology: Principles and Applications of the General Theory of Relativity."

Abdus Salam

Dr. Salam, the first Pakistani to win a Nobel prize, had been considered by many of his peers for the past several years as a likely winner for his work in electromagnetics and particle physics. He said that he was "absolutely delighted, thrilled and overwhelmed" to share the Nobel physics prize with the Americans, Drs. Glashow and Weinberg. Although none of the three had collaborated on their most recent work, Dr. Salam said he had corresponded with Dr. Glashow and written a paper with Dr. Weinberg several years ago.

The 53-year-old scientist, born in Jhang, Pakistan, was educated at Cambridge University in England where he got his doctorate in physics. The winner of many honors, he is currently professor of theoretical physics at the Imperial College of Science and Technology in the University of London, director of the International Center for Theoretical Physics in Trieste, Italy, and is chairman of the United Nations Advisory Committee on Science and Technology.

According to fellow scientists, he is currently devoting much of his time in attempts to raise the level of scientific knowledge and to train more scientists for work in developing countries. When informed of his Nobel award, he said: "My first reaction, of course, is the greatest gratitude to Allah, who has guided our thoughts jointly in the way the truth lies in finding out the laws of nature."

Georg Wittig

"At my age, you don't expect honors or awards anymore," 82-year-old Prof. Wittig said at his home in Heidelberg when he was told of being a co-winner of the Nobel chemistry prize. Completely surprised by the honor, the scientist said his prize-winning work was accomplished three decades ago.

Dr. Wittig, professor-emeritus of organic chemistry at the University of Heidelberg in southern West Germany, said: "The development of the method named after me—the Wittig Synthesis, also known as the Wittig Reaction—I worked on 30 years ago." The chemical process he devised is a method of linking carbon and phosphorus, opening up new ways to synthesize biologically active substances.

Dr. Wittig, the 24th German to win the chemistry award, and Dr. Herbert Brown, who shares the chemistry prize and is the 21st American chemistry winner, were honored for independent work in related but different fields. Asked about his plans for the prize money, Dr. Wittig said, "I will give the money to my daughters."

Herbert C. Brown

Dr. Brown, professor of chemistry at Purdue University in West Lafayette, Ind., was reached at an Exxon research laboratory in Linden, New Jersey, for his reaction to becoming a co-winner of the Nobel prize for chemistry. "If I had known about it, I would have stayed at Purdue to get the news!" he exclaimed. An ex-

pert in hydrocarbon chemistry, he is a consultant to Exxon and frequently travels to New Jersey in this capacity.

Born in London, the 67-year-old chemist has lived in the United States for most of his life. He acquired his master's degree at the University of Chicago and his doctorate there in 1938. He then was appointed chemistry instructor at his alma mater and later at Wayne State University in Detroit before he joined the Purdue chemistry faculty in 1947. A dozen years later, he was named to the top chemistry professorship at Purdue.

In addition to being lecturer for the Chemical Society of London, he has received the American Chemical Society Award in Synthetic Organic Chemistry, the Linus Pauling Medal and the National Medal of Science. He is married to the former Sarah Baylen, a chemist whom he met as a classmate at the University of Chicago. They have one son, Charles, who is a chemist.

Dr. Herbert C. Brown

Physiology and Medicine

by Lawrence K. Altman

The Research

An American and a Briton won the 1979 Nobel Prize for physiology and medicine for developing a revolutionary X-ray technique that gives doctors an astonishingly clear look inside the living human body. In the six years since its introduction, the technique, known as computed axial tomography, or the CAT scan, has been used in the diagnostic evaluation of the ailments of millions of patients.

The $190,000 award, which the two men will share, was made by the Nobel Assembly of the Karolinska Institute in Stockholm to Allan McLeod Cormack, 55 years old, a physicist at Tufts University in Medford, Mass., and Godfrey Newbold Hounsfield, 60, an electronics engineer at the British company EMI. Mr. Cormack, who was born in South Africa, came to this country in 1956 and is now an American citizen.

The CAT scanning technique, in which a fully conscious patient lies on his back while an X-ray tube rotates around his head or other parts of the body, allows doctors to take pictures that reveal specific slices of the anatomy in more detail than possible through any other nonsurgical technique.

The award was one of the most unusual in the 78-year history of the prizes. Among the reasons for that were the following:

¶Neither laureate has a doctoral degree in medicine or any field of science.

¶After a long debate that delayed the announcement for an hour, the 54 voting members of the Nobel Assembly vetoed the choice of their own selection committee. The identity of the original nominee or nominees was not made known. Swedish national television reported that the delay was presumably due to a split between two factions within the Nobel Assembly, with one favoring discoveries in basic science and the other discoveries with more direct application to everyday medicine.

¶The two researchers have never met. They did their research independently of each other.

274

The prize recalls the first Nobel Prize in physics, in 1901, which went to William K. Roentgen for his discovery, in 1895, of the X-ray, which also revolutionized the practice of medicine. In the interval, medical physics has become a specialized field of medicine, and the CAT scanner was awarded a prize in the medical category because it reflected developments in mathematical physics that had their greatest application and significance in medicine.

The CAT scan has been called the greatest advance in radiology since the discovery of X-rays. But the award is sure to set off a controversy among health care experts and government officials over the use of the new device. Critics say that the equipment is too costly for many hospitals and contend that it is sometimes used when simpler and cheaper methods might suffice. Proponents say that it has revolutionized the practice of neurology and other fields of medicine since it was introduced in 1973. The Nobel Committee said in its citation: "It is no exaggeration to state that no other method within X-ray diagnostics within such a short period of time has led to such remarkable advances in research and in a multitude of applications" as CAT scans.

Two thousand CAT scanners, which can cost $500,000 or more each, have been sold in more than 50 countries, and 1,110 are in use in this country. An EMI spokesman said the company had sold more than 1,100 units, including more than 600 in the United States. In addition to EMI, there are four other chief manufacturers of CAT scanners: General Electric, Technicare, which is a division of Johnson & Johnson; Pfizer, and Siemens.

Dr. Ronald G. Evens of the Mallinckrodt Institute in St. Louis said that "modern neurology and neurosurgery cannot be practiced without a CAT scanner" because it has so changed patient care. It has drastically reduced the number of painful, and sometimes dangerous, tests that were needed to diagnose tumors, birth defects and other brain conditions. CAT scans can diagnose strokes, but the diagnosis can also be made through other tests and therefore the cost-effectiveness has been questioned.

It is the application of the CAT scan to detection of problems elsewhere in the body that is the subject of considerable controversy. Because the body scanner was introduced in 1975, and because advances in ultrasound and nuclear medicine have been made in recent years, sufficient data have not been collected to adequately compare the techniques and to answer key medical questions about their relative values. Dr. Evens said that there was little, if any, controversy about the usefulness of the CAT scanner in diagnosing a number of disorders, among them those affecting the kidney and certain lymph nodes near it; abnormalities of the spine, such as those resulting from injuries resulting in bone fragments that might tear the spinal cord and cause paralysis, and for cancers and infections and other problems of the face and the pelvis.

He said that the CAT scan shows "high promise" for determining whether surgery could be done for lung cancers and disorders of the liver. However, he said, questions remain whether CAT scans will replace other studies for these purposes.

As studies have shown when and for what conditions scans are medically useful, the key question in the controversy has come down to: How many machines should there be in each geographic area?

Asked how he viewed the debate, Mr. Hounsfield said in a telephone interview from London that the answers to the economic questions must await further studies. "We are still learning," he said, adding that he was studying even newer uses for the device, which he began developing in 1967.

Mr. Hounsfield and Mr. Cormack received the prize along with other laureates on Dec. 10, 1979, the anniversary of the death of Alfred Nobel, the inventor of dynamite, who left his fortune for these prizes. The awards are in chemistry, physics, economics and literature.

Allan MacLeod Cormack

When he was in high school in South Africa, Allan MacLeod Cormack wanted to be an astronomer but he realized that he would have to study physics for a career in that field.

That led him to the study of both engineering and physics at University of Cape Town and graduate work in theoretical physics at Cam-

Professor Allan Cormack, co-recipient of the Nobel Prize for Medicine, is seen here with his original CAT scanner.

bridge University. Although it did not lead him into astronomy, he said, he is still very much interested in that subject.

His entry into medical physics and the research that led to the Nobel Prize took place more than 20 years ago with a six-month tenure as a medical physicist at Groote Schuur Hospital in Cape Town. He took the position, he recalled, partly because the law required the hospital to have a physicist to oversee use of radioactive isotopes and other medical applications of physics.

Mr. Cormack became interested in the use of radiation in the diagnosis and treatment of cancer but was perplexed by some of the deficiencies in the technology of that day.

"I asked myself, how can you give a dose of radiation if you don't know the material through which it has to pass?" he said, referring to the response of tissue to radiation.

The idea that led to the Nobel Prize award was planted there, he said in a telephone interview from his office at the physics department of Tufts University in Medford, Mass. It led him to some theoretical calculations and, a few years later, to reports in The Journal of Applied

Physics on the mathematical formulas needed to compute the absorption of X-ray radiation by various tissues of the body. These reports were an important factor leading to the award. After that he continued research in that field, but largely as a hobby. His main work was in theoretical physics research on the interactions of subatomic particles.

He was born in Johannesburg, Feb. 23, 1924, took a bachelor of science degree at University of Cape Town in 1944, a master's degree in 1945 and followed that with two years of postgraduate study at Cambridge University. Like his Nobel Prize co-winner, Godfrey Hounsfield, he has never taken a doctoral degree.

In 1956 he went to Harvard University as a Research Fellow, joined the physics faculty of Tufts University in 1957 and became a United States citizen in 1966. He is married to the former Barbara Jean Seavey. They have three children: Margaret Jean, a graduate student at Yale; Jean Barbara, a music major at Tufts and Robert Allan Seavey Cormack who is in high school.

The physicist, formerly chairman of the Tufts University physics department, is teaching introductory physics this year. He is described by friends as a heavyset man of medium height with a pungent sense of humor. From time to time he has taken up such outdoor sports as rock climbing, tennis and, more recently, sailing in New Hampshire.

Godfrey Newbold Hounsfield

Godfrey Newbold Hounsfield was deeply involved in electronics even as a youngster growing up in a rural part of Nottinghamshire, England, in the Depression of the early 1930's. He was the youngest of five children. His father was an engineer turned farmer.

"On a farm you can get very bored," the slender, mustached scientist said in a telephone interview.

At the age of 13 he built a record player, putting it together extemporaneously from a collection of spare parts. In his mid-teens he built his own radio sets. In World War II he served as a radar lecturer at the Royal Air Force College's radar school.

After the war he attended Faraday House Electrical Engineering College in London and, shortly after his graduation in 1951, he joined the research staff of EMI Ltd., an international complex of more than 80 companies in the electronics, music and entertainment fields. He worked at first on radar and later on computer design.

It was research on the design of computers capable of recognizing printed characters, he said, that led him into research on new X-ray techniques and the development of the system for which the 60-year-old scientist was named a Nobel Prize winner. Although he and his co-winner, Allan MacLeod Cormack, were pursuing the same scientific concepts and, at one time, lived no farther apart than London and Cambridge, they worked entirely independently and have not yet met. Like Mr. Cormack, Mr. Hounsfield has never taken a doctoral degree.

As a project engineer on the EMI research staff he was head of a design team that created the first large, solid-state computer to be built in Britain. This led to research on a thin film, large-capacity memory store for computer use, related research on character recognition and the origin of the concept of the computed axial tomographic (CAT) X-ray scanning system for medical diagnosis. For the past 10 years Mr. Hounsfield has concentrated on research on new X-ray techniques.

The courteous, soft-spoken scientist, described by an acquaintance as "quiet, really an introvert," has won at least 25 awards for his research, most of them in the last decade. He was described as appearing to be almost amazed at each new honor.

In 1975 he was made a Fellow of the Royal Society, Britain's highest scientific honor, and was also presented the Prince Philip Medal of the City and Guilds of the London Institute, an annual award for outstanding achievement in science, technology and industry. Mr. Hounsfield, a bachelor, has devoted many years to long distance walking—"rambling," as he put it —in Britain's Lake District, mountain areas and on the continent.

"He is brilliant, but in nonscientific matters a little bit absent-minded," said a business associate in the United States. "If you ask him to meet you at a hotel, you need to remind him of it. It's not discourtesy, he just might forget."

Chronology
of Science Events

Jan 2   Findings of HEW-sponsored research suggest that routine fetal monitoring may not be effective, safe, and cost-saving; suggest fetal monitoring is inaccurate diagnostic tool.

Jan 7   Study by psychologist Paul Reichelt shows that providing adolescents with effective contraception will not markedly affect their sexual behavoir ● One hundred forty-seven nations will participate in year-long Global Weather Experiment to study seasonal weather cycle of earth's atmosphere.

Jan 9   Worldwide drive to detect gravity waves, predicted by Einstein's General Theory of Relativity, intensifies following landmark experiment offering first strong evidence of their existence.

Jan 10 Recent meeting of American Association for Advancement of Science focused on upcoming industrial trends, role of low-level radiation in causing cancer, air pollution and climate, and agricultural productivity.

Jan 14 *New England Journal of Medicine* reports strong evidence linking heredity to peptic ulcers; an estimated 10% of Americans have peptic ulcers at some point in their lives.

Jan 16 Rediscovery of lost Kingdom of Ebla shows 4,500 year-old state had many parallels with modern living. 15,000 clay tablets of records expand knowledge and confirm existence of entities whose historical reality were open to question ● New studies find traditional beliefs about what makes people happy are incorrect; reveal that love, marriage, sex lives, job satisfaction and personal success are determining factors.

Jan 19   Drs. Donald Johanson and Tim White announce discovery of human ancester *Australopithecus afarensis* with unexpected combination of small, ape-like head and fully erect body.

Jan 21   Consortium of nations conducting advanced fusion research drafts plans for large and costly experimental power plant using a fusion device which would solve world's energy problems for long time if successful.

Jan 25   Data from Soviet and American Venus probes show planet as "hellish" spot with extreme temperatures, sulfurous atmosphere and massive thunder and lightning.

Jan 29   Massachusetts Institute of Technology Professor Maurice S. Fox reports his study on breast cancer shows that radical surgery is no more effective than more conservative, less mutilating treatment followed by radiation therapy.

Feb 1   White House panel concludes that although ultimate prospects are "bright," no more than 1% of U.S. electricity can be generated from sunlight by the end of the century.

Feb 5   Discovery of perennial teocinte plant that crossbreeds with corn, creates hopes for agricultural revolution.

Feb 6   Princeton University Museum of Natural History geologist John Horner announces discovery of previously unknown species of duck-bill dinosaur *Maiasaura peeblesorum*.

Feb 8   Scientists report Pioneer spacecraft has discovered vast chasm extending hundreds of miles across Venus' equatorial region.

Feb 10   Dr. Dennis Gabor, winner of 1971 Nobel Prize in Physics for his invention of holography, dies at the age of 78.

Feb 15   World Climate Conference reports withdrawal of irrigation water needed to feed world's billions in next century, will probably halt discharge of major rivers into seas • Deep Florida lake has yielded discoveries that give rare opportunity to study complex interactions of climate, animal and plant ecology back to more than 12,000 years ago.

Feb 18   World Climate Conference participants confirm that smog and dust from industrial Europe and China are responsible for mysterious haze that hangs over Alaska, Greenland and the Arctic Ocean every spring.

Feb 20   New research challenges long-standing notions that obesity is caused by genes, laziness, greediness, or low-metabolism.

Feb 21   World Health Organization plans to immunize all world's children against six childhood diseases by 1990.

Feb 24   World Climate Conference, at conclusion of its meeting, expresses concern that increased use of fossil fuels might alter climate sufficiently to require radical changes in world agricultural and energy production.

Feb 26 Solar eclipse is viewed by thousands in U.S.; spectacular display with bright corona is caused by solar storms.

Feb 27 Voyager 1 nears rendezvous with Jupiter after 18 month voyage; transmits new information about its moons.

Feb 28 Mayo Clinic Study indicates that incidence of stroke has declined dramatically over last 50 years ● Voyager spacecraft discovers existence of intense auroral activity on Jupiter, similar to earth's aurora borealis.

Mar 1 Voyager 1 spacecraft discovers electrically-charged particles circling Jupiter as well as new type of very-low-frequency radio emission emanating from planet ● Ancient Nubian artifacts yield evidence of oldest recognizable monarch in human history; findings suggest Nubians reached advanced form of political development as early as 3300 B.C.

Mar 3 Scientists say recently discovered plasma cloud circling Jupiter at orbit of its satellite Io appears to be composed of extremely hot, electrified sulfur particles excited by energies in excess of 500 billion watts.

Mar 4 European Organization for Nuclear Research to build accelerator 20 miles in circumference in hope of producing three long sought atomic particles ● New photographs of Jupiter's moons by Voyager spacecraft reveal for first time long dark streaks that could be fault lines on Europa, and huge bulls-eye feature on Io, innermost satellite of Jupiter.

Mar 5 Voyager photographs of Jupiter's four largest moons give scientists first clear impression of their colors and most detailed view of their surface characteristics.

Mar 6 Voyager spacecraft survives intense radiation surrounding Jupiter and begins first close-up exploration of planet and several of its moons; transmits high-resolution photographs of Io's surface ● Worldwide weather study, conducted during five weeks ended February 20, indicates that enough of atmosphere can be observed to make possible substantial improvements in weather forecasting.

Mar 7 Photographs transmitted by Voyager spacecraft depict Jovian moon Io as one of the most perplexing bodies of solar system; planet appears to resemble Earth more than any other known body. Voyager also transmits first close-up photographs of Ganymede and Callisto, two largest satellites of Jupiter.

Mar 8 Voyager spacecraft discovers thin, dark ring of rocky debris circling Jupiter well within orbit of innermost moon Almathea. Ring is estimated to be 18 miles thick and more than 5,000 miles wide.

Mar 9 Photographs transmitted by Voyager 1 reveal existence of large, young volcanic mountain on Io, indicating that Io, like Earth, still is an active body with molten interior ● Study conducted at University of Florida and Veterans Administration Center, indicates that healthy men often stop breathing for periods up to 54 seconds when they sleep; researchers are unable to explain why phenomenon, known as apnea, occurs.

Mar 13 Dr. Arnold J. Friedhoff and colleagues at New York University School of Medicine report that some drugs taken by pregnant women as treatment for serious mental illness might cause permanent changes in brains of their children.

Mar 14 100th anniversary of the birth of Albert Einstein.

Mar 15 Scientists at Haystack radio telescope, Westford, Massachusetts, report detecting black hole at core of Milky Way Galaxy that is five million times as massive as the Sun.

Mar 19 Deep-sea drilling ship *Glomar Challenger,* boring into Emperor Seamounts, chain of volcanic islands 6,000 feet below surface of North Pacific, finds that islands are counterpart of today's Hawaii, formed by volcanic activity on ocean floor.

Mar 20 Findings described at American Heart Association Annual Conference on Cardio-vascular Disease Epidemiology, indicate that moderate consumption of alcoholic beverages may help curb heart attacks ● Scientists report that hypertension is group of diverse maladies rather than single ailment; disease is major factor in heart attacks and strokes.

Mar 21 Study conducted by American Health Foundation, and funded by National Cancer Institute, indicates that major killer diseases that afflict Americans have roots in childhood.

Mar 22 Dr. Mary D. Leakey reports discovery of footprints of two creatures who appear to have walked exactly as modern human beings, in Tanzania, dated at more than 3.6 million years old. Footprints are oldest known marks of human-like creatures on Earth; Dr. Leakey says discovery confirms that human ancestors were fully bipedal 1.5 million years before earliest-known appearance of toolmaking and of brains larger than those of apes.

Mar 27 Participants in International Conference on Endangered Species, say raising of rare species by "farming" them in protected and carefully supervised environment may help stem decline of threatened wildlife resources.

Mar 28 Radiation is released in accident at Three Mile Island Nuclear Reactor in Middletown, Pennsylvania.

Mar 29 Report in *New England Journal of Medicine* links lead contamination too mild to produce overt symptoms of illness to brain damage in children.

Mar 31 Researchers aboard Woods Hole Oceanographic Institute deep-diving submarine *Alvin* and Miami University research vessel *Gilliss* discover creatures that live inside 10-foot tubes of their own making; creatures have no mouth, gut or eyes and their anatomy is so novel that some specialists consider them entirely new animal kingdom phylum.

Apr 1 64-year-old Norwegian explorer Thor Heyerdahl to retire from making unusual ocean-going voyages in craft modeled on primitive vessels; Heyerdahl believes he has proved his point that all ancient pre-European civilizations could have intercommunicated across oceans with primitive vessels.

Apr 2 Delegates from 31 nations meeting at Convention on International Trade in Endangered Species of Wild Fauna and Flora, conclude conference and sign treaty prohibiting or restricting trade of rare or threatened species among member countries.

Apr 3 Recent studies indicate that placebos relieve pain in 30–40% of patients but tend to be widely used and misused by medical profession.

Apr 4 Three recent studies prepared by Doctors Christopher Tietz, Mark Belsey and colleagues at the World Health Organization, Geneva, downgrade link between use of oral contraceptives and heart-attack incidents.

Apr 5 National Sciences Academy report questions safety and effectiveness of benzo-diazepines (flurazepam), widely used as sleeping pills; finds prescription sleeping pills should be used for only few nights at a time and in limited numbers.

Apr 10 Stanford University researchers have discovered that cells from fetus appear in mother's blood as early as the 12th week of pregnancy; finding lends hope to possibility of developing a simple blood test to detect birth defects and of unraveling some of the mysteries of pregnancy • Doctors Richard F. Squires and Claus Braestrup have discovered that many brain cells have special chemical structures (or receptors) on their surfaces that interact successfully with such benzodiazepine drugs as Valium, Librium and Dalmane, without producing undesirable effects. Scientists believe that these structures serve as brain's own natural tranquilizers.

Apr 11 USSR launches Soyuz 33 with Soviet cosmonaut Nikolai Rukavishnikov and Bulgarian Major Georgi Ivanov aboard; Soyuz will dock with orbiting Salyut space station, which contains cosmonauts Vladimir Lyakhov and Valery Ryumin.

Apr 16 National Audubon Society appeals to proprietors of tall structures to douse their lights on foggy nights, since migratory birds tend to crash into lighted structures on cloudy nights; U.S. Fish and Wildlife Service survey has found that 536 buildings were involved in 80 million bird deaths per year.

Apr 17 A ten-year study by sex researchers Masters and Johnson indicates that homosexuals are not significantly different from heterosexuals in their responses to a wide variety of sexual stimuli.

Apr 18 Team of professional and amateur archeologists, participating in a two-year round-the-world expedition known as Operation Drake, discover sunken trading ship *Olive Branch*, and remains of ill-fated 17th-century Scottish colony of New Caledonia at Caledonia Bay, on Caribbean coast of Panama.

Apr 24 Borimir Jordan, classics professor at University of California, and John Perlin, solar energy historian, have found evidence that Greeks and Romans made extensive use of solar power to heat homes, baths and greenhouses after wood, then the main energy source, became scarce.

Apr 25   Dr. Sadao Ichikawa of Saitama University in Japan reports that spiderwort, a common roadside wildflower, is a more reliable indicator of effects of low-level radiation than currently used mechanical counters.

Apr 27   Massachusetts Institute of Technology scientist Dr. Ronald G. Prinn reports atmosphere of Venus appears to be ferment of exotic chemical reactions in which sulfur predominates.

May 1   Endorphins, opiate-like substances, have been identified as part of the brain's natural pain-control system. The chemical may be linked not only to pain and emotion, but also to natural responses to shock and even to the sexual urge.

May 7   The honeybee is facing a threat from a relatively new kind of insecticide containing methyl parathion.

May 8   Scientists link interferon, an anti-virus substance, to auto-immune diseases, in which the body's own defense mechanism turns against itself ● Dr. Anne R. Somers, specialist in family and community medicine, finds that marriage is good for health and longevity ● Submarine dives by Drs. Roger L. Larson and Robert D. Ballard have encountered hydrothermal activity, which caused eruptions of extremely hot metal-laden water from ocean floor ● Fossils discovered in Burma suggest that anthropoids may have originated more than 40 million years ago in Southeast Asia.

May 15   Recent investigations by Drs. William J. Hamilton 3rd and Curt D. Busse suggest that the human body may not have biological capacity for the heavy meat eating that is typical of many modern societies. ● Dr. Alan Walker of Johns Hopkins University, using microscopic analysis he invented, finds that not until advent of Homo erectus, species immediately ancestral to Homo sapiens, is there evidence of omnivorous diet.

May 20   Scientists pinpoint galactic source of radiation bursts in Large Magellanic Cloud near Milky Way Galaxy.

May 22   Researchers at the University of California have produced a computer whose responses are paranoid, to help uncover unsuspected aspects of paranoia ● Yale University Medical School researchers find insulin activity in human body is very sensitive to small amounts of the stress hormone adrenalin.

May 24   A virus has been linked to the cause of juvenile-onset diabetes.

May 28   Federal Council on Environment Quality reports the use of off-road vehicles, such as trail bikes, has an adverse effect on ecosystems in the United States.

May 29   Work by Belgian chemist Dr. Ilya Prigogine indicates a possible loophole in the Second Law of Thermodynamics, allowing impetus which pushes life to further evolution.

May 30   Pioneer Venus 1 spacecraft discovers a mountain range on Venus with peaks higher than Mt. Everest.

May 31   Ecological studies in the Amazon River Basin indicate that very large parks may not be the only way to preserve the greatest variety of wildlife species ● Wisps of gasses on Io, a satellite of Jupiter, detected by Voyager 1 spacecraft, are considered further evidence of volcanic activity there.

Jun 3   Five-year study disputes the idea that doctors prolong life at any cost in people dying of chronic diseases ● Thirty thousand residents in Amish communities of Lancaster, Pa., are immunized against polio because of six confirmed cases of the disease in the area.

Jun 5   A study of medical histories of 52 married middle-aged couples finds doctors are more responsive to male complaints, and that men receive more thorough examinations for specific complaints ● Scientists conclude, after study of Voyager spacecraft data, that the Jovian moons Io, Callisto, Ganymede, and Europa are distinct worlds whose characteristics are unknown elsewhere in the solar system ● UN Environmental Program report shows that number of insect and animal pests that have become immune to pesticides is rising swiftly and poses grave future problems for both world health and global food production.

Jun 6   Astronomers suspect image of a quasar has been split by the gravity of an extremely massive object roughly midway between quasar and earth. (If true, this would represent the first manifestation of gravitational lens predicted in Einstein's Theory of Relativity).

Jun 8   Scientific research team identifies at least 2 regions of Mars where liquid water may exist just below surface and where conditions may support some forms of life.

Jun 17   Conference of archeoastronomers, at conference in Santa Fe, New Mexico, report finding, at wide range of sites, evidence of alignments in ancient structures suggesting calendars, and say early Americans integrated motions of the planets into their lives and their view of the world.

Jun 22   Dudley Observatory scientists Drs. Joseph Erkes and Ivan Linscott discover that turbulent galaxy Messier 87 is emitting rapid-fire radio pulses with each carrying energy that 10 million suns would radiate.

Jun 26   Two-year analysis of data gathered by '77 joint US-USSR expedition finds high fish population of the Bering Sea results from previously uncharted current from the Pacific Ocean that brings to the area large amounts of nutrients ● Specialists at Ames Research Center in California report that present levels of intelligence might have been reached 60 million years ago if rapid evolution of nervous systems in the early development of life had continued.

Jun 27   Pennsylvania University Drs. Herbert A. Blough and Robert L. Giuntoli report success in treating genital herpes simplex (a venereal infection) with the drug 2-deoxy-D-glucose.

Jul 3   Anthropologist Dr. Suzanne Chevalier-Skolnikoff finds that infant apes' vocalization progress stops at an early age, and notes that the variance in vocal development is a vital factor in developmental difference between apes and man ● Voyager 2 spacecraft nears rendevous with Jupiter, and photographs Europa, a satellite not explored by sister craft Voyager 1.

Jul 4 Health specialists contend that unnecessary use of smallpox vaccine is responsible for outbreaks of the disease, which otherwise seems to have been eradicated almost everywhere in the world.

Jul 6 *New England Journal of Medicine* reports over five million Americans visit 20,000 U.S. chiropractors annually, despite the medical profession's dubious view of chiropractic ● Analysis of solar measurements by the Royal Greenwich Observatory, covering years 1836 to 1953, leads some physicists to suggest that the sun may be in a period of decline.

Jul 7 Study of Voyager 1 spacecraft data reveals extremely tenuous sulfur dioxide atmosphere on Io, one of Jupiter's major satellites. The haze of gas may rise as high as 100 miles, although the density is one ten-millionth that of earth.

Jul 13 University of South Carolina archeologists uncover site of long-lost 16th century colony of Santa Elena, once capital of Spanish Florida.

Jul 15 *Glomar Challenger* bores two miles below sea floor of the Pacific Ocean to sample record left by a variety of life that existed over millions of years.

Jul 17 California University (San Francisco) biochemists successfully use DNA splicing to alter genes in a bacteria strain to produce human growth hormone ● Recent studies by Princeton University physicist Robert H. Dicke indicate variations in the sun's magnetic field, not sunspots or other phenomena, affect climatic conditions on earth.

Jul 20 Study finds that the most common form of bacterial meningitis is contagious and warrants precautionary doses of antibiotic drugs in susceptible children.

Jul 25 National Science Foundation reports that divers exploring the under-ice environment of two freshwater lakes in Antarctica have discovered algae growing near bottom that thrive on less sunlight than any other known plants.

Jul 27 Birth of the first hybrid ape is reported, supporting recently advanced theory that new species sometimes arise from the juggling of genetic material over a few generations.

Jul 31 Scientists at Tokyo University report converting sunlight directly into electrical energy, achieving efficiency as high as 30%, higher than that of most existing solar cells ● Dr. Randy Thornhill finds some male scorpion flies assume role of transvestites to steal food from other males and present it as their own courtship gift to female flies ● Brigham Young University paleontologist Dr. James A. Jensen finds a nine-foot shoulder blade belonging to the biggest dinosaur ever discovered, in southwest Colorado.

Aug 6 Massachusetts General Hospital study finds that cancerous tumors induced in guinea pigs avoided the animals' normal immunologic defenses by living in self-created cocoons.

Aug 7   Dr. Gordon G. Gallup Jr. finds that pre-adolescent chimpanzees, when presented with a mirror, begin to recognize themselves in 3 or 4 days. (Such self-awareness was thought to be a human characteristic exclusively).

Aug 8   Scientists at the U.S. Geological Survey say that the August 6 earthquake in northern California occurred along a fault zone with persistent creep, which presumably eases strain and the chances of a major quake.

Aug 10   Technical papers presented at the 15th Intersociety Energy Conversion Engineering Conference suggest that solutions to global energy problems have already been found.

Aug 12   University of California professor Dr. Burney J. LeBoeuf reports Northern elephant seals, once near extinction, lack genetic diversity to cope with new diseases or environmental changes.

Aug 16   Outbreak of hepatitis is studied in North Carolina to learn if new and virulent strain of virus has emerged.

Aug 21   Scientists say steps must be taken to stop waste of helium, whose unique properties of refrigeration are essential to development of technologies based on superconductivity, by which global energy starvation can be held at bay.

Aug 28   National Disease Control Center experts have traced infantile paralysis outbreak among Pennsylvania Amish to earlier incidents in the Netherlands and, possibly, Kuwait ● Entomological research shows that the larvae of caddisflies weave intricate microscopic nets that filter material from water, providing food for larvae. The National Science Foundation wants to determine if the insect's water-filtering activities can benefit man.

Aug 30   Pioneer 11 spacecraft scans Iapetus, a moon of Saturn, but fails to disclose why one side of the satellite is six times brighter than the other.

Aug 31   Pioneer 11 spacecraft fails to disclose evidence of a fifth ring circling Saturn, as had been hypothesized by astronomers ● H. William Menard, director of U.S. Geological Survey, says that if suspected oil reserves below the floor of the Atlantic Ocean exist, they could amount to 15 billion barrels.

Sept 1   Solar storms disrupt radio transmissions from Pioneer 11 spacecraft, threatening to reduce the amount of data and quality of pictures being transmitted about Saturn.

Sept 2   Pioneer 11 sends back first photographs of Saturn after surviving bombardment from fine particles within the planet's rings, and indicate that an additional small moon and another ring of debris may be orbiting the planet ● International teams of 300 scientists, headed by 1978 Nobel Physics co-winner Dr. Samuel Ting, have proven the fundamental theory of matter known as quantum chromodynamics, which assumes that a particle of strong force, 'gluon,' holds together groups of quarks which make up stable atomic nuclei.

Sept 3 Photographs of Saturn's satellite Titan taken by Pioneer 11 reveal greater variation in color than expected by scientists, and indicates that Titan's atmosphere is a heterogeneous mixture of gases and molecules.

Sept 4 Scientists at the University of Minnesota are exploring the use of the common cattail as a source of energy for communities in wetland areas.

Sept 5 American Cancer Society reports many doctors are responding to patients' wish for less radical surgery in treatment of breast cancer, when the disease has not progressed too far ● NASA states an oversight thwarted efforts of Pioneer 11 spacecraft to transmit crucial data concerning Titan, when the agency failed to inform the USSR of its plans, and radio interference of a Soviet satellite drowned out transmission of data.

Sept 6 Salt Institute public relations director H. Lincoln Harner states that the reduction of salt in the diet should be a matter between physician and patient, and not a matter for individuals to try to 'treat' themselves.

Sept 7 Pioneer 11 scientists confirm eleventh moon circling Saturn and a second new ring, and further report that data on the satellite Titan was not lost due to interference by a Soviet satellite, but rather degraded by a solar storm and by poor earthbound communications.

Sept 8 Recombinant DNA Advisory Committee recommends to National Institutes of Health that 80% to 85% of current studies with DNA or 'gene-splicing' research be exempted from strict Federal guidelines.

Sept 11 Studies conducted by Washington University team on Vietnamese refugees living in the U.S. finds that adaptational problems differ among ethnic groups, that women are more vulnerable than men to migration-caused stress, and that many symptoms of illness among refugees are psychosomatic.

Sept 13 Chinese Institute of Vertebrate Paleontology Deputy Director Dr. Woo Jukang says that it is clear, from new findings, that the Peking Man, classed as a form of Homo erectus, hunted game, cooked game over fire, lived in bands of 50 or more and was talkative ● New England Medical Journal reports on research linking genetic abnormality to a specific type of kidney cancer in which 10 family members were affected over three generations.

Sept 15 Expert panel convened at National Institutes of Health concludes that the decision to use estrogens to treat menopausal disorders should be made by a woman after she has been clearly advised of potential dangers.

Sept 16 Study by Stanford University researchers finds that superior physical fitness and habitual exercise programs do not guarantee protection against sudden death during or after exercise.

Sept 17 China undertakes a drive to eradicate schistosomiasis (snail fever) by 1985. The disease, caused by a parasite, afflicts 2.5 million Chinese and is often fatal if not treated.

Sept 18 Johns Hopkins University scientists use quantum mechanics and quantum chemical analysis to construct blueprint of fundamental molecules of certain drugs, to permit synthesis by laboratory chemists ● Rockefeller University scientists use biofeedback training methods to train posture of patients with scoliosis ● California University researcher Robert A. Daniels, diving in coves off Antarctic Peninsula to observe fish behavior, discovers what may be the first recorded case of true altruism in lower animals—in the fish Harpagifer bispinis.

Sept 21 U.S. launches High Energy Astronomy Observatory to scan heavens for cosmic and gamma rays in continuing effort to learn more about past and possible future of universe.

Sept 24 Chinese specialists seek causes of exceedingly high incidence of specific cancers in certain localities. Overall cancer incidence in Shanghai area is the highest in the world.

Sept 25 Some 10,000 men in China are taking 1 of 3 birth-control preparations containing gossypol, a substance which appears to prevent production of viable sperm without affecting the body's hormone balance, and also seems free of any potential cancer hazard.

Sept 27 Mayo Clinic study finds that large amount of Vitamin C offered no therapeutic benefits in 150 advanced cancer patients tested.

Oct 1 Dr. Arthur Upton, director of the National Cancer Institute, citing "incomplete evidence" linking diet to cancer, advises Americans to eat less fat, drink less alcohol, eat more fiber and avoid being overweight.

Oct 5 Mexican Pemex authorities and U.S. contracters fail to stop gushing oil well in the Gulf of Mexico, and believe that the spill might continue for months.

Oct 9 Australian Numerical Meteorology Research Center weather scientist B. G. Hunt postulates that during the Late Precambrian Era, 1.5 billion years ago, the Earth spun 2 or 2½ times faster than it does now, profoundly influencing the climate. ● N. Y. Botanical Garden botanists say a 40-acre, virgin hemlock forest in the Bronx garden, is threatened with extinction after existing on the site for 20,000 years. ● Federal drug abuse research cites a growing use of imported marijuana which is often 10 times as potent as the domestic product.

Oct 10 A team of scientists at the National Institutes of Health and Rockefeller University, using cells of mice, have successfully injected a single gene into a defective living cell, curing that cell's fatal genetic flaw.

Oct 12 American Allan McLeod Cormack and Briton Godfrey Newbold Hounsfield win the 1979 Noble Prize in physiology and medicine for developing the CAT scanner.

Oct 16 A Study by Daniel Adams concludes that cheetahs, now an endangered species living only in Africa, once roamed the North American plains and may have originated there. ● The Nobel Prize in chemistry is won by Herbert C. Brown and Georg Wittig, for development of compounds which facilitate chemical reactions. The physics prize is shared by Steven Weinberg and Sheldon L. Glashow, both Americans, and Abdus Salam, the first Pakistani to win such an award.

Oct 17 Scientists at Mexico State University, using high-altitude balloon with ultrasensitive instruments, detect stream of antimatter from space.

Oct 18 The CIA predicts oil shortages will occur when the world economy picks up in the early 1980's, and that the Communist bloc will become a net importer of crude oil, instead of a net exporter.

Oct 23 American scientists are buoyed by success of an experiment to increase the nearly-extinct whooping crane population by introducing captive-laid eggs in nests of sandhill cranes.

Oct 25 A nationwide, federally funded study implicates nitrous oxide ("laughing gas") in a significant number of health problems among dental workers.

Oct 30 NASA launches its first spacecraft designed for study of earth's magnetic field and crustal anomalies ● Three physicists at Los Alamos Scientific Laboratory and Dr. Harold Agnew, former director, challenge Dr. Zhores Medvedev's thesis that a large nuclear accident occurred near Kyshtym in the Soviet Union in late 1957 or early 1958.

Oct 31 The President's Commission of the Three Mile Island accident concludes that such an accident was inevitable, at Three Mile Island or elsewhere, given the inadequate training of operators and the confusing procedure.

Nov 1 Some scientists believe that a "superbolt"—a lightning flash so powerful that it can release as much energy as a small nuclear weapon—may have been responsible for the flash of light that an American reconnaissance satellite detected in the area around South Africa on September 22 ● Dr. Jesse Roth is the first winner of the new $100,000 Lita Annenberg Hazen Award for clinical research achievements in the understanding of diabetes.

Nov 4 Scientists attending a two-day symposium at the University of Maryland say technologically advanced civilizations are so rare that mankind's may be the only one in this galaxy.

Nov 6 1,400 Federal employee participants in a computerized "health hazard appraisal" program, conducted by the Center for Disease Control, are receiving ten-year life expectancy projections after filling out a detailed questionnaire.

Nov 7 Experts begin exploring practical applications for the discovery by Soviet mathematician L. G. Khachian of a method by which computers can find guaranteed solutions to a class of very difficult problems, known as "Traveling Salesman Problems".

Nov 13 Criminologists and scientists are divided over question of validity, accuracy and use of voice stress detectors that some claim can spot deception in human speech.

Nov 14 Astronomers Drs. John P. Huchra, Marc Aaronson, and Jeremy Mould report the universe is expanding twice as fast as previously believed and may only be 9 billion years old.

Nov 15 Drs. Walter Gilbert and Frederick Sanger receive 1979 Albert Lasker Medical Research Award for contributing to understanding of chemistry of heredity. Dr. Roger Sperry receives award for studies in function of the human brain, and Sir John Wilson also receives award for contributing to a worldwide campaign against blindness.

Nov 29 Study of some 26,000 pregnancies casts serious doubt on the safety of sexual intercourse during pregnancy.

Dec 5 More than a third of dental X-ray machines and almost half the breast X-ray machines examined by the FDA in a 45-state survey emitted unacceptable levels of radiation, according to the General Accounting Office.

Dec 8 Harvard University Professor Frank M. Cross reports papyrus rolls found in Jericho are the oldest legal documents known to have originated in ancient Palestine.

Dec 11 RCA Corporation reports losing contact with satellite Satcom 3, after maneuvering it into permanent orbit.

Dec 17 Several large-scale experiments are planned to test theory that particles of matter forming nuclei of all atoms—protons and neutrons—disintegrate radioactively, so that all matter will eventually disappear.

Index

PHOTO ACKNOWLEDGMENTS

We would like to thank the following people and organizations for the use of their photographs: P. 3-11, 14-16 Jet Propulsion Laboratories/California Institute of Technology/NASA; p. 18-20 NASA: p. 23, 25 (top) Jet Propulsion Laboratories/California Institute of Technology/NASA; p. 25 (bottom) Clemens of Copenhagen; p. 26, 27, 29-32, 35 Jet Propulsion Laboratories/California Institute of Technology/NASA; p. 38 Kitt Peak National Observatory; p. 39 J. Bedke, Hale Observatories; p. 40-42 Kitt Peak National Observatory; p. 47 (top) Los Alamos Photo Laboratory; p. 47 (bottom) D. Stark; p. 49 Los Alamos Scientific Laboratory; p. 50 (top), 51 R. Little; p. 50 (bottom) G. Keene; p. 53 General Atomic Company; p. 54 Princeton University Plasma Physics Laboratory; p. 55-58 Lawrence Livermore Laboratory; p. 59 Sandia Laboratories; p. 62-64 Dupont; p. 65 James Colleson/Black Star/Dupont; p. 67 Elizabeth Wilcox/Columbia Presbyterian Medical Center; p. 69 New York Hospital/Cornell Medical Center; p. 70 Elizabeth Wilcox/Columbia Presbyterian Medical Center; p. 71 New York Hospital/Cornell Medical Center; p. 74 (top) Dr. Robert Kastenbaum; p. 74 (bottom) National Institute on Aging; p. 75 Gray Panthers/© Julie Jensen; p. 77 National Institute on Aging; p. 79 Albert Einstein College of Medicine; p. 80 National Institute on Aging; p. 83, 85, 87 © Phyllis Crowley; p. 90 Linda J. Soled/Cornell University Medical College; p. 91 National Institute of Allergy and Infectious Diseases; p. 92, 93 Dr. Richard P. Novick; p. 95 (top) Columbia-Presbyterian Medical Center; p. 95 (bottom) Center for Disease Control, Atlanta, Georgia; p. 98, 99 National Institute of Mental Health; p. 102 Montefiore Hospital and Medical Center; p. 104 New York University; p. 106 Montefiore Hospital and Medical Center; p. 108 Miles Laboratories, Inc.; p. 111 New York University; p. 114-115 New York Hospital/Cornell Medical Center; p. 117, 119, 120 National Institute for Burn Medicine, Ann Arbor, Michigan; p. 124, 125, 127 NIA Gerontology Photo; p. 130 United Press International; p. 131 Culver Pictures; p. 133 California Department of Fish and Game; p. 137 The Aluminum Association, Inc.; p. 138, 140, 142 Grumman Energy Systems, Inc.; p. 143 Schwinn Bicycle Company; p. 146 Susan Cottingham/Town of Crested Butte; p. 148 Wes Light/Town of Crested Butte; p. 150 The New York Times; p. 151 Henry Truebe/Town of Crested Butte; p. 152, 153, 154 (top) Wes Light/Town of Crested Butte; p. 154 (bottom) Crested Butte Archives; p. 156 Debbie Hooks-Drake/Town of Crested Butte; p. 159 J. Goerg/New York State Department of Environmental Conservation; p. 160 United Press International; p. 162 U.S. Environmental Protection Agency; p. 163 United Press International; p. 165 EPA-Documerica/Charles O'Rear; p. 169 Food and Drug Administration; p. 170 Dr. Irving J. Selikoff; p. 171 The American Cancer Society; p. 173 United Press International; p. 176, 180 Sylvia Plachy; p. 184, 185, 187, 189 Society for Animal Rights; p. 192, 193 Center for Disease Control, Atlanta, Georgia; p. 205 New York Hospital/Cornell Medical Center; p. 209, 210 Emily Burrows; p. 212 University of Rhode Island; p. 216 Dr. Samuel A. Corson; p. 218-220 American Humane Association; p. 223, 224 United Press International; p. 227 Dr. Myron Winick; p. 230 (top), 231 Bill Dupuy/Jackson Laboratory; p. 230 (bottom) George McKay/Jackson Laboratory; p. 235 (left) Mary H. Clark; p. 235 (right) William H. Clark; p. 239 United Press International; p. 242-253 Southwest Cultural Resources Center; p. 256-259 Brigham Young University; p. 262, 264, 266, 267 The Cleveland Museum of Natural History; p. 271, 272 Harvard University; p. 273 © Susan Lapides; p. 276 Purdue University.

One Dozen Markers
only $3.48

Actual size

- Pitch-black water-base felt-tip markers—
- Made of unbreakable plastic
- Separate cap fits in back of pen
- Medium point—perfect for general use
- Easily erasable from laminated surfaces

To Order:
Please send name & address plus quantity desired (by the dozen) along with check or money order payable to Bobley Publishing Corp., 311 Crossways Park Drive, Woodbury, New York 11797. Kindly include any applicable taxes.